Rehired, Not Retired

Books by Dilip Saraf

The 7 Keys to a Dream Job: A Career Nirvana Playbook!
Reinvention through Messaging: The Write Message for the Right Job!
Pathways to Career Nirvana: An Ultimate Success Sourcebook!

Rehired, Not Retired

Proven Strategies for the Baby Boomers!

Dilip G. Saraf

Career Transitions Unlimited

Only for those who dare to practice what we preach...®

iUniverse, Inc.

New York Lincoln Shanghai

Rehired, Not Retired
Proven Strategies for the Baby Boomers!

Copyright © 2006 by Dilip G. Saraf

iUniverse books may be ordered through booksellers or by contacting:

iUniverse
2021 Pine Lake Road, Suite 100
Lincoln, NE 68512
www.iuniverse.com
1-800-Authors (1-800-288-4677)

ISBN-13: 978-0-595-36258-5 (pbk)
ISBN-13: 978-0-595-67359-9 (cloth)
ISBN-13: 978-0-595-80703-1 (ebk)
ISBN-10: 0-595-36258-3 (pbk)
ISBN-10: 0-595-67359-7 (cloth)
ISBN-10: 0-595-80703-8 (ebk)

Printed in the United States of America

This book is dedicated to the two men in my life that made it worth living:

Govind Vitthal Saraf and David Eugene Arnold, Sr.

"When you sell man a book, you are not selling him just 12 ounces of paper, ink, and glue—you are selling him a whole new life."

—Christopher Morley, author (1890–1957)

Contents

Preface

"Happiness is a state of consciousness which proceeds from the achievement of one's values."

—Ayn Rand, author, philosopher (1905–1982)

This book resulted from working with career professionals who came seeking advice. Most of those in career distress wanted to know how to deal with any one of the following challenges that they faced: how to reengage in the current job market, how to deal with their impending or current retirement[1], or what to do with the continued dissatisfaction in their tenuous or stultifying jobs. Nearly all were in the baby-boomer age. Baby boomers are those born between 1946 and 1964, comprising nearly 75 million Americans, representing 25 percent of the U.S. population in 2005. Assuming that nearly half want to work or did work and are near retirement, this number now swells to nearly 37 million!

A radical shift in the job market began in late 2000. This is when the off-shoring's impact and the dot-com's spectacular collapse were reverberating throughout the economy. In the Silicon Valley, which was ground zero for the meltdown that started in 2001, a number of factors changed inexorably since then. Elsewhere, yet other factors created a sudden economic whiplash in the job market, as we then knew it.

Many Internet start-ups that were hyped up with no rational business model backing them up began to fall like dominos, swallowing in their wake paper fortunes of brash entrepreneurs. Thousands of high-tech jobs that were the models of safety, security, *and* glamour for technology workers in the U.S. began to be sent overseas to cheap—and much more productive—labor markets of India, China, and even Europe. Manufacturing jobs that were once the bastions of middle-class job security began to vaporize and quickly disappear from the U.S. job market. In the process, the national unemployment rate rose

---

[1] An average employee in the U.S. goes into retirement with $58,500 saved (July '05 data). See Appendix-I to appreciate how cash flow in the "retirement" years can influence your living standard. This appendix clearly shows how getting a good job after "retirement" can dramatically change quality of life during your twilight years.

to over seven percent. In some regions that have been the high-tech show cases, as the Silicon Valley in California, the unemployment rate quickly shot past the double digits, with no end in sight.

Interestingly, this job loss was not isolated to the U.S.. Across the globe, a new force suddenly began to shape how jobs were created, forging new employment compacts. The playing field got leveled, the world became flat, and suddenly most geographic, political, and national boundaries disappeared—at least for commerce. Primary factors that were responsible for the "Flat world" and its implications to the global economy are eloquently described in Thomas Friedman's *The World is Flat: A Brief History of the 21st Century.*

Something else also began to happen as a result of these forces. Those who were in the workforce for 20-plus years began to see job loss at a higher rate than others. They also found reemployment much more difficult in the emerging job market. This loss of jobs for the older workers was not just limited to the U.S..

The Effects of Boomer "Retirement"

The phenomenon of the aging population and its impact at both the macro and micro level is now a world issue. Why? The U.S. is not alone in its demographic anomaly with the baby boomer population described above. Japan, Europe, South America are also major geographies affected by this factor. In Japan nearly a third of its population is in the 60-plus age group and in Europe, nearly a quarter. The rampant unemployment across the entire labor pool in these regions is another matter, which exacerbates the plight of the jobless senior professional. The cultural norms and labor laws of those countries make finding jobs for the elderly workers even more difficult than it is in the U.S.. When those from an aging population suddenly face a stalled cash flow resulting from job loss or having to retire when they are not financially ready, they find it difficult to sustain their standard of living. With rising costs, continuing population growth, resource limitations, and skewed demographics that favor younger citizens, the clout of the elderly continues to erode despite their large numbers. Being out of work in large numbers makes them powerless to fight the tide that they see as against them.

Their diminishing economic clout and their growing dependence on social services make their situation unique. The flattened world exacerbates this plight. How? As the retirees now dissave to sustain their living standard, the money available for economic activities starts to dry up. When they were employed, that money came from the savings and the retirement accounts that grew as they advanced in their careers. In a nation's capital market this has serious and far-reaching implications. The flat world now makes the reverberations of this national factor globally visible. So, the impact of an aging population being out of work is far more serious than most are willing to admit.

On the social front there is an entirely different set of forces at work as a result of the boomer phenomenon. Some of these forces are listed below:

- A dramatic shortage of skilled employees
- A loss of institutional knowledge that resides in senior employees and decision-makers
- A depletion of company (and union) retirement funds and health plans
- A dramatic increase in the need for services for the retirees and the elderly
- A huge drop in public- and private-sector workforce, including civil servants
- A decrease in overall productivity as more experienced workers are replaced with their less skilled counterparts and those who belong to a different generation (see Gen-X and Gen-Y factors in Chapter-4: The Baby Boomer Advantage) and who hold a different set of values
- A growing indifference to the human aspects of dealing with customers as younger employees increasingly rely on technology to do this important aspect of their jobs.
- A disappearing "human moment" at work, often resulting in increased stress and brittle relationships.

Senior executives have not yet come to appreciate the impact of this phenomenon as it affects their organizations' immediate well being.

Reinventing for Reemployment

In the U.S. alone, of those laid off, many are in an awkward age bracket where they are too old to find suitable employment on the one hand and, maybe, too young to retire on the other. Most of them are baby boomers. As the unemployment began to mount its affect on the baby boomers was profound. They felt lost. They needed a different approach to their re-employment and transition.

A variety of factors made this group seek re-employment. The most notable among these factors were the increase in life expectancy, now at the unprecedented 77.5 years in the U.S.; an increasing uncertainty in corporate promises of retirement and medical benefits; rising medical costs; and lack of adequate health-benefits coverage. Compounding these factors were the economic uncertainty prompted by sudden swelling of the U.S. national debt since 2000, continued erosion of the dollar, and growing balance-of-trade deficits.

Yet another factor that emerged from this flux was that many, who came out leaving their jobs behind them, suddenly realized that they were unhappy in their past jobs anyway. They were unfulfilled. This awareness of unfulfilled purpose grew for many as they advanced in their careers, feeling that they were not doing what they should have been doing—nourishing their soul in the purposeful pursuit in which they were engaged. Having now lost the main source of livelihood and then realizing that what they were engaged in was a mercenary existence anyway, caused many to recoil in dismay. This realization awakened them to a new reality of what they had to offer. With what salt was still left in them, they had better look at opportunities that not only gave them an ongoing source of income again, but also, more importantly, the ones that nourished their soul with something purposeful that excited them. At this stage of their lives money became secondary.

They also came to realize that they perhaps continued amid growing inner discontent in their jobs, primarily because they did not want to surrender their security and expose themselves to uncertainty. Many dismissed the idea of a late-life career refresh simply because it insulted their sensibilities, in addition to scaring them in an era of growing uncertainty. A career refresh in its negative connotation entails starting over at a new place of employment with no seniority status and the privileges that go with that seniority. Here, one starts with the shortest span of vacation after the first year of service, a benefit many find insulting after having worked decades long at a job or in a career at their previous place of employment.

Nearly 80 percent of those working are in this state of resignation. And yet, they continue doing what they do primarily because of the inertia or being in a state of denial over their ongoing unhappiness and plight. An involuntary job loss is a good juncture for re-assessment on many levels. Once you are out and are no longer beholden to your employer, it is easier to be objective and to reassess your job, career, and how you want to spend your life so that you feel nourished. The need to reassess a career and how much happiness one derives from it is most pronounced with impending retirement or at a juncture of being just out of work. This is when all perspectives about job, career, and life's purpose come into sharper focus for most.

What was the impetus for the topic of this book? Much of what is in this book—and the three past titles published in 2004—was triggered by what happened starting in early 2001. This is when the job market was quaked by the economic forces that turned it upside down, both in the U.S. and abroad. From that tumult, what emerged was exploding awareness that career-related matters did not get the attention they deserved in our lives, and when they did, it was usually when we were in a crisis mode. What brought this realization in even greater relief were the dotcom meltdown and the spiral of economic setbacks that started in 2001, when nearly 15 million Americans were in some kind of job-related quandary. The events of September 11, 2001 were yet another reminder of our fragile existence.

Of the many clients who came seeking relief, some were out of work; some underemployed, some underpaid, and many had just simply given up looking and had started pursuing whatever got them a paycheck. The common theme was that *all* were distempered and discomposed by their fate. The peak *unofficial* unemployment rate at the end of 2003 was nearly eight percent (official rate was nearly six percent nationally), with perhaps three times that number of people who were in some kind of job-related quandary. Pundits often argued about the stated facts and realities. This may also have been so because the traditional measurement methods for a job market, turned upside down, no longer made sense in this flux. In this unemployed pool the baby boomers dominated. This was a wake-up call. Interestingly, the statistics about those unemployed in the baby boomer age group was remarkably consistent in other international geographies mentioned earlier.

Working with a large number of the baby boomers, who had otherwise resigned themselves to "retiring" in the U.S., what emerged was that reinventing their value proposition worked in almost every case. The success rate with the reinvention was far greater than that when a person merely decided to find another job in the same line of work or to do anything that was available that got them a paycheck. This was particularly true in careers where local jobs were shrinking because of the global workforce. Without reinvention, the desperate ones often surrendered to temporary and hourly jobs as sign twirling, working as greeters at retail chains, or even pursuing well-cautioned scams as "envelope stuffing." The reward in almost every case of personal reinvention was not just finding a job but also a dream job and something that brought purpose in their life; a first for many. Appendix-I shows financial implications of the two approaches.

This book was prompted by the reinvention successes of those who had originally pursued opportunities that they could not conquer. And, yet the same baby boomers were able to reenergize their life with a different message that galvanized their campaign to redeploy. In many instances they were able to claim the job—their dream job—by changing their attitude, looking at the opportunity differently, crafting a message of reinvention, and approaching the opportunity with confidence. This is, in essence, what this book presents as object lessons.

Breaking Through!

Although there was no limit to the list of barriers the job seekers perceived as blocking them from reaching their goal, some were common. Those who were laid off after being in the same company for many years felt that they were too old to compete with those of the younger generation (Gen-X or Gen-Y). Many felt that their formal degrees were not relevant to the jobs that interested them; some did not even have degrees. This feeling was common despite their well-paying ex-jobs that they had for many years. Some felt that they were burnt out by being in one industry, especially high-tech, too long and were ready to transition to more meaningful jobs with "stability" as might be available in other industries, notably biotech. In making such transitions they lacked industry experience. This list of barriers is truly endless in the minds of those who immure themselves in their limiting beliefs. Transforming the limiting beliefs into liberating beliefs was what reinvention provided. To many, it was a gift at a time when they needed it the most.

The purpose of this book is twofold. One is to equip those who stumble their earnest efforts to get their dream job by letting their limiting beliefs get in the way. To those in this group the book shows how they must change their mindset first. The book shows them, in the same vein, how an untapped resource—their genius—deep within, will mantle them with powers and transport them. Once the power of this resource is accessed, a magical force transforms them on how they think of themselves. All the prior limiting beliefs that shackled them from achieving their dreams are now transformed into convictions that liberate them by virtue of their transformed attitude and approach. They can now play their cards far differently than they ever thought possible by now being armed with this transforming attitude and mindset. Once so mantled, they are able to achieve exceptional rather than expected outcomes, far beyond the reality of their *entrenched* capabilities.

This book is written to inspire many who concoct any number of excuses for inaction, who fear defeat in doing anything *new*, and who surrender in their pursuits of what could otherwise be their dream job. What is presented here as a prescription can remove the perceived barriers that block their pathway to their dream. It clearly shows how those who have the insights and the innate skills to create *new* value in a position can overcome all the objections that appear daunting at first glance. The book shows examples of clients who pursued these opportunities that appeared out of reach on the surface, but quickly conquered them by using simple yet powerful strategies.

Yes, these strategies are simple. And yet, they are not easy. They are simple because they entail having to change an entrenched mindset and attitude by accessing your deeper gifts; they are not easy because they entail having to change a view of yourself and look at the opportunity in an entirely different light. It is your repositioning of yourself for the same job by now viewing the opportunity in a perspective that matches the changed view of yourself. This is the breakthrough that will be apparent in each case that is presented throughout the book as an object lesson.

The second and more important message in this book is that to achieve joy in a job and a fulfilling career, the alignment between what you truly yearn to do and what you end up doing on the job is critical. Thus, unless there is a structured process to discover and then articulate what brings you inner joy and then to align that discovery with the job at hand, this realization will remain elusive. The book shows how to tap into *that* force—your genius or inner voice—and to not only conquer the opportunity you are after, but to also structure your work for achieving self-actualization—career nirvana—that everyone dreams about.

Much of what is presented in the book stemmed from real case studies that I encountered during my coaching practice in the Silicon Valley and through-out the world. This practice entailed both career coaching and life coaching. Career coaching required taking a look at how to approach the career issues; life coaching allowed working with clients to change their view of themselves and empowering them with transforming their beliefs and giving them the tools and the rules to manifest differently. The challenge is universal, mostly stemming from the basic human condition. It crosses cultural, geographical, gender-based, and age-based factors. The process entailed cutting through all the veils that we surround ourselves with and getting through to the essence of who one is. There is something universal about working to earn a living as an integral part of the human condition; it is our primordial need. True, many practices that govern employment rules are grounded in local laws and cus-toms. Regardless, the basic forces that drive one's need to be productively employed are more or less universal. What this book has to offer will be valu-able in any situation almost anywhere in the world.

Why a Tome?

The size of this book may intimidate some at first glance. One reason for its bulk is that the book embodies material that evolved from everyday needs of those who were in transition and who fit the profile of the intended readers—mid-career professionals and baby boomers.

The other reason is that there are actual examples of résumés and cover letters that clearly show a variety of situations that require specific responses and messages. There are 32 examples of well-written cover letters alone that resulted in positive responses from the targets. The actual examples of the résumés and cover letters are expected to give direction with specific points of view (POV) on how to generate winning messages.

Experience shows that readers would rather have something that they can use directly with some changes than to have to fashion something new to fit their need. This is so because they usually have their priorities in another area—finding a great job! Experience also shows that having a rich assortment of real-life scenarios helps generate new ideas and POVs quickly for creative messages that can then be fashioned with confidence.

The Book's Message:

The following bullets summarize the main points of this book:

- A transition late in life can be a positive life-changing opportunity if you know how to exploit it that way.

- Being out of work and looking for a new job or changing careers late in life for better purpose-alignment require a well-disciplined process grounded in personal discovery

- A résumé is about tomorrow and not yesterday! It must convey an unambiguous message of value.

- Your value proposition must be based on who you are and not what you have done in the past.

- Your inner voice is articulated through your genius as Unique Skills in your résumé. A value proposition based on your genius is timeless and highly resilient

- In an economy where the job market is driven by technology-based automation, new jobs grounded in hyper-human work will never be eliminated

- In an off-shored climate the high value jobs remain unidentified and unclaimed

- In the "flat world" new jobs will require an improved understanding of human needs than that of technology management.

- The process of reinvention involves finding innovative ways to articulate messages that change people's perception of how you create value and, more importantly, how it *must* be created.

- Those who see an impending retirement for themselves and are interested in continuing for a few more years at their current employer must proactively present their case to their chain of command and explore how they can continue beyond their current engagement and possibly reengage without interruption so that the employer benefits from it. A consulting contract can also be forged through this dialog.

Using these and other concepts presented here and object lessons, I hope that you are able to engage yourself in endeavors that give you a new lease on your career and life and recapture your dreams that somehow got lost in the shuffle.

As in my previous books, ♠ before a section represents topics worth revisiting to get better ongoing insights. Similarly, a * represents an important topic.

Acknowledgements

Once again, those who helped me most in developing the contents of this book are my clients. Those who agreed to try new avenues to job search and career management provided the test bed for many ideas that are at the core of what is in this book. So, thank you for placing your trust in my hands to help you in ways that otherwise would not have been possible. As always, my loving wife, Mary Lou, and our son, Raj, helped me with their diligent efforts of editing what is in this book and making sure that what I wrote was clear enough for anyone to follow! The table of Retirement Cash Flow in Appendix-I is due to my friends S. G. Kane and S. S. Naik.

Silicon Valley, CA

Chapter-1: The Retirement Dilemma

"I am indeed a king, because I know how to rule myself."
—Pietro Aretino, satirist, dramatist (1492–1556)

Introduction

Historically, most of the working population looked forward to retirement. Most were employed during their adult life making a good living and worked hard at it. Until the end of the past century, and certainly till about the mid 1970s, most relied on their employers to take care of their welfare and job security. Assured employment was the unspoken covenant on which most idealized their working world and many realized it until then. Those who struggled through the Great Depression and came out of it to find themselves a job and who had their entire career ahead of them, enjoyed the security of lifelong employment and guaranteed retirement benefits, later fortified by the Social Security system.

All that began to change rather suddenly starting about the mid 1970s when lifetime employment was replaced with "employment at will." Even then there was some expectation of ongoing employment in most instances. Even that came to an abrupt halt when the economic downturn and the resulting job losses suddenly exploded in early 2001. The events of September 11, 2001 and the ensuing course of geopolitical and economic fallout sealed the fate of the employment models, until then considered invincible in the minds of most.

Long before these events loomed, there was a phenomenon in the making. During the years 1946–1964, following the end of World War II, there was an unprecedented population explosion in the U.S. and also in many other nations equally affected by the fallout of the war. That population surge was so significant that those born during that period came to be labeled as the "baby boomers" in this country. This surge of population carried with it its own economic fallout. As these babies grew up, the economy began to be driven by the needs of those who fell in this demography and, no matter what the adversity, if anyone engaged in an economic activity that took care of the ongoing needs of this demographic group, they were assured of success in whatever endeavor that engaged them.

Enter the New Millennium. Now, the economic landscape is vastly different than what it was when the baby boomers began their life in this country—and elsewhere—nearly 50 years back. The employment picture is now uncertain. The "employment at will" model has taken true hold of the agreement between the employer and employee. The world has become flat which means that jobs go where resources are and not the other way around. Jobs chase people around the world, which has now resulted in a massive job-market upheaval the U.S. and other Western countries. The work is now flowing to India, China, and other Asian countries, where it is getting done efficiently and effectively. Those most affected by this trend are in their baby boomer years. Why? Because they have the hardest time retooling themselves to find alternate employment.

A Global Crisis

The fallout of this phenomenon is not limited to the U.S.. It is spread throughout the world wherever the population demographics mimicked the pattern most noticeable in the U.S., Japan, and the countries in Europe and South America are also affected by the fallout of the aging population exposed to the unemployment threat. Those who are actually facing unemployment as a result of the world becoming flat are at highest risk.

When a large segment of a country's population is suddenly subjected to economic forces that expose it to being out of work with no prospects of finding easy employment, the overall impact of that prospect is long term and catastrophic beyond anyone's immediate grasp. At a macro level, when a growing pool of workers goes from earning and saving to spending by dissaving, the whole economy sees its jolt. To make matters worse, most want to continue their lifestyle. The aggregate effect of this shift in the flow of capital can be significant at the national level.

Another dimension of this loss is at a social level. The mature professional brings a certain human element to their work that is getting increasingly rare with the erosion of experienced workers. Their abundant capacity to deal with human issues that organizations face every day far surpasses that of their younger counterparts. With increased technology insertion in our workplace and a rapidly growing population of younger workers, the "human moment" is rapidly disappearing from the corporate world; we are accelerating the demise of the human enterprise!

Yet another factor is the productivity of older workers. Recent studies have shown that in the U.S., younger workers waste nearly twice the amount time in unproductive behaviors (gossiping, moonlighting, etc.) than their older counterparts. This has an effect on productivity of the organization. Also, older workers were likely to stay for twice as long as their younger counterparts. This factor alone can save corporations significant retraining costs.

At a micro level, the affect is even more significant. First, psychologically, someone coming out of work, especially involuntarily, recoils by continuing to live in the same style as they were when employed. For pride if not for being in denial, many rationalize that being out of work at a late stage in their career entitles them to continue their lifestyle. So, typically, many react to this changed economic condition by borrowing against their homes or retirement accounts to affect as if nothing has changed for them. The reality is that each person so displaced now is living on "borrowed" money. The social pressure from their employed colleagues further exacerbates this condition.

How can you change the balance when the tide of events is against you? One way is to get back into the workforce and be employed again. It is, of course, difficult getting back to work when the job market has changed—the very reason for your being out of work—and not having any clue on how to get into the workforce again. A different approach is needed to change the balance of power in your favor. So, what is the prescription?

A Prescription

One avenue to get back into the workforce is through reinvention. Looking ahead rather than looking back the world presents opportunities that are not obvious. When one type of job disappears another one pops up if one is willing to use their imagination and creativity to explore and adapt themselves to the changed environment. To some the very idea of reinvention is daunting. And, yet, those who do it are largely successful. One reason perhaps is that most do not realize that in our everyday life we use less than five percent of our true capacity or capabilities. Using the deep reservoir of latent capabilities that we all have, it is no longer inconceivable to fashion a new "package" that better aligns with what is needed (current jobs) and what you can do based on your inner capabilities (not just based on what you did in the past). So, if one takes the forward-looking view of how to redefine and redeploy oneself, the task of reinventing does not appear that far fetched anymore. In fact, with this attitude, it becomes fun and a challenge.

One key element of the reinvention is our own genius or inner voice. This is a gift we *all* have that allows us to change what we do in ways that is not apparent to many. Once we are able to own this endowment and figure out how to manifest it for the task at hand, we can refashion what we do (not who we are) in a chameleon-like manner.

This book is about how to do this transformation at a later stage in one's life.

Two Views

There are two views necessary to fashion a reinvention: one entails the outside-in view, the other, inside-out. In synthesizing a composite that serves both worlds, it is necessary to fashion a reinvention that is an amalgam of both. These views are of how you see the world as an oyster of opportunity.

The inside-out view deals with what you have done in the past and how that relates to the opportunities that present themselves in the emerging ecosystem. This is primarily a retrospective view; a view typically presented in traditional résumés that are chronological in format. The other view—outside-in—is from looking at the same emergent world and then discovering new opportunities at the intersection of your current interests and the spoken or hidden needs. Although each view is tempered by your own perspective of yourself, looking at them somewhat independently provides a richer view of possibilities.

In the outside-in view there is an inevitable list of companies that are desirable, but do not have openings in the areas that interest you. The best approach to take, then, is identifying an opportunity based on what the company is not doing or should be doing and pursuing it by using one of the approaches suggested in the later chapters (see Chapter-6: Building Your Platform). In making a case for this target company with your value proposition and an insight that you have developed, the two views come together to craft a reinvention that can often work well.

Summary: Chapter-1: The Retirement Dilemma

This brief chapter outlines the conflict—and challenge—faced by mid-career professionals who are too young to retire. This discussion is not limited only to the aging baby boomers, but applies equally to those who are fighting their mid-career stagnation, with or without a job. The baby-boomer label refers to the age of those born between 1946 and 1964 and only to the U.S. geography. In reality, those on either side of this age and also those who reside and work in other geographies face similar challenges. The ideas suggested in this book apply to all and are not limited those in the U.S.. This problem is global.

The problem of working people getting out of the workforce too early—before they voluntarily decide to do so—has implications that go far beyond the plight faced by the affected individual. At the macro level the cumulative effect of a county's population going out of work is economically negative. When an increasingly large unemployed population goes from steadily saving to dissaving, the effect on the capital flow at the national level is noticeable. At the individual level the effects are devastating. This book's prescription is at the individual level and is aimed at empowering those who feel that they need external intervention—a government handout—to help their cause. This book debunks that notion.

The mainstay prescription of this book is reinvention. This is prescribed at two levels: an outside-in approach, where you take a look at the emerging opportunities that go beyond what is obvious and stated; and the inside-out approach, where you decide how to move forward with a value proposition based on who you are. A successful reinvention occurs at the intersection of these two views.

Chapter-2: Tools and Rules for Transition

"Significant problems of today cannot be solved by applying the same level of thinking as when we created them."

—Albert Einstein (1879–1955)

Introduction

This chapter provides the groundwork for those entering a transition. Transition is a challenging period that underscores preparedness more than finesse in accomplishing what one sets out to achieve. This chapter has three main topics to help make a transition productive and fun:

- Managing Transitions
- Getting Organized
- Understanding Yourself

This chapter also provides tools to cope with hurdles faced during a transition; tools that provide some sense of control during the process.

Managing Transitions

Managing a personal transition comprises understanding the forces that drive it. How best to deal with these forces common to all transitions can make these transitions meaningful, even rewarding, and provide some degree of control to those facing them. It is this control that makes the transition a positive experience. The following discussion presents the anatomy of a transition so that it is not a mystery.

Forces that are manageable drive personal transitions. Although no one can control the events that prompt a transition, understanding how to manage a career transition, or for that matter, any transition, is critical to create a positive outcome. In our increasingly uncertain world, transitions are the norm and not the quiescent life that we all yearn for.

The following discussion is presented to demystify the various factors that manifest during a transition.

♠ What is a Transition?

A transition is a journey through which we travel to get to the destination, navigating through both time and emotional space.

During transitions our life is changing; not ending!

Career transition can cause major trauma, especially if it involves finding employment in a tanking economy. Navigating through such a transition can present a challenge that many are not prepared for. We can approach a transition one of two ways. One is to go and retreat in utter defeat and find someone to blame, sue, or go begging after. In other words, to become a recreant! The other is to take stock, find strength, and summon our innermost resources to discover what we are made of, develop new insights, and go on to conquer something to surprise even ourselves. It is to this latter group this book will be most helpful! This book is written for and is expected to be most helpful for those who deal with their career transition using the latter approach.

Regardless of the support we have around us, both emotionally and otherwise, we can control how we are affected by these transitions. The difference in the way we deal with these transitions and how they affect us is a matter of our preparedness, attitude, and our emotional constitution. We cannot control what happens to us in specific situations, but we can control how *we* deal with them! We can become victims or martyrs as easily as we can victors and masters based on choices that only we can make. It is also a matter of what tools we have in our arsenal to deal with such situations that give us control over how we can do things differently and achieve the right outcomes. This book provides many such tools.

Transitional Nirvana

Before we discuss Transitional Nirvana, let us first discuss *Nirvana*.

Nirvana is a Sanskrit word that has to do with a state of bliss, and a state of existence where one is free from cycles of pain and suffering. In some Eastern philosophies, our existence consists of cycles of pain and pleasure. Unless we find ways of breaking this cycle we are stuck in it. Attaining Nirvana means breaking that cycle and finding bliss in our existence. Career Nirvana is a state of that bliss as it relates to our work life and it is achievable by practicing some of what is presented here.

Adapting or even adopting what is presented here is a way to become free from career-related cycles. This is *not* a religious practice; rather it is a practice based on inner spiritual need and drive. As human beings this is our primordial need!

♠ Emotional Price

Emotional price is the non-physical energy expended in making a transition. Interestingly, though, the expenditure of the non-physical energy translates into physically depleting a body. Why? The physical, mental, and emotional resources are intertwined in our being, more than most realize.

When people are emotionally charged-up they are able to do amazing physical feats. When they are physically alert, their mental acuity is high, and when they are mentally sharp, their eyes twinkle. So, all these manifestations of existence are one and the same, except that what causes us to mobilize each is different. When one is challenged, as when going through a major transition, it is important to keep the three energy centers in harmony. The need for emotional energy is high when undergoing transitions so it is important to keep a reservoir of the other two.

As is depicted in Figure-1, equilibrium between the physical, mental, and emotional energy centers is critical to overall health and harmony at any time, especially during a transition. This is why during a transition maintaining a regimen that allows this balance is critical.

Another way to look at the emotional price paid during a personal transition can be expressed by a simple relationship:

Emotional Price = Resistance to change + Resilience

Thus the emotional toll is high when our own resistance to change is high; ergo fighting the change is bad. Lowering our own resistance to change can go a long way in stretching out the emotional reservoir to deal with the transition. How? One way is to accept the inevitable and then positively look at how to adapt to the changing circumstances quickly. The concept of the Change Curve, Figure-2, describes how change happens and how to manage a transition through this change. Using some of the recommendations offered there, it is easy to make this change speedily. Secondly, the emotional toll is inversely related to resilience. The higher the resilience—the ability to bounce back from a trauma—the lower the emotional toll during a transition.

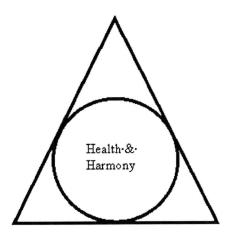

Mental·Energy

Health·&·Harmony

Physical·Energy

Emotional·Energy

Figure·1:·The·Energy-Balance·Trilogy

Detailed discussion on resilience is deferred to the next section but it is important to know here that there are exercises to become more resilient. They appear immediately following the discussion of the three additional factors that come into play during a successful transition:

♠ How We Manifest to Others

There is a triad of factors integral to a successful transition. These three factors influence how others perceive you. Becoming aware of each will allow for an effective transition. There are three factors:

- Managing your resilience
- Managing your chemicals
- Managing your fear

Each of these is now discussed in the following sections with specific tools to help provide a better outcome during a transition.

Managing Your Resilience

Resilience is a quality that allows you to bounce back from an impactful episode of a personal nature (trauma). Resilience lets you regroup and re-engage inner resources in a meaningful way to mobilize actions to move forward. One way to look at the power of being resilient is to look at its opposite: stiffness or rigidity! The classic metaphor of the mighty oak falling down in a gale-force wind and the supple willow plant bending in its path and yielding to its power, has much to convey in the way resilience can work. Those who are not able to yield to the powerful forces, temporary as they might be, can end up surrendering rather than finding themselves challenged by recognizing the power of these forces and then developing strategies to deal with them to rise to the challenge. Fighting these forces takes enormous inner resources, and then, when their power abates, there is no reserve left with which to move forward. Yielding to the forces on the other hand, gives the person a chance to regroup and then move ahead as their power wanes; it always does after a certain time!

To further understand resilience, knowing its components is a good start.

♠ Components of Personal Resilience

The following components are critical to assessing one's resilience in a transition:

- Knowing the situation and having a healthy perspective on it
- Having a deep understanding of yourself and confidence in your value
- Having a good support system: personal, professional, and social
- Ability to take action despite uncertainty and clarity

➢ **Knowing the situation and having a perspective on it:** Being open to different possibilities of how you can go through the transition can be a great resource in developing a healthy perspective. It is normal to not only take such setbacks personally, but also to *personalize* them. The difference between the two is, when you take something personally, you are holding yourself accountable for what happened to you and taking action to move ahead. This is healthy. However, when you personalize an adverse situation, you are trying to look at what you might have done differently to avoid it. The latter is a matter of mere speculation. For example, if you have just been laid off and you believe that if you had done something differently you could have prevented it, you are personalizing the outcome.

➤ **Having a deep understanding of yourself and confidence in your value:** This is the hard part. This is so because we identify our worth with how others value us. Our job is one measure of this value. When that is threatened it is easy to doubt our own value. Losing a job is a temporary setback. What Socrates said nearly 2500 years back is still relevant today:

"Remember that there is nothing stable in human affairs; therefore avoid undue elation in prosperity, or undue depression in adversity."

If this is the first time that you have lost your job and have to deal with such a transition, consider it a wake-up call. If you have done this before, it is time to learn new ways to deal with what you knew from before. If you have never held a job—as a fresh graduate might—then it is time to find out what your value is. Having a deep belief in your own value, worth, and ability to engage productively is key to developing confidence about yourself.

➤ **Having a good support system:** Having a good support system or network is also key to successfully navigating through rough periods in one's life. Such a support system provides emotional, financial, mental, and physical resources. Its absence can be devastating. One client suffered some setbacks during the period following the 2001 meltdown. His wife of 15 years constantly kept reminding him what a failure he had been and how his friends had succeeded despite the economy! He finally had to see a therapist just the get through each day!

➤ Most underestimate the size of their overall social and support network. The support system consists of personal, social, professional, and other connections. These connections are important in opening up additional resources. For example, if you know someone who works at one company, that person can be tapped to getting more information on the hiring manager or the job of interest.

A detailed discussion on networking is presented in Chapter-8: Marketing the Product—You!. A graphic depiction of the Networking Universe is shown in Figure-7 in that chapter.

➤ **Exercising the ability to take action despite uncertainty and clarity:** In tough times it is easy to get paralyzed by overwhelming possibilities of actions and not knowing what actions are appropriate and when. Making a methodical plan and then discussing such a plan with someone within the support system can be a good way to move into action. They can also act as your checkpoint for progress. Once you start moving with a plan, you will feel less stressed and more in control, even though you are seeing little or no "action" initially. Remember, there is an inevitable delay between taking the right action and seeing its impact; much like a wall-mounted thermostat taking time to actually change the room temperature.

Going With the Flow

Resilience can also be termed as "going with the flow!" The following story illustrates how this quality can help through life's ups and downs:

> A very old Chinese Taoist story describes a farmer in a poor country village. He was considered very well to do, because he owned a horse, which he used for plowing and for transportation.
>
> One day his horse ran away. All his neighbors exclaimed how terrible this was, but the farmer merely said, "Maybe yes, maybe no." A few days later the horse returned and brought two wild horses with it. The neighbors all rejoiced at this good fortune, but the farmer just said, "Maybe yes, maybe no."
>
> The next day the farmer's son tried to ride one of the wild horses; the horse threw him and broke his leg. The neighbors all offered their sympathy for his misfortune, the farmer again said, "Maybe yes, maybe no." The next week conscription officers came to the village to take young men for the army. They rejected the farmer's son because of his broken leg. When the neighbors told how lucky he was, the farmer replied, "Maybe yes, maybe no…."

The moral of the story, of course, is that the meaning of any event in our lives depends upon how we perceive it. Things do happen and we must learn to take them in stride.

Resilience Exercise

The following prescriptive exercise is designed to assess your resilience.

Managing your Resilience: Exercise

To evaluate your own resilience respond to the following items. Circle the response closest to what you believe to be your own measure of it. Then add up the score at the end.

Situational Perspective:	High 10-9-8-	Mid 7-6-5-4	Low 3-2-1

Situational Perspective:

I have a sense of why I am in transition
Knowing what I know, the inevitability of why I am transitioning now was
There are less competent people still working and enjoying their jobs, and the extent to which I can disregard it is

Self-Understanding:
Despite my current situation my confidence in my abilities to be usefully employed is
In spite of difficult economic conditions my ability to reinvent myself to be productively engaged is
If I am unable to find something that fits my skills, my ability to re-deploy myself is

Support System:
The degree of support I can derive from my own support system is
My ability to grow the current circle of contacts quickly, is

Taking Action:
My confidence in my ability to plan and move ahead with action is
If the plan needs adjustment based on the outcomes, my ability to revise it is

Total Score

If your score is 60 or higher, you can be considered resilient (be honest)! Practice behaviors that move you to a higher score.

*Managing Your Chemicals

This is the second factor that needs managing during transitions. It has to do with how others react to you. We, as chemical-generating organisms, are able to generate, among others, two hormones, and, in turn, *induce* the same in others. These two hormones dictate how others respond to us. Since job search is a social activity involving others, this is important.

The two chemicals contrast each other by their very nature and how they affect physiologically and psychologically: one is epinephrine, more commonly known as adrenaline, responsible for helping us generate instinctive responses in times of threat and danger and the other is beta-endorphin, considered many times more powerful than even morphine—a highly analgesic drug or a painkiller. Adrenaline helps generate fear, whereas beta-endorphin helps us become euphoric and joyful.

We are able to *induce* in those with whom we interact *their* adrenaline and beta-endorphin, creating an interesting dynamic. For example, if we are tense and self-absorbed with our own pain, we induce in those who come near us *their* adrenaline. Adrenaline has one major affect on those who are experiencing its release: flight or fight! People are uncomfortable if you heap on them too much self-pity and your pain in your interactions with them. Nature blessed us with this gift to react properly in the presence of fear.

When one is confronted with a life-threatening situation, the release of their adrenaline causes them to instinctively fight or flight to save themselves from the imminent danger. So, if you cause others to release their adrenaline in your interaction with them, they simply walk away—flight would be too rude—rather than offering help! When people are suffering personal problems, as can happen from a job loss, career-related setbacks, or misfortunes, their natural tendency is to indulge in self-pity, and tell everyone their woes. So, when meeting someone in a social setting when you are in such a state, rather than launching into a tale of woes as soon as shaking hands, try practicing an alternate behavior.

The preferred way is to start a pleasant conversation—talking about *them*. If you connect with the person, they will sense your body language and perhaps ask questions that may lead to a conversation where you bring up your needs. Even if the other person does not "get it," keep that interaction pleasant. If you, on the other hand, come on too strong with your woes, they may shun you from then on. You have caused them to release *their* adrenalin. In fact, in many interactions people will not generally remember what was said (facts) but how it was said (emotions) or the affect (how that made them feel).

On the other hand when you come across to others as *genuinely* optimistic, positive and outwardly focused, their own reaction to your demeanor results in their body releasing the other hormone, beta-endorphin. This release causes others to experience joy and warmth around you. And, who does not want to be in that state?

Putting others in this state can be a learned behavior!

Managing Your Chemicals: Exercise

The following exercise is designed to help you evaluate your response in different situations and how others may respond to you.

Managing Your Chemicals: Exercise

This exercise we will explore your natural tendency to "induce" the good (endorphin) or the bad (adrenaline) chemical in your interaction with others. Respond with honesty to make this work for you. An adrenaline inducing interaction is likely to result in people walking away from you!

Behavior	(Endorphin Good	Adrenaline) Bad
In my social interaction with others I am more apt to start with my woes.		X
In my social interaction with others I begin first by asking about others and then sensing how I should hold my end of the conversation.	X	
If others tell me how great things are for them when I know I am struggling, I feel uneasy.		X
In a social group, when I know that I am in a bad space, I withdraw rather than using it to energize me.		X
When I want someone to help me in my job situation I do not waste time with pleasantries; I get right to it.		X

When I face defeat, as a rejection in a job opportunity, I withdraw from social activities and mope.		X
When I am turned down for a job and I realize that someone I know might be able to pursue it, I keep that information to myself.		X
Even when I know I am flubbing an interview I have the ability to smile and keep my cool.	X	
As I get more and more into my job-search campaign and fail to produce a positive outcome, I feel down.		X
I try to find faults with others and tell them so.		X
I generally believe that life sucks.		X
When a series of things go bad during an early part of a day, I assume that the rest of the day will follow suit.		X
No matter how down I am I have the ability to make someone happy.	X	

If you have many X's circled on the right side of the column, clearly, you need to work on your attitude. Marking your own X on the "Good" side conveys that you have a healthy and positive attitude in the way you are approaching your transition.

Managing Your Fear

The third and the final factor discussed here, that helps in transitional success, is the ability to operate without fear. How? When there is uncertainty, especially job related, there is angst, which can create fear. This emotion deeply affects those who let it run their lives. Fear creates its own adrenaline! This again creates others to see you as someone they want to avoid. Fear is something not kept inside ourselves as most think, it is something that is apparent to anyone who sees us; we wear it even without our knowing it. It is much like a strong perfume we wear that we can no longer smell! Fear impedes one's thinking and power to reason.

Fear surrounding job uncertainty can be managed since it is not instinctive fear. *Instinctive* fear is a gift that we are given to save our lives. It is an internally driven response induced when we know that our life—not our *existence*—is threatened as when someone confronts us with a gun in their hands, or a wild beast we may encounter at a camp unexpectedly. This instinctive fear puts our body in an automatic mode and impels us to react to it by flight or fight. Even under those life-threatening situations, the outcome is far more desirable when you are able to think rationally, and then act rather than react in panic. The only challenge is getting your mind into the thinking mode. Our response to *existential* fear can be managed to provide us the ability to create the best outcome.

During life's transitions certain approaches we choose to adopt can help us. Recent studies have shown that those with an open mind, positive outlook, and without fear are more likely to come out ahead faster in these transitions, than those who retreat, sulk, blame others for their woes, and move in fear. Fear and negativity around a situation can affect our mind by occluding it. An occluded mind is limited in its capacity to perform. Whereas someone who is fully engaged with emotional, mental, and physical resources can deliver so much more! This is why the first requirement in a transition is ridding of the fear factor! This is particularly true of job or career transitions.

Reminder: To successfully leverage one's internal resources and to mobilize untapped potential, becoming aware of the fear factor and overcoming the deepest fears are critical for a speedy transition to success.

Managing any transition *process* can be a rewarding experience, even though the episode prompting it itself can be emotionally traumatic.

An Antidote to Fear

One way to steel yourself in situations that require your full faculties is to work on the fear factor as a habit. We are all scared of some things that we avoid doing. One way to build your immunity to being fearful is to constantly do something that makes you afraid and hence makes you shun it. So, doing something different each day that scares you can quickly overcome your fear surrounding having to deal with such matters. If you are afraid of making cold calls, making a few cold calls, starting with the easier ones, can prepare you to handle the anxiety surrounding cold calls. Making a list of items that instill fear and then finding ways to deal with them, one at a time, can quickly build your immunity to fear. This is a life skill. It is instructive to know what Laird Hamilton, the person who pioneered the dangerous sport of Big Wave surfing said about his constant exposure to deathly danger: *"I know if I scared myself once a day, I am a better person, and I think that everyone would be. I think that it is a part of actually existing."*

Dealing with Sleeplessness

During intense transitions it is normal to experience anxiety. Intense transitions can be those prompted by a job loss, an impending termination or layoff, or anything that creates uncertainty, which leads to fear as we just discussed. Sometimes, this fear then drives certainty—the inevitable actually happens—which culminates in dread! During such episodes it is normal to experience sleepless nights, or awaken in the middle of the night in sweat, and then lying awake with eyes wide open, wondering about what is next and finding meaning behind what is going on. In the quiet of the night, all negative thoughts multiply unchecked and create a paralyzing emotion from within. As the situation deteriorates due to a declining economy, personal setbacks, and other factors, it creates further anxiety that impairs normal thinking. This is now a vicious cycle and it permeates our daily existence. Its effect is to slowly attack our own self-confidence and an ability to master our own destiny in an insidious and pernicious way. This fear that causes sleepless nights also vitiates our daily performance in all that we do to get out of the very situation that creates these nightmares. The best way to deal with this quandary is to recognize that such angst is common to most who have to face similar challenging transitions. Holding positive thoughts and painting pictures of blissful outcomes from these transitions can be good tools to combat these negative forces. Of course, thoughtful and visionary planning, diligent execution, and course correction, as learning is derived from ongoing efforts, must fortify such positive imagery. Any action to be effective, however, must be directed to clearly conceived ends.

Focusing on planned actions and holding the belief that the universe provides us its lessons through these travails and that our life is not complete without these lessons is an affirmation that, too, can help us. Such lessons make us strong and are proving grounds for our own inner strength of character. Accepting defeat in the face of adversity and retreating do not complete the intended lesson; they merely defer it. Additionally, one's self-confidence and esteem take a beating in this early admission of defeat. Maintaining a regimen, a plan, and diligent execution of the plan are important for success and for early positive conclusion of such transitions. Remember, *"Only the brave make the dangerous tenable."*—John Fitzgerald Kennedy.

Managing Your Fear: Exercise

This exercise is designed to assess your ability to manage fear in situations that are not life threatening. Existence-threatening situations—loss of status, job, and money—do not warrant a response that is steeped in fear or one that is fear induced. In such situations it is normal to be in a state of quandary. But this is *different* from feeling fear!

This exercise measures your ability to operate under fear in stressful situations at a job interview, social interactions with others, especially with those whom you consider to be in positions of power, and where the outcome of the situation can affect your future.

Managing your Fear: Exercise

Factor/Score (write your response number for each item listed below):	Fear Factor		
	High 10-9-8-	Middle 7-6-5-4	Low 3-2-1
1. When I am called upon to prove my abilities, as in an interview or a test, I become afraid			
2. When I am in interactions with others where my abilities can be challenged, I become paralyzed with fear and my fear of failure or exposure is			
3. For an interview or a presentation no, amount of preparation can rid the feeling that, if I fail, terrible things can happen to my future			
4. No matter how hard I try, I cannot seem to shake the feeling that somehow, what I know and do not know will get exposed, and I will be humiliated			
5. I am so anxious to make a good impression on those who matter to me, that I often leave feeling as though I have, in the end, done poorly, because of my high degree of apprehension			

6. No matter how well I do in an important interaction (as an interview), I leave feeling that given another chance I would do even better

7. In important meetings, I feel as though the other person is in control and I am solicitous to them

8. For an upcoming job interview, I keep reflecting on the past situations where I flubbed them, and keep thinking that it could happen again

9. In an important social or business interaction, my palms are sweaty before a handshake

10. I often fear losing most of my possessions if I stay out of work too long and the degree to which this bothers me is

Overall score:

Fear Rating:	70 and up	High degree of fear
	50–70	Somewhat fearful
	30–50	Healthy fear level
	30 and below	Almost fearless

Practice behaviors and thoughts that move you to the lower scores.

♠ A Transformational Strategy

To move ahead successfully during a transition, at a personal level, being positive and optimistic greatly help. Here, success is not necessarily landing a job immediately or getting what you are after but, rather, being able to manage the transition process with some adventure, fun, and personal control over it. Studies have shown that, over time, if you are positive and calm in taking on a challenge in the face of a series of defeats, you will end up on top, largely by being open to adventure, being optimistic, and holding the belief that you are in control, no matter how many setbacks you repeatedly encounter. The only possible caution here might be that of avoiding *repeated* setbacks by using certain approaches and methods that cause them. There, finding a pattern and learning from that pattern are critical to moving ahead positively. Behaviors that generate new avenues of hope must replace patterns of defeat. This is why identifying these patterns is critical before they take hold. In any *adventure* failure is common. Our giving up and stopping to pursue new avenues of trying is what makes these failures permanent!

Frequent bouts of hopelessness and your sense being out of control are some of the worst feelings during the process of a job search—especially if you are out of work and looking. This sense will be exacerbated in a tough economy as well as when you face special challenges as being perceived as too old to be looking. This age factor is a common thought in the minds of those especially transitioning during their mid-career setbacks. As disappointments mount to what appear as seemingly perfect jobs, with each setback, rejection, or lack of response, your self-esteem plummets. As your confidence retreats, you start becoming a victim and loose your sense of control. You may even give up hope if the same cycles repeat and retreat in despair!

Having a confident and properly vetted message of value and then a strategy that goes with that are important during long bouts of dry spell, when you do not even get in front of decision makers to state your case; the gatekeepers do not let you through. This is why having an aggressive campaign—the one that bypasses the gatekeepers—works in that if enough messages are out there for someone to see, someone will see one and you will get your audience that you are looking for.

Studies have shown that those who maintain their perspective in such situations are better able to engage the full arsenal of their resources: wit, energy, intellect, memory recall, and composure. In one study, when simple puzzles were given to a group of adults, researchers found that those who were comfortable within their own selves, fully relaxed, and ready to take on the challenge for fun, were consistently able to find clever ways to beat the odds and get the right answer. Those who were apprehensive, unsure, and afraid, invariably ended giving up in frustration or taking too long by sequentially dealing with each element of the puzzle. Those who remained calm and were fully engaged with all their resources were able to marshal their intuition and insights and were readily able to find some key or clue that gave them the edge to succeed more quickly. The research also found that those who approached their life positively overall, were far more likely to be able to deal with any adversity as a victor than as a victim! Similarly, in a job search, a positive outlook goes a long way in making you more desirable to others, and helping you reach your goal.

Staying positive and celebrating even minor successes and building on what works in a given situation can create a virtuous cycle. Success releases its own endorphins inside your body, which can help you far more than anything ingested externally in moving ahead to success! Remember what Herm Albright said: *"A positive attitude may not solve all your problems, but it will annoy enough people to make it worth the effort."*

Impediments to Transition

A job loss is often a cause for many changes in one's personal life. When everything is "normal" in a life, issues remain in the background and life sails "comfortably."

A sudden job loss can change that. In some cases its suddenness is immaterial. In a family situation, where two spouses share deeply ingrained but differing views around jobs steeped in their cultural upbringing, there is a potential for problems. These problems surface when even one spouse suffers a job loss. If the couple has not communicated individual views around jobs and what their job means to them personally, the changed circumstances can recoil in a surprise. Overcoming this difference and reconciling the two views after the job loss can take a surprisingly large effort and can affect their marriage or relationship.

Marriages or unions that involve spouses or partners from different cultures are particularly prone to this surprise. One client's wife was from one of countries in the Pacific Rim. She held the belief—but never communicated that to him—that his worth was tied to his job and how much money he brought home from it and that she was to manage the family finances. When his income suddenly stopped, following a well-publicized layoff, she continued *her* lifestyle because she believed that his losing the job—even in a tanked economy—was his fault and that *she* should not have to suffer for it. They could not agree to a scaled-down lifestyle after the job loss, and his top priority became saving their marriage.

A job loss can send shock waves in one's personal life. Understanding priorities and then deciding how to move on in a job search can take more time and effort than may be anticipated. Not addressing more important issues before embarking on a job search can be a frustrating experience because of the constant impediments they pose for an effective job-search campaign.

If the situation during your "normal life" does not warrant an audit of how each spouse feels about changed circumstances such as a job loss, it may be prudent to explore these views and communicate them to each other so that when setbacks do occur, there is little or no discord. This simple measure of prevention will allow one to then move ahead during a transition with full focus.

A Philosophical Insight

During transitions people find their lives becoming intense. Everything hits them hard and they start seeing things in a different light than they did when everything was going well for them. A transition is a period of learning and growing. It too is a period of finding new meaning in the way our lives impact other lives. Some even see a major transition as a near-death experience with an epiphany!

One rule worth reflecting on during such transitions is the rule of universal giving. In essence, this rule states that if you want something, you have to learn to give it in your own way to one who does not have it. In times of our own needs it is difficult to be giving to others. The following true story is probably an object lesson of this universal rule:

A Universal WGACA Story

WGACA stands for what goes around comes around. Often in our lives we encounter instances where we do not treat others in the spirit of the Golden Rule: treat others as you would want others to treat you! This is often perpetrated by our own selfishness, the values we adopt, and the choices we make in our own daily lives. During life's transitions you will encounter situations where lack of simple human courtesies may incense you. You may never hear from an interviewer who gave you all the indications that you would be offered the job. You may never get a call back from repeated messages you left in response to something you had sent for a job opportunity. You may never hear from your "friends" because now you are in need.

The following story is a true tale of how a simple act of doing the right thing selflessly can result in something good at a later time. When times are tough and things do not seem to be going your way, it is easy to transfer your wrath to others. Don't! As this story illustrates, you have the power to break that cycle and do the right thing!

> His name was Fleming, and he was a poor Scottish farmer. One day, while trying to make a living for his family, he heard a cry for help coming from a nearby bog. He dropped his tools and ran to the bog. There, mired to his waist in black muck, was a terrified boy, screaming and struggling to free himself. Farmer Fleming saved the lad from what could have been a slow and terrifying death.

> The next day, a fancy carriage pulled up to the Scotsman's sparse surroundings. An elegantly dressed nobleman stepped out and introduced himself as the father of the boy who had

been saved. "I want to repay you," said the nobleman. "You saved my son's life."

"No," replied the farmer, waving off the offer. "I can't accept payment for what I did." At that moment, the farmer's own son came to the door of the family hovel.

"Is that your son?" the nobleman asked.

"Yes," the farmer replied proudly.

"I'll make you a deal. Let me take him and give him a good education. If the lad is anything like his father, he'll grow to become a man you can be proud of. And, that he did. In time, Farmer Fleming's son graduated from St. Mary's Hospital Medical School in London, and went on to become known worldwide as the noted Sir Alexander Fleming, the discoverer of Penicillin.

Years afterward, the nobleman's son was stricken with pneumonia. What saved him? It was the very Penicillin that Fleming had invented. What was the name of the nobleman? It was none other than Lord Randolph Churchill, whose son, Sir Winston Churchill, went on to achieve greatness in his own right. Someone once said, What goes around comes around. Work like you don't need the money. Interview like you do not need the job; love like you've never been hurt; and dance like nobody's watching.

The moral here is to learn to give, even when you are lacking in some key resources. Give in your own way and accept nothing in return! If the boomerang effect does not follow immediately, it will in its own way and *you* will know when it happens.

<u>WGACA Exercise:</u>

Looking at my own current situation I have the following (can be more than one) to give to others who can benefit from it:

#1)
Describe it:

I plan to give it by:

#2)
Describe it:

I plan to give it by:

My own personal thought on WGACA is (this is optional)

♠ The Change Curve

The change curve is a nearly universal representation of any transition that involves human affairs. A typical change curve is shown below:

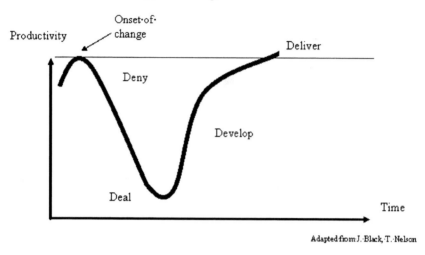

Adapted from J. Black, T. Nelson

Figure-2·The·Change·Curve

The nature of the curve suggests that when we are going through a change, we go from being in one state *before* the onset of change, through becoming aware of the change, and then going through a transition process following that change. This dynamic even applies when the change is positive. For example, when someone gets promoted or wins a lottery jackpot, they need to adjust to their new state by going through a similar regressive transition.

Becoming aware of how change takes place using the representation of the curve helps those undergoing a transition to manage it. The idea behind the change curve is to get past the stages that take you away from being productive and away from a state of good mental and emotional balance to another state of equal or better balance, past a zone where you backslide during the transition. This typically happens through a series of learning and coping experiences. The faster you transition through the curve and the shallower the curve, the easier it is dealing with change in a positive way and getting to the "other side." With things manageable and that are within your own control, you can make the depth and the width of the change curve "valley" to whatever *you* want.

There are specific interventions to accelerate the passage through the change curve—especially the valley—to the next state in a four-state continuum. These four states are labeled in Figure-2 and described in Table-1, which also describes the interventions for a *job* transition. The idea is to get to the next state on the curve quickly and to come out reenergized and ready to take on the new challenge by letting go of the past (the death of the past) and embrace the new (rebirth). For transitions other than those involving jobs similar steps can be identified.

From State	Symptoms	To-State	Intervention	Tools	Comments
Denial (Inability to face reality and to prepare to act in a constructive way)	Not accepting loss; denying reality. Anger; blame; regret	Deal	Support group; counseling, family members.	Discard past reminders; make plan. Use Tool-1 and Tool-2	Just talking about the loss can help!
Deal (Accepting what happened and finding ways to move ahead.)	Unproductive activities; frustration; feeling lost or even overwhelmed	Develop	Create structure, prepare a plan, engage in activities, and follow the plan.	Get organized. Daily schedule; measure progress and activities. Reward yourself. Use Tool-3, Tool-4 and Tool-5	Use help from others to create accountability for yourself!
Develop (Defining specific actions to move forward and creating accountabilities.)	Feeling encouraged by progress; can see forward movement	Deliver	Coaching; support groups; increased emphasis on metrics Increased networks.	Expanding original plan to greater details based on what works. Use Tool-6, and Tool-7	Focus on your strengths that allow success in specific endeavors. Finalize résumé(s) and Marketing Plan
Deliver (Delivering outcomes that are measurable, culminating in a goal previously envisaged.)	Feel good about the changed state and about accomplishments	Ready for next Performance Level	Doing postmortem, Learning from the transition and realizing what works for you.	Keep daily activity log; measure activity/progress. Reward yourself with something promised earlier. Use Tool-8	Once you have mastered this concept, future transitions are easier. Keep weekly track with Tool-8.

Table-1: Understanding the Change Curve—Accelerating Change

Understanding the change process and how it can be managed is key to staying positive and hopeful during any transition. Table-1 can help those in a job transition and who can use it to move through the change with minimum disruption and feeling good about the future! Tool-7 and Tool-8 are in the author's *The 7 Keys to a Dream Job: A Career Nirvana Playbook!*, and refer to the Marketing Plan and the Activity Tracking Log respectively.

As one can glean from this table, a transition *can* last for an extended period of time, depending on circumstances. This is apparent from looking in the Tools column, in which the tools shown here are available throughout the book, starting with the next section. The best approach to accelerating change is to go through the book and spot these tools (see Index) and come back to develop a better understanding of how to manage the change and create the most effective outcome.

*Tools to Accelerate Transition

The following tools can help you better deal and prepare for the transition. They are designed to help you emotionally accept the change and to take you through your change process:

➤ Change State (Tool-1)

➤ Transition Statement (Tool-2)

➤ Positioning Statement (Tool-3)

➤ My Truth! (Tool-4)

Each one is described below and can be used to accelerate the transition:

Transition Statement

A Transition Statement is an answer to the question others may ask. Why are you looking for a change? This change could be a new job or something else. This statement is your honest response to others to help them help you. It also clarifies why you are seeking the change. An effective Transition Statement is brief, non-defensive, positive, and blameless. The following examples are illustrative:

"Recent merger of Electronic Industries and Dynamic Enterprises resulted in consolidating their separate operations. My position was eliminated as a result, and now I am out looking for a new one."

"Recent economic downturn forced my company to move its operations overseas, leaving only administrative and management jobs in the US. I am now looking for a design and drafting position nearby."

"After my marriage I decided to take time to start a family and raise kids till they were of school age. All three of my children are in school now and I decided to enter the workforce as an interior decorator and I am looking for opportunities nearby where I live."

"I recently immigrated to the U.S. on a green card. I was an architect in Europe for a number of years and am now looking for similar work here."

An example of a poorly written Transition Statement is also presented here for illustrative purposes (actual example from a workshop with disguised details):

"My boss at General Electronics was an idiot. He never appreciated my value and the hard work I put in there. I was not alone in this. When things got tough he just decided to lay people off and I was one of them. He is still working there and I am here looking for a job."

A Transition Statement should be both written and fit for oral delivery. The language and how it is presented are, of course, different. A written statement presented orally can sound stuffy.

Most Transition Statements are presented when meeting someone. The following samples can help someone who is struggling with the two versions:

Written

After HP merged with Compaq the two organizations were restructured to eliminate duplicate positions. Recent off-shoring trends have further affected the workforce at the new company and, as a result, I am no longer employed at HP. I am now looking for opportunities in the IT support areas in a company that is interested in making its infrastructure more effective.

Spoken

You probably already know about the big merger between HP and Compaq. This has resulted in ongoing reduction of the workforce. As this was going on, off-shoring further impacted those who were in the IT and software areas there. I recently left HP and am looking to leverage what I learned there into an opportunity of making overall IT more effective in a company that recognizes it, and am excited about the possibilities that are now out there!

Laid off vs. "Fired"

While composing a Transition Statement some may wonder how to do it if they were "fired" instead of being laid off. The difference between the two categories for being unemployed is that being "fired" is also called Termination for Cause. This implies that the company had a reason to terminate and let someone go because it believed the person did something to deserve being fired. Being fired is different from being laid-off. The latter is the circumstance resulting from economic conditions and the former a case of some untoward incident that compromised one's being employed at the company. This may also include "performance" issues. Some companies routinely let go the "bottom-ranked" 5–10 percent performers. See Chapter-3: Managing Transitions: The Under-Performer Syndrome.

Sometimes these terminations occur for political reasons. The best approach is to first state the reason for looking to make the transition. "*I recently left General Electronics as a result of some changes*" can work in a Transitioning Statement, primarily because the transitioning statement is forward looking. If, however, when someone asks face-to-face and presses for details, the best approach is to present the facts in a positive way. Also, not engaging in an elaborate explanation is wise, otherwise the explanation alone may raise some eyebrows. Many understand how political some organizations are and getting fired is not uncommon. Some companies "fire" a particular employee to protect their ability to claim unemployment insurance; if they resign, they are ineligible for it. In this chapter, My Truth!, described later can also be used to write down the lesson from this episode for future learning, if there was any!

Most companies have a process for terminating employees for "cause." In many cases the cause ends up being some expedient to get rid of employees that the current chain of command brands as wayward. Often, many creative and highly regarded performers suddenly get classified into this category, and once this happens, they suddenly fall into disfavor and even become pariahs. The department manager finds some reason why they should be removed and starts the proceedings by giving them oral and written "Notices of Concern."

Once this train of events is set in motion, it is often too late to avoid a firing. The best course of action in such cases is to find another job outside quickly and then ask your company for an exit package. Such packages are often generous–up to six months of pay—and are your best way out of the situation. If such a process gets initiated, the best policy is to not fight what is happening and start looking. It is often much easier to find another position when you still have a job. See Su's story presented in the boxed text in Chapter-3: Managing Transitions: If You are Unhappily Employed and Looking for a Change.

Tool-1: Change State

Change-Transition Exercise
  In my own case of transition, I am currently in state (From Fig. 2):

  Reason why I am in this state:

  Things I am going to practice to go to the next state:

  I will know I am there because:

  Things I am going to do beyond the next state:

Tool-2: Transition Statement

Now write your own transition statement in the space below:

Your Transition Statement

Written:

Spoken:

Positioning Statement

Similar to the transition statement, a Positioning Statement tells what you do. It is a short pithy statement of how you create *value* in what you do. It can also be called an elevator speech. A positioning statement has a format of "I am a…." sentence.

Here are some examples of Positioning Statements:

I am an electronic circuit designer with over 10 years designing complex analog, digital, and hybrid circuits. I have designed both board-level and chip level circuits in a variety of applications and have led many creative teams that have delivered pioneering circuits and devices in a wide range of applications over the years.

I am an administrator with over five years in an office of a major law firm. I can manage a large office and lead all administrative, minor accounting, and organizing functions to make it a smoothly functioning support group for the overall business it serves.

I am a marketing communications specialist with over 12 years in an industrial-controls manufacturing company. My specialty is new products and I develop novel marketing campaigns to make them highly visible and desirable in the marketplace as they become ready.

I am a lawyer with over 13 years in a large high-tech corporation. My specialty is contract law and I can handle general law affairs of a large organization with a staff of 15 or more, supporting the legal matters in today's environment.

I am a nurse with over 20 years in a world-renowned hospital. My specialty is pediatric cardiology, and I have worked with some of the most famous names in this field.

One word of caution: these Positioning Statements are examples of more formal statements presented better in the written form. An elevator speech is better designed for an oral delivery. Reading a statement designed for a written presentation can make it sound stilted. Please make sure that you have two separate forms of these statements, preferably both written out so that they have the same message but sound appropriate when presented. See Transition Statement.

Tool-3: Positioning Statement

Now, write your own Positioning Statement:

Positioning Statement

Written:

Oral:

"My Truth!"

"My Truth!" is a private and personal statement. Sometimes you do not want to divulge all that surrounds your current situation. Sometimes even you are not sure what you want, other than just a job. It is a good idea to be clear about the truth so that you are honest with yourself. The better you are aligned with what you communicate and what your own truth is, the more authentic your campaign and more honest the outcome. Most have the innate ability to spot the misalignment between your words and how you present them.

Also, as just presented in Laid-off or "Fired", you may want to use this exercise to capture your learning from the episode that resulted in your getting fired and how you want to present it to the outside world.

This statement is confidential and need not be discussed with *anyone* if you choose not to.

During a job-search campaign, there will be moments of reflection, doubts, and apprehension, especially for a campaign that drags out because of the economy or other factors. Having an honest "My Truth!" statement will act as a touchstone that one can come back to, to verify the authenticity of your campaign. If your campaign is misaligned with this statement, then there is a reason, and the reason can be found on *that* page. Experience shows that regardless of the economy, a misaligned campaign can take much longer than can be explained by examining the components of it clinically!

Yet another reason for this intimate disclosure stems from the principle that if you deeply believe something, put it down, and own it; it has the power and ability to manifest. You can create your own future! Carrying the written thought will now become part of your being, and the universe has the obligation to owe you that gift. Just try it!

Some examples follow:

Since my husband's layoff, things have become tough financially. He is too depressed to start looking and I do not know how long that is going to take. To support my family I need to get back to what I did 15 years ago: doing office work and answering phones. Once he gets going again, I may not need the work.

My son is planning to go to an Ivy League college in a year. If he does get accepted, I need nearly $100,000 more than what I have already set aside in the college fund. Right now, I need a job in case I have to come up that extra money.

If he gets a scholarship or ends up at a community or state college, I may decide to go into my own business then.

My current boss is giving me signals that I am not going to advance further in this organization. I need to find for myself if I can move up in an organization where I am appreciated and rewarded with positions of responsibilities. I must explore to see what is out there, before I decide to take an entirely different route, as going into my own business.

Recent losses in the stock market have financially wiped me out. I need to find some startup that is promising, so that I can see it through its IPO and then cash out on my options. Once I hit the $1 million in cashable stock, I am out of there.

After working in high-tech for sixteen years I have realized that I made the wrong choice. I need a more stable and hassle-free work environment. I am going to pursue teaching at a small college or community institution. I already have the credentials I need to do this

Tool-4: "My Truth!"

Write down your own statement now!

"My Truth!"

♠ Getting Organized

One of the more commonplace topics of concern for those getting ready to launch a job-search campaign is how they should get organized to run their campaign and how this should all come about so that there is efficiency, purpose, and discrete identity to it as a process. Most run their campaigns from homes or home offices. Some have the luxury of doing it from the offices of the outplacement service providers through their employers, at least for a while. No matter how one is organized, it comes down to having a different structure to their activities than they did before entering this period of transition. Those who manage their job searching from home or home office are often troubled to realize that there is no space between the demands on their time for job-searching activity, and their obligations as someone who is running a household. They are physically there, so anyone can interrupt. They feel guilty for not being helpful, so they give in. This habit can interfere with their productive campaign.

The following suggestions can help a productive job search, working from home.

Sanctum Sanctorum

For a productive campaign having an office is helpful. This could be a quiet area in a corner of a large room, dining table (which may be difficult), or a room with a door and a complete set up. The following guidelines can help you create such a space:

1. Set aside some space that no one can intrude casually. Create some rules in your household around how you plan to work in the space you have designated for this purpose and how those who come across it should treat it.

2. If you have a room with a door, make it clear that when the door is closed you are not available.

3. Make a routine for your job-search activities and follow it. This provides the structure. If you are out of work and looking, it is easy to not have that structure. If you are working but looking for a change, you need to develop discipline.

4. Organize your workspace so that it is set up for efficient job-search activities. Your computer, binders, and all support materials should be easily accessible from where you sit to do most of your work. See Chapter-9: Acing the Interview: Having Ready Access to Material.

5. If your space is limited, share the space with others in a time-share mode: if you have a student who needs to do homework on your computer at night, structure your schedule for the early hours of the day or during the school hours.

6. Remove TV and other *video* entertainment set-ups from the space where you plan to work. These distractions can be time intruders and will tempt you to lose your focus on what you should be doing. Keep them in a separate room so that you have to make an effort to go watch TV and where others in the household can catch you!

7. If you need a variety in your workspace, find some alternate arrangements and use them throughout the day or week to keep you going. Often, sitting in the same place of work creates monotony resulting in less productive outcomes. Consider your local library or a park nearby.

Tool-5; Getting Organized

My Needs for Getting Organized

Make a list of your needs to run an effective job-search campaign from home and discuss it with the members of your household:

1)

2)

3)

4)

5)

6)

7)

8)

9)

10)

What do *you* have to do so that, as a family unit, you are going to be able to have your needs met. This is not a "give me all"; it is a give and take! Do not dictate your terms to others since you run the household; do this as a process of negotiation. Discuss what's in it for them, (WIIFM, where "M" stands for me).

Structured Distractions

In major transitions, often our life is turned upside down. This is particularly true in job and career transitions. During a job-search campaign, encountering bouts of intense moments can become routine. When these moments sneak up on you, you must learn to just walk away from the flux before getting overwhelmed. This is no reflection on your ability to handle stressful situations; it is learning to deal with stress without yielding to it. One way to deal with such moments of intensity is to have a temporary escape. Indulging in some fun distractions can be refreshing. Taking up a hobby, or attending a yoga class can be helpful at times that are hard to manage. In your routine, work in some fun so that you continually recharge yourself and get back to where you are needed. In episodes of intense angst, just walk away and immerse yourself in an impromptu fun activity. Make time for it and move scheduled things around so that you can make this happen, *just for you*. Take time to talk to some family member if they are around and check what they are up to. Here, too, try the endorphin route instead of the adrenaline option (discussed earlier).

Often, those who are unable to engage in a serious job-search, find excuses for not being able to commit to their search activities as there are pressing projects around the house that require their attention. Interestingly, some of the "pressing" projects can be on their "list" for years and yet they suddenly take preemptive priority!

One way to deal with this temptation is to tackle a project as a reward for some agreed on accomplishment, as long as the project is time-bound and short. "Completed résumé: go finish project #1. First call in response to a job opportunity: go start project #2, etc." Having a prioritized list of projects as your rewards can be a disciplined way to avoid getting run over by pending projects.

Organized Abandon

Many approach their job search (especially those out of work or looking for a change) as a chore that they have to do to somehow get what they are looking for or get something close to it. Looking for work or change in a tough economy is no picnic. So, they approach their search with resignation and surrender rather than approaching the search with determination and resolve. The end result of such a campaign is a so-so job that either may not last very long, or may end up being a regret. If, however, a search is approached with a certain degree of organization, planning, and energy, with high expectations, there is likely to be a pleasant surprise! You need to provide an environment where you get "lost" in the process of job search. Many creative avenues are presented in this book in later sections, that will allow for targeting exciting jobs that *you* want. Some of these jobs may not even exist (see Chapter-8: Marketing the Product-You!: Unconventional Approaches, for example). Organized abandon is a state where you are approaching the process in a creatively structured space and mindset, free to explore what your unfettered mind lets you pursue. The results may surprise you!

Managing Creativity

Much of the material in this book evolved from creative moments that clients encountered during their journey to find something better for themselves: better job, better career, and better work-life balance. This is especially noteworthy because the state of the economy and job market in the Valley, and above all, their own state of mind as baby-boomers, dictated a less ambitious expectation during their adventures. Many felt that approaching career transition in a state of quandary was not making them productive, although many started in that state. One factor that mobilizes creativity is our own inner power that we all posses but seldom use. One manifestation of that power is our own genius. This is further discussed in Chapter-6: Building Your Platform: Résumé Elements. Tapping into this natural gift transforms everything around us, allowing us to approach a given challenge in ways that we do not usually attempt. The mentioned clients were intimidated by the very idea of tapping into *their* genius and their creativity and yet when they understood the concept they quickly owned it. Then they started practicing behaviors that transformed their thinking.

Why do we need to be in a creative space during a career transition? In a creative space we surrender our familiar (algorithmic) routines to pursue more risky (heuristic) adventures. Algorithmic routines in a job-search process would be the familiar approaches we adopt to quickly find what we are looking for. A heuristic adventure, on the other hand, would be where one takes risks, finds a clever way to do something using an approach never before contemplated. What does this mean? In a job-search context this means developing an ability to avoid the obvious and taking a different path to conquer the set goal. With this attitude the goal itself now is loftier! This approach does not require abandoning the familiar. The mix of the familiar and the adventurous will evolve based on what works and the degree of comfort one develops in an approach. In heuristic adventures there is no set path, it must be created! And, for that to happen one needs a creative space.

How does one get into a creative space and shed their normal instinctive self. What we presented in previous sections so far is a start: getting organized, having a disciplined routine, and so on. Additionally, there is yet one factor that dominates our being left out of this creative bliss, and that factor is our own fear. Fear is normal. But fear makes us behave in an instinctive mode; and this does *not* put us in a creative space allowing our mind to explore possibilities. We discussed fear in more detail in Managing Your Fear earlier. In a similar vein fear shuts out creativity and makes us like everyone else; *undifferentiated*. Operating at one's true potential requires absence of fear. Ridding fear allows one to tap into their Essence, which is their pure inner self. And it is this Essence that has the ability to intuitively approach a problem in ways that are not possible with linear, sequential, and logical reasoning. Being creative then follows.

Your Telephone Connection

The next item for a successful and effective organization is how one is connected to the outside world. A dedicated telephone line just for the job search business is critical. This line should have an answering device with a professional and personal greeting in your own voice. More lines for routine incoming calls and for family members to call out are the next priority. *Do not* tie up a phone line on an Internet connection if you plan to use that line for incoming business calls. Have DSL or cable service for a high-speed Internet connection. If you cannot afford such a service, then think of going to a library or a facility that gives you access to one. For more discussion on this topic see Chapter-9: Acing the Interview, specifically, The Telephone Call.

Having Ready Access to Material

During an interview call, having ready access to files and correspondence is critical.

There are, of course, a variety of ways of keeping such information, so that there is ready access during critical times as an incoming interview call, which can come without any notice. With hard drives obsolescing the old-fashioned paper files, most keep their important files now on their PCs.

For job-search related matters, here's a low-tech alternative that is more effective:

A three-ring binder, big enough to hold important outgoing responses to job openings and other correspondence, is such an alternative. Thumb tabs organize it, alphabetically, with each company response filed under its respective name. Each stack of papers, under a tab, consists of the cover letter, résumé, any company research, notes, and other materials. All generic responses go under an "Other" tab. Why is this a preferred organization? Simply because it affords the most convenient, reliable, and simple arrangement of files for ready access, regardless of what the PC decides to do at a critical time! Yet, another psychological advantage is that having a stack of papers in a binder creates visibility to what is in the "Pipeline," as we discussed in the marketing chapter. Having a spreadsheet summary at the start of the binder provides the visual summary of the pipeline for effective administration of the overall process.

When an incoming call comes on the "Red Phone," answering it promptly and then holding the conversation from the designated place, can give an edge to ace the interview. It does not matter now if the PC is on, the three-ring binder should be right next to the PC! Putting on the headset, opening up the three-ring binder to the tab for the company calling and launching into a professional conversation, with a smile in your tone can begin immediately! With your hands free to take notes, a relaxed, poised, and engaged conversation can now take place without any distractions!

The other advantage of having a three-ring binder for all outgoing job responses is that it is available to be taken wherever it is needed, for studying without the technology paraphernalia. Maintaining the discipline, by constantly organizing the materials, to keep it slim and uncluttered with extraneous information that becomes obsolete, are critical as the outgoing responses mount in a long campaign!

Having the PC as a *back up* for files and folders is a good idea. Here, too, keeping the entire system well organized and managing similar sounding file names, especially for résumés, are critical. This naming problem can result, when in a hurry, in sending as an attachment the wrong files. The best antidote for this confusion is to keep all versions of a résumé separate and carefully naming them, so that they are not confusing during harried moments. Anything that has become out of date or obsolete must be periodically purged, regardless of the size of the hard drive! As will be discussed in Chapter-6: Building Your Platform, having multiple flavors of your résumé is a good idea. Each flavor can evolve over time as you learn new ways of presenting your message. Each revision must be tracked carefully by labeling your résumé with the version number, which can be located in the bottom right corner with a size eight (or smaller) font. This simple discipline will allow you to correctly respond to a caller, who may have an older version of your résumé, by simply asking them to check the number printed at the bottom right corner during the conversation, and then clicking open that document on your PC screen.

Your Time

Your time, when you are home, is expected to be a free for all, based on the routine that you practiced *before* your transition. This *must* now change. One way to enforce this change is for you to make your own time schedule, mark it on your calendar, and honor it. This approach is particularly important to those who already have a job and are looking for a change. Another aid to this discipline is dinnertime discussions with family members on how they can help you through this transition by respecting your time. If you are out of work and home most of the time running your campaign, post your *daily* schedule on the refrigerator for all to see.

One of the major challenges job seekers—especially the unemployed—face is when they awaken each morning they are overwhelmed by what lies ahead. Some are paralyzed by how this makes them feel. This feeling can lead to despair and even resignation, resulting in your just turning on the TV upon your waking. Once you get into this mode, pretty soon this little indulgence can result in your TV marathon ending with the *evening news*, punctuated only by occasional eating and restroom breaks!

A good antidote when this happens is to plan your next day *before* going to bed and to draw up a schedule for the entire day, hour-by-hour. This is why planning is so important. Making such a schedule and mentally accepting each item on that schedule can create visual images of what your next day might look like. Once again, an old-fashioned paper calendar with appointments broken down by quarter hour is a good visual aid as a tool. Now you're going to bed with a purposeful tomorrow. As soon as you're out of bed you know what to do! With constant adjustments to what works, a discipline to start your day can be in place. This discipline may also let you sleep better and force you to wake up at a designated time.

Staying Focused

Just as staying organized is a challenge, which you can deal with by keeping your space and time organized throughout your campaign from the get go, as we just discussed here, staying focused, too, is a challenge for many. In the age of the Internet it is easy to get distracted by things that pop up either on the screen or in your mind during your regular activities, especially as you are doing research on job opportunities, companies, and people on the Web. The way many Websites are presented, it is easy to find reasons to stray from the main research topic at hand and explore something by digressing. As you digress from the main topic to something else, yet another distraction takes your focus away from *that*, and on and on. This is called zigzagging!

One way to avoid zigzagging is to, once again, manage your time on the Internet. Once you keep your time there bounded, and have committed yourself on your calendar to research a certain number of topics, during that time, make sure that you honor that and hold yourself accountable. Keep a notepad to jot down distracting ideas, topics, and things of interest that you encounter as "pop-ups" either on the screen, or in your mind, or otherwise. Consider getting back to them as a reward for having done something well, completing something, or accomplishing a goal. Interestingly, if you make such an ongoing list of things you want to explore later while you are in the middle of a task, many items on that list simply become irrelevant when you revisit them at a later time! Remember, that just because no one has imposed a deadline on your assignment does not mean that you can take forever to accomplish it. To that point, if you are deadline driven, create your own and honor them!

Your Expectations

Managing your own expectations is important in a job-search campaign. Let others in the household know what you expect from them and approach this transition as a team effort where the roles of each team member of the household are clear. When a routine is established and everyone honors each other for their time, space, and commitments, giving a reward is a good way to reinforce the discipline. Without this discipline you will have many excuses and little progress on your campaign.

Keeping Your Cool

During a career transition it is normal to feel as if nothing is in your control. On a less blessed day, it is not unusual to experience a series of setbacks, frustrations, and mortifying lessons. Such days are especially prone to one making more mistakes in sending messages, résumés, and interacting with others. On such days, it is best to recognize what is happening and manage the day so that there is some control over what is going to happen from then on, at least for that day. It is not a good idea to surrender in defeat and withdraw. Especially on such days, being vigilant helps! This also means deferring critical actions that can wait for the next day or a better day, which may just be around the corner.

Rewarding Yourself

As the campaign gets going and you get in the groove of your routine, you need to reward yourself for staying on track, keeping your commitments, or accomplishing a goal that you set out to conquer. This could be as simple as calling a certain number of people, sending a certain number of résumés, or following up on certain networking contacts. Decide your reward before you complete the task and then go get it.

♠ Understanding Yourself

Career transitions are often marked by reflection and examination. Life's transitions are opportunities presented to us—gifts—that allow these indulgences. When undergoing such transitions, those who use these opportunities for engaging in self-discovery and in better understanding of their own purpose in life, find such episodes refreshingly rewarding—looking back! Although in the moment these episodes are stressful, looking back, most accept these opportunities to be a blessing.

This discussion on understanding yourself is presented here for two reasons: One is to help those who are in a transition understand themselves better so that they become aware of how they handle their situations on a recurring basis, and the second, more important reason is to help them understand and manage some of their repetitive behavior patterns that can be puzzling and even frustrating to them. These patterns deal with their interactions with others. This is important to know in a job search where your social and professional interactions with others determine what happens next. This section is presented not so much to *change* who you are, but, more importantly, to make you aware of how you may come across to others. Once that is known, you may choose to *manage* that behavior to create outcomes that are more in line with your expectations.

Professional Evaluation

Professional evaluation is a service available from career counselors and other service providers that can provide insights into your career planning, especially if you are at a crossroads. Those choosing a particular academic path also go through this as a part of their career planning process in high school and college. Career assessments are tools used by professionals and there are many available. Generally, do not expect to find anything new here from these assessments; just validation of what you already knew about yourself or that you suspected to be part of your experiences. Typically, such assessments provide a structure and a language for formally communicating these messages. One benefit is perhaps, understanding of your talents in a broader perspective of the overall job market, and how the currently available jobs can provide an outlet for such talents. New job categories are created continually and there are literally thousands of them. Having a ready list and some linkage of this list with your own talent is a good resource for your own insights. Yet another tip: most of these assessments are available free from a government Website that is updated frequently (see below).

Career Assessment

Many tools and assessment instruments are available for career targeting and planning. Strong Interest Inventory instruments can provide a solid, dependable, career-planning tool. The Strong Inventory measures participant's interests in a broad range of occupations, work activities, leisure activities, and school subjects. Its validity and reliability far exceed those of any other interest inventory. There is a family of Strong/career planning tools commercially available. These tools should be used to help those making a career decision, including:

- Those considering a career change
- Employees seeking more satisfying work within an organization
- Students exploring career options
- Organizations looking to retain star performers and key staff
- Midlife and older adults planning their retirement

A summary of various Strong-based tools is listed on http://www.cpp.com.

Another Website, managed by the U.S. government, is http://www.onetcenter.org, which provides free career assessments.

Personality Testing

There are many tools available for personality tests. One can get immersed in this pursuit and end up getting confused at the end. A simple and proven test instrument, however, is presented here. It is quick, inexpensive, widely available, well understood, and widely applied, so if you ask someone within your circle what Type they were, more than likely you would get a response.

This is the Myers-Briggs Type test. This is available on the Web for free from many providers.

Myers-Briggs Type Testing

The MBTI® is the most widely used personality-typing instrument presently in use. It is provided in several different languages and has been proven to be statistically valid and reliable. Many corporations, universities, governmental agencies, and the military use it to enhance team performance, communications, and organizational development. Individuals also use it to better understand their behavior and ability to interface with members of their family or teams.

The MBTI® was developed at Stanford University in the early '30s by the mother and daughter combination of Isabel Myers and Katherine Briggs in an effort to operationalize the theories of the renowned psychiatrist Karl Jung (*Uyng*). It was used successfully during World War II in placing civilians in jobs required by the war effort. It has since been revised several times and is constantly being tested for validity and reliability. There is a whole industry based on this theory and how it is practiced.

The instrument itself addresses an individual's preference for *four* personality traits.

The first acknowledges the individual's preference for Extraversion or Introversion. This dichotomy indicates how individuals view the world around them and whether they are energized by others and their surroundings or prefer to address the inner world of ideas and concepts. Being Introverted is different from being shy, which is a different quality; there can be shy Extraverts. Remember this is just a preference, not an either or. Everyone has a varying degree of both. In fact, this shading applies to all four traits.

The second dichotomy considers how individuals take in data or information. This can be either through the concrete method of Sensing (looking at data or using analytical means) or the more abstract method of Intuition. Differences between individuals in this area can create significant problems regarding how reality is viewed and, consequently, how individuals view each other.

The third dichotomy is the only one that is affected by the individual's *gender*. It indicates how the individual uses information in making decisions. The more logical and objective method is referred to as the Thinking function and is preferred by 60 percent of males. The more value related and subjective method is referred to as Feeling and is preferred by 60 percent of women. These differences can create significant communication difficulties at home and at work and understanding this decision-making process can greatly enhance the functioning of an organization or family unit.

Finally, the Judging/Perceiving attitudes indicate how an individual organizes and operates in the outside world. This dichotomy is usually the easiest one to spot if you are Type watching. The Judging type will be systematic and decisive, while the Perceiving type will be noncommittal and open-ended. They like to decide at the absolute last minute! Differences in the way we conduct our lives can be quite annoying to those of the opposite attitude and need to be understood.

Each of the four attributes is independent of the others. These are determined by a self-administered test that has been validated over millions of samples and that has been refined and made more reliable over the past 50-plus years.

Why is the Type important in a job-search situation? For one, it dictates your approach to the job search. Job search is an activity that primarily involves dealing with the outside world and people in that world. Psychological Type plays a profound role in determining approaches that are likely to work for a job seeker. There are 16 MBTI® Types based on the four combinations of each type randomly grouped together. These types are shown in Table-2. While details of each type can be found in many sources, this discussion is limited to how each group of attributes influences your job-search approach.

Whether you are an Introvert or Extravert, you have "Extraverted functions," and these are very important during job interviews. For Introverts, these functions are auxiliary and less important aspect of their conscious personality. Reasons for this include:

- The reason for outward-focused activity in job search.
- The statistical prevalence of Extraverts in our society, resulting is what is come to be known as a "Western Extravert Bias."
- The need for communication and interaction as core job-search tools. While our introverted forms of communication can play some role, these tend to be relegated to second place in the job-search process.

In the table below the letters representing each dichotomy appear in groups of four, and what each letter means is summarized here for ready reference. Taking only one of the four letters, in groups of four, make up the 16 Types listed below:

I/E	Introvert/Extravert	Getting·your·energy·(inwardly·or·outwardly)
N/S	Intuitive/Sensing	Getting·your·information·(intuition·or·from·sensing)
T/F	Thinking/Feeling	Making·decisions·(mind·or·heart)
J/P	Judging/Perceiving	Individual's·world-view·(black/white·or·shades·of·gray)

ISTJ	ISFJ	INFJ	INTJ
ISTP	ISFP	INFP	INTP
ESTP	ESFP	ENFP	ENTP
ESTJ	ESFJ	ENFJ	ENTJ

Table·2:·The·16·MBTI·Types

Career Transition Styles

How different Types handle their transition process is largely driven by their makeup. Since looking for a job is an Extraverted activity, extraverted styles dominate behaviors. Also, certain jobs require certain personality characteristics to be done well. A mismatch there can result in much grief for both the employer and the employee. Therefore, your ability to understand this match is critical in your acing the interview and managing the selection process.

Job search involves Extraverted activities. Even though one may have a Introverted type personality dominant in their makeup, the Extraverted attributes become auxiliary to that person. For example "Perceiving" is an extraverted (outward-directed) category because it has to do with how you interact with the outside world. One can perceive either by Sensing or by Intuiting. Same holds for Judging, which can be based on Thinking or Feeling. Thus there are four auxiliary characteristics that are present in any person as shown here, along with their "themes":

SP   "Ready, Fire, Aim."

NP   "Look at all the jobs out there; I am overwhelmed."

TJ   "Here's what I can do for you; everything must close."

FJ   "We can be good together; I like you, what's with you?"

The following is a brief description of each of the four styles; see also Table-3 on the next page:

SP Style: This style is driven by perceptions formed by data-driven activity. The focus is on taking in, looking at, and wanting data. S types look at raw data, form opinions, and perceive the outside world based on that intake. Since there is infinitude of possibilities with the data flowing in, SPs often get overwhelmed and react by rationalizing that even if they hit a few of the targets with their "shot gun" they will land soon. So they engage in wanton activity: sending countless résumés, calling every possible lead, going to every job fair just to name a few possibilities. One antidote for SPs, then, is to plan, strategize, be selective, and take some risks.

NP Style: If SPs are mired in data, NPs are sure of their own insights! Intuitive types abhor structures and they take great pride in their ability to synthesize something from nothing—their own intuition. They see things that often simply may not exist. They will pursue opportunities and wonder why no one is responding to their "insights." This is further exacerbated if they are also language limited or poor communicators. N types are particularly poor at teaming and sharing a view with others; they have a hard time following the "pack." NPs tend to care less about their appearance and social norms, so they are at a disadvantage in social and corporate surroundings. Those pushing the far side of 50 can look older than they really are for this reason. So, if an older NP wants to go looking for a job and get ready for an interview they should care about their appearance and social behaviors.

TJ Style: TJs are thinkers. They are at the core of the corporate world's executive cadre. The need for logical reasoning and closure is so dear to these Types that they find it difficult to deal with the FP types. Their focus makes TJ blind to people who factor in every thing they pursue. TJs are poor at small talk or getting to know the person who is interviewing them; they want to get right to the point. They see people as a means to an end—their ends!

FJ: FJs are excellent relationship builders. Their networks are large and productive. Seeking harmony can be to the detriment of this Type, so they have to learn to manage that. You do not have to like everyone who comes across your path in the job-search campaign. Sometimes functional relationship can get you by. Some times F (harmony) can conflict with J (closure) in a relationship, so FJs have to learn to live with "enforced agreement." One strategy FJs can use to favorably impress their interviewers is to show solid logic and an ability to draw conclusions without much rambling and digression. Since the J aspect drives for closure, being aware of the other person's Type can help.

Table-3: Transition Styles for Four Categories (Note your Type. Look for the two letters in it in the Category column below.)

Category	Transition Style	Behaviors	Antidote	Comments
SP (Sensing/Perceiving)	Bias to action: Just Do It	Respond to raw data; look for more data; little planning; action without closures; ISTPs are more likely to search the Internet than network	Look for patterns; form strategy; form theories, think before acting; review results, learn. Form structure for closing open items; create self accountability	Before getting into action, prepare a plan on how you are going to get the most from each step, a planning step.
NP (Intuitive/Perceiving)	Anything goes with anything	Aversion to traditional structures; desultory habits; lack of follow-through, forgetful. In tough job market "an absent-minded professor" is a liability.	Invoke your SJ style for structure and reality. Recognize that others do not share your "insights"; be patient with those who are more "S" than you	Solving problems that others do not see is a typical NP trait. If you must solve a problem, make sure it is recognized first.
TJ (Thinking/Judging)	Executive outlook	Plan and execute transition; goal-driven; people blindness; no subjective values; controlling. "Black or white" outlook; feelings have no place	Know when to let go; seek out feeling and show sensitivity to people issues; relax; hiring is a people process.	TJs tend to connect well with higher-ups because of ethos. Remember, though, that your hiring manager is the one you have to report to!
FJ (Feeling/Perceiving)	Relationships driven	Easy networking; more tactical, less strategic; can take the feeling aspect too far and create discomfort with those who are ISTJs in the interview chain	Think strategy; logic; manager assertiveness; temper your people connection with being detached in getting too close to others too early	FJs do well in people jobs as customer relations, HR, training, front-desk. Leverage these attributes if you are seeking such opportunities.

Type: Practice Exercises

Exercises based on Types:

You are an NP. What is your normal approach to your different steps of the job search and how would you increase the effectiveness of your campaign if you knew this?

You are an SP. What is your normal approach to your different steps of the job search and how would you increase the effectiveness of your campaign if you knew this?

You are a TJ. What is your normal approach to your different steps of the job search and how would you increase the effectiveness of your campaign if you knew this?

You are an FJ. What is your normal approach to your different steps of the job search and how would you increase the effectiveness of your campaign if you knew this?

Summary: Chapter-2: Tools and Rules of Transition

This foundational chapter covers many topics critical to the success of a positive transition as well as for the career management process. In fact, internalizing what is presented here can be a life skill that can help in any transition, not just in a career transition! At its core, it prepares you to understand the most fundamental factors common to any transition. Mastering what is presented here can make the difference between running a mediocre transition campaign and a well-organized one that is sustainable in any job market or economy and at any age for those transitioning.

- Looking for a job, either when you are nearing retirement, laid off, or in any other situation, is a transition and must be approached with a process that can be managed to provide the outcome you desire. During a transition your life is changing and not ending!

- A transition is a life's journey that can be *planned* for by reaching the right destination. This journey can be made adventuresome with some risk-taking and following proven methods.

- Recognize your own fear and work diligently to rid it. When you wear your fear others can see it, while you cannot. How fear affects what you communicate keeps getting in the way of what you wish to achieve.

- The emotional price you pay during your transition (any of life's transitions) is proportional to your own resistance to change and inversely to your resilience.

- Resilience is your ability to bounce back in an adverse situation and function at your full potential.

- In your interactions with others you release two chemicals within your own body—endorphins (good) and adrenaline (bad). The same chemicals are induced in those you interact with and it is these chemicals that dictate how you come across to them. You can manage which ones you want to release, both in you and in others.

- Remember What Goes Around Comes Around: WGACA! People may mistreat you during this critical period in your life. They will get their just deserts, but you must manage yours on your own!

- The Change Curve shows how you can transition faster and with minimal pain and suffering. Practice the coping strategies. Five tools that will help you accelerate transition are presented in this chapter.

- Getting organized—physically and mentally—is critical to launching and sustaining an effective campaign. Physical organization includes your workspace and arrangements, while mental organization includes your attitude and expectations. Develop a disciplined approach to your work.

- Career assessment and personality testing are some tools available for those who want to better understand their preferences. Myers Briggs® Typing tool is useful in understanding your own social style during your job search and how you use that knowledge to manage your own behavior and how you are able to connect with others during your transition, where social skills rule.

This chapter has six exercises to help accelerate the change process and make the transition easier.

Chapter-3: Managing Transitions

"Change before you have to"
—Jack Welch, Chairman, General Electric (1981–2001)

Introduction

This chapter is about managing your transition regardless of how you get to the point of making that transition. What a particular transition looks like depends on your starting point as is described in this chapter. As a part of that transition, one of the important elements is how to get your job-search campaign going.

The approach presented here is for *any* job market. A bull market, where everyone is hiring and there are more jobs than available resources, can seduce many to take the easy route and grab what comes their way. Even in such a market, following what is presented here can give you an edge, resulting in a better outcome. In a bear job market, what is presented here can make the difference between getting a mediocre job and a long wait, to getting your dream job much faster.

There are 15 categories of those in their baby-boomer years looking for a change in their careers:

1. Those about to be unemployed

2. Those on notice with limited time to find something within their own organization

3. Those with "performance" issues and an imminent Notice of Concern

4. Just out of work

5. Out of work for a while and looking

6. Employed (unhappily) and looking for a change

7. Employed, doing well, but feel lost

8. Work-Visa holders (H1-B)

9. Re-entering the workforce because of a need

10. Have never worked and feel out of touch, but now must earn a living

11. Volunteered during the immediate past, but now need a job

12. Worked in another country and now looking here for opportunities

13. Worked as a consultant in the past and now looking for a full-time position

14. Want to do something on your own

15. Coming out of retirement

For those who fall into the last category, reading this material, especially the first part in this chapter, will help through the initial transition and for preparing a plan of action. Reading the rest of the book will help with different ideas to make this plan more actionable.

Presenting these categories does not imply that job seekers are not unique. They are, and each one has specific needs. However, at a *macro* level these needs can be aggregated for each category and then, once the preliminaries are dealt with, as they are presented here, more specific needs can be identified as they are in later chapters to customize each campaign.

Each of the 15 categories spells a characteristic that requires a different approach to a job-search campaign. Why? Mainly because the factors that drive a campaign are comprised of ingredients that have different points of focus. For example, someone just out of work has a good sense of what is happening in the job market more than someone who has never worked. So, the former would have some familiarity with how to do a quick assessment of where the jobs and opportunities are, whereas the latter needs to first have some sense of what they are good at or want to do. A secretary (a now dated term deliberately used to show when this person last knew the job market) and an administrator (Administrative Assistant) in today's workforce are two different entities in many ways. So, someone who wants to go back as a "secretary" needs to learn new skills, understand today's market, and then create materials that position them correctly for their campaign.

Regardless to which category a job seeker belongs, the first step in moving ahead is getting ready!

♠ Getting Ready

The first step after coming to grips with having to look for a job, regardless of why, is to make a plan for moving ahead. Inform as many people of your new status as "actively looking for opportunities," as is possible and as quickly as possible after your "grieving." This applies more for those who have lost their jobs than those who are looking because they are searching for better opportunities (categories 6 and 7). In this latter case discretion is the watchword, as we shall see in the detailed discussion for this group of job seekers. For those out of work and looking, informing others hastens getting out of the denial state. Being positive and keeping good humor takes special energy and disposition in this state, but it can be a learned behavior and it is the best strategy during this transition.

Once this burden of "secrecy and shame" is lifted, it is much easier to solicit help from others to move ahead. Your support group may be instrumental in giving helpful input in a variety of areas, including contacts for financial advisors, career counselors, job leads, and hiring managers. Thank them for their concern and input. When you do use their input—and even if you don't immediately find it useful—thank them in some special way so that they remember it. This etiquette needs to be extended to all those who provide you this support, even your closest friends and relatives, to ensure that the flow of this goodwill continues. See *The 7 Keys to a Dream Job: A Career Nirvana Playbook!*, Key-7: Job-Search Etiquette, for more on this topic.

At this point surveying the job market by visiting more popular job boards on the Web can be insightful. The next step is to identify which job families are worth targeting. A job family is a group of jobs that share the same or nearly the same competencies or has many common skill requirements.

Writing different résumés of two or three flavors to address targeting multiple job families is covered in a latter section (See Chapter-6: Building Your Platform: Multiple-position Résumés).

Regardless of the category to which a job seeker belongs, the following steps are necessary for getting ready to move on with the search:

- **Emotionally accepting** the situation and thinking positively to move ahead,

- **Soliciting Spousal support** may sound superfluous, but it is very important. Some spouses (or partners) become passive aggressive when their mate is looking for a job, especially from a jobless position. Some even become hostile and demean them creating major problems in building confidence and good job-search campaign. If necessary, seeing a marriage counselor or a therapist can be of help, too!

- **Informing** all those around you that you are now looking for new opportunities,

- **Survival planning** for a realistic period during which your cash flow may be limited and fortifying your financial needs with lines of credit when the going is still good,

- **Compiling a list** of all those who can help you in your search and reconnecting,

- **Searching** for open positions on job boards and then forming a plan of action,

- **Understanding** what is happening to jobs (see Chapter-6 for Leveraging Job Trends),

- **Expanding** your targets by resorting to unconventional approaches (Chapter-8),

- **Preparing a résumé** for each category of targets (typically three flavors); Chapter-6,

- **Physical preparations** to get things organized so that you can show your readiness for the job search. These include getting an interview wardrobe, getting your car ready and reliable, organizing so that if you need someone to take care of the household needs as watching your child, infirm, or looking after a pet while you may be out and about, especially for an interview.

- **Mentally readying** for the fact that in a tough economy it might not always be possible to moving linearly ahead on a career ladder. This is particularly true if you have lost your job or are at a risk of losing your current one. In some cases you may have to reengage as a contractor or consultant and then look for a full-time position in the same organization. In some cases even these positions may be a step or two lower than your last job.

- **Baby-boomers** are particularly vulnerable, especially those out of work, to the competition from those much younger than they are. Emotionally this can be challenging. This is so because those with less experience somehow become more desirable hires than someone like you who brings a wealth of knowledge and experience. See how this is neutralized or even preempted by using the concept presented in Chapter-5: The Baby-boomer Advantage, Table-5: Hyper Human Work.

Now, having learned these basics about how to get situated for a successful job search, let us focus on the 15 categories of job seekers and identify what needs to be the specific process and strategy for each one.

If You Are About to be Unemployed

Depending on each individual situation, those about to be laid off face two immediate challenges even before getting organized to move on. They are described in the following two sections.

♠ Dealing with the Loss

If you were just notified of being laid-off, you need to accept the news and must deal with your loss, even though you still may have a job. You may have your job from that point on for anywhere between a few minutes (you may be escorted out immediately upon notification) to several months. In either case you are technically out of work. Legally you are not terminated until you can no longer go back to your place of work, but still you are out of a job. No matter how long you had been anticipating this, or especially if this came as a total surprise, there is a degree of shock for which few are prepared when it actually happens.

Some companies routinely let go a percentage of their "lowest ranking" employees (see "The Under-Performer Syndrome" below). Others announce that businesses that are not meeting financial performance goals, regardless of the talent that is staffing them, will be closed and affected people laid off. Although both categories of out-of-work job seekers now have to deal with finding themselves a new job, their circumstances are different, and how they feel about the new status will be colored by their own frame of mind. This will show in the way they project themselves: the language they use, the attitude they wear, and the confidence with which they move forward. The window that they choose to view the world now lets the world see them through that very window. This is why it is critical to get past this state of mind and start behaving positively as soon as one is able.

Burning Your Bridges

After learning of the impending unemployment, many get emotionally distressed. In such a state it is difficult to be rational and think logically through the best course of action that can protect long-term prospects and success. Many, in a fit of pique, hastily react negatively to what has just happened to them and take actions that create more problems downstream for their own success. Some make assumptions about who might have conspired for their being out of work. Based on these assumptions, they hastily act in a way that compromises their relationships with the very people who might have come to their future aid had they been more diplomatic.

There is a subtle and interesting human dynamic at play here that most do not recognize or use to their advantage: If someone has indeed done you harm and was the cause of your grief, your alienating that person is exactly the wrong move. Getting back at them directly in ill will and humor would be a wrong move. Why? If that person has caused your termination in an underhanded way, the guilt that person carries may help you. This may sound counterintuitive, but what is at play here is the psychology of guilt. Now, if the need comes for that person to do something for you, they might go out of their way to be helpful and kind to you, since they no longer see you as a threat. If you still feel revengeful then you must wait for an opportunity to return in kind at a later time. Remember the law of Universal Giving (WGACA story in Chapter-2). Do not waste your valuable time and energy in the moment on negative people.

Bottom line: never burn your bridges and relationships in which you have invested your lifetime in a moment of irrationality. Most terminations and situations surrounding them are irreversible. Do not compound your misfortune by emotionally reacting to a perceived injustice. Even if the action seems perfectly rational in the moment, defer the impulse until you compose yourself and think of its consequences. When in doubt *avoid* attacking or trashing others.

The "Under-Performer" Syndrome

It is particularly difficult for those who are coming out of organizations that lay off their "low performing" employees. In such organizations even if those that are laid off for other reasons—as can happen if a business is closing because of market conditions, or a reorganization—feel that they, too, are now branded as "low performing!" This self-opinion further compounds the negativity around a job loss.

The best way to overcome this feeling of perceived inadequacy in the face of personal defeat is to be reassured by acknowledging that most performance-measurement systems, even in well-managed organizations, are highly political, arbitrary, inconsistent, and subjective. This is why when positioning for job searching, it is a good idea to state that whatever it is that you do, *you* consider yourself tops—as opposed to stating how you were *ranked*. Another way is to say what you are best at doing. For example, if you are an financial analyst, you may want to present yourself as someone who is an ace financial analyst and then say that you are best at presenting incisive analysis for a business in a highly volatile market. This may resonate with the employer if they are facing a volatile market and your research indicated that prior to your presenting yourself. The other suggestion here, too, is not to blame anyone or try to explain why you were not "ranked" at the top or let go ("They didn't know what they were doing").

Those on Notice

Often, larger companies that are downsizing are putting employees on notice and giving them a fixed amount of time to find suitable positions from within. During this period, typically three months, employees on notice can scour the company's internal postings to see what is appropriate for them to pursue. Then they contact the respective hiring manager and present their credentials for a face-to-face interview, holding high hopes that they will be selected to continue their employment. Often these hopes are illusory.

The False-Hopes syndrome

Those who have limited time to find alternate positions within their company hold out the hope for being offered something worthwhile. This expectation is further fortified by their belief that their tenure with the company would give them priority and special consideration. As a result, they keep pursuing opportunity after opportunity within their own company during this "grace" period. Familiarity with their own organization leads them to believe that their tenure should be enough for their potential hiring managers to be fully aware of their credentials and value, and that their marketing of themselves should be limited to making a few phone calls. Many keep going back to their office to find something useful to do rather than focusing on their own plan to launch a viable campaign. They fully expect to be hired back and continue their employment uninterrupted!

Nothing could be further from the truth. The hiring managers are looking to fill open positions with the best candidate and not the most available or familiar. Invariably, if hiring managers do not find exceptional candidates, they wait until they are able to open the position for outside applicants. In this case you have lost a golden opportunity to present yourself in a favorable way to the hiring manager who might have looked at your candidacy with greater weight if it were presented more professionally, in a more compelling way, and with a bit of a more studied campaign. The insidious effect of holding out hope that you would be rehired is that once the "grace" period is over, you have to launch a more serious campaign from the start anyway for the outside job market. Often, this gets harder after three months of holding false hopes and rejections. More often than not these interviews are given, if at all, more out of courtesy.

A word of advice: always enter the "grace" period following the notification as a period where you have a renewed chance to make an impression with the hiring managers *within your own company*. This effort in no way should be underestimated because you are now looking from within your own familiar ground. Always prepare as if this were a competitive and open *outside* position and, depending on circumstances ("low ranking" for instance) for being on notice as an opportunity with minimum chances of success. Most companies show a success rate of "rehiring" within the grace period of less than 10 percent. This means that 90 percent of the positions were filled with candidates from the open market, even when their skills posted on the job requisition were identical to the ones for candidates who were notified and were given the grace period.

The other indignity faced by those given the grace period is that many times hiring managers set up interviews with anxious candidates and do not show up for them. They rationalize that the interviewees are inside the company and have nothing to do and should understand busy managers being suddenly unavailable. If this happens more than a couple of times, complain to the HR recruiter and decide if you really care to hold out further hopes of being "rehired" by your own company.

Imminent *Notice of Concern*

Many organizations engage in weeding out otherwise excellent workers merely because they simply do not get along with the new management or that they face changes that make it difficult for the employees to adjust to their new environment. Gradually, they fall in disfavor with the management and become a liability. Despite their past stellar employment record the new management does not give them the time or coaching necessary for their re-integration. The management feels uncomfortable with their continued presence, even though their performance is otherwise excellent.

In many such situations the most common approach management adopts is to find some ways to make the employee's ongoing performance an issue and give a oral notice of concern. This can take place in a variety of ways. Initially, the employee is made to feel uncomfortable by being excluded from most common departmental courtesies as meetings, celebrations, and memos or emails. Then they start getting no-win assignments, whereby they are unlikely to perform well on them despite their stellar history.

When this treatment continues for a while, the expectation is that the employee will leave on their own and clear the way to someone else in their place. If this uncomfortable situation continues, the employee's immediate supervisor finds some reason to give a "written notice of concern," whereby the employee gets a surprising list of "inadequacies" that suddenly become apparent to the management. In some cases, particularly for otherwise excellent employees, this can be something as trivial as not using the right font in an overhead presentation to showing up to a meeting a few minutes late. The idea here is to legally protect the course of action that the employer has chosen to take so that the employee in question can be terminated (for cause).

For most employees this is a no-win situation. Continuing to fight under the circumstances makes working conditions unbearable. Quitting in disgust is often untenable because then they become unemployed, finding it difficult to land another job, especially in a difficult economy. Anyone leaving voluntarily can also compromises qualifying for their unemployment benefits.

The best course of action in such situations is to detect events and their import early in their tracks and take preemptive action. The problem most face in such situations is that they go into denial over the initial treatment. They rationalize by convincing themselves that they are imagining what is happening to them. They also reason that the boss is in a bad mood and would get over it if they change their attitude towards the boss.

Once things have gone on a wrong track the first step to take is for you to have a meeting with the supervisor and confront the issue. If no clear answers are forthcoming and the issue is not resolved to satisfaction, you must start looking for a job *outside* the company. Even though there may be open positions for someone with your qualifications inside the company, the current management can block your move to another location.

Even if a marginally better job or position outside the company is viable it is a good idea to pursue it with some priority. Having a job and looking is always an advantage and you must learn how to parlay that into a new job.

Once a job is in hand, the best approach is to go to the boss and ask for an "exit package" by stating that it may be mutually beneficial if you two went your separate ways. You do not need to disclose that you now have another job. Most companies are relieved to accommodate this request and are willing to give up to six months severance package to avoid legal troubles. This is, of course, negotiable.

The alternatives to this approach are not pleasant. Employees may be downgraded in performance, eventually hitting the bottom five percent. This then forces "a termination for cause."

When there is a discord between an employee and the employer and the situation deteriorates to where disciplinary process rules the conduct between the two, some are tempted to seek the help of an attorney. They feel that with the help of a third party using their legal clout there is some advantage to be gained. Generally, this is not a good idea. It is often difficult to find a good lawyer who will champion your cause. Once you bring in a third party with a legal clout, all dialog suddenly ends. Any settlement that is likely can be quickly dissipated by the legal costs. This may also make it difficult for you to find future employment. The best approach to maintain a healthy dialog between you and your manager (including the HR) and fashion the best package that is available. Most are surprised by how easy it is to get what they want by objectively presenting your case and then finding some common ground on which to settle. Some companies have arbitration agents and some even have ombudsmen who oversee ethical matters of the company. Seeking their assistance can also be a good choice.

Just Out of Work

Surprisingly, this category applies to both, those notified and immediately terminated and those continuing for a period after notification. Each one is briefly discussed below.

Out of Work and Terminated

Some companies do not believe in waiting to terminate immediately upon notification. In fact, some are so hasty in the way they remove employees, that employees get invited to a group meeting. Someone remotely familiar stands up and announces that they are all now no longer employees of the company, and are escorted out with a packet in their hands, giving details of their severance. This abrupt process leaves many in shock, especially those who had no clue that this was coming.

Out of Work, Awaiting Termination

Some companies notify their employees of the impending termination and let them continue coming to work for a period of time. Sometimes, this period can be as much as three months. This, in essence, is being out of work with an agonizing period of being allowed to go back to place of "work" and finding some common ground with those who are still employed there. The sooner you reconcile to the reality of being out of work and stop going to "work," pretending that everything is normal, the better off you are in moving ahead.

Like all major changes, the fear of the unknown is a substantial factor and hurdle in coping with unemployment. When we lose our job, we may experience a "death" similar to someone who is close to us passing away. Some even characterize this loss as a near-death experience when they rely on their jobs so deeply, well beyond their financial needs. The grieving process, as a result, varies from person to person but must be dealt with by first becoming aware of it by getting out of the denial state. To keep going back to work, even when you know you have no job and staying there merely because you are allowed to, prolong the denial stage. Actively making arrangements for alternate employment is the best antidote for this temptation.

Out of Work for a While and Looking

If you have been out of work for a while and looking, it is easy to start getting discouraged after a few months. As this period of inability to generate action and move ahead approaches the first anniversary of being out of work in a tough market, it is easy to slide into a funk. A feeling of despair, hopelessness, and defeat can often follow this. With these feelings, it gets progressively harder to reenergize the job-search campaign and redirect it or find a new approach to pursue with any conviction.

And yet, that is what is needed to galvanize the job search with action, new energy, and a new direction. It is easy to slide into an approach to the job search that incrementally leads to feckless efforts by developing hopes that were unrealistic to start with. Metaphorically, it is akin to turning up the gain or volume on a piece of music that is bad to start with; it does not get better that way. Thus when things do not produce results over a period of time, merely increasing the activity such as sending more résumés, will not generally work. And, why does this happen?

♠ Switching from a Sprint to a Marathon

If the original campaign was started with a willy-nilly approach followed by ongoing tweaking over a period of time, then a less than positive outcome should not be a surprise. You need to attack the job-search campaign with earnest from the get go. One way to approach this is to treat it more like a marathon than a sprint after giving it a fair chance. Why? Because if the campaign does not result in the desired outcome within a reasonable time—three months in a tough job market—you need to buckle up for a long and rough ride. This is why a patchwork résumé and a weak campaign are not a good way to start a job search, especially in a tough market or a in a deteriorating economy. With a willy-nilly approach, continued rejection or inaction result in increasingly frustrating experiences. These defeats cause diffidence in your ongoing efforts, which create more defeats, triggering a vicious cycle. If you are financially limited, the impact of this train of events is further exacerbated.

Even with adequate finances, this transition can be challenging at the emotional level alone.

This is why for those whose finances do not provide them the staying power necessary for a marathon campaign, it is all the more critical to have spent the time getting the campaign on the right footing from the get go, especially in a tough job market and especially for the mid-career professionals. Ironically, those with constrained finances try to shorten their campaign by hastening the *front-end process*—cobbling together a résumé, haphazardly sending it out even though it is not presentable, and without a marketing plan, and resorting to a shotgun approach, just to get things going, as if in a panic. Such a start takes forever to result in a meaningful outcome, even when the job market is reasonably good. Launching a job search in fits and starts makes the overall campaign that much more stressful and feckless. Some even pay for résumé-blaster services that send out their résumés by the thousands, just to get the word out. This is counterproductive. Most recruiters and employers simply delete such unsolicited blasts. This is why it is critical to take the time to get the campaign properly in order and vet it before launching, especially when one's financial horizon is limited.

The other strategy, too, might be to ramp up a campaign with a deliberate plan so that learning occurs as early inputs provide actionable feedback to improve ongoing messages. Additionally, a properly organized campaign laid on a solid foundation makes it easy to switch from a sprint to a marathon.

How to regroup if one has already started their campaign in a less than desirable way and has now come to realize that it is floundering after several months into it? The first step is to recognize what is happening: it can be called trying to solve a management problem with a technical solution.

♠ Solving a Management Problem with a Technical Approach

When a campaign is weltering in setbacks and defeats and appears stuck without reasonable action, the first step is to recognize that this is happening. The second is to take immediate action to negate its effect and recover from it. It is easy to keep hoping that something would change by working harder or tweaking here and there. The wrong thing to do is to translate defeats and frustrations to anger and anger into irrational behavior, and then into fear. This is a never-ending cycle that spirals into a doomed campaign.

In the management lexicon, there is a principle that is used in solving a problem and taking action. That principle is based on solving a given problem using the proper strategy. To solve a management problem, no amount of technical expertise can come to its rescue; management skills and not technical talent must solve it. A technical approach in this case is akin to incremental changes to an already doomed campaign. The management approach is to change the fundamental nature of the campaign and then march ahead.

There is a famous quote of Einstein's that captures the spirit of what is presented in this paragraph: *"Significant problems of today cannot be solved by applying the same level of thinking as when we created them."* The significant problem in this context is that all the past actions have been to no avail. The first thing to do, then, is to start from the beginning and adopt a radically different approach. The best place to start this is to review the whole campaign, its lessons, and extract as much learning from it as is objectively possible to fold it into the next generation of *different* actions. Do not engage in actions that merely increase the speed with which you do the wrong things.

The first step in reenergizing the campaign, then, is to identify what jobs are realistically within your reach. For this, starting fresh and compiling a list of jobs that appear within your past experience, talents, and objective are a good start. It is also a good idea to look at the trends to see what has happened to the jobs in a particular job family, so that you can extrapolate what the outlook is over the next few months or years. (See Chapter-6: Building Your Platform; Leveraging Job Trends.)

Once the correct job is identified, the next step is to ensure that an invigorating résumé is positioned for that job and provides a competitive advantage in the market. After this is done the remaining actions are similar to the sequence listed in the previous section except that there are some additional factors. The following steps are recommended to *reenergize* a tired campaign.

- **Emotionally accepting** that things need to change and then thinking positively to move ahead with renewed energy, despite past rejections,

- **Identifying patterns** that frustrate moving on to next steps in the job search and replacing them with behaviors that create meaningful action,

- **Reconnecting** with all those around you and communicating to them that you are still looking for new opportunities,

- **Revisiting the list** of all those who can help you in your search and reconnecting with positive and optimistic perspectives. Communicate to them what is now different,

- **Searching** for open positions on job boards and then forming a dynamic plan of action; constantly making adjustments to the message and tactics based on a plan,

- **Developing** an understanding of what is happening to the job market (trends); changing the message in the résumés and cover letters to reflect this understanding *individually,*

- **Positively and creatively** listing the preceding period (out of work) on the résumé as when you were engaged as a consultant, volunteer, or part-time employee,

- **Expanding your targets** by resorting to transformational approaches with even more commitment (see Chapter-8: Unconventional Approaches),

- **Preparing your résumé** for each category of targets and then fortifying each transmittal with a well-researched and highly targeted cover letter (see Chapter-6 and Chapter-8),

- Increasing overall reliance on **networking** and spending more efforts on network-related activities and responses than in the past,

- Being more open to **consulting**, part-time, and ad-hoc assignments to generate engagements even though they may be short-lived and ill paid,

- Being more open to **flexible assignments** where a job requires a broader skill-set not normally contemplated and perhaps at a salary below what was considered "normal,"

- **Developing an alternate trade** or ability to generate work that pays, while simultaneously looking for a job within your career,

- **Seeking professional help** by getting in touch with reputable professionals in the career management field, screening them for a match and then making a small investment in their services. Many, often underestimate how effective good professional help can be. If a good coach can give you a jump start and shave off months of trial and error, landing you a great job, a few hundred dollars spent can be a good investment.

One approach to overcome the feeling of inaction and to move from a sprint to a marathon is to first map out a portfolio of skills that are in ready demand for a trade job. These skills can generate some relief in your ability to generate quick income by engaging in activities that harness them while continuing to look for jobs within your career. By being able to generate income while continuing to look within the main career, one is able to do more selective targeting and allow more time to land a job in a difficult economy. This is particularly fruitful when one or more of the skills stem from natural gifts or trades.

In one instance, one client, a software program manager, was skilled at remodeling kitchens and redoing residential wiring. So, starting with his own neighbors and friends, he first moonlighted with small jobs—his regular "job" was to look for his career job—earning some income in the process. Soon, he was able to generate enough action to allow him to sustain his regular lifestyle and continue to look for work with confidence and a positive attitude. He was able to manage the trade work on the weekends and other times so that the interference from this activity was minimal in his efforts to find a job during weekdays. He soon landed at a job that engaged him well. See section under Résumé "Dos and Don'ts" item #5 in Chapter-6: Building Your Platform.

Another approach to looking at the entire campaign to evaluate what might be done differently is to revisit "My Truth!" discussed in Chapter-2: Tools and Rules of Transition. Going back to the statement used in Tool-4: My Truth in that chapter can help shed some light on whether you are running an authentic campaign.

If You are (Unhappily) Employed and Looking for Change

This discussion is presented with the following points of focus:

➢ Finding the root cause of your unhappiness

➢ Change within the same company

➢ Going outside, but within the same industry

➢ Going outside, but to a different industry

Finding the root cause of your unhappiness is critical before making any plans expecting to change that state. Why? If the cause of your unhappiness is stemming from actions (or inactions) of your own making and the situation that is causing you the pain is exacerbating, then it is time you took control of the situation. The suggestion here in not that one party is entirely to blame for what is happening. If you end up as "you against the system," then do not assume that you cannot change what is affecting you. Your course of action may entail changing your view of the situation, taking charge of it, and then systematically setting a course of action that brings happiness back into your work-life—and in, turn, your personal life. The bonus for taking this approach is that you learn how to hold yourself accountable for your own happiness—a very basic life skill. This assessment is, of course, not a black and white call. But, making an honest appraisal of what is causing you to be unhappy is always a good start.

Being objective about yourself is difficult. Self examination in an objective manner is, however, achievable through a variety of avenues. Talking to a friend you trust, going to a career coach, or talking to a mentor are some of the ways that this can come about. Becoming self sufficient in such a discovery, even with outside help, is critical in achieving long-term happiness.

If the main cause of your unhappiness is mostly of your own making then changing jobs within the same company, going outside looking for a different job, or even changing industries, as is discussed in this section, would do little to change the ultimate outcome of what happens as a result of the transition. Many employees are too easy to blame the company or the system for their ongoing woes and pain. Very few realize how much power they have to create their own reality.

Getting to your own reality in an escalating or deteriorating situation can often be difficult. This is especially true for those who do not have inner resources and a good support system to undergo personal self assessment and who can get some objective advice that is actionable.

See Su's story in the box. Also see previous "Imminent Notice of Concern" presented earlier in this chapter.

In a tough economy, companies decide their future quarter-by-quarter. With the continuing trend of outsourcing and off-shoring, there is increasing pressure on those who form the core workforce of any company. This is why more and more are working long hours just to stay off the "radar" in a tough economy.

Surveys conducted in tough times indicate that as many as 80 percent of the employees are unhappy enough to consider leaving their current job. This is despite their not knowing where they might be headed. Many feel under appreciated, overworked, and stuck in dead-end jobs. See Figure-6: Degrees of Engagement in Work, in Chapter-5 and the discussion about how people engage themselves in their work.

This working environment forces many already employed to pursue other opportunities but they are scared to overtly do this. Yet another reason is that they are being worked so hard that they are exhausted from that alone, unable to pursue anything else for want of time and energy.

Whatever the reason, whatever the motivation, and whatever the situation, in uncertain times more people want to change than when times are good. This is perverse!

Unhappy Su

Su Chang came from Taiwan and got her MBA from a major university in the U.S.. After several stints at different employers and in different industries for nearly a decade, Su started working at a major high-tech company in the Silicon Valley. She was a market analyst and was quickly acknowledged as a top performer and earned the respect of her colleagues and superiors.

Although Su was a great worker she kept to herself and her work. She did not socialize much although she enjoyed social events and participated in them dutifully as the occasions arose. As most first-generation immigrants, especially those of the Asian descent do, Su kept work as her only focus. She also did not gossip about others or engage in idle banter about the company, colleagues, and others.

On one occasion Su's VP, her boss's boss, presented some market data to the company's CEO and with a great sense of accomplishment, distributed that material to his group. Some of the material came from Su's analysis that she had done a few moths back. As Su was perusing the material that looked familiar to her, she spotted a minor error in the way one of the assumptions about the data was presented; an error not of *her* doing. Su took that error as a personal failing and decided to take action on what had been wrongly presented to the CEO. She sent a terse email directly to the VP mentioning the error and that it be corrected immediately. Su did not copy her boss on this email as she thought it was unnecessary.

Although there was no response to the email either from her VP or indirectly from her boss things immediately began to change for Su. From that week on Su stopped getting invited to any meetings or events that involved everyone else in the department. He boss began making it awkward by excluding her from key developments or assignments. Later that year Su's performance review suddenly took a nosedive in the way she was rated on it. Before this episode, Su was always ranked at the top five percent with most items scored at 4.5 or 5 on a scale of five. In a very short time Su became the departmental pariah.

As Su became more and more alienated from the mainstream activity of the department she began to feel increasingly isolated and started feeling depressed. She started seeing a therapist, who put her on antidepressants. Things were spiraling down fast and Su had trouble keeping her job performance up to a level where she had performed in the past.

After nearly two years of this treatment and increasing isolation, Su's boss finally had a meeting with her when she gave Su a "Notice of Concern." The notice did not list any specific actionable items that Su could change.

As a result, Su got even more depressed and decided to leave the company.

Even as Su left the company she did not realize what went wrong and what she could have done differently.

Su could not see that sending an email to her VP about a minor error that was insignificant was not the way to handle what had happened. She should have considered, instead, going to her boss and personally discussing the gravity of the error and then asked for the boss's advice on the correct course of action. This simple oversight and lack of judgment cost Su dearly in many ways.

For those considering a change in tough times or even otherwise, the following checklist can provide guidance:

- ✓ **Chose the company first, job second:** Decide first where you want to be working and then chose opportunities that are available, rather than getting a "better position" at a company that may turn out to be a "sweat shop." Being selective about where you work has far more impact on your own well being, long-term, than any salary increase. The added stress of a worse environment is never worth the extra money. Besides, never leave a job out of spite to get at the current employer and land in a situation where you may be worse off. Only you end up being punished by this move.

- ✓ **Explore intra-company transfer:** If you have tenure with the current employer and are unhappy, try to relocate within the same organization if possible. This change may revitalize you without starting over in an uncertain situation, particularly in a down economy! For tenured employees, this also protects their vesting.

- ✓ **Research appropriate opportunities:** After making a list of companies to work for, look for what opportunities appear appropriate to be making the move and taking the risk. Do not assume that your looking around will remain secret for long. This may merely accelerate your departure from the company and you may prematurely end up being out of work, just because of the way you handled the job change.

- ✓ **Move up and not sideways or down:** Once the target job is identified— try moving ahead and not down on your career path when seeking a change—make your résumé to position yourself for that opportunity and other positions similar in stature.

✓ **Find people you know in target companies** to present you to the potential hiring managers. Sometimes finding a contingent recruiter might be a good idea. Even in tough times, some companies do retained searches. If your position is one of those that are in demand at the time you are seeking a change, contact reputable retained search firms and position yourself from that vantage point. See Chapter-8 for discussion on Working with Third Parties to understand how contingent and retained recruiters work.

✓ **Research companies** that interest you and then send a well-crafted letter to someone high up to make your case, *without* your résumé! Ask for the recipient to meet with you to discuss this further. See how this can be done by reading Chapter-8: Marketing the Product—You!

✓ **Go in the stealth mode:** When the interest of the target employer gets heated up and you start being away from your current employer, handle your absence, phone calls, and messages with discretion. If the word leaks out that you are looking, all of a sudden you may be out of work. This may compromise your ongoing efforts to land the new job— employers are typically more interested in pursuing those who have jobs, and less in those who don't.

✓ **Make yourself visible:** This may be paradoxical to "going in the stealth mode" from above. It is not. Here the suggestion is to becoming professionally more visible in the industry forums. Find out where your prospect companies are participating. See if your own organization will sponsor you to participate, attend, or otherwise let you in on the action. Present papers, volunteer, or take some role at these gatherings. If you make a mark, you may get naturally closer to someone from the target company who may seek you out. Let them chase you if you can arrange that!

✓ **Prepare a plan and stick to it.** This plan must include actions, timetables, and enough details to force you to maintain a certain level of active work on the job-seeking front. The reason for this approach is that it is easy to fall into the trap of getting consumed by your current job. See Chapter-2 on how to get organized for an efficient campaign.

✓ **Be assertive *and* patient:** Once discussions begin, conclude them with great finesse and alacrity. Stay firm, make your points and wait. If you play it cool and show patience, you will surprise yourself on how well this all works. In your discussions and throughout the process, do not betray your unhappiness with the current employer, find some plausible reason why you are seeking a change and stick with it. Do not bring into discussions your current employer in a disparaging manner.

✓ **Seek advice of a professional career counselor** to help you through the transition in getting your résumé ready, polishing up on the interviewing skills and all other job-search related matters. At times, you may feel torn in your loyalties (see below).

✓ **Take some time off** if you cannot get away from your demanding boss to organize the initial part of your campaign. Having to work hard and long hours can be an excuse for not getting started and focused on a campaign. Talk to your family about allowing you some time to be "home" on vacation and help and support you in the organization of a campaign.

Some, who are looking for a change while holding a job, still feel as though they are betraying trust by looking around. In today's mercenary climate, you should look after your own welfare, giving full measure of your job commitment to the current employer, nothing more. Never fall in love with a *company*; it cannot love you back!

Within the Same Company

There are many benefits to staying in the same company when times are tough. For one, established seniority in that company is protected and there are benefits to be derived from that long term. If a particular place within a company is problematic, then one way to find some comfort is to seek a change where things might be different.

Regardless of the reason, it is a good idea to keep an open eye for a deteriorating situation. We have our own radars that allow us to detect this in advance. This is why waiting for things to improve once something takes its course in such situations is not a good move if you are already thinking of a change. Waiting for the right thing to happen merely creates increased competition.

Make your résumé as if you are going to look for a job outside the company. Start making discreet enquiries about opportunities within the company, especially if the company is a large one with many operations spread out geographically. Explore to see if the company is expanding in any area that interests you, even though the general economy is shrinking. Be the first to be in line for such opportunities. It might even be worth your while to propose such ventures to the right managers.

There is yet one more reason for leveraging your tenure in your own company that is subtler than is apparent to some. This is further presented in more detail in this chapter in a later section: Employed, Doing Well, but Feel Lost.

The following list summarizes your actions for an intra-company opportunity:

1. If you are disillusioned within your operations, trust your instincts and move on to finding something without waiting for things to get better; they usually don't! If the outside climate is also deteriorating—as the economy—do not postpone for things to get better. Find an opportunity *within* the existing climate.

2. Decide what you want to do if you stayed in the same company and then look for those areas within the company that afford such positions. Explore to see if such a position would be a résumé builder or a résumé killer. A résumé builder makes your profile look good as you advance your own career. Such an opportunity, even though it may be short, can be a good springboard for going out when the timing is right.

3. Make a résumé as if you were looking outside and start checking out what is available so that you have a better sense of the market. Do not hesitate to approach your competitors discreetly or even through a recruiter.

4. Contact search firms and recruiters for advice and retain one to see if they can place you within the boundaries of your requirements. This can be done in parallel if you are able to keep this process in a stealth mode. This is often hard and the timing of this in the process can be critical.

5. Become visible inside your company so other managers can see you in situations outside your own work environment. Present papers, participate in shows, attend company events where other mangers are likely to congregate and discuss emerging opportunities.

6. Start reading company's plans carefully and suggest opportunities to your management with constructive ideas. You might be tapped when the management decides to pursue one of these in the near future.

7. Maintain good relationships with your immediate chain of command and let them know that you are looking around for the right opportunity and that it is not a reflection of how you are being treated. Here, make sure that this message is not presented in a disingenuous manner.

8. Keep doing your job well and do not complain, even as things start getting worse.

9. If you are under severe stress in your current job and are looking for a change, set a timeline. Start ratcheting-up your outside search. Staying in the same situation under stress can be detrimental to your health.

10. Develop close relationships with a few you can trust. You need support during this time of change. Be *very* careful whom you tell what you are up to, especially within your own company. This can create more problems and you might be eased out if you go about telling everyone what you are up to!

Outside, but Same Industry

Once you decide to go outside, you need to do things a bit differently than if you were to stay and explore alternate venues within the same company. Having a job at a good company and being in good standing there certainly helps. The idea is to leverage this into a job in another organization when the going is good. This is why the sooner your "radar" detects something is going in the wrong direction for you either at a personal level or for the entire company or its operations where you are vested, the sooner you need to make your move to protect your position of leverage. The following summary of actions can be used as a guide to start your search process.

➤ Once you have decided to leave your employer make sure that you have good relationships with key people upon your departure. Your references are going to come from your current employer. So, if you need to do any relationship mending to protect this, start doing this early and do this somewhat naturally. Taking someone to lunch or remembering their birthday and taking part in it socially may be a good start.

➤ Make your résumé after ensuring that every claim in it is fully supportable and make sure that it shows your contributions to the key areas where there is general interest outside your company. If you have developed proprietary knowledge that has gone on to become a major factor in your company's success then make sure that it is mentioned specifically. If you were a major player in such a cause, then the industry mavens through your publications, awards, and visibility in the specific community probably already know your name. Never keep quiet about your major contributions and accomplishments. Trumpet them. If you do not blow your own horn someone will use it for a spittoon!

➤ Start aggressively attending industry events for your company. If you are not asked, see if you can wangle your way into such events by doing something on your own as writing a paper or developing a showcase on your own imitative. You will then be more likely to be asked to be a presenter at such events.

➢ When you do attend such events, socialize and find out about companies that you plan to target as your potential employers and find out the key players and get to know them at these events. These are golden opportunities for such connections.

➢ Contact a search firm and let them know what you bring to the party and see if someone there can represent you to the competitor of your company in a way that is ethical and moral. If you have an established name within your industry it makes the job of someone who is representing you much easier and compelling.

➢ Talk to the customers, suppliers, and channels of the target company where you want to explore and find out something from them that you can leverage into your cover letter or campaign. Since you are already in the field it is much easier to have access to such information.

➢ Find out what the target company is pursuing in new initiatives and make a presentation to its management through a prospecting letter or a message so that it gets an audience. See the letter shown in Chapter-7: Write to the Point with Letters: Sample Letters (Unconventional Approaches), specifically the one to Enterprise Computers by Charles Smith, as an example.

➢ Research the target company's past endeavors where they were not successful and find out why. If the new initiative has a similar flavor remind them in a subtle way that you know why it failed in the past on similar ventures and that you can help them this time. If presented appropriately this can be a key to your success at the target company.

➢ Ask for an exploratory meeting with a key manager at the target company if your research shows that it is doing something that needs your experience and expertise.

➢ Campaign in a stealth mode, so that you protect your position where you are currently enjoying a good reputation. In tough economic times if the word gets out that you were looking you might not be there long.

♠ Outside, but Different Industry

Going outside the industry is not as difficult as most think. Why? There are many common and transferable skills that can be leveraged into other industries. In fact, many job competencies are industry transparent. Common examples are accounting, finance, human resources, logistics, security, IT (some aspects), program management, and most administrative functions, just to name a few. In addition there are many process-based skills that are even more amenable to cross-industry jobs. For example product development process, customer order entry process, to name a few.

There is also another benefit in doing a cross-industry foray. When one sector of the industry is tanking, another one that uses similar skills can be on the upswing. For example when high-tech and IT industry were in a slump starting 2001, many other industries did not share its ravages. High-tech and IT producers had cut their spending significantly, yet the biotech, healthcare, and service industries continued their momentum because they had the money to fund their growth curve. So, if you were an IT specialist, migrating to any one of these industries could have been to your advantage. You just need to learn some of the transferable skills, as we shall discuss presently.

Transitioning from High-tech to Biotech

With the ongoing outsourcing and off-shoring in the high-tech industry, there is growing interest from those leaving it for entry into biotech. Biotech is perceived as having the same entrepreneurial spirit that the high-tech has had and there is some kindred connection that compels those who are tired of the cyclical nature of the high-tech industry to seriously consider it as a viable and attractive alternative. Much of the biotech industry that makes devices and produces items for human benefit shares its armamentarium with the high-tech world, and that factor alone has much to do for the lure of migration from high-tech to biotech.

There are seven areas in what is generally regarded as "Biotech" industry. They are listed below with brief descriptions of the areas they each cover. More information is available from www.bio.org a Washington D.C. organization that acts as a clearinghouse of all that is biotech. Biological Industries Association (BIO) is an industry group for the entire biotech activity.

1. Pharmaceuticals: drug discovery, disease cures, drug delivery

2. Medical devices: biomedical devices including pace makers to lab instruments

3. Diagnostic equipment: MRI, screening and diagnostic equipment

4. Bioinformatics: an amalgam of biology and IT (integrates computer science statistics to generate molecular maps of genomes)

5. Life Sciences: cancer research and other health-care matters

6. Healthcare: hospitals, clinics

7. Agra Business: genetically altered foods, wine, cheese

Each area has needs for functions that are common to any business such as IT, HR, training, sales, and marketing. In addition the opportunities for specific functions exist as in project management, software, quality assurance (QA), product development.

Those coming from the high-tech world find two compelling selling features in what they bring to migrate to biotech:

- High-tech brings a more disciplined approach to many biotech jobs stemming from the way many of the processes are done in high-tech,

- Many jobs across the two industries are transferable with some training,

A brief discussion on each of the items is presented here.

During the past decade the high-tech industry has been mutated into a commodities producer. With the pervasive Internet, wireless technology, electronic games, and automotive applications, most high-tech output is directed towards consumer markets. This has forced the industry to adopt practices, processes, and disciplines that routinely allow it to spit out a highly complex consumer products in a matter of months, nine to18 months is typical for high-tech. Biotech, on the other hand, takes much longer to take its products to market. Many of these are driven by regulatory requirements, as the FDA approval, adherence to GMP (Good Manufacturing Practices) and other factors. The fact still remains that biotech still could use some discipline in its processes that high-tech pioneered during the past two decades.

The opportunities in biotech, thus, are for those who can see the connection between such processes in the two industries and are able to exploit that connection to their advantage.

The second factor of transferable skills is applicable not just to biotech but also to any other industry. This is because of many functions inside an organization require skills that are industry transparent as we just discussed earlier. Many academic institutions now offer training in many of these areas so that those looking to make a transfer can seriously consider such opportunities with certifications from such institutions if they are required for a job.

As a professional community, biotech tends to be a bit parochial on how it takes in "outsiders." In many jobs a Ph.D. is expected—even required, particularly if you're in the mainstream function as drug discovery and clinical trials. But, there are many opportunities that can be captured with same or similar training as one has, going into high-tech.

♠ Transitioning from High-tech to Other Industry

The same argument offered in the biotech context applies to the other sectors. As service sector becomes more and more a part of the overall economy, job opportunities will become more and more aligned with the manufacturing and white-collar jobs from other sectors. There will be fewer boundaries in job opportunities between different sectors with time.

During the past decade, many high-tech executives migrated to other industries for no other reason than to disseminate the disciplined approach and management rigor of the high-tech to other industries. One high-tech executive migrated to a little known construction material supply company and succeeded in making it a highly visible, profitable industry leader that went on to win the Malcolm Baldrige Quality Award for overall excellence in the early Nineties. The following job categories is a partial list of common areas between the high-tech and other industries:

- General management
- Program management
- Customer support
- Logistics
- Sales
- Marketing
- IT
- Human Resources
- Operations

The key to success in making a switch from high-tech to any other industry is to find the points of leverage in the skill sets and transferable skills so that one can present a compelling value statement when making a cross-industry transfer.

Many professionals are told that to switch industries taking a lower-level—even entry-level—job is a good strategy. Although this approach appeals to logic, it discounts some key factors that give leverage to those transitioning out of some industries as we just discussed here. Knowing what strengths the industry has that you plan to leave, regardless of what cycle it is in, and how those strengths can benefit other industries, where your interest lies, can provide the leverage you need to make an appropriate transition.

For further discussion on making cross-industry transfer see "Playing Golf with Tiger Woods" in Key-3: Presenting Yourself, in the author's *The 7 Keys to a Dream Job: A Career Nirvana Playbook!*

Employed, Doing Well, but Feel Lost

There is a significant population of those in the workforce doing well and that has gathered certain momentum in their careers. They have had challenging career assignments, their track record is sovereign, their ambitions high, and yet they feel, looking around and ahead, that they need to do something out of the ordinary to change their career path and pursue other avenues to career growth. Typically, these professionals are in their mid 30s and early 40s. Their vision for themselves is that of a CEO or as someone heading a major business making an impact on the world around them. They also see themselves as being far more capable than those running their own business, starting with their own boss. And, rightfully so!

Typically, these professionals have gone through a variety of early assignments and have done well in them varying from, for example in a high-tech company, product development, consultative sales, product management, to leading major projects. They may even get assigned as a lead to some major account and will continue to do well even in that assignment. Since they were not career sales professionals, they look forward to getting out of this assignment to move on to advance their careers. The problem: they are doing so well selling and managing customers that the company does not see them as anything else! They are too valuable in their current role. If they continue to stay where they are assigned they may stagnate there or leave the company just to find themselves another career path. This, too, gets difficult as their résumé now has sales as their most recent assignment. This dilemma is not faced only by those who end up in sales through a variety of tracks; it is just a case in point and the most common.

Some feel that to break the cycle of getting stuck in an area where they sought an assignment to slake their professional curiosity about it and to round out their careers that they have to preemptively take their career path in their own hands. One such way, as they see it, is to get an advanced degree— an MBA if they already do not have one—and repackage themselves as whomever they choose to become and pursue opportunities outside of their company, once they get that degree. They are even willing to pay their way for the degree, often in thousands or hundred thousand-dollar range.

One reason why pursuing an MBA, or any other degree, is not necessarily a solution to the situation is that, unless you are clear of the path that you wish to pursue *after* the degree, the same cycle can repeat and you are back to where you started, just a few more years older than you were the first time. Pursuing a degree is often an escape rather than a means to advance your career in *some* cases.

There is yet another thought that we presented in a previous section—If You Are (Unhappily) Employed and Looking for Change—and the same is repeated here with even more emphasis. Why? Because of what we already said: you are doing well and have gathered career momentum. Leveraging that momentum in your own company has benefits that are subtler than are apparent to some. When you are looking for an outside opportunity, the scope of what you can pursue is limited by what you have already done. Your accomplishments will be on your résumé, and outsiders will judge your value by your track record more than anything else. Within your own company, however, the story is a bit different. Many, who worked with you, have known you as well as your potential and your ambitions. They will also know you for your drive.

These factors cannot be articulated on a résumé or gleaned through your employment intake process. Even sophisticated and rigorous selection assessments lasting a few days, sometimes used as a part of employee intake process cannot identify these qualities. It is much easier to leverage that personal capital within your own company than with an outside employer. This does not mean that you cannot venture out and get a major jump in your position going out. No! This merely suggests that for all those looking within their own companies underestimate the advantage they have, because of the momentum they have created in their careers.

The following suggestions are offered to those who are at career crossroads and wondering if they should stay in their company or venture out:

➢ Let your boss know that although you are doing well in the current assignment you need to establish a timetable to seek another career move within the same company and seek an opportunity to advance your career. Openly discuss the possibilities and explore what can be mapped out. In large organizations this is not only possible, but also very likely. After having an initial discussion with your boss and seeing no action, send a written message (email or memo) so that there is a reason for your boss not to ignore your request.

➢ Find a mentor within your own organization. Bosses can be parochial in their visions and may not be able to see the bigger picture for you or the company. Find a mentor in another organization of the company, not your own. With a stellar record this should not be a major challenge.

➢ Find and cultivate a mentor outside your own company. This is someone you admire, know, or have worked with in your own career path.

➢ Define what you want to do as a next step and find companies that offer those opportunities. More than likely you may find this difficult. Another avenue is deciding which company that you find attractive to advance yourself—based on your research—and decide what you could offer this company. Write a letter with a point of view (POV) to someone in a high position and seek an interview. See in Chapter-8: Marketing the Product-You! Sample Letters: Unconventional Approaches, specifically the one to Enterprise Computers by Charles Smith, as an example.

➢ With your good track record, you should be able to do the same (point # 4, above) in your current company. If this succeeds, you may get to head a brand-new operation that you envisaged.

For those who fall in this category of professionals, career transitions can be challenging yet fun and adventuresome pursuits. They often find it particularly difficult to seek out someone who can provide objective input. Doing trial and error can be frustrating, expensive, and off the mark and hence should be avoided. You can also lose valuable time in the process.

The best answer will invariably come from listening to your own inner voice and following some of the recommendations made here. Seeking the help of a competent career counselor, too, can help. The other consideration is making a move when the going is good. In uncertain times, things can change rapidly and some advantage can be lost if a new boss suddenly appears on the scene, or the company's fortunes change through no fault of yours.

Work-Visa Holders (H1-B)

There are many in the U.S. who are here working (or were) on a work visa. Especially those who are on H1-B status, face particularly challenging times when they lose their jobs under the threat of becoming "out of status." Typically within 30–90 days after losing their jobs, immigrants can come out of status depending on how their termination is structured. In some cases the time clock starts the date after the last paycheck. So, one of the actions you can take as a visa holder is to check to see if you have any latitude in the way you are terminated and how your final paycheck is cut.

After losing a job it is bad enough to be looking for another job when one has financial constraints, losing immigrant status puts a different complexion on the challenge. This is because immigrants do not have financial resources typically available to those already established in this country. If the visa deadline puts you "out of status," it portends deportation. This is a hard deadline that is not negotiable. Borrowing from others and liquidating any assets can overcome financial limitations. Immigration status, now, becomes your driving factor in the job-search campaign.

In addition to pursuing a suitable job, those in this category have to recognize that employers are not willing to readily hire H-1B holders because the conditions are so much in their favor in a job-parched market. It costs them money to sponsor a visa, and there is legal help needed to accomplish this, which some companies are not willing to foot if they can avoid it.

One avenue to delay deportation deadline is to contract some agencies that will, for a fee, keep you as their employee and contract you out where there are jobs. Thus, you are on their "payroll" until something more substantial becomes available. Any implications of this arrangement and the costs associated with this contract have to be carefully considered, especially since this involves immigration and legal matters. Be careful of promises that sound too good to be true, especially if they entail having to front money—thousands of dollars—to accommodate your case!

Re-entering the Workforce Because of a Need

After being out of work for a while (several years) reentering the workforce can be daunting for the baby boomers or mid-career professionals, especially in a tough economy. During a period of employment draught this feeling can quickly escalate to despair. For a trade position, certifications or licenses are critical. If the skills are rusty, consider being an apprentice to someone in the trade by looking at ads in the local papers or community billboards. Also, consider visiting super stores as Home Depot, Lowe's and other major chains, which sell home-improvement materials for job leads. Those who are buying materials are likely in need of some handyperson help.

When entering the workforce as an office worker or a professional, checking how current your skills are is critical. If you are looking to enter or reenter the workforce as an office support person—an administrator, a receptionist, or a legal secretary—look for the open positions and their job descriptions posted on job boards. Usually the descriptions will spell out certifications and other professional requirements for the open positions. Search on the Web to find out how to obtain these credentials with the least amount of effort and investment. Investigate and pursue only those that have enough clout, that mentioning the source of your credentials can give you the leverage you need in a job interview.

The next step is to start networking. If you are established in a community, your social connections can be of help here. Be open and forthcoming to those you know and solicit their help and support in getting names and contacts that can help you further your cause. Join local support groups that churches and other religious organizations sponsor. Attend networking events that are organized around job search. Call local outplacement organizations and businesses that support these activities and go to their meetings. Start looking for ads and postings and start applying to see what kind of responses you get for your campaign. Start the campaign on a small footing with a few responses initially. That way, if you need to change your message or approach, you are not entirely shut out of the entire job market. In a tough economy, community organizations and libraries hold clinics for the unemployed to help them with leads, résumé writing, and connections with local employers. Attend such events, and even volunteer, to expand your circle of connections.

When you have been out of the workforce for a long time, getting back into the mindset of working can be cultural shock. Start socializing with those who are working to get a sense of their life and compare it to yours. This will get you mentally ready to fine-tune your overall attitude to looking for a job. There are many who hire you for your attitude and then train you for skills. The other way does not work for them. Southwest Airlines is one of those employers that has championed this approach to hiring its crew, especially flight attendants.

Yet another consideration for reentering the workforce is evaluating if a flexible or variable work schedule may be of interest to you. Airlines, libraries, and hospitals allow this possibility.

Job sharing is a fairly recent alternative that can allow sharing of your job with someone that potential employer may find compatible with its culture. Typically, partners for such an arrangement have to be initiated from your end, and the discussion needs to take place early in the process.

The following checklist is compiled to summarize how to reenter the workforce after a long hiatus:

- ✓ **Decide which profession** to pursue and what that profession now looks like in today's market
- ✓ **Identify what credentials** are needed to qualify yourself for a job in the profession and get the credentials
- ✓ **Make a résumé** that differentiates you from everyone else
- ✓ **Start networking** by attending social community and job-related events
- ✓ **Write unsolicited letters** to higher-ups in organizations you are interested in working and ask them for an informational interview
- ✓ **Contact local outplacement companies** for information on support groups and for help on how to get ready to reenter the job market. Brush up on interviewing and business etiquettes

✓ **Get your image polished** with some accessories that make you look professional

✓ **Get a business card** with a clever tagline

✓ **Create and execute a marketing plan** (See Chapter-8: Marketing Yourself!)

✓ **Showcase your value,** and not your need

✓ **Seek professional advice** from a reputable coach or professional counselor. Make this small investment.

✓ **Become a volunteer:** Participate and lead activities at local community events that are organized to help those looking for work, as mentioned in the beginning part of this section. This way you will not only become visible, but also get valuable leads for jobs.

✓ **Network** by attending organized weekly networking events and volunteer there

Volunteered in the Immediate Past, but Now Need a Job

Increasingly, this category of baby boomers is rapidly getting on the job market and finding it challenging to reengage in ways that they find worthwhile. In their past they did not need a paycheck, as their spouses, majority being men, earned a good wage. However, as their spouses' prospects appear growingly uncertain, including threats to their pension, benefits, or the job itself, they are contemplating getting back to bulwark their joint future.

Until now, they could afford to volunteer as their future seemed secure with just one paycheck. Yet another reason why many professionals who volunteer are trying to get out of non-profits, especially from the human services organizations, is that the future of these organizations has suddenly become difficult due to cutbacks in government programs, decreasing charitable donations, and overall indifference to the cause of volunteering.

Getting back into the workforce after having little or no experience in the corporate world can be difficult, particularly since these individuals do not know how to package their value proposition outside the context of their charity and volunteer work. So, one of the major challenges is how to package the message and target the right employers for opportunities.

One of the most logical transitions such individuals can make from charitable or non-profit organizations is to other "non-profits" that have a business mission and that are not founded on charity. Such organizations include major hospital chains, human service agencies, as the Red Cross, and even many foundations that work with non-profit, human service agencies and organizations. Universities and academic organizations are also possible targets.

If the ultimate objective is to land a corporate job, this approach may provide the necessary transition point or a bridge so that, if the desire to work for a corporation continues to call you in that direction, it would be natural to make such a transition at a later and appropriate time.

Never Worked

This, perhaps, is the most challenging of all categories for job seekers. The motivations are obvious: the most compelling can stem from the economic need. An ill-provided widow, someone who lost their savings for medical or other reasons, including circumstances beyond their control, and a variety of other everyday reasons, all require that we seriously consider entering the job market to make ends meet or even to keep us engaged and purposeful. The first key question is always what career or job to pursue so that the objective for entering the job market is met.

There are various ways to identify what job or industry to choose from to launch your career. This is perhaps the most challenging task. With so many choices, it is difficult to identify which path to take. Even after such a choice one wonders what if that path turns out to be not a good choice? All these questions always create perplexing panoply of challenges one faces.

Here are some suggestions:

1. **Look from within yourself** to find out if something that someone does, you wish you could do. Talk to that person even if you do not know them; they might find it flattering.

2. **Look at the economic climate** and find out what the current job trends are. Find out emerging jobs that are going to create more opportunities in the next five-ten years than just going after jobs that you are familiar with by association. Some job families are now dying rapidly as offshoring trend continues, particularly in the high-tech area, and in the service industry.

3. **Look for action:** Since you are out of work for a prolonged period or have never worked, your objective is to get *any* reasonable job so that you have recent work history. See where paying jobs are, even though they may be faddish, trendy, or temporary. Some income, with work experience and the fact that you are employable can be leveraged into better, more stable

jobs soon after the first wave of stints plays out. If you hold the dated belief that once you get a job you should stick to it, get over it.

4. **Take tests** that determine which professions you might be good at. Caution: these tests are not that precise and often take much effort, time, money, and energy. If you find a good counselor ask if there is something that they recommend. See in Chapter-2: Tools and Rules of Transition: Personality Testing.

5. **Arrange for an informational interview** with someone you know who works in the area that interests you. By having a first-hand discussion with this person, or better yet, meeting them in their own office setting to see how they do what they do, might provide insights that are otherwise hard to come by. See in Key-7: Informational Interviews in the author's *The 7 Keys to Dream Job: A Career Nirvana Playbook!*.

6. **Job versatility:** If there is no particular preference, try to find a job that has many allied skills that are transportable to other jobs. For example, if you become a customer service representative at a service company and learn skills to do that job, it is easy to transfer to a manufacturing or product oriented company to work as their customer support person, or at a professional office as the front-desk person.

7. **Job satisfaction:** Look for what gives you the freedom and job satisfaction to offset the extra salary you would not be making. Merely going after money can create problems later on when you discover that you cannot stand the job after you get used to the money. Remember that you do not have the seasoning of a veteran career person in the job. Because of this, you must work yourself into the chosen job and make your value known. This is why selecting the right opportunity is critical. Do not blindly go after big money.

8. **Large vs. small:** In economic uncertainty, target large organizations, where there is ample opportunity to move around or look for growth. Smaller businesses are vulnerable to uncertainties and have limited growth opportunities. Smaller organizations also have less patience to train someone. If conditions are favorable, local, city, state, and federal government jobs are also worth considering. They often have examinations or tests that one must pass to qualify.

9. **Explore volunteering** locally. Many well-connected citizens volunteer their time at such agencies, making it easy for you to socialize and network for leads, connection, and opportunities. If you are feeling desolate

and that is what is prompting you to look for a job more than your financial status, this may just be the right avenue to break onto the scene!

10. **Contact your local chamber of commerce.** Usually they have information on community events, jobs lead, and opportunities.

11. **No résumé?** Since you never worked before the likelihood of a presentable résumé is slim. Instead approach opportunities with letters, as shown in Chapter-7: Write to the Point with Letter: Sample Letters.

12. **Send letters** (without résumé) to hiring managers and top company officials with ideas you have about how to make their businesses better. These ideas do not need to be anything esoteric or highly researched. If you, as a consumer or customer, envision an opportunity inside a company because of the experience you've had with it has been disappointing, leverage that into a suggestion with specifics so that you can get attention of someone who can see you about it in person. You can present that suggestion as an employment opportunity. See in Chapter-7: Write to the Point with Letters: Unconventional Approaches.

13. **Business Ventures:** If you look around and see how things have changed socially and economically, you will find some opportunities that are not obvious. eBay is a source of income for many who take the time to learn how to make an income from the veritable forum for individual entrepreneurs—from your own home. If you create something artistic or something that has an untested market, eBay is a great avenue to explore if you can generate action. Many entrepreneurs have started their own businesses to support those who auction on eBay, such as selling packaging materials, serving as a collection point for the merchandize, which they then place on the site for auction, or as a broker to sell on the auction site.

With growing baby boomer population, someone in their age group could start a service that helps them in their everyday social—or other—needs. One enterprising baby-boomer woman, who lived in a development, started her own dating service, modeled after the one started to cater to younger generation. She organized social events for those who were interested in finding themselves a partner or companion, paid a fee to attend the social events which she organized at her place. Soon, the business took off and she was moving ahead to establish this business as a national franchise. More information about this topic is provided later in this chapter under *Going on Your Own.*

Getting into the job market or working to earn a living after a long break or for the first time at an advanced age can be a mortifying experience. One way to get back your confidence is to start behaving like a professional by changing your routines and then starting to execute the steps in the above list. Getting a professional wardrobe, a stylish haircut, a manicure to boost one's image can go a long way in reestablishing one's image in the professional world. Also, socializing with the type of people with whom you want to be associated can prepare you to explore if that avenue is to your liking before getting too involved or making a major commitment.

Worked in Another Country but Looking Here

If you have worked in another country and have come to the U.S. on a Work Permit or a Visa, then looking for a job at a level you can perform is a good start. There are various challenges that immigrants find disheartening, especially in a tough job market.

The following is a checklist of items to be aware of so that your job-search efforts are productive:

- ✓ **Job-board postings**: Visit some well-known job boards and find out what jobs are available that come close to the one you held back home. Although you may have done some of the work that is spelled out in the job posting and familiar with the skills or even have all the skills listed, the way of doing things in this country may not be the same as they are done back home.

- ✓ **Get certified**: Getting certified formally brings your skills at parity with others who will compete with you for a particular job. For example, if someone who has done accounting in India is now looking for the same work in the US, the accounting practices differ in the two countries, although the basic principles are the same. Getting a certificate in accounting would bring your accounting skills at parity with those competing with you. Your basic aptitude for numbers is already validated by your previous education, training, and past experience. You can also get a jumpstart by volunteering with some organization to do its accounting work.

- ✓ **Identify coursework**: Some jobs require being skilled at certain subject matters. For example in software there are now courses being offered in Java, Microsoft, Sun, and Oracle, SAP, to mention a few. Find out from the job openings which of these are in high demand. More importantly, find out which ones are going to stay. Then call the agencies that offer these courses and enroll to get certified. Also spending some time getting more skilled after taking the coursework can go a long way in making you more valuable in the job market.

✓ **Make your résumé:** Prepare a résumé that makes a compelling message around your skills. Show how you bring value as a result of your experience abroad and leverage that into your new pursuit. For example applying to a company with a German parent and stating your ability to speak fluent German can be an advantage. Use professional résumé writing resources to make yours culturally transparent; often the language in a résumé can betray one's recent migration to this country.

✓ **"Tribalize":** This may sound odd, but if you just migrated from another country, you have some connections here that go back to your roots (tribe). Leverage them in your pursuits for jobs.

✓ **English and etiquette:** Many immigrants struggle with English as it is spoken in the U.S.. Even though they may be coming from a country where English is commonly used as a business language, their understanding of colloquial English is lacking. This can create barriers in the interview—especially the telephone interviews—where the interviewer may have a hard time understanding them. Enrolling into any program that is offered by many universities, educational organizations and communities on English as a Second Language (ESL) may be appropriate. When at home, listening to local TV or radio stations that broadcast English programs in preference to the ones that broadcast in your own language can be a good thing. Speaking English at home, even if you have to force yourself to do that also helps. This way you will become natural at understanding local dialects, colloquial dialog and English as it is spoken in this country. Also, reading books on business and social etiquette is a good habit.

Understanding social norms is important for being considered integrated in the culture. Reading nationally syndicated newspaper columns on etiquette and advice can give a good understanding of the topical issues and cultural norms quickly. See *The 7 Keys to a Dream Job: A Career Nirvana Playbook!*: Key-7, for Job Search Etiquettes.

Worked as a Consultant, Looking for Full-time Work

There are some who have worked as independent consultants for a long time in the past and have not had a traditional job. They were retained by a variety of "clients" over the years and during that time did successful consulting stints in one or more related areas of expertise. They have now reached a stage in their lives where they want a secure job and a steady income. In a tough economy this becomes a normal practice, just as its converse happens when the economy gets hot and there is suddenly a demand for a particular consulting skill.

The challenge in finding a desirable job here is twofold: The first is the difficulty in finding a job of any respectable flavor even within your own area of expertise because your résumé does not show the expected entries of employment chronology; the second, of course, is that having done well-paying stints in the past of various durations, it is difficult to reconcile to a lower compensation.

One way to overcome the first hurdle is to write the résumé as if you were "employed" during your consulting tenure by an employer, even if that happens to be your own company. Your company name can appear as the employer and the engagements you've had in the past can show as experiences during the time. This part of the Professional Experience section of your résumé now looks similar to the one who held a traditional job. If you have had different employers with whom you worked as a consultant, then list them chronologically as if they were your employers who engaged you in a full-time job. The idea here is to make your résumé look like a familiar presentation of your chronology so that no red flags are in the way of your getting the interview. During the interview you need to present your experience as one might if they had a job in a conventional sense.

The second hurdle—compensation—is easier. You need to accept the market rate for the going jobs in your category. The best way to assess the current rates is to visit one or more Websites that post salary and rate information as salary.com. Although this may be disappointing for someone who generated high income for a number of years, you have to reconcile to the current market conditions now.

Going on Your Own

As the job market gets tougher, those wanting go on their own increase in the numbers. Why? For one, there are fewer jobs to begin with. Secondly, those who are in their 40s and 50s and beyond, assume that entering the job market as a full-time employee may be a long process and then they may have to surrender to this possibility anyway. So, they preempt that possibility with a decision to go on their own—mostly as a consultant. There are several ways to venture on your own. The following checklist can serve as a summary of these opportunities:

✓ Independent consulting

✓ Becoming an independent agent: real estate or insurance

✓ Writing a book

✓ Buying a franchise

✓ Developing a franchise

✓ Owning your own business

✓ Buying a business

✓ Going as a partner in a joint venture

✓ eBay (selling some unique items that have market)

In each of the categories, follow your own instincts as to what will be most rewarding. Do not follow a path based on making money alone, by imitating someone else's success with their venture. They succeeded in what they did probably because they loved what they did. The prime criterion should be your love for the venture, and not the money. Initially, all ventures require much effort to get going. In a tough economy it takes even more and requires longer to get going. Under these circumstances the only thing that sustains those in it is their love for what they started, and their belief that they'd make it work. If one starts a business because of the lure of money and it fails to materialize, there is nothing to sustain the hope that given some more time and more energy the venture would succeed. If you see some business that looks successful and you have an interest in it, the best format to launch should be based on what you know already works, rather than reinventing the format ("Replicate, not innovate!")

Do all the necessary market research before embarking on making the final decision and committing funds to a venture. Seek professional—lawyer, accountant—advice.

Let us briefly review each of these possibilities and look at the pros and cons.

Independent Consulting

This is perhaps the easiest and most prevalent form of entrepreneurship. As a professional you have already accumulated skills and experience in a specific area. Some companies have internal consultants who have clients with whom they work. It is these who underestimate what it takes to become a consultant and make a go of your consulting business. Why? This is mainly because there is a captive clientele inside the company that is going to use available services. Even if your services are not comprehensive there is a demand for it inside the organization, depending on how your services are structured. There is also a good support group you have available from inside the functional area of your department where you reside. You do not have to go marketing your services and wait for the phone to ring. So, if you are a reasonably successful consultant inside an organization, you are probably optimistic about starting your own consulting business.

One of the hardest areas and a surprise to those just starting out in their consulting business, is how hard it is to find clients. Marketing takes a major effort. Unless you have a highly differentiated value proposition and the demand is high for what you offer, there is no easy way to get clients. It takes several years to establish your practice and reputation. Even with these drawbacks consulting offers some benefits:

- More freedom and flexibility in your work life
- Small financial investment and low commensurate risk
- High income potential
- No one to be accountable to but yourself
- Learn new skills constantly to stay competitive
- Collaborate with other professionals to expand your skill set

On the negative side:

- Your previous income level may not be immediately realizable
- You will do most of the work yourself; no colleagues or support
- You may put your personal finances at risk
- You may miss some job opportunities if you are going into a tough economic period
- You may not be able to work with all clients and may be out of work in an instant
- Your cash flow may be erratic and business cyclical

One avenue to mitigate these risks and challenges is to first engage as an employee of a successful consulting organization that specializes in your area. This makes it easy to understand many aspects of this industry. As you develop your clientele you can decide if at a later time you can start your own business and use the client references to get yourself business based on your reputation and work.

Another avenue is the contracting route. Here you engage with a contract agency, which places you in their client organization. If you are working more as a consultant, then you can build on that experience and decide if you are ready to go this on your own at an appropriate time.

There are many good books on the business of consulting. The consulting methodology is something with which the practitioners of this trade have to become familiar. The consultative process is more of a science than an art. And yet, there is much to be learned by doing things your own way. These books are a good place to start reading up on this topic and learning about the trade secrets of being a consultant.

Independent Real Estate or Insurance Agent

When jobs are scarce, becoming a real estate or insurance agent appeals to many as people's desire for buying and selling homes and securing insurance remains nearly constant. In both cases and other similar ventures, explore to see what the ratio of these professionals is for every 1000 people in the community you wish to serve. Although housing is expensive in many communities, there may be a long wait before you are able to generate income by becoming an agent. No matter what those who are trying to lure you in this profession promise, consider yourself out of much action for at least twice the amount of time they think you need to generate cash flow. There are also no guarantees; you have to hustle! If you cannot visualize doing this work you probably will regret going after this line of profession. Your chances of success are greater if you can find someone who is willing take you under their wings and show you the ropes.

Writing a Book

Many dream of writing a book and publishing what they have learned over the years so that others can benefit from it. Sometimes it is not even what you have learned so much as having something deeply personal to share with others. Publishing a book brings instant credibility to your authority, regardless of how well the book does. Good sales just make you more known.

It is often publishing the book that is more challenging than authoring it. There are many excellent books on this topic. In summary, with desktop publishing, there is a segment of the printing and publishing industry based on print-on-demand (POD) technology that makes it easy to publish as few as 10 or a 100 copies of a professional-looking book for a cost of as little as $10 per copy with some set-up costs. This way you do not have to stock a large quantity of books; they can be printed as needed. Many companies offer graphic design and layout, some offer editing, photography, and printing and binding.

They also offer assistance with copyright, registration with book wholesalers, the formalities with the Library of Congress, and sales and distribution through traditional and online booksellers. Some will even coordinate publicity and signings.

As a marketing tool, books can be invaluable. A professional-looking book can establish an aura of authority that can boost sales and credibility for the author in promoting their work. Being published, having a book in print and available for sale, can boost self-confidence and credibility. A small-business owner can become an author for under $1,000.

The following are summary tips:

- Identify a topic that you can write about and explore what the market is if you wrote a book about it.

- It is much easier to write a book about what you know and stream it into the pages of your manuscript than to research all sorts of topics and write about what that research means in your book. Such topics tend to be time limited by the nature of the information. This book is an example of the streaming effect. What appears on the pages is how I felt about the topic and very little is researched or interpreted. What is presented here is a result of my direct experience with my clients in the current (three years) market.

- Writing a book can be a task that requires painstaking effort, especially the first time. Start with an outline and discipline yourself to write a few pages each day. The book will be done before you know it. Once about 50 or so pages are done in the text form, the remainder of the book goes much faster. Often, writing the first draft is the easy part; getting it through the rigorous editing and production process can be a time-consuming endeavor.

- Try self-publishing the book. It is much easier. Desktop publishing has made book writing and publishing much easier.

- Create your own Website and post the book and promote from there. Sell it on eBay.

- Once the book becomes popular, a traditional publisher may publish and promote it.

Buying a Franchise

Buying a franchise can be the easiest way to enter into your own business with a proven model of success developed by the franchiser. Starting a new business is risky. The franchiser has taken much of that risk out and has made running that particular business more or less formulaic. This does not mean that there are no risks; there are risks but the magnitude of those risks are greatly diminished and the uncertainty of the product or service success is already established in the general market. This does not always and necessarily mean that the specific demographics in which your franchise will be operating is a proven concept yet. You have to vet that aspect of it. And, that could be your biggest risk.

Generally, there are two types of franchises:

Business Format Franchise is when a franchiser licenses the rights to sell a product or service and provides proprietary methods for operating a business, including logos, systems, and training. Fast food, mailing outlets, convenience stores, and gas stations fall into this category of franchising.

Product or Trade Name Franchise is where a franchiser sells the rights to use a trademark or brand name as part of existing business. Beverage distribution or brand-product outlets as dealerships fall into this format.

While you take out the risk of testing if a particular format or service sells in a particular market, you pay for that risk mitigation through entry fees. Most franchises are priced so that the start-up costs exceed the cost of setting up a similar business. Since the set up is formulaic, though, it is a proven approach to success, all other things being equal.

Developing a Franchise

Many dream of this idea that involves creating a new business model, testing it, and then developing a replicating process so that you can develop a franchise from this replication concept. Each franchise is identical and is typically run by entrepreneurs. The franchiser can benefit from the initial hard work by both getting initial franchising fees from each franchisee and then annuity payments as each franchise continues to flourish. You own the name and the model so it is hard to copy. The following checklist suggests what to look for in order to develop your business.

✓ **Know what you are getting into:** Start small, prove the concept at the pilot level and then develop a more robust business model that is replicable.

✓ **Talk to franchise consultants:** This will ensure that you have expert input that your concept is new and that it is scalable.

✓ **Reach out to thought leaders:** The people who understand, support, and can stand behind your venture with some clout are good to find. Hook up with incubator programs and alliances that allow you to leverage resources and time. These leaders are now your potential board. Hook up with the local chamber of commerce and venture capital firms.

✓ **Understand the law:** Different states have laws that vary. You may need legal help in making sure that both you and the franchisee are protected.

✓ **Know your professional limitations:** Hire the best leaders. You may be good at new concept and taking them to the pilot stage. Once you have a scalable model, stakes are different. Make sure that you have a professional management team to run the operations.

Starting a Business

For many, starting your own business can be an exciting venture, especially if the offering is something that is novel, or trendy. This can be a gratifying undertaking and in some respects, much like raising your own child and nurturing it to success. Those starting out in a new business underestimate the effort that goes into making the business a going concern. The investment is usually more than most estimate, the time it takes to break-even is longer than expected, and there are surprises along the way that require contingency planning and resources, not apparent in a conventional planning methodology. Fewer than half of new businesses survive past the first two years of operation and fewer than 20 percent survive the first five! The most notorious of these is the restaurant business. The failure rate for restaurants in the first two years is 90 percent!

Before entering a new business careful study of demand, business model, competition, capital availability and management of its operations are critical to launching it. Evaluate all options before entering into a business venture, especially when the economic conditions are challenging.

Buying a Business

Buying an established business is an attractive option for those who are not good at estimating what it takes to get a business going. To use a metaphor, it is like jumping on a moving train rather than getting in one waiting to leave the station; you don't know if it ever will! Each year hundreds of thousands of businesses in this country are bought and sold (there are over 12 million businesses in the US).

Buying a business offers some flexibility. You can run the business yourself or find someone who can run it for you and compensate that person for doing so. A running business can be evaluated by going through its history, talking to its customers and suppliers and checking out its reputation in the community.

Buying a business already established that can be improved upon requires that the buyer has a good understanding of the business and instincts, and what would differentiate the acquired business from what it is. This requires a vision and leadership expertise. Before closing a deal, make sure you have done due diligence and researched all liabilities, as you take the business on as your own.

Partnering (with your Spouse)

Going into a business with a partner can be a fun venture. If you can pool your resources including your capital, management talent and expertise, this can be a profitable and productive venture. This can be done in any of the formats discussed above. Good understanding of partnerships and good relationships with the partner(s) are critical to the success of such an arrangement. A contract is also critical to a successful partnership.

If your spouse already has a business or an idea for a venture, it is tempting to be partners. As long as an agreement of roles, responsibilities, and monitoring of ongoing operations to the satisfaction of both can be worked out, this can be made to work. Keeping the household relationship separate from the business is difficult, but can be made to work with some ground rules set up before starting the arrangement.

♠ Formal Aspects of Entrepreneurship

For legal purposes a business can fall into any one of the following categories:

- S corporation
- C Corporation
- Sole proprietorship
- Limited partnership
- Limited Liability Company (LLC)

Each type offers certain advantages and tax structures. Any further discussion on these areas is outside the scope of this material and the reader is advised to consult several good references on these topics and engage a legal counsel or a Certified Public Accountant (CPA) for further exploration. Table-4: Entity Comparison Charts summarize particulars and entity tax specifics merely as guidelines and *not* as legal representations.

* Entity Comparison Charts

Table-4 shows the five different types of entities that can be formed as businesses and their relative operating obligations. Use these as a starting point to explore how you may want to consider structuring your future business and what the attendant issues are for each choice. There is no free lunch. Consult a professional before deciding on this critical matter so that you are not surprised later. These are legally binding entities and, once you are set up, you are obligated to meet all legal, fiducial, and business requirements.

♠ Coming Out of Retirement

Coming out of retirement can be prompted either by sudden change in financial circumstances or by the need to engage productively, at least part-time, in a purposeful pursuit. Many go into retirement because they feel that retired life is something to be experienced, savored, and bragged about, since much is made of not working after a certain time in one's life. It's an image and an idea many hold and look forward to. Someone once defined retirement as being able to do what you want. So, if you want to go back to work, you can redefine *that* as retirement, without feeling guilty about it.

There are a few who, when they experience retirement in its full manifestation get disillusioned by its emptiness and lack of stimulation, both physically and mentally. If, on the other hand, the need is purely financial and was not foreseen at the onset of retirement, it is a different matter. In either case you need to go through the material in Getting With the Program in chapter-1, so that your intent is clear and you can move ahead with purpose. Remember that this, too, is a transition back to work. How this transition is handled depends on how long you have been in retirement.

The following list can be a good reminder for starting your process to get back to work from retirement:

1. Be honest about the reasons for going back to work after testing the fruits of retirement

2. If you are out of work and in retirement for a while (more than two years) potential employers can be apprehensive in a tough job market. You may have a hard time getting interviews unless you are aggressive in your campaign

3. In your résumé try not listing the most recent period as that entailing retirement. See if you can justify that period as doing volunteer work, consulting (even just a little), or starting a new business

Notes:

Table-4: Entity Comparison Charts

CHARACTERISTICS	S CORPORATION	C CORPORATION	SOLE PROPRIETORSHIP	PARTNERSHIP	LIMITED LIABILITY COMPANY (LLC)
Continuity of Life	Indefinite	Indefinite	Cases on death of proprietor	Ends if 50+ percent of partnership interest is sold/exchanged within a 12 month period	Generally no
Management	Centralized; Board of Directors; Corporate officers	Centralized; Board of Directors; Corporate officers	N/A–one owner	General partnership: not centralized, limited partnership generally centralized	Can be either centralized or not centralized
Liability of owners	Generally limited to assets in corporation	Generally limited to assets in corporation	Unlimited	General partnership unlimited, limited partnership, general partner unlimited, limited partner limited to investments	Limited
Tax Return Form	Form 100S	Form 100	Form 1040 Schedule C	Form 565	Form 568
Taxability of income	Generally	To corporation	Taxable to proprietor	Taxable to partner	Taxable to member
Double taxation of income? (Corporation and Shareholder)	No, unless former C corp. and built-in gains apply	Yes, taxed first at corporate level, and then shareholder	No	No	No
Deductibility of losses	Generally deductible by S/H, liabilities do not increase basis for deducting losses except for S/H loans	Deductible by corporation	Deductible by proprietor	Generally deductible by partner to extent of basis; Liabilities may increase basis for deducting losses	Generally deductible by member to extent of basis; Liabilities may increase basis for deducting losses
Passive losses	May not offset active or portfolio income (limits apply at shareholder level	May offset active but not portfolio income of closely held corp. but not personal service corporation	May not offset active or portfolio income	Cannot offset active or portfolio income (limits apply at partner level)	Cannot offset active or portfolio income (limits apply at member level)

CHARACTERISTICS	S CORPORATION	C CORPORATION	SOLE PROPRIETORSHIP	PARTNERSHIP	LIMITED LIABILITY COMPANY (LLC)
Tax Year	Generally must use calendar year or make Sec. 444 election	May select any fiscal year if not a personal service corporate	Must use tax year of proprietor	Generally must use fiscal year of majority interest partner/make Sec. 444 election	Generally must use fiscal year of majority interest partner/make Section 444 election
Register with Secretary Of State	Yes	Yes	No	Yes	Yes
Necessary Documentation	Articles of Inc., bylaws, minutes of the board, stock record	Same as S-Corp	Minimal	Partnership agreement	Articles of organization; Operating agreement
Distribution to Owner	Nontaxable to extent of basis in stock	Not deductible by corp., ordinary income S/H	Nontaxable	Nontaxable to extent of basis in partnership	Nontaxable to extent of basis in LLC
Liquidation Distribution	At corporation level treated as sales of property, gain passes though increases shareholder basis, trigger built-in gains tax	At corporation level treated as sales of property, gain to shareholder if full market value exceeds stock basis	Nontaxable	Generally, nontaxable; Cash distribution in excess of basis will trigger gain disproportionate distribution of Section 751 assets may trigger gain	Generally, nontaxable; cash distribution in excess of basis will trigger gain disproportionate distribution of Section 751 assets may trigger gain
Maximum Tax Rate	Taxed at individual shareholder level; If corporate-level tax applies: @1.5 percent.	Generally taxed at 8.84 percent.	Taxed at individual level	Taxed at individual partner level	Taxed at individual member level, at LLC level-annual LLC fee based on total income
Minimum Franchise Tax (even with losses)	$800	$800 1st yr.= $300 2nd yr. = $500	None	General Partnership— $0: L/P - $800	$800
Self-employed Income to Owners	No	No	Yes	General partners; not limited Ps	Yes
Classes of Stock/ownership interest	Limited to 1 class; can own subsidiaries	Unrestricted	N/A	Unrestricted	Unrestricted
Number of Investors	Limited to 75	Unlimited	N/A	Unlimited	Unlimited
Eligible investors	Individual, estate, certain trusts, & 501©(3) charitable organizations.	Unrestricted	N/A	Unrestricted	Unrestricted

4. If you're serious about getting back to work, slowly wean yourself from your retirement activities and social circles that indulge in that lifestyle. You need a fresh mindset.

5. Try volunteering at least part-time to engage yourself in productive activity. A productive mindset is critical to searching for a good job, even part-time.

6. Take some refresher courses that will not only update your skills but will also get you in a social circle with more creative and energetic people. You need to see yourself more as someone willing to learn and venture out than as someone who is tired of new things.

7. Network with established professional associations and renew your memberships that may have lapsed as a result of your retirement. Many offer discounted fees for retirees.

8. Start mentoring younger professionals who come across your path. This will energize your campaign and give the fillip you need to make yourself feel useful.

9. Give talks at the local groups and associations that are attended by those looking for work. You have an advantage because of your unique situation. Leverage that experience in your presentations.

10. Explore tutoring opportunities for the young. This, too, can be an energizing experience and can be a résumé builder. Tutors can make good money.

If you get tired looking for employment after a while and are frustrated you may explore the idea of buying a business or a franchise. This may entail your having to invest money—probably your life savings—to get this realized. Be very cautious when it comes to risking your retirement money on *any* venture, even when it may be completely legitimate. Evaluate risks and go with caution. Never give money to anyone whose credentials are suspect.

Notes:

Summary: Chapter-3: Managing Transitions

This chapter starts with an explanation of why all job seekers are the *not* same. Where one starts is important in defining how to move ahead. At the macroscopic level there are the 15 categories of job seekers as identified in this chapter. At the microscopic level each individual job seeker needs their individualized approach to moving ahead. These nuances are presented in subsequent chapters. Each category of professionals in the baby-boomer age group must approach their job search with the prescriptions defined under their category. In this chapter we cover the following categories of job seekers in the baby-boomer age group:

Identify to which of the 15 categories of job seekers you belong

1. If you are about to be unemployed

2. Those on notice with limited time to find something within their own organization

3. Those with performance issues and an imminent Notice of Concern

4. Just out of work

5. Out of work for a while and looking

6. Employed (unhappily) and looking for a change

7. Employed, doing well but feel lost

8. Work-Visa Holders (H1-B)

9. Re-entering the workforce because of a need

10. Volunteered in the immediate past, but now must have a job

11. Have never worked and feel out of touch but now must earn a living

12. Worked in another country and now looking here for opportunities

13. Worked as a consultant in the past 10–15 years and now looking for a full-time position

14. Want to do something on your own

15. Coming out of retirement

Regardless of the category (of 15), getting ready involves:

• Emotionally Accepting your new state

• Informing those who matter

• Compiling networking contacts list

• Searching for the right open positions

- Understanding the job market (Including trends)
- Expanding your repertoire of marketing space (guerilla, unconventional)
- Preparing a résumé (must be market aligned; see Chapter-6: Building Your Platform)

If considering going on your own read the implications of different entities in the Entity Comparison Charts

Chapter-4: The Baby-boomer Advantage

"A great many people believe that they are thinking when they are merely rearranging their prejudices."

—William James, author (1842–1910)

Introduction

The baby boomer generation is in a unique position to exploit the current dynamic of the job market in ways that others cannot. Although the baby boomer age currently can be 40 on its low end (60 on its high end) of the spectrum, anyone on either side of the range and beyond shares this advantage. In a broader sense, they can also be called mid-career professionals. In these days of increasing life-expectancy (currently nearly 80 years and growing) even a 65-year old out-of-work professional can be considered a mid-career job seeker!

What most lament as their disadvantage, especially the baby boomers in transition, is, in reality, an edge that they can exploit in their career. How? By featuring it in ways that serves them. It is normal for anyone to state the obvious and find an excuse to rationalize it and then compound it by compensating for it in ways that puts them at a further disadvantage.

For example, a 50-year old marketing professional with outstanding track record, but someone who is out of work and competing with the much younger job seeker is first going to find ways to excuse their age and then present a reason why they are out and looking. To make up for their situation, they are likely to offer their outstanding value at a bargain price. This is simply the wrong strategy because the employer is then going to think less of them and that is why this chapter is presented. The reason for this chapter is to provide some insights many could use in their transition to help them better position themselves in what they want to achieve.

Job Movement

To understand the current job market flux, especially in the U.S. and in many of the industrialized geographies where the flattening of the world has displaced knowledge workers, especially those with substantial and valuable experience, it is important to look at historical evolution of the job market.

In the U.S., nearly a century ago—1900 A.D.—the agriculture sector employed nearly 95 percent of the working population. To a large extend the same labor situation existed in other parts of the world in that era. Although industrial revolution had already started taking its share of the labor market, including the rapid expansion of the railroads throughout the continental U.S. in the twentieth century, nearly half the labor pool was engaged in agriculture, including the logistics and supply chain for its overall contribution to the economy. The knowledge work occupied the remainder of the work force. As the agricultural technology evolved and mechanized farming became more common, that factor gradually dwindled and at the end of the century agriculture employed only about two percent of the labor pool in the U.S. This dramatic reduction in agricultural employment over nearly a century happened despite increased food needs and the U.S. acting as the breadbasket to the world.

Similar forces are now shaping up for the knowledge worker. In comparable terms, the knowledge worker in the manufacturing sector constituted about 48 percent of the labor pool in 1950, about fifty years ago. Today the knowledge worker in the manufacturing sector makes up nearly 17 percent of the working population. Following the previous example of the decimation of the agricultural labor pool, the same can be inferred of the knowledge worker in another fifty years—or even sooner, considering the velocity of events—where the total amount of labor force in the knowledge sector would be down to two percent.

Alarming as this statistics appears, it is not far fetched. During the past fifty years a reduction by more than half of the knowledge workforce forebodes a trend. If this category of labor pool suffers the same fate as the agricultural worker in another fifty years or so, then it is not difficult to contemplate that the knowledge worker will shrink down to, once again, two percent of the workforce.

What does this mean to the knowledge worker of today, and especially to those who span the mid-career age group?

Increasing Automation

One reason for the reduction in the ranks of the knowledge worker is of their own making! How? As the knowledge work rapidly created more sophisticated technology, rules-based work began to be automated. We see ample evidence of this in our everyday world. As the computer technology began to do routine human tasks, computerized machines began to replace humans. We started seeing this trend in banking (ATMs), call centers (automated call taking), progressively capable software applications that replaced humans in large numbers no longer needed for that task. This onslaught of automation continues today relentlessly.

The result is that despite increased service-sector opportunities that replaced manufacturing jobs, there is a net reduction in even service jobs during the past decade, despite an increase in the population that demands such jobs. From 1993 to 2003 there has been a net reduction of nearly 19 percent of service jobs despite a nearly 10 percent increased population. This trend is also going to continue unabated as more and more sophisticated applications continue their march against the labor force.

So, where are the jobs going?

For one, the flat world has created a labor arbitrage situation that did not exist prior to just a few years back. The off shoring and the relentless trend towards automation are now whipsawing the existing labor force at an accelerated rate. As rapidly as these jobs are disappearing, there are new jobs being created by virtue of the same forces that are decimating the human labor. How?

The inescapable fact of the emerging dynamic is that as long as the humans rule this planet, the need for human work is not going to abate. Automation of rules-based work merely moves the jobs that require human touch—hyper human work—upstream. By merely suppressing the need for this work its existence is not going to be negated. In fact, it is going to manifest as a latent and pent-up need.

Hyper-human Work

Hyper human work comprises tasks that only humans can do. A century ago what machines could do was limited by the technology available at that time. With time, sophistication grew and human intervention began to slowly decrease and both the quality of work and productivity increased steadily. However, what did not increase commensurately was the rise in the overall human experience. As automation increased human experience became more and more rare.

Regardless of the degree of automation in every task there is going to be a component of human interaction that is going to be indispensable. Merely ignoring its existence is going to delay the quality of the human experience. Table-5 below illustrates this well.

A good example of hyper human work is customer help desk. In most cases customer support comes from response centers staffed by an army of trained operators who are programmed to answer customer queries using a script tree. Increasingly, these tasks are being off shored, mostly to India, because of the cost advantage.

#	Traditional Job	Hyper-human job	Skill Required	Comments
1	Administrative Assistant	Office manager /Administrative Response Specialist	Broad knowledge of office skills, managing key relationships, customer savvy	Skills move from "machine awareness" to "people awareness"
2	Loan clerks	Personal finance concierges, Investment counselors	Overall knowledge of personal financial needs and awareness of different avenues of leveraging personal wealth	May require higher level of educational qualifications
3	Electronic Technicians	Personal Productivity concierges	How to work with electronic appliances and how they communicate	Moving from PCs and workstations to networked installations that enhance personal productivity
4	Travel agents	Experience designers Travel facilitators	Personality and life style assessment. Global cultural and geopolitical awareness	Multi-lingual, multi-cultural skills; understanding how families plan vacations
5	Telemarketers	Marketing information experts	Psychological and cultural understanding of customers, persuasiveness	Skills move from hard selling to understanding the persona at the other end and their needs

Table-5: Transitioning to hyper-human jobs

When a company does not view each customer contact with a strategic intent it is missing out on valuable opportunity to upsell. Usually, when a customer calls such a center there is a problem. Most companies want to dispose of such encounters with minimum investment and move on to their "core competencies" as generating revenues with the products they make and sell. They see this as cost of doing business and in some cases a "necessary evil."

If a company, however, takes a more strategic approach to such an opportunity, it will situate itself with a different arrangement for a customer complaint. By carefully routing incoming calls into packets of segmented opportunities and staffing each segment of call handlers with a different mission, an incoming call can quickly become a gift to itself in many situations. So, instead of having "mechanized" call-center responders, if a company replaces them with customer concierges, a calling customer can walk away with a whole different outlook on how a company handles their complaints and have a different view of its attitude towards customers. Thus, a company looking at automation to save labor can re-think the new opportunity with a hyper-human attitude and come out ahead.

What does this mean in a job market? Having this hyper-human perspective will give new ammunition to differentiate oneself when approaching an employer for a position, open or not. The Department of Labor (www.dol.gov) publishes in its *Occupational Outlook Handbook* service-oriented jobs that are going to be automated in the next decade. The table (Table-5) provides some insights on how this is emerging in some jobs. Also, to explore where new jobs are these days visit www.jobvoyages.gov and check out where some of the emerging jobs are and how they relate to what you want to be doing. This Website is a result of collaboration between the Department of Labor (DoL) and the Department of Education (DoE) to help those looking for emerging jobs.

As is apparent from the discussion of the nature of hyper-human work and the strong human content that is inherent in them, those who are most qualified to handle such jobs have maturity and relationship building experience. This is why hyper-human work is typically best staffed by those with years of experience behind them. Baby boomers have a clear advantage in reconfiguring jobs as they exist now and reemphasizing their hyper-human content in a way that makes them strong contenders for those jobs. In the emerging economy the baby boomers are better advised to not count on corporate or social resources to protect their livelihood. The strategy to succeed in hyper-human economy is to inject "life, emotion, and the human richness" in every job and find avenues to build relationship to enhance that job through increased human contact. No one is better qualified to do this well than the baby boomer generation.

The Baby-boomer Edge

As more and more consumers become aware of the importance of the basic human interaction in this growingly impersonal and automated existence, those who bring this richness in any transaction are going to be in demand. Even though a job description may not expressly state the need for a human element in an interaction, the one pursuing such an opportunity will have a distinct advantage if they can articulate this need in unambiguous ways. Growing use of technology and increased automation in all our commercial interactions have resulted in alienation of the most basic human needs: warm, caring, human, and emotional response to our plight as consumers in this increasingly mercenary existence. Somehow, it is much harder to the younger generations (Gen Xers and the Gen-Y workforce) to display that dimension. To most, this comes with age and experience and for having lived a life of challenges and hardships, which many youngsters dismiss as those resulting from one's own actions. Those on the other side need a sympathetic ear to continue the communication in such times when the situation demands it. Baby-boomers are far more capable of such empathy than their younger counterparts and this is their advantage.

The baby-boomers must communicate to a business where they have an interest in pursuing employment the value for this human quality, which they have in abundance, and position themselves to their advantage so that this differentiates them from the rest.

How to do this even in non-existent jobs is shown in examples of letters and résumés throughout this book, especially in Chapters-6, 7, and 8.

Summary: Chapter-4: The Baby-boomer Advantage

This short chapter highlights the challenge faced by those who have been in their career for about 20 years and have acquired a dimension in their experience that is not easy to come by without having lived it.

Increased life expectancy, desire to contribute in a purposeful way, and the financial pressures are compelling many experienced professionals to rethink their career plans—and their value propositions.

There are some key forces that are changing the job market structurally. Increased automation, dramatic rises in productivity, availability of highly productive labor force globally, and concomitant rise in the expectation of the human dimension in all our business transactions. What this implies is that jobs that have a high touch component are going to be replacing those being performed with high-tech methods. In the emerging economy hyper-human work is going to have increased role in the way jobs are going to be defined. In fact, those who are able to identify jobs that are not apparent and refocus them with this emphasis are going to get attention in the way their message is viewed in the emerging economy.

How are the hyper-human jobs going to be defined and compared to the existing jobs? Using the Department of Labor projections, Table-5 outlines some commonly known jobs that will have their hyper-human counterparts in the emerging economy. This table highlights a trend that shows that emotionally rich and human-contact interactions are going to be key in the future of the value-creation process. No one is better equipped to handle this challenge than the baby-boomer generation and a mid-career professional. Their upbringing, experience, and awareness of the human element in the business are going to be central to their future success.

Chapter-5: How Your Genius Helps You

"Every one is born a genius, but the process of living de-geniuses them."

     —Buckminster Fuller (1895–1983)

"A man does not live by bread alone."

     —A proverb

Introduction

The new Millennium brought with it unprecedented challenges in career management. Why?

The implosion of the job market, off-shoring of many high-tech jobs, and job consolidations stemming from mega mergers and acquisitions all came to a head as the new Millennium got underway. At the end of 2001, nearly 15 million in the U.S. were in some way affected by these economic forces directly. This meant that either they were out of a job, were under the threat of a layoff, or were displaced by the implacable forces of the economy.

As traditional jobs in all industries were undergoing this mutation, job seekers, working or not, were desperately trying to reinvent themselves to make their future secure by leveraging their career momentum. As the job market was reshaping itself from a jolt high on the Richter scale, many new opportunities emerged. Those who were able to spot them, pursued these new avenues with confidence and got themselves on a new career trajectory. However, most did not understand this dynamic and were relegated to looking for jobs in the traditional way using Jurassic methods.

This book emerged from experiences working with nearly 2,000 professionals who were facing career challenges. They came from all walks of careers, ages, backgrounds, and professions: high-tech executives, engineers, lawyers, airline pilots, and medical technicians, to name a few. The theme across these diverse constituencies was the same: how do you develop a message that cuts through the traditional notion of how most think about a career. And, more importantly, how do you manifest your career in a different way, given that the past career path has no prospects?

Reinvention is nothing new. To redeploy one must explore where in the emergent scene their talents cross paths with the opportunities that are now exploitable and help create economic value. When one manifestation of a career is transformed into another it is a reinvention. This can also be called a career *avatar*. Avatar is a Sanskrit word and it means a different manifestation of the same basic platform in a way that creates value in a mutated way.

"Winging" your mind

In this rapidly changing economic climate it is critical that we learn to quickly change how we manifest to keep us gainfully employed. We have much more to offer than we often realize or acknowledge. Our own internal thoughts, prejudices, and limiting beliefs throttle our efforts to see ourselves beyond our past accomplishments. Our internal barriers, thus, sabotage our efforts to take on a different career avatar. Often, we create these barriers by programming ourselves at a cellular level; we deeply believe that we are incapable of something or unworthy of a lofty goal.

The main cause of the internal barriers in our pursuits is our attitude and how we perceive what is happening to us in words that we express. Our thoughts translate into words that we harbor, marshal, and articulate. Thus, our verbal abilities limit our thinking than its converse! It is also perhaps because we surrender our ability to verbalize our thoughts to what we can comfortably articulate; we limit our thinking purely by virtue of our nurtured abilities; verbal ability is a nurtured skill! It is unfortunate that we let the nurtured skills trump our natural gifts. Why? Simply because it is that we do not know how to articulate these gifts in a way that serves us.

Our subconscious thoughts drive our actions and our actions are expressed in words we choose to use in expressing our thoughts. For example, those who are disenfranchised by economic forces—out of work, cannot find ready employment—are frustrated with their efforts and how the system is treating them. They have a frame of mind that defeats their own pursuits. Their experiences working within the system create a defeatist mindset especially in a tough economy. These experiences seep into their subconscious and their thoughts now become increasingly negative and their words, progressively more self-defeating. Those who hear their messages naturally shy away from them by not returning their phone calls, avoiding contact, and passing them up for those who reflect a better message. This happens despite their impeccable qualifications and stellar employment histories.

We can unshackle our mind by thinking different thoughts and materializing them by conscious actions. One way to achieve this is by empowering our mind and programming ourselves to stay away from thoughts, influences, and people who bring us down, including your negative self.

Another way is to explore what makes us "tick." Those who feel disenfranchised by being economically orphaned after having lost their job or their means of support, often feel like a martyr or a victim. This is a natural reaction to what is happening around them. As a result they feel comfortable manifesting as a martyr in their social interactions with others. This attitude conduces an exactly opposite effect than what they intend or expect.

How? Those around us are influenced by how we make them feel. When we are down on ourselves and are trying to get others to pay attention to our woes through martyrdom, the effect is opposite. People cannot deal with it. It is analogous to when someone tells you they have a terminal disease, or that they are homeless. Most cannot muster enough empathy to deal with it honestly enough to make that person feel genuinely comfortable or to even comfort them in some human way.

The same is perhaps true when someone is in a state that is its exact opposite: when they have achieved success. Most offer their obligatory felicitations and join in to celebrate, but very few are able to share the success in a genuine gesture of goodwill and admiration. The interesting fact of the human condition is that even in success we need validation, even though success itself is one!

What does this mean? Whether in success or in defeat we are pretty much on our own. The only ones, who perhaps can sympathize with our pain or join in victory, are our closest loved ones, and sometimes even that is suspect! This also means that we must develop our own coping strategies with such circumstances. They are a fact of human condition. What Socrates said nearly 2500 years ago is still valid today, *"Remember that there is nothing stable in human affairs; therefore, avoid undue elation in prosperity, or undue depression in adversity."* We are programmed to be martyrs to our plight and then expect those around us to commiserate when we are down and celebrate when we are up.

Thinking differently

A more empowering approach is for us to program ourselves differently. Before our plight spirals down to a full-fledged funk, it is a good strategy for us to program ourselves to a different course of action. There are many choices we make, especially during times when our luck is not on our side, such as when suffering unemployment and when we face rejection, which tends to perpetuate our condition more than helping it. One such choice is joining a networking group or a support group for those who are unemployed. This is not necessarily a bad thing, but those who come together in such forums have different expectations of what the group can provide. Merely exchanging business cards with those in similar situations or having them review your résumé is bootstrapping. Such occasions are positive in that they assure you that you are not alone in this journey and that others share your plight. But, this is not enough. What is needed is an inspiration that allows you to break your cycle of feeling comfortable within the group and continuing your efforts to move ahead.

The best and the only place for that inspiration is for it to come from within; the most handy yet the most difficult source for it! Why? In our culture of sound bites, instant gratification, and quick fixes, we look to others to provide us what we seek, even though we know, deep down, that it does not exist and that they cannot provide it. Sure, we hear an inspiring speaker—we are hooked on them—to give us inspiration. Some even do. But, what does not happen is that that inspiration translating into changed behavior and a habit that allow you to move ahead in a positive way. We keep hoping that in view of our plight we are deserving of some divine consideration that will deliver us from our predicament.

The following table is an attempt at showing how you can program yourself to think differently so that you can extricate out of this situation yourself and make a habit out of thinking differently—from being a martyr to a master.

The following table shows how you can affirm yourself in a positive way:

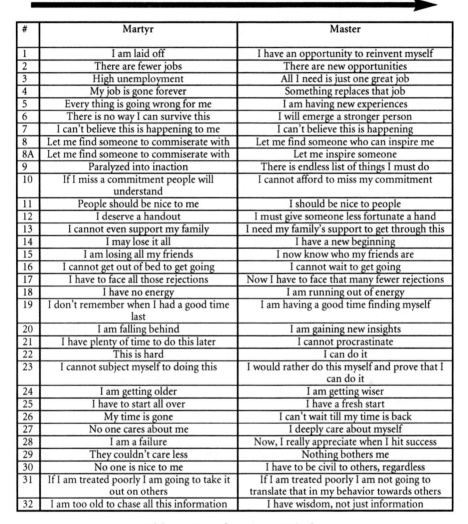

#	Martyr	Master
1	I am laid off	I have an opportunity to reinvent myself
2	There are fewer jobs	There are new opportunities
3	High unemployment	All I need is just one great job
4	My job is gone forever	Something replaces that job
5	Every thing is going wrong for me	I am having new experiences
6	There is no way I can survive this	I will emerge a stronger person
7	I can't believe this is happening to me	I can't believe this is happening
8	Let me find someone to commiserate with	Let me find someone who can inspire me
8A	Let me find someone to commiserate with	Let me inspire someone
9	Paralyzed into inaction	There is endless list of things I must do
10	If I miss a commitment people will understand	I cannot afford to miss my commitment
11	People should be nice to me	I should be nice to people
12	I deserve a handout	I must give someone less fortunate a hand
13	I cannot even support my family	I need my family's support to get through this
14	I may lose it all	I have a new beginning
15	I am losing all my friends	I now know who my friends are
16	I cannot get out of bed to get going	I cannot wait to get going
17	I have to face all those rejections	Now I have to face that many fewer rejections
18	I have no energy	I am running out of energy
19	I don't remember when I had a good time last	I am having a good time finding myself
20	I am falling behind	I am gaining new insights
21	I have plenty of time to do this later	I cannot procrastinate
22	This is hard	I can do it
23	I cannot subject myself to doing this	I would rather do this myself and prove that I can do it
24	I am getting older	I am getting wiser
25	I have to start all over	I have a fresh start
26	My time is gone	I can't wait till my time is back
27	No one cares about me	I deeply care about myself
28	I am a failure	Now, I really appreciate when I hit success
29	They couldn't care less	Nothing bothers me
30	No one is nice to me	I have to be civil to others, regardless
31	If I am treated poorly I am going to take it out on others	If I am treated poorly I am not going to translate that in my behavior towards others
32	I am too old to chase all this information	I have wisdom, not just information

Table-6: Transforming a Mindset

This table is presented at showing how easy it is to reprogram yourself to think differently on the same topic and how easy it is mobilizing yourself into action despite your setbacks.

The suggestion here is not intended to stop going to the myriad support and networking groups; often they are the only immediate source of help and understanding! But, it is more for a deeper self-reliance and an important and often overlooked, additional avenue to seek relief.

Another such avenue is pursuing those who are already successful, working in the field of your interest and who are willing to share their thoughts and insights. Busy and successful individuals are difficult to access, and, that is the point. You must first identify who they are and track them down. You must explore avenues to get their attention and get them to see you and understand their perspective. Why should they give you their time? Because by virtue of who they are, the simply do. All you have to do is to approach them properly.

This is not to suggest that going to the networking and support groups is a bad idea. No! On the contrary these groups are invaluable in fleshing out leads, getting everyday information on what is going on in the job market front, and, in general, staying plugged into the overall process. But, what is often detrimental is the mindset that they foster and what you can potentially become by staying with them longer term.

One example of how staying with the mindset of those who participate in the networking groups for those out of work is how participants transfer their priorities into actions that are often counterproductive. One example of such behavior is hunkering down and saving money in job-search activities. This is good but, when taken to extremes, it can be counterproductive. Their cohorts perpetuate their desire to bootstrap their efforts, often without seeking competent help, often delaying their efforts to reach conclusion to their job-search process. For example, an average résumé in a tough market can result in many rejections or complete lack of action. Tweaking such a message by soliciting help from within the support group can only have marginal impact. Such resources are not able to provide breakthroughs needed to make the résumé different in a crowded market; the best they can do is for it to make it like theirs! If they are struggling to get interviews, what does that say about their message? What this means is that your résumé must receive a total makeover, which can only come from working with a professional. And yet, many job seekers do not venture to spend a few hundred dollars on the right professional to get the résumé presentable to pull themselves out of their predicament.

A Breakthrough

One way to break through the morass of common impediments is to find some inspiration from within. Your own confidence can be a source of this inspiration. The message that one puts out in a state of diffidence is muted in its power. It is riddled with ambivalence, doubt, and absence of focus. A challenge presented by this condition is called the messaging challenge. It is described below and how to overcome this challenge is also presented at the end of this discussion.

♠The Messaging Challenge

Throughout this book, *message* (verb) refers to the action of communicating functional value. Messaging is an adjective or gerund from that verb. It means the sum total of communication by written, spoken, and unspoken words that get into the stream during the job-search campaign to generate the intended action. It also includes *how* a message is sent!

A typical messaging challenge one encounters in a career transition is presented graphically in Figure-3.

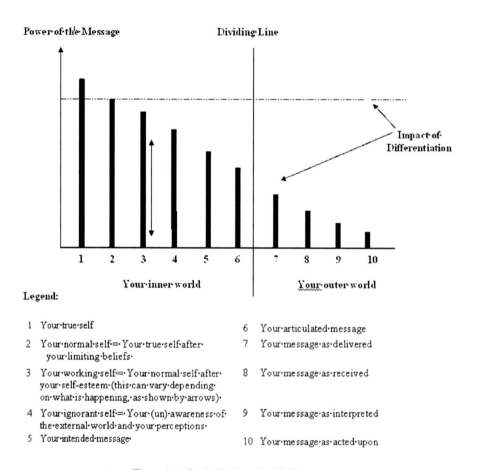

Figure-3: A Typical Messaging Challenge

Power of the Message   Dividing Line

Impact of
Differentiation

1 2 3 4 5 6 7 8 9 10

Your inner world   Your outer world

Legend:

1 Your true self

2 Your normal self = Your true self after your limiting beliefs

3 Your working self = Your normal self after your self-esteem (this can vary depending on what is happening, as shown by arrows)

4 Your ignorant self = Your (un) awareness of the external world and your perceptions

5 Your intended message

6 Your articulated message

7 Your message as delivered

8 Your message as received

9 Your message as interpreted

10 Your message as acted upon

With every messaging opportunity there lies a challenge. Most of these challenges are limitations grounded in a variety of factors. Figure-1 shows, in graphic form, some of these challenges. Although this graphic is conceptual, its implications are real. Table-7 shows how to overcome some of the challenges stemming from messaging limitations. The messaging challenge stems from the fact that those who are trying a craft a message about their value are immune to their own charms! At the heart of this challenge is objectifying your gifts or genius. The process of objectification entails giving expression to what is otherwise difficult to communicate so that those receiving this communication can experience it or relate to it. In the job-searching context it is the essence of the résumé to objectify a job seeker's value so that the potential employer can understand what is presented that is unique; this may not be easy. Why? This is simply because it is difficult for those in the thick of it to be objective about themselves. This challenge is further multiplied by the emotional nature of the transition process itself.

In a tough job market the messaging challenge appears amplified even further. Partially, this amplification comes from the dynamic that surrounds the job seeker. Job search, whether for those employed and looking for a change, or for these out of work looking to get back is an emotional venture. It subjects the person in transition through an emotional roller coaster. In an emotional state people have trouble being objective about themselves and their communication, further diminishing the message. This aspect of the messaging dynamic is *not* depicted in the figure, primarily because of its difficulty.

A tough market, surprisingly, can also provide an intrinsic opportunity to amplify this same message. How? As we will discuss, a highly differentiated message gets amplified once it crosses to the right of the Dividing Line, especially in a tough market, as will be presented. But first, let us look more closely at this diminished-message syndrome and how to devise countermeasures to bring it back to its original power. The discussion of what is presented in Figure-3 follows:

The bars in the graph conceptually depict the power of a potential message that could be generated from the person engaged in the process. This depiction dramatizes the gap that normally exists between the intent and the outcome, but most are not even aware of it. The following break down is aimed at prescriptively helping the reader understand the driving dynamic and how to overcome the forces that go against the intent of the person in their message. Conceptually, this graphic depicts nine barriers to a "pure" message. Each barrier in a sequential process attenuates the power of the preceding message, as is described below.

Your True Self represents what the phrase implies. This is the true depiction of the power that you, as a job seeker, possess in the way you create value for others. Your true self can create a "pure" message. Your most compelling value creating elements and how you deliver that value are embodied in this concept. This embodiment includes your genius, your inner drive, intuition, divine inspiration, and your motivation to create something that leaves behind a legacy. If all of this capability can be articulated in a message, the message itself would be quite powerful. This is, of course, a very difficult thing to do, even for highly skilled writers.

Another way to look at the coherence that comes from your true self is when your subconscious, conscious, and super conscious minds are in harmony! And, when they are, there is nothing stopping you!

Your Normal Self is your true self after your limiting beliefs take away from your ability to fully manifest. Limiting beliefs stem from judgments you make about yourself ("no college degree, too old, etc."), your abilities, and other factors that are more founded on irrationality and apprehensions. They further diminish the power of your message stemming from your true self. That is why the height of the second bar is smaller than the one to its left. Through self-awareness, coaching, and forming new habits, it is realistic to nearly eradicate limiting beliefs. As limiting beliefs are identified and worked on, the power of your message receives a boost, and an improved message then helps, in turn, to dispel your limiting beliefs, creating a virtuous cycle. This is why testing your limiting beliefs and challenging them are so powerful.

Your Working Self is the product of your normal self and your self-esteem. Self-esteem is the confidence and satisfaction you have in your self. Depending on what is happening around you, your self-esteem can vary. Self-esteem is sensitive to the events that challenge your worth, as well as those that validate it. It is driven by how you perceive others treat you. When you suffer a job loss and its fallout, it is normal to have low self-esteem. When things are going well for you, it is also normal for you to feel validation, which boosts your self-esteem. How you come across to others while undergoing cyclical ups and downs in what you do, can modulate your self-esteem, and consequently your message that you create, carry, and communicate.

This is why in a career transition, coming out of denial and moving forward with positive intent are so critical to a successful outcome. Those who dwell on their past defeats and personalize the outcomes, continue to harbor negativity around their efforts, which militate against their best interests. The real negative influence of this factor permeates downstream in an insidious way. This means that as the height of this bar varies, the heights of the bars to its right also vary accordingly.

#	Power Level	Attenuating Factors	Antidote	Tools	Comments
1	Your True Self	None	None	None	You are operating at your Essence
2	Your Normal Self	Limiting beliefs, biases, judgments, prejudices	Suspend judgment, take risks, reach out, discover	Coaching, identifying defeat patterns, past learnings	An honest appraisal of past patterns can yield powerful insights
3	Your working self	Self-esteem, confidence, current situation	Reflect on past victories, change routines,	Separate patterns from episodes, experiment with new ideas	This is the most variable part of your messaging make-up. On bad days, retreat!
4	Your ignorant self	"Unconscious incompetence," become more market savvy	Openly discover external market conditions, challenge your knowledge, network	Network with those who are one or two levels above your experience and status	Move to "conscious incompetence" and then work on it.
5	Your intended message (See Ralph Waldo Emerson quote in Comments column)	Inability to extend your reach beyond your grasp, open-mindedness	Reach out to opportunities just outside your comfort zone and pursue them with vigor	Find mentorship with someone you admire and solicit help to extend yourself	Going out with aggressive messages can be a good start. *"You don't know how far you can go until you go too far"*
6	Your articulated message	Language skills, fear of being perceived as arrogant,	Write down your message and own it by constantly working at it	"Elevator speech," writing skills	By working with your message you can develop ownership
7	Your delivered message	Delivery mechanism, process	Practice different deliveries, knowing audience	Looking at different delivery modalities	Practice written telephone, and interview skills
8	Your message as received	How the message was sent and to whom	Use methods consistent with the intent of the message; know your audience,	Make a list of different communication channels for your campaign, use appropriately	Do not casually use different methods of communications without knowing the intended consequences
9	Your message as interpreted	Competition, overall environment	Carefully target message after research and work at it	Résumé template, Unique Skills, great cover letter	Entire message should be in harmony and cogent
10	Your message as acted upon	Perceptions of those acting	Vigorous post-message campaign	Follow-up, solid interviews, differentiation	Ratchet up your message as you navigate

Table-7: The Messaging-Challenge Prescription

Your Ignorant Self is the product of what you do not know and how you integrate what you do know into your thinking about yourself. It is easy to see how market or target ignorance can impair your value proposition. For example, as a fresh graduate, you will typically have a short résumé. What you do have on the résumé is typically limited to your past experiences, which may have no direct connection to the current pursuit. Unless you are able to make that connection, what is on the résumé is just filler. It is not difficult to make a connection between the past and the needs of the market so that a résumé reader can see how what you bring can add value to their cause.

In one instance, a fresh graduate with a degree in communication was looking for a job in a tough market. After stating her objective at the top of her résumé, as someone looking for a position at a company in employee and customer communications, she listed her most recent experiences. These stints were at retail chains as a sales clerk, shipping dock, and so forth.

Information such as what she had on her résumé could not help her in being positioned favorably in a tough job market, primarily because she was not able to connect her experiences with the value proposition she was claiming: communicating better with others. If, instead, she had written the same stints as connected to her academic and professional pursuits, the résumé would have had a far more impactful presentation. For example, she could have packaged her stints as showing how, by improving the communications with whom she worked, she was able to improve her effectiveness, which helped the company in better working conditions. This is not a difficult thing to do; it just requires an enlightened perspective. This is the ignorance part that can hurt you in your messaging efforts. Please see the second example in the résumé showcase of Chapter-6: Building Your Platform, to see how a makeover dealt with a similar hurdle for yet another fresh graduate.

The other constituency of job seekers most affected by this syndrome is those who have been out of work for a long time or those who have never worked. Same considerations apply in these instances, where connecting the value proposition to the potential needs at the target opportunity can transform your positioning.

Your Message is the message you *plan* to create and to present to the outside world about your value-creation process. It is interesting to note that the state of your mind has much to do with how you message for yourself. Once again, the size of the bar that represents the power of the message, is lower than the preceding bar because most have difficulty thinking of themselves in objective terms. Most are afraid or at least apprehensive about thinking of themselves in ways that may come across to others as self-aggrandizing or boastful. This apprehension about your "worthiness" of what you may put out, further attenuates the power of the message that is being formulated.

Your Articulated Message is what finally appears in written or spoken form. This is the verbal message. Due to language limitations, poor presentation skills, and lack of objectivity, it is easy to overshoot the mark on the conservative side, resulting in a timid, muddled, hesitant, or even a diffident message. This is why the height of the bar that represents the power of this message is lower than its proceeding counterpart. This is the message that goes to the outside world.

One of the more common practices adopted in writing résumés is that many do not write impactful messages that differentiate them. Their refrain is that once they get in an interview they would explain what they intended to convey in their otherwise trite message. The problem with this logic is that in a tough market you cannot get that far without a compelling message to begin with. Some try to compensate for this weakness by persistently calling the recruiter after sending their résumé that carries such a message. They plead with the recruiters to give them a chance so that they can convince the hiring managers of their true worth. This further impairs their prospects for the job.

Any message of import in a job search must be reviewed before it is sent out or delivered. Many use their own editing talents to improve the message. One of the most insidious aspects of vetting your own message, once written, is that you are no longer able to read what you wrote in the same way as someone else might. Why? Perhaps because you already know the intent of the message and as a result, no matter what is in front of your eyes, it will read the same as you originally intended. This can be called the *believing-is-seeing syndrome*. Others see it differently. This is why critical messages must be vetted by objective eyes for intent and impact.

Your Message as Delivered includes knowing how different delivery mechanisms and modalities can help or hurt a message. Timing is critical, especially in oral messages. If you have any doubts, just look at how stand-up comics place their entire message delivery and timing to carry them in their routines. A great line delivered poorly with a wrong sense of timing can land flat on a warmed up audience.

Your Message as Received shows that when the target audience receives the final message, after it crosses the Dividing Line, how it interprets the message is driven by a variety of factors. How it is presented, how does it compare to other messages, who is reading it, what are they required to do with it, and so on. It, as a result, gets further diminished in its power.

By differentiating, this message can be amplified by virtue of how it is received. This includes: a great cover letter, how it was sent (courier/email), who received it, among other variables. The gray bar on top of the dark one, Figure-3 shows the power of differentiation at this level of the message in its travels.

Your Message as Interpreted signifies someone reading your message and acting on it usually contextualizes it and accords it a degree of importance based on, once again, a variety of factors. If you are sending a résumé and a cover letter, both messages had better be complementary. The message in the cover letter should be more in concert with the company's immediate value-creation needs, in a way that other candidates failed to leverage. If these two messages lack a degree of coherence and resonance for the target company, their value is further diminished as is shown in the figure as bar with a smaller height.

How your message is interpreted at this stage is a function of other messages that compete with it. If the entire résumé and the cover letter produce a message that resonates with the person who is interpreting it, the amplification of this message can be substantial as is shown conceptually by the gray bar on top of the original dark bar.

Your Message as Acted Upon is the final step that creates the response to your message and the degree of enthusiasm it is accorded, is a result of all the previous factors. If the final impact of all the factors discussed so far is not high, the response is also going to reflect that in the action that resulted from your efforts. Additionally, those at the receiving end of the message naturally believe that any message presented in pursuit of an opportunity needs to be discounted. The writing style (much "fluff") of many who write their messages during career transition promotes this notion.

The interesting aspect of this messaging model is that if the sent message is carefully prepared, it has the power to amplify, not attenuate, as it goes to the outside world. This was presented at the beginning of this discussion and is shown in examples throughout this book, How does this amplification occur? It occurs primarily because of the differentiation that it creates. A well-articulated message, that is coherent, consistent, and cogent, stands out from all the others and has a tendency to amplify itself, as a result, not attenuate. This realization and its consistent bearing out in one of the toughest markets, is what prompted this model!

If you have played the differentiation strategy well throughout your interactions during the hiring process, your message can get a substantial boost in its power by virtue of how it is acted on. This is shown as a gray bar of significant size on top of the original dark bar. This rendition and model dramatize the differentiating power of a well-delivered message, and how it gets amplified, as it travels progressively through review and selection process.

Throughout this book, many examples of how to generate highly differentiated messages are provided in a variety of situations.

Your Genius to the Rescue

Most people often have misapprehension around the term genius. They relate genius to extraordinary physical or mental powers that only few have. An Einstein, a Picasso, a Mozart, are all viewed as geniuses in their own right and this intimidates most who view themselves as "ordinary" in comparison. Although this sense of being ordinary is true, it does not mean that they lack special gifts. In our context, we define genius as a special gift that we each have that allows us to do things in *unique* ways. This is our natural gift. In a dictionary sense it stands for *a strong inclination, a peculiar, distinctive, or identifying character or spirit the associations and traditions of a place, a personification, or embodiment, especially of a quality or condition.* Thus the concept of genius applies both to a place and a person and it is universal in its manifestation. To each of us it is a source of light within. It's the light that shines on our path to our purpose.

One way to achieve the level of messaging power indicated by the gray bars on top of the black bars of diminishing height is to use this source of light that exists from within all of us: our genius. Our genius is thus our innate gift that is integral part of our existence and something that is unique in the way we manifest it. We often underestimate the power of our own genius, perhaps because we live with it daily. What makes the ratcheting tattoo of job requirements, especially in a tough market, daunting is that we surrender ourselves to our own limitations and refuse to consider ourselves worthy of these positions. Bulwarking our existing skills with our genius and creating a message of value that overcomes some of the more challenging job requirements works well. The gray bars shown in the figure conceptually depict this notion. A message steeped in your genius can greatly amplify an otherwise mediocre message. When we operate without our genius, we are subjecting ourselves to dealing with life's challenges without wearing the armor that defends us. Applying skills that are not steeped in your own genius is tantamount to an ersatz existence; an authentic existence stems from your genius!

The question now is not if you should operate within your genius, but how to identify your genius and then articulate it in a presentable way.

Genius Demystified

The character of your genius is that it allows you to package your skills in a form that creates excitement in the readers' minds. How? The first and the foremost presentation of you is a message, usually on paper, for most professionals. There are some exceptions as it might be in the case of artisans—or even artists—who express themselves with the objects they create. But, for the most part, the starting point is a message on paper. This may sound contrary to the notion that most hold of it as residing in one's mind. Often, what resides in a mind is a jumble of vague messages that are not crystallized. Once these messages land on paper and are forged to shape with diligent attention as to their verbal content, they represent with some power, the author's identity. An identity that can mobilize and even inspire its author and reader alike to action.

One effective way to crystallize something concrete from clutter is to put it in writing in unambiguous terms. Committing one's identity on paper is an excruciating exercise. Why? Objectifying one's true purpose in a compelling way takes effort and can be a frustrating experience. Most do not have the appreciation, the means, or the patience for it. Thus, they maunder through life with messages made up as they navigate through their daily encounters, transmitting these messages to those who cross their paths. This is a poor way to have others pay you the attention that is deserving. Giving form and expression to an idea that is in one's mind are often difficult. Part of this difficulty is presented in the Messaging Challenge and is shown in Figure-3. Part of this difficulty also comes from one's inability to bootstrap their true potential by digging deeper in their past and abilities. This is also integral to the messaging challenge shown graphically in that figure.

Metaphorically, writing your own message of value that is objective and yet compelling without unnecessary verbiage and flowery language is like a surgeon's inability to perform surgery on their own body. It can be done but it is not effective. You need someone to help you in the process; someone who knows how to get to the quick. And, this is not an easy task.

This need of reducing one's being in a verbal message is preposterous to some. And, yet when they are able to see themselves reduced in verbal form on paper, they are transformed beyond their fondest hopes. For one, words have the magic that creates a colorful message about what they convey. If this message is steeped in realism and yet it carries an imaginative message of value creation, its impact is undeniable. Of course, one can also write their message in a "fictional" way to create the same excitement in a reader's mind and get their attention. But, such an approach will not endure beyond the first impression.

Each message delivered to a reader creates its own expectation in the reader's mind. If the reality of subsequent encounters with the reader does not match these expectations, their disappointment will be too difficult a barrier to overcome to go past that initial encounter. Thus, you have defeated yourself by over representing yourself in the readers' minds and thwarted any chances of further relationship with them.

Why? Again, the idea here is not to transform your message by flowery language, but to create a message from a transformed mindset, an entirely different proposition. If you were to go to someone who writes good copy and ask them to write for you what you do, in as colorful a message as is the person capable, such a message can look impressive on its surface. But, without the substance to back it up and, without the power to support its weight, which must come only from deep within you, such message will ring hollow and will not take you beyond the most casual first encounter.

The idea here is that it is not the message that transforms its writer, it is the process of objectifying their genius—their soul—that does. Once transformed, they unleash their true power to do things that are otherwise not possible to achieve and what appears to them beyond reach. As they objectify their genius and gradually begin to own it, the process creates an evolving and crystallizing message. Owning their genius in a language that inspires them becomes more and more comfortable with time. The confidence it generates from projecting it drives the pursuit of a goal otherwise beyond reach, attainable.

Usually, a résumé is the most common form of presenting you and what you do. This is the first—and the foremost—expression in a verbal form of what your purpose is in the context of how you create value for someone who matters in your pursuits. Wrapping this value statement in your genius is a convenient way to create a compelling message. Why? Your genius is your ticket to achieving your true purpose. Your genius connects the very existence of your being with your soul. The soul receives its nourishment by your allowing it to pursue its calling and aligning what you do with what it yearns. Your genius is the extension of your soul in a material form. Your genius is a vehicle that allows you to manifest your true purpose, which emanates from your deepest core—your soul. Nothing can be more powerful than this force that an individual can marshal. Nothing!

Despite the power your own genius can create and despite the levels of achievements to which it can propel you in your endeavors, many do not operate with its benefits. Why? It is so perhaps because the idea of owning their own genius is foreign, even scary to them. Besides, most of the assessments that are available, as tools, for individual discovery often do not create a compelling ownership, perhaps because they lack the face validity, or that perhaps because the outcome is too obvious, or even that they are too general. They also, often, lack the light-bulb moment of truth or the "aha" factor in their first awareness of it, its realization, application, and impact. Most assessment and discovery tools or instruments are not fluid *and* specific enough to accommodate the myriad possibilities that allow those engaging in such diagnoses to truly buy into the outcome and follow it with conviction in an actionable way. Many assessments are undertaken or administered to sate the curiosity or are provided as course of required testing or assessment in professional development.

It is difficult for many to manifest as their soul intends them to. However, for its companion, their body, it is easy for most to address their bodily needs: they eat healthy foods, they exercise, and they maintain a regimen of rest and activity and so on; all bodily needs commonly agreed to for a healthy corporeal life. To many, addressing the care of their soul is an elusive pursuit. Some even vitiate it by cranking up their religious rituals, which often has an exactly the opposite effect—the connection between religion and true spirituality is tenuous at best! Caring for our soul is often less urgent and yet, it is very important. Somehow, our urgent needs seem to always preempt our important ones!

If maintaining their existence in tune with a healthy body, properly maintained, gives them an edge, aligning their soul with their pursuit will give an edge that is beyond description or measurement. This is where the commonly expressed belief of our using less than five percent of our true capability perhaps comes into play. For many, this is difficult to understand because they believe that they are already giving all that they have in what they do. Metaphorically, this is like pushing a car uphill sideways, which is a very difficult task because of the mechanics of it.

What they fail to realize is that they are misaligned with their true purpose and hence they have to make and expend enormous efforts to achieve what they set out to do. This misalignment causes stress. This stress affects, in turn, our physical well-being. Recent studies have shown that stress affects our physiology at a cellular level. Continued stress causes cell damage that results in hair loss, baldness, premature aging and listlessness.

One countermeasure of such stress would be the rewarding work they do. If work causes additional stress, there is no relief and people succumb to early aging, morbidity, and even premature death. What accelerates this condition is how they treat their stress that results from this misalignment.

On the other hand, when work nourishes their soul, it has a healing effect that goes down to the cellular level. Nourishing work, derived from aligning one's genius to the purpose at hand, can heel damaged cells and repair abused body parts. if they are aligned with their very being in what they set out to do, the power with which they are able to apply themselves is infinitely more manifest. And, this happens without "effort." Using the same metaphor of the car, this is now akin to pushing the same car downhill by *rolling* it, a much easier task! When one is operating at their being, they are fearless, they have all their resources mobilized and coming to their aid.

Actually, when you are truly aligned, the whole universe aligns behind you! Things start happening in amazing ways. It is as if the Universe makes it dear for you to search and own your genius first, but once you discover it, articulate it, and then own it through your struggles, it bestows upon you unprecedented rewards.

Staying within the ambit of one's genius in all that they do is critical to their professional success. Why? Again, the most powerful manifestation of a being is when their true purpose is aligned with their task. One way to create that alignment is to first objectify the genius and then show the connection of that spark with the value-creating needs of the target. Done in earnest, this approach invariably results in an endeavor that leads to achieving self-actualization or nirvana.

Evolving Your Genius

Your genius has two components: one innate and the other nurtured. The innate genius is your gift that is inborn. Most become aware of it in their early adolescence and have the option to follow a path that allows them to channel that talent to their benefit. However, often, material and social factors vitiate such pursuits. Why? After all, many consider economic earning power to be the most important factor in their lives. Many professions do not allow for the kind of earning power that is considered comfortable, and as a result, some shun such professions early in their development. They often do this even without having any taste of their abilities to see what can be achieved by harnessing them. This resignation thwarts any possible opportunities they have to operate from their genius in what they pursue unless they stay close to the professional calling that allows them to use their genius in some way.

Even if they pursue a path that allows them to fully harness their genius, there are other skills that are adjunct to it that need to be developed to make the portfolio of skills sellable. If the genius is kept as a central focus of one's pursuit, the adjunct skills that are developed tend to complement the genius, and, together, they create a formidable value proposition as an economic package. Thus, for someone to fully harness their genius they must identify those skills that complement their natural gifts and allow them to leverage their overall value proposition.

Figure-4 shows how the innate genius and its nurtured counterpart play together to complementarily reinforce each other. Thus, being aligned with your genius in what you pursue makes your genius stronger or more compelling. On the other hand, if it is not channeled, it languishes, and, in the process, brings you much stress, unhappiness, and material wants. Now, why would anyone want *that*?

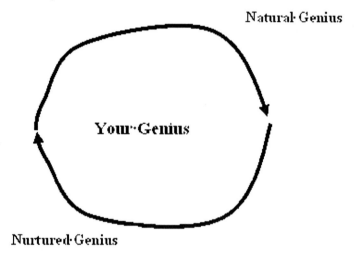

Figure-4: How Genius Grows in a Positive Environment

As the figure indicates, your genius can grow as you grow your professional abilities in the right environment. This growth comes from honing your skill in that is steeped in your genius and the increasing confidence that comes from its success as you develop in your profession in an environment that is supportive. Some of the elements of this environment are:

1. Basic alignment of purpose
2. Self-confidence of operating within your genius
3. Supportive boss
4. Nurturing colleagues
5. Possibilities for growth
6. Long-term prospects

Each of these factors is essential to harnessing and growing your abilities to operate within your genius.

Genius and Obstacles

The purpose of this book is to help those who give up pursuing their dreams because "obstacles" get in their way of achieving what they set out to do. These obstacles could be external or self-perceived. In either case they are perceived as insurmountable.

Once you own your genius, however, it is relatively easy to overcome these objections by focusing on how you can use your genius to leverage your position even when others who compete with you have advantage by virtue of their material accomplishments. These material accomplishments include educational background, specific experience, skills that are perceived as essential to a job, and so on.

For a given position how your genius plays a part in compensating for the perceived lack of requirements is shown in Figure-5: The Genius Connection.

The heavy lines in the figure radiating from the star in the center show a strong influence of the genius in the way it affects a positive outcome. The light lines show that the genius does not influence the outcome as much. The following attributes of a job or position *may* go into making a selection:

1. Length of experience

2. Specific experience

3. Educational background

4. Skills required

5. Indefinable characteristics

6. Physicality

7. Industry knowledge

8. Potential of success

The Table-8 shows how these requirements can play a major part in a selection process and how properly presented genius can overcome these requirements. This table is based on anecdotal data working with over 1,000 clients, who used this approach to job search and were successful in their pursuits.

The table represents only a small sampling of job requirements that can be neutralized by properly articulated genius attributes. These attributes are typically presented as Unique Skills in a résumé. See examples in chapter-6: Building Your Platform.

#	Selection Criteria	Weight 10= Highest	Genius	Genius Counteraction	Comments
1	Length of Experience	7	Passion	Very High	Often passion for a particular job neutralizes length of experience
2	Specific Experience	1	Proven Ideas	Low	Ideas that are proven in allied fields can compensate for this requirement
3	Education	6	Imagination	High	Related education can replace demonstrated abilities to create new value
4	Skills Required	6	Maturity	High	Maturity is not always age related. Showing good judgment is important
5	Indefinable Characteristics	10	Specific company insights	Highest	Having an in-depth understanding of the company needs are critical to a position
6	Physicality	5	Value Creation	Moderate	These are illegal in the U.S. but there are unwritten rules at play.
7	Industry Knowledge	4	Transferable skills	Moderate	A strong genius attribute can neutralize specific industry knowledge
8	Potential for Success	8	Learning Skills	Very High	Ability to learn quickly can be a great neutralizer for any doubts about future success

Table-8: How Genius can Counteract Selection Criteria

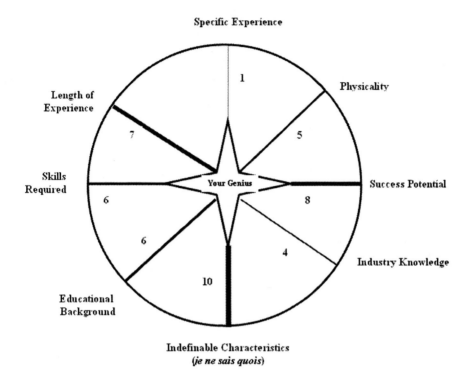

Legend:

- The labels around the perimeter of the circle represent typical selection factors.
- The radial lines represent the connection genius has with these factors
- The weight (1–10) a radial line represents how much influence genius has on a particular selection factor (Heavy lines show heavy influence)

Note:

1. Job requirements are different from selection factors. Often these factors override job requirements as is shown in examples throughout the book.

2. Physicality refers to all physical aspects that are factored in the selection process, as age, race, gender, appearance, physical attributes, etc. Many of these may be illegal.

Figure-5: How Genius can Play in Job Selection

From Hunting to Farming

One of the fallouts of an uncertain economic climate and the job market is that those looking for opportunities pursue them in a reactive way. This is similar to what hunters did at the dawn of the human existence. The hunting metaphor stems from what the hunters did in the Stone Age to meet their basic food needs. They set out of their caves each day to look for their quarry to bring home their daily need for food and nourishment. On days that they did not find any prey, they came back hungry and then tried it again the next. As days wore on the hunters got increasingly more desperate in their attempts at finding sustenance and were willing to settle for things that they would not otherwise, when they had the choice. Having the ability to store a kill for a few days brought some relief, but the basic habit did not change until farming became a way of life.

As farming became a technology in its own right, man's dependence on food became less reactive and desperate. In a way, the ability to productively farm was the genius that man "found" by using the knowledge of farming, crops, and the soil—technology in essence—that relieved the daily stress of foraging for food.

The same metaphor holds true for job searching in one's career. This is not limited to job searching when you are out of work and looking for a job, but it also applies when managing a career. The process of managing a career involves planning, and making intelligent and deliberate choices so that there are options from which to choose.

Developing career options comes from knowing what your value is and how it compares in relative terms in a competitive marketplace. Your genius is central to this process because this single factor is a major force in creating differentiated positioning in a competitive world. To move from hunting to farming, metaphorically, requires a robust message that differentiates your value proposition from the rest. A message that allows you to package your value in a way that has an interested audience represents a robust value proposition.

Examples of how to move your mindset from hunting to farming are presented in Chapters-6 and 7 for a variety of professions to emphasize the concept of how changing the way your value message is packaged transforms you positioning.

Transitional Challenges and Reflection

In a typical situation those engaged in their everyday work life are often consumed by what they do. Their job takes their energy and attention on a daily basis. They do not have the time to pause and reflect. As a result, many often surrender to their situation even if they are not happy in it. They resign to their condition and rationalize it by arguing that this is how things are.

Many often doubt themselves and wonder if they are imagining what is happening to them; they live in a surreal world; zoned out, as if on autopilot. Their activities are guided by a series of programmed commands that get them through their workday. Just to stay in synch with the world around them they have to make an effort—pretense. They live in a world stemming from their surrender to their own plight and their resignation to deal with it to change what is happening to them. They become slave to their paycheck in their jejune existence.

They don't have to! In this age we are so focused on getting things done at any cost and at a pace that we often do not have or take the time to slow down, think, reflect, and listen to ourselves. Pausing, analyzing, reflecting, and getting some objective insights by talking to someone else can be a great way to change the status quo. We are often slaves to our own needs and are afraid that if we pursue another line of thought, that we may compromise our brittle existence. We become so afraid of losing our material belongings that they end up owning us, instead.

As a result, we do not engage in reflective insights that allow us to identify our genius, articulate it, and then find a better alignment between who we are and what we must do. We also do not have the courage to pursue our own dream shaped by listening to what is happening to us in our everyday existence and how that is slowly eroding our esteem, or even killing out spirit.

In this context there is the parable of a boiled frog that is worth repeating:

> The frog's physiology does not have a thermostat that senses slowly changing ambient temperature. So, if you put a frog in a pot of water and slowly bring that water to a boil the frog will boil itself to death without jumping out of the pot.
>
> If however, the same frog is dropped into a pot of heating water, it immediately jumps out because it cannot stand that sudden jump in its ambient temperature, even though the water is nowhere near the boiling point. Thus, the frog does not have the ability to detect slow changes that are deadly enough to kill it, much as we do not respond to a slowly eroding environment around us by inuring to a degrading but toxic environment that we would not become part of if we knew it beforehand...

The best approach to looking at your situation is to reflectively review your status and then compare it to what you had imagined it would be before you entered the situation. If there is a difference between the two that is affecting you emotionally and your well being and enjoyment in your job are compromised, then it is time to make a change.

There are seven levels of engagement in a job. Below is a ranking of increasing engagement in a job starting with the most superficial to most engaged. They are briefly described as we come to the end of this chapter:

➢ Pretense

➢ Compliant
➢ Resigned

➢ Forced
➢ Engaged

➢ Aligned

➢ Authentic

Pretense is when you are doing your job merely to show others that you can hold a job and earn a paycheck. This engagement stemmed from your need to earn money, show to the world around you that you are worthy as a human being and that you are "normal." You typically go through your day hating nearly every moment of what you are doing and wish that you were doing something else, but do not have the will power to extricate yourself from the situation or believe that there can be a better existence.

Compliant attitude to work is when you surrender yourself to the situation you have signed up to somewhat willy-nilly and wish that you were somewhere else doing something else, but you have no idea what that is. In terms of stress, this situation creates high stress.

Being **Resigned** to your work or job stems from shame and social pressure that you put on yourself for having to work and having to be busy earning money. This is one step above being compliant in that you have some will that forces you to put energy in what you do, if for no other reason than your mere sense of duty. You get some satisfaction from what you do but the general attitude is that of surrender to the situation and giving only what you must to get by.

You have **Forced** yourself in a work situation because of your own commitment to show that you can conquer the assignment at hand. Personal pride, ego, and a sense that others are going to judge you on how you brave through this assignment or the job forces you to apply your energies in an unhealthy way that produces results but at an enormous price that you pay in stress, exhaustion, and expending a great degree of effort. Your effort is often not appreciated.

Engaged is when you are able to focus on the job in the moment you apply yourself and are able to give most of your energies to work and produce good results. Each task requires having to marshal enough fortitude before commencing and once engaged you are able to see through the task to its end. You often produce good results.

Aligned is when you are able to not only stay focused on the task or job but are able to think about it even during you own accord, when away from work. You are thinking about what you are engaged in during the times you are not required to. You also spend more time at work beyond what is normally required.

Authentic application of self to work is the ultimate seduction. Here you are doing what you do, because of your complete alignment in every aspect of what you do and you cannot separate work from your being. When you are engaged in an authentic work relationship, there is the least amount of stress you feel in what you do. Work is pure joy!

The purpose of this book is to help you move from the mercenary existence to the one that offers joy and authenticity. This condition applies both to the job or anything that you do as an enterprise. This book is aimed at showing how using your genius helps you achieve an authentic existence in your work life. An authentic existence in work life translates into a much better work-life balance, a virtually stress-free life, and a better quality-of-work life.

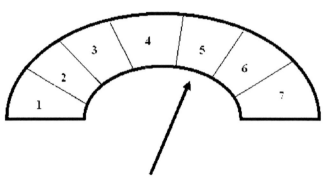

Legend:

1. Pretense
2. Compliant
3. Resigned
4. Forced
5. Engaged
6. Aligned
7. Authentic

Note: More than 80 percent of those working are to the left of the arrow in how they are doing their jobs.

Figure 6: Degrees of Engagement in Work

Transitions are a great time to engage in this reflective abandon. Even if you are well situated in your job indulging in this personal self-analysis is a good way to renew yourself. Often people dislike their jobs and decide to move on to another company, career, profession, or industry. But, before casually undertaking such a major change it is a good idea to evaluate the source of unhappiness that prompts the change. The following is a list of factors that can help in this analysis:

1. Company values
2. Company culture
3. Colleagues/peers
4. Boss
5. Fit
6. Prospects
7. Meaning of work

In the ensuing chapters we will explore how your genius can come to your rescue and put you on a path of renewal.

A dream job involves engaging at level "5" or above. Ideally, you want to be at level "7" where there is no difference between your being and the work that you do. The following list of factors defines what constitutes a dream job:

1. Sense of purpose
2. The job itself
3. The opportunity
4. Future potential
5. Compensation
6. Company
7. Company culture
8. Colleagues/co-workers

Genius and Your Platform

A platform is a unique concept of branding and keeping the integrity of that brand across different *avatars* during a career transformation. An avatar, as already explained at the beginning of this chapter is one manifestation of your career. (An avatar, as described there, is a word of Sanskrit origin and means that the basic entity has morphed into another manifestation to accomplish a particular mission.)

An avatar typically applies to human beings but can also be applied to inanimate objects in a general context. Thus, when someone completely changes their career and manifests as a professional with a different calling card, they can be seen as an avatar of their past manifestation. In the case of inanimate objects, a food processor and a blender can be considered as two different avatars of the same basic food preparation appliance. When you witness avatars the manifestations are unmistakably different and yet, their soul remains the same.

Most consider changing careers by tweaking their résumé. This is often difficult because the transformation cannot be credible without a message that goes well beyond what is in the resume. Also, it is much more difficult to fashion a résumé to change a career in a major way without incorporating many elements in your transformation that go well beyond what can be typically put in a résumé or is expected to present.

Enter the platform concept. A platform is a complete representation of a message that incorporates it so compellingly that it leaves no doubt in the reader's mind that the message must be acted upon favorably. A résumé is one element of a platform, albeit an important one. A résumé with genius as its centerpiece can provide a ready means of creating different avatars based on the genius. A platform can be viewed as an integrated system with articulated elements that are interactive. This means that each element of the platform affects all others and also that each one contributes its own message to the overall outcome. A résumé based on one's genius creates a means for a powerful platform. The following typical list constitutes a platform:

➢ Résumé

➢ Supporting materials as portfolios of past work

➢ Letters of recommendations and references

➢ Stories of leadership

➢ Website

In the next chapter this concept is described more fully.

Summary Chapter-5: How Your Genius Helps You

In any economic activity the message that one creates in getting others to pay attention to it and that results in someone paying for the services that message represents is central to the economic value exchanged. Most struggle in crafting their value message primarily because they lack the perspective that empowers them to create the message, particularly when it involves their own talent. In this seminal chapter we define genius as any attribute that makes you stand out from others. The following are key elements of this chapter:

The Messaging Challenge is the gap between who you are (True Self) and the actual response you get from the value-proposition message. The model developed graphically shows the 10 levels of message diminution as a result of personal limits that can be overcome by tapping into and articulating your genius. Crafting a message wrapped in your genius allows you to diminish the gap between your True Self and how you manifest.

Genius is presented as a parameter with a capacity to grow rather than as something that is fixed from the start. The nature and the nurtured components can create virtuous cycle in the right environment that only you can create by how you apply it in what you do in the first place.

How to extract your genius using a tool is explained in the next chapter.

To be engaged with your full genius in your career one must recognize that there are various levels at which you are capable of engaging:

➢ Pretense

➢ Compliant

➢ Resigned

➢ Forced

➢ Engaged

➢ Aligned

➢ Authentic

Most operate in their jobs at Level-5. When you are engaged at the Authentic level your genius is fully at play and your work becomes aligned with who you are and becomes purposeful.

Your Platform is how you build your elements for creating and delivering your message of value. Two critical elements of this platform are your résumé and your cover letter. This is discussed in more detail in the next chapter.

Chapter-6: Building Your Platform

"By words the mind is winged."

—Aristophanes (c. 448–385)

Introduction

A platform is a vehicle that communicates your overall value to a targeted audience. A platform in the context of career management or a job search comprises many elements. The most crucial of these are the résumé and cover letter. Other elements of a typical platform are your references, your Website, a portfolio of your past work, and so on.

A résumé is your proxy. But, since it is a message, it must have the ability and power to move the person in front of it to act as if it were you. The message in your résumé is at the heart of how you create value for the target employer. Together with the cover letter, this integrated message speaks much about how you think of yourself and project that thinking. This message must have the power to move its reader to take the next step that brings you closer to getting hired. In the pervious chapter, which dealt with your genius and described how it helps create a message that differentiates, much was written about how to amplify the power of such a message. This chapter shows *how* to create such a message.

The job market has experienced a sea change, especially since rapid off shoring and outsourcing began to change the employment scene. Yet, not much has changed about how résumés are still written and presented. This is perhaps because those writing them have not changed their mindsets about what a résumé really is and does. In the new paradigm, central to a résumé is how your genius shines through its message. We all possess this attribute, allowing us to do things uniquely. And yet, we do not know how to leverage this force for ourselves or even acknowledge its existence. In this chapter, we present how to craft a résumé for effective messaging using a design that has evolved and proven in one of the toughest job markets in remembered history. This résumé design uses individual genius as its centerpiece.

Cover letters are in presented in the next chapter.

Organization

This chapter is organized along the following main topics, to help quickly focus on the area that is most important to building a platform and creating an effective message:

- Understanding the Target Market
- Résumé writing
  - ➤ Résumé Purpose
  - ➤ Résumé Elements
  - ➤ Common Resume Challenges
  - ➤ Multiple-Position Résumés
  - ➤ Executive Résumés
- Résumé Showcase

Each bulleted topic is presented in this chapter to help understand the material, with tools and examples provided for immediate success.

Understanding the Target Market

To really understand a market, the best way to get acquainted with it is to visit it! By going to popular job boards one can quickly assess what the jobs are and their flavors. The job and position descriptions of an open job allow you to assess what needs to be presented to properly respond, so that it is viewed favorably.

One way to create differentiation, is to not only respond to what is already in the job description, but to go a step further in the way the job itself is going to emerge. This is called job trending. Job trending is sending a message to prospective employers that for *their* long-term success, merely meeting stated job requirements is not enough; future needs also must be addressed! This forward-thinking approach can help capture the imagination of prospect employers in ways your competition may fail to!

We discuss this further in Writing Your Résumé, in this chapter.

♠ Leveraging Job Trends

Introduction

The job market, starting with high-tech, started experiencing a structural shift even before the dotcom meltdown began in late 2000. It did not take long to spread that contagion to other industries quickly. This inexorable shift in jobs continues today and most job families are affected by it, although some more than the others. A job family is a cluster of jobs that share common skill requirements. Some job families may take time before they show signs of change. Here we'll explore what that shift is, and the trend of that shift, and more importantly, what that means to someone who has to manage a career.

The Global Economy

In an ironic twist, the success spawned by the creative minds of the Silicon Valley became the source of their own grief. How? As the Internet became more pervasive in the late '90s, global communication became a commodity. It was no longer necessary to wait for expensive and unreliable means of communicating at a functional level, where one exchanges large quantities of information freely and near-synchronously around the globe and around the clock. Factors driving a major shift that started affecting jobs in high-tech and related industries are listed below. Other industries will follow suit, and soon:

> ➤ A large technology pool of inexpensive and expert talent available overseas, especially India, that speaks English.

> ➤ A large labor pool of manufacturing talent available in China and the Pacific Rim countries. Both these factors accelerated the off-shoring trend.

> ➤ Many companies started outsourcing key functions they once took pride in performing themselves. Manufacturing was one, among others. This resulted in consolidation of such functions across the entire industry within a sector, resulting in highly narrow job competencies to keep labor costs down.

> ➤ A fundamentally shifted mindset that is now examining the way we behave in the corporate world and the economy to create value and build wealth. The operating mantra shifted from local job creation to global value generation.

> ➤ Major technology players as HP, IBM, and Motorola realized that producing consumer goods as PCs, hand-held digital products, and communication devices was not their core competency that differentiated them in the marketplace. These goods had become commodities with

short life cycles; some had even become fashion statements. Original Equipment Manufacturers (OEMs) shifted to outsourcing their products to Original Design Manufacturers (ODMs). ODMs provide both product design and manufacturing resources to a major brand. Global players now merely put their labels and provide logistical and marketing channel resources to get the products in the hands of consumers and end users. They also build alliances with other players in the marketplace to enhance customer experience and capture greater value. The focus is now closer to the customer than it is on the side of production (see next bullet).

➢ Organizations began to realize that the value creation process had shifted from back-end to the front-end activities. Traditional back-end activities had been manufacturing, support, operations, and logistics. Front-end activities, on the other hand are understanding the customer, market knowledge, order entry process, and managing the customer account. More and more organizations realized that outsourcing the back-end activities and tightening the management of the front-end activities would provide a competitive advantage to create a business model that would sustain itself as more and more back-end operations got outsourced.

➢ A shift in emphasis from selling products to services and after-sale activities. Starting in the mid 90s, companies as IBM, GE, and HP recognized that as products became more and more sophisticated, customers needed increasingly more help in understanding how to use these complex products in an environment that produces value beyond what was obvious to them. It was, thus, not enough to merely make a product sale, but also to create an ongoing revenue stream and profits by providing services and solutions to customer accounts and manage those accounts to make sure that they grow on both fronts: product demand and services.

➢ A shift from constantly having to upgrade technologies for speed and functionality to squeezing out the most value from what is already in place and living with what is sufficient, versus what is the best and the fastest! This single factor was perhaps why the high-tech implosion accelerated, starting late in year 2000.

➢ A shift in organizational managers' thinking in the way employees create value: employees are now expected to create an *ongoing* value stream, and not just carry out their work for a paycheck, regardless of how it impacts the *immediate* bottom line and wealth creation; ongoing wealth creation became the operating principle.

♠ Off-shoring and Outsourcing

The practice of outsourcing and off-shoring has come into sharper focus during the past few years, particularly starting with the incidental dotcom implosion in early 2001. During 2003 about 250,000 jobs, mostly high-tech and knowledge jobs, were "off-shored" to India and other countries as China, Indonesia, and the Philippines. Exactly how many jobs were lost to off-shoring is a matter of debate. Some jobs have even gone to Russia and the Eastern European countries. Unbeknownst to many, off-shoring to India began in the early '80s, with many manual computer tasks—digital toil—being shipped for low-cost processing. Only in the past few years has this trend taken on an exponential proportion, brought into sharper focus by the intense media interest and rampant job losses that go well beyond those lost to off-shoring. See below, the "Hype" phase! With time, increasingly higher-value work is going to India.

The off-shoring and outsourcing of jobs are two somewhat different practices that an organization can adopt. Outsourcing is where an organization decides to stay focused on its core competencies and farms out its more routine functions to those who can do them more efficiently, *regardless* of the geography. Typically these functions include payroll, security, front lobby administration, mailroom, and other routines. Outsourcing practice has been a management alternative since the late '80s, which accelerated in the '90s. This trend is not going to change. More and more companies are going to find ways of consolidating their routine tasks and finding ways to cut costs to become more efficient in what they do. This cost advantage is what keeps them competitive; they are not so much strategic practices, as they are survival tactics.

Off-shoring is a different matter: companies have found that some functions, even core functions, can be "off-shored" by keeping a pool of labor forces overseas that can do many jobs more efficiently, allowing them to develop an ongoing capability to perform critical tasks competitively. India has emerged as one country with resources that can support many such initiatives. Major Fortune-500 companies in the past few years have "off-shored" many white-collar jobs to India and other countries. This practice is not limited to call centers and administrative functions; it has now pervaded almost all knowledge work, which now includes even radiological diagnostics, using some of the physicians trained to interpret medical tests and MRIs. This trend will not reverse; it is, in fact, going to accelerate.

Many complain about the low cost of knowledge work in India. By some estimates there is a 6–10:1 salary advantage for comparable skills between India and the U.S.. Considering the overhead and other costs, the net saving can easily be 4:1. But this is not the whole story, particularly in software. Not only is the salary of a comparable software professional less by a significant factor in India (compared to the U.S.), the efficiency of production is much higher to boot! How is this possible?

One reason is that, in the U.S., we focused on cranking out constantly revised, complex, and functionally cumbersome software during the pioneering phase of the software and the personal computer industry. India, on the other hand, focused on streamlining software development methodology by adopting a disciplined approach. This is much analogous to what happened to the automotive industry in the '70s when the Japanese ate Detroit's lunch by beating them on the quality of their automobiles at a *lower* cost.

In software there is a methodology for improving the effectiveness of how it is developed. In this methodology there are five levels at which this development can take place and it is called Capability Maturity Model (CMM). In this model, Level one represents the most rudimentary approach to software development, and Level five, the most evolved. The ratio of the outputs between the two levels is typically *tenfold*!

Much of the U.S software development process, on average, operates at level 2+, according to experts. The level at which India produces software is at level-4 or even level-5. Currently India has the most number of level-5 software development centers in the world! This means that the output difference, *not* accounting for quality issues, is two to five times what is produced here! This is a significant factor to combat. This is why software and IT projects will continue to gravitate to India in the future, despite any political backlash from the migration. The force is economic and compelling for software.

The rate at which the off-shoring trend across a broad skill set, not just software development, is going to accelerate will depend on a variety of factors. When an initiative captures public attention, as off-shoring has, since the early Millennium, it is usually in its early stages of "hype." As a result, many perceptions about the advantage of off-shoring are distorted. Why?

Let us take a closer look.

Any major "new" management initiative evolves before it is adopted as a valid and accepted business practice across a wide range of industries. If such an initiative dies down after much media attention and hype, it is looked upon as a management fad. Recent fads were reengineering, empowerment, and team building to name a few. There are four stages in the evolution of a new initiative:

- Hype
- Disillusionment
- Redeployment
- Integration

The first phase "hype" is when there is much public focus on the issue and there are constant media reports about the initiative, including its political ramifications. Many companies jump on the bandwagon and follow those who are "successful" adopting the new fad. Soon there is a backlash as a result of the hyped activity. The gains are not what they expected, there is political backlash, there are hidden costs, and there are social pressures and so on.

Enter disillusionment, the next stage! During this stage many companies back peddle the initiative and retrench their positions. On the off-shoring front, recently Dell and IBM have backed off and pulled some of their functions back into their U.S. operations. This trend will continue as will the trend to outsource, as more and more tasks and functions are identified during this shakedown.

Redeployment is where organizations learn the true cost of implementing an initiative and use that learning and other factors to develop their long-term plan on how to stabilize their operations and benefit from the positive aspects of the trend. During this stage, the initiative looses its media interest and pure economic rationality and organizational considerations drive their fate. The off-shoring trend is not yet seen this stage, but is expected to see it within the next year or so. The off-shoring initiative is one of those inevitable economic forces resulting from the global economy spawned by the Internet. The irony here is that those who made the Internet a commercial success have been hit the hardest by its emergence!

The final stage is integration, where the initiative matures and so do peoples' perspective on it. Their long-term benefits tend to become visible. This horizon is a few years away for the off-shoring trend.

The idea presented here validates the concept of the Change Curve of Figure-2 presented in Chapter-2.

High-tech has suffered the most impact by the off-shoring trend. It is estimated that in the coming years about one in seven jobs in this industry (mostly in the Silicon Valley) is going to be off-shored, mostly to India. In 2003 about 250,000 jobs were lost to India as mentioned before. Even though there were some three million in the U.S. labor pool who had lost their jobs (and nearly 15 million out of work or underemployed!) in the past three years, each one of them thought that *their* job had gone to India. This is called perceptual amplification!

The reality, though, is that as companies find better ways to manage global resources, more and more jobs are going to go overseas. It is estimated that by 2015 about 3 million jobs are going overseas. But by the same token, new jobs are going to be *defined* right here. Typically those jobs are more "upstream" in the value chain. This means getting closer to the customer and developing business models that are more service based. This trend has implications that are worth considering for the future well being and management of one's career.

Outsourcing now has become so common in the handling of the supply chain that for those viewing it as an attractive management alternative; it becomes much more palatable to just call it "sourcing." Once you take this attitude your approach to managing your career changes whether you are inside a company working and worrying about your job security or from the outside trying to get in with the right value proposition.

♠ Career Implications

The factors listed have now resulted in an inescapable shift in the way organizations are considering how to fill open positions. Some are making a conscious effort to take the emerging trends into account; others have to be reminded by those looking for opportunities in these organizations. In a bear market employers are selective. It is no longer enough to be the best at what one once did; what they now need to demonstrate clearly is that skills presented in a résumé will benefit the target organization's *future* needs. Being aware of the emerging trends and the way future job competencies are shaping up will give job applicants an edge in their search. Table-9 in this chapter is a partial list of traditional and emerging job competencies for some job families. Using this map of forward-looking competencies, job seekers must now position themselves for a favorable consideration—even an edge—during the hiring process.

♠ Integrating Job Trends in Your Message

Integrating job trends in a message is an advantage that must be exploited in each opportunity. Why? There are three reasons:

- Most posted jobs do not reflect today's reality. They're often constructed by "copy and paste" of the past ones, often dating back a few years!

- Most applicants responding to job openings try to match what is already described in the job posting. Having a message that goes beyond this description, and the one that captures an employer's imagination gives an edge!

- Demonstrating an understanding of how a position can create greater value by integrating broader aspects of a job can create a competitive advantage.

Job trends are an important element of the overall message of a job-search campaign. For example, for a software developer, especially in high-tech, the very nature of the development process has changed dramatically in the U.S. Much of the work is now parceled out to India and overseas. No matter how great you are at developing software, unless you understand how this trend of off-shoring is going to affect the potential employer, you are not going to have a long-term job there. Even if a company does not have any language in the job opening about off-shoring now, responding to an opportunity with the knowledge of this trend is an advantage. This insight can be presented in the following way in a Career Objective:

Before

Career Objective: A position as a software development lead

After

Career Objective: A hands-on technical lead in software responsible for: collaborating with customers to capture their requirements, organizing teams and setting up projects that include off-shore resources, managing overall projects to ensure that the final solution is delivered to delight the customer, and managing the entire product life-cycle for a profitable revenue stream.

A more detailed discussion on Career Objective is covered in résumé writing, which follows. Letters that reflect these messages are in the next chapter.

Creating a résumé for a job with an employer that supports outsourcing or off-shoring requires specific messages. One cannot present a message without awareness of the needs. For example, if someone is looking to migrate from a traditional manufacturing organization, an OEM, to a company that supports outsourced manufacturing, even to the same OEM, the skill set required in the new position is different from the one expected in the comparable position at the OEM. Why? This is mainly because the focus of value creation in the two organizations is different. The OEM, typically, requires a broad set of skills to achieve the manufacturing capability. Working across a broad cross-functional organization is critical to make this position create value for the OEM. For the outsourced manufacturing organization, however, the focus is the depth of a given function more than the broad knowledge because this is how the outsourced business achieves cost benefits: doing repetitive operations at minimal cost. The résumé and the cover letters must incorporate this awareness in unambiguous messages. One example of the two flavors of résumés, albeit in the contracting domain (vs. job domain), is presented in *The 7 Keys to a Dream Job: A Career Nirvana Playbook!*, Key-7, under Contracting.

♠ Differentiating Yourself

Throughout this chapter we have and will continue to emphasize that differentiating is a key strategy for a successful job search. Differentiation does not just start during the marketing process; it goes way back with the first piece of a message—the résumé! Even before the résumé is written, how one thinks has much to do with how it all ends up being differentiated.

The concept of differentiation is hammered throughout this book. It is presented in various sections to show different aspects of this theme. For example, knowing the job trends can help in creating a differentiated message in each résumé.

The next section presents how to differentiate with your résumé message.

Notes:

Table-9: Emerging Job Trends in Today's Economy: A Sampling

	Traditional Job	Traditional Role	Emerging Job	New Role	Drivers	Opportunities in
11	Account Manager	Sell to generate revenues, protect accounts/revenue streams standing	Relationship Manager	Understand customer drivers, value transfer equation, long-term relationships, alliances	Customer loyalty, cost of landing new accounts, cost of defections	Customer intimacy
12	Business Development Manager	Promote business, create new revenues, make profits, and expand	Opportunities Seeker	Explore what is NOT happening and ID avenues to catalyze it	Current value creation not supporting expectations competition, commoditization	Alliances, value loops with suppliers, consolidation
33	Component Engineer	Define and specify components/vendors	Applications Engineering	Define new applications for components, creative single source	Simplicity, reliability, alliances, partnership	Alliance creation in value chain
44	Customer Support	Post-sale customer support	Customer Experience Champion	Understand customer needs, use, issues, and know how to close	Product complexity, customer impatience and expectations	
55	Does not exist	N/A	Account Executive Process Steward	Promote organization-wide process to match large accounts with senior execs to manage discovery, relationship, and growth,	Large accounts are orphans left to the will of the Account Managers; account defections, lack of long-term visibility	Global and strategic accounts
66	Facilities Manager	Construction, utilities, services, space allocation, special facilities, regulatory	Facilities Overseer	Real-Estate Custodian, strategic planning, Hoshin, energy incentives, subcontracts	Cost; globalization, work habits, virtual orgs, regulatory compliance incentives	Subcontracting services
77	IT Specialist	Design and support IT infrastructure with the latest and the greatest	IT Resource	Make available what is installed, increase investment effectiveness	Installed capacity, low availability, utilization, and capital, increased hurdle rates, IT as a business partner	IT effectiveness; welding business ops to IT
88	Maintainability Engineer	Product life-cycle, downstream costs, logistics	Revenue protection engineer	Find creative ways to enhance product's overall appeal in its long-term life	Throwaway designs of the past, environmentalist, back-to-basics	New models of maintenance logistics, self-help diagnostics

##	Traditional Job	Traditional Role	Emerging Job	New Role	Drivers	Opportunities in
99	Marcom Specialist	Develop product/service communications and collaterals	Marcom Generalist	Guerilla approaches to reaching end users, creating product excitement/demand vacuum	Limited budgets, multiple avenues, savvy but time-constrained end user, highly customized real-time collaterals	Customer-intimate campaign capabilities, HP's new INDIGO venture is a case in point. Print-on-Demand collateral
10	OD Specialist	Organizational development, teams, training, leadership development	OE Catalyst	Project Teams, PM Methodology, Career Ladders, reward structures, Operating Protocols, Six Sigma	New Team Paradigms, Structure (PMOs), Alignment, Cycle Times	Organizational effective initiatives
111	Procurement Manager	JIT, quality, multiple sources, vendor ship,	Supply Network Catalyst	Supply chain integration value capture, ecosystem dynamics, transform resources to provide package goods.	Complex ecosystems, dynamic world economy, M&As, cheap labor	Cultural training, values, supply network dynamics value exchanges
112	Project Manager	Lead product/service development, deliver against set objectives	Profit Center, autonomous units, line of business, accountable to customers/supplier	Value-chain network, team leadership, cross-functional cooperation, subcontract management; customer experience	Web capability, team dynamics, life-cycle, Earned Value, Global workforce	New team paradigms; PMO and benchmarking
113	Product Development Engineer	Translate inventions into profitable product suites, platforms and derivatives	ODM Specifier	Liaise between R&D, emerging component technologies, capabilities, and ODMs for differentiated products.	Major players are now brand promoters, not operational participants, technology commoditization	Prototype capabilities in-house and ODM development.
114	Production Planner	Develop detailed work/material flow /logistics, inventory	Production Overseer	Align demand with capacity, shift loads, global cost awareness	Global resources, ODM	Integrated planning.
115	R&D Manager	Lead creative teams to generate new product stream, new platforms, future revenue streams	Innovations Catalyst	Establish a new core competency for innovation. Establish organization-wide process for innovation	Slow inventions, lack of continuity of new platforms, future value and competitive advantage	Leveraging innovations across entire organization not just in R&D.

##	Traditional Job	Traditional Role	Emerging Job	New Role	Drivers	Opportunities in
116	Reliability/Maintainability	Predict performance	Product Experience Engineer	Technology life, value alternatives, availability, value experience	Emerging technologies; value alternatives	New approaches to Product Design; manufacturability.
117	Software Developer	Translate requirements into code, then rework as needed; keep doing version iterations to create complex, hard-to-use s/w	Product Developer	Translate Customer Needs to Requirements, liaison, teaming, validation, customer champion, disciplined development	Process integration, accountability, cost, schedule, customer experience, and globalization.	Extreme programming, Capability Maturity Model (CMM); S/W Reuse Coaching/Mentoring. Off-shoring integration.
118	Software QA	Validate code, document, Configuration Management	Product Assurance/Support	Liaise between customer and developer, strategic testing, life cycle, customer experience	Process integration, Outsourcing, India connection, CMM,	Extreme Programming, Software Reuse
119	Technical Writer	Develop materials to help customers with product use.	Product-use facilitator	Create print, Web and other deliverables with interactive capabilities; up-to-date materials	Web, complex products, Limited training, language barriers, product changes.	Multi-media skills; knowing how users need information managed/delivered.
220	Test Engineer	Design test scenarios to validate new products, assure compliance, support complaints.	Test Champions	Participate early in design process; help create test simulations, test as an ongoing process and then final testing.	Cycle times, test capabilities, Automated testing; computerized simulations, test costs and time.	Outsourced testing.
221	Training & Development	ID Needs, develop content, deliver training	Training Management	ID opportunities, find resources, TTT Line managers, monitor how it impacts bottom line	Emphasis away from Level-1 measurements,	Developing training designs to affect the bottom line Level-5 not just Level-1
222	Usability Engineer	Product use; User interface	Customer Experience Engineer	Ease of use, post-purchase experience, clever/creative applications	Consumer disillusionment value expectations, innovation	Speaking customer and user language in final deliverables.

Résumé Writing

Résumé writing is an art. It is also a science. Writing one's own résumé is one of the most challenging undertakings, because on the one hand, it is hard to be objective, and on the other, it is important to showcase accomplishments in a way that creates clear differentiation in a crowded marketplace. The other difficulty comes from packaging accomplishments and then creating a message around them so that it appeals to the decision maker or hiring manager. Yet another frustration that enters in creating a résumé is that, once it is complete and circulated for a critique, it is hard to find anyone who does not have an opinion and a specific comment about it. Having spent much time and energy creating a "self-portrait" in an emotionally charged state, it is hard to ignore all the advice that is offered, and at the same time manage the process to get going on the job-search campaign!

♠Résumé Purpose

The purpose of a résumé is to create a value message that benefits the target employer. Merely having a message of value is not enough to get to a hiring decision. Why? Having an unambiguous value message is a start. But, more importantly, showing a clear benefit flowing from it is the next requirement. The difference between a value statement and a benefit is that one flows from the other, but for which further action is required. A simple example may illustrate this point: Suppose you purchased a self-help book. Assuming that the book is well rated in its genre, you receive value, once the transaction takes place. However, for the benefit to ensue from the book, you must put to practice what the book espouses in your own life. Otherwise, there is no benefit, other than, perhaps, the book's adorning a bookcase.

The value-creating process requires an alignment between the résumé message and the needs of the target employer. Thus, if your genius is at the heart of the résumé message and this message resonates with the target employer, at first blush, you have a dream job opportunity that is worth pursuing. This is why having a soulful message in a résumé is so important for finding that dream job everyone yearns for.

A résumé design, based on your genius at its center, changes all other aspects of how it is written, presented, and viewed. This is the new design of a résumé that is at the heart of how messaging must emerge in this new job era. The discussion on how to translate the value proposition based on the genius so that it is a benefit to the potential employer, is a matter of doing research on its needs. Translating these needs into cogent messages goes beyond what is in a résumé; it is the place for the cover letters. They are covered in Chapter-7: Write to the Point with Letters. The following discussion is presented on how to achieve résumé transformation successfully.

♠Me? Genius? Why Not!

We just discussed in Chapter-5: How your Genus Helps You in you message. Many often wonder how knowing their genius can help them. In other words, if they are operating with their genius already on their side, engaging them in their pursuits, how is it going to help them in their further professional growth? Here we define genius, not as some transcendent intellectual capacity, but rather, as something that creates unique value, your gift to do something better than others can do it, as already presented in Chapter-5.

Many consciously think of their genius as their gift that allows them to do what they do better, differently than others, and aligned with their own purpose. No amount of extra effort by someone else who does not possess such gift can compensate for what your genius can help you create. When your genius is aligned with your work, things flow naturally and create amazing outcomes, effortlessly. Additionally, being aligned with the natural genius, work seems joyous. This means that there is virtually no work-related stress that causes so much grief—even morbidity—to so many as they continue to drudge through their jobs. Aligned with work, manifesting your genius is the state of *nirvana* that everyone yearns for. You resonate!

What does this mean in terms of a career, job search, and particularly messaging; the main thrust of this chapter? It simply means that the sooner one is able to extract their genius (See Genius Extraction Tool, later in this chapter), articulate it, own it, and translate it into a compelling value proposition, the better their chances are of finding this elusive nirvanic joy that everyone is after.

Once this genius is discovered, owned, and applied, its manifestations are many. Genius, consciously recognized, mobilizes new opportunities. It is the catalyst that provides a new dimension to your job search. Unlike merely job-driven skills, which have limited reach across different jobs, your genius is truly a universal currency that sees no job-related boundaries. Even when cutting across industries, genius-based skills can help in creating a credible message if the correct language is used to wrap value around your genius. This is shown in the Résumé Showcase at the end of the chapter. This means that you are able to mold your value proposition to the opportunity at hand in a versatile way to apply it to create value. Merely having job-focused skills does not allow this versatility; it does not make for a compelling résumé. In the absence of this critical element in a résumé, it tends to lack soul. No amount of flowery language can then compensate for the lack of appeal stemming from that deficit.

Résumé as a Storytelling Tool

There are a few myths about a résumé; let's disabuse them at the outset.

First, a résumé is about yesterday, or looking back.

Most write their résumés by capturing their past and starting their résumés with a "Summary" statement. Such a statement, of necessity, is backward looking. Typically, those who have been working for a number of years accumulate a variety of skills and their experience is replete with assignments that look like a veritable smorgasbord of projects, tasks, and accomplishments. Such a presentation can show a lack of focus. A résumé should start with a focused message about what you want to be doing *tomorrow*. Starting a résumé with a compelling Career Objective does this well. A Career Objective is not just a job description; rather, it is a compelling statement of how one creates value for the target employer.

Second, it is all about you!

Most start writing their résumés by looking back at what they have done and then listing chronologically their assignments (not accomplishments). This approach results in an accurate chronology of one's past but fails to present how value is created for a potential employer or how leadership will be marshaled to address the challenges at hand. Even more important, is how one has successfully managed a career to progressively deliver increasing value in each job! Metaphorically, it ends up more like a collection of rummage or job assignments pulled together for a flea market, rather than a showcase for an upscale department store that presents a carefully scripted story for a select clientele and a theme. This story and the theme for the résumé have to be derived and assembled by research, from a list of target companies.

Third, it should be a compilation of all past experience with data, for an expert reader in mind.

The résumé should list only that which supports your value proposition, which is the Career Objective at the top of the résumé. Any work experience of skills that do not directly support this value proposition should be relegated to the background, de-emphasized so as not to detract from your focus. This detraction may creep in, for example, from being in the workforce long enough to be seen as "too experienced!" In this case, take your experience back to the time when your job still strongly supported your value proposition and list all your previous experience before this point under *last year* just listed *and prior*. To wit, if a career spans 30 years, direct experience you have, which supports the value proposition may span 12, and if you are writing the résumé in 2006, the chronology could list job details going back to 1994. All the preceding experience is listed under a single heading as "Prior–*1994*," with a line or two for each company and some relevant detail. See attached illustrative sample résumés in this chapter in the Résumé Showcase.

Also, the writing should be presented so that anyone with some familiarity with the subject matter can understand the content, not *just* experts. Presenting the accomplishments in a *story* format, creating intrigue, and avoiding acronyms, special terms, and gobbledygook, can compel the hiring team or the decision maker to read a résumé! Anyone reading it should understand its cogent message. This is a true test of a well-written message. Specific tools, languages, or techniques used (all nouns) in a particular technology or specialized task can be listed as "Skills Used" followed by a string of these nouns, separated by commas (see examples in the Résumé Showcase).

A Branding Tool

One way to get attention in any market is to differentiate the product or service. If it is *you* you're selling, it, too, could benefit from the same treatment.

Why not, indeed! Few consider themselves worthy of a brand image! "It is only for the celebrities and the rich," they rationalize. In any economy there is value in differentiating. Differentiating comes from branding and identifying a few unique characteristics that provide value over and above their competitors. The value you create in the job in which you are engaged is not a one-time benefit to the employer, but rather, it is the stream of benefits on an ongoing basis. A brand can be built over time. Clever messaging can also create it; messaging that resonates with the buyer.

How does one do this in a résumé?

One way to brand yourself is to show how different you are from the pack. Showing this uniqueness crisply and compellingly can serve as a branding tool. Our genius, as we presented in a previous section in this chapter and in Chapter-5, can be a means of creating this uniqueness. We all have our own genius about us in some way. Pulling this out, articulating it in a compelling way and then calling this something that is not off-putting and that does not create an aura of arrogance, are good ways to present the brand that differentiates you. This is discussed in more detail in the Unique Skills section below.

Another way to brand is by creation of an image.

Image creation goes beyond the words on your résumé. Image has to do with how you present what you create. That includes how the résumé is presented, how you present yourself, how you dress and speak, among your other attributes, cultivated or otherwise.

Having laid this foundation for the philosophy of good résumé writing, let's go back to the storytelling aspect and see how such a story can now be presented with the foregoing guidelines, element by element.

♠ Résumé Elements

A good format for telling a story and a format that provides a consistent, yet flexible framework for the writer, consists of the following elements:

- Career Objective
- Experience Summary
- Unique Skills (your genius)
- Technical Skills
- Professional Experience
- Educational Background
- Professional Development
- Other Accomplishments
- Key Words
- An Optional Headline or Tagline

Each element from the above list is discussed at length below.

Career Objective

This is a forward-looking, focused statement of a value-creation process that, at once, commands attention by its imaginative phrasing and concise presentation. This statement makes a few claims about how you create value for the target employer in a couple of lines with a bolded position title to grab visual attention. A career objective is *not* just a position title. A sample below can show the power of a well-crafted Career Objective:

Before

Career Objective: R&D manager in high-tech or software

After

Career Objective: A **Leadership position in R&D** responsible for: Catalyzing technology visions, and then quickly turning them into high-revenue products; uncovering unusual applications of existing technologies, and discovering new approaches to unsolved problems to mainstream emerging technologies; creating an environment of innovation *throughout* the organization

In this example, how the applicant immediately differentiates by articulating value creation in the R&D labs *and* outside, is much more specific and compelling.

A colon following the phrase *responsible for,* as is shown in the example above, allows for a list of responsibilities to be presented, separated by semicolons and commas. If the entire construction does not represent a grammatical sentence, there may not be a period at the end.

There is another phrase that crops up often in a job search and it is worth discussing in this context. That phrase is Positioning Statement. A Positioning Statement is a "today" entity. A Career Objective, on the other hand has a "tomorrow" focus to it. For example, if you left recently as a legal counsel of a retail chain, your Positioning Statement may be packaged as*: "I am a legal counsel with extensive business experience in today's retail climate and can leverage my past experience to make a growing retailer successful in today's highly regulated and litigious climate."*

This may not be the same as a Career Objective that appears on this person's résumé. This is primarily because what this person wants to do tomorrow may be different than what is reflected in the Positioning Statement. Please see Résumé Showcase later in this chapter for an example résumé (Résumé #19: Palmer Shoens), to more fully understand this concept.

Experience Summary

This is a summary statement that highlights overall experience and supports the *claims* made in the Career Objective. This element is about four to five lines in length, different from *Professional Experience*, and is in addition to it.

For example, in the case of the R&D manager previously noted, the Career Objective can lead to writing an Experience Summary using the following observations. There are three claims in this Career Objective: first, catalyzing technology visions and then quickly turning them into high-revenue products; second, deploying existing technologies to solve problems; and, third, mainstreaming emerging technologies. Here is a well-presented Experience Summary:

Five years, most recently at HP-Labs, leading creative engineers and scientists, translating proprietary and patentable inventions into new product offerings to lead technology markets. Previous four years at various HP divisions working directly with GMs offering innovative solutions to problems using mature technologies that resulted in creating $2B in new business. Two years defining ways to accelerate diffusion of new technologies to lead the marketplace.

The function of Experience Summary is to showcase the relevant past that supports the Career Objective claims. As mentioned, this element is separate from, and in addition to, Professional Experience. Why? This is because the latter is a chronological—and hence sequential—presentation of a career history. Experience Summary, on the other hand allows editorial freedom threading through the entire career, and pulling out parts that are relevant to support the claims of value, regardless of when they occurred. As an example, if a particular claim is supported by one year of the most recent experience doing a particular assignment, by two years, five-years back, and by one year, eight-years ago doing the same task, then a total of four years doing this task can be claimed in the Experience Summary. Without this element the reader has to mentally do this arithmetic by carefully reading the résumé, something for which most on the hiring side do not have the time. And, even if they did, they may not get it in the way you would want to present it.

♠Unique Skills (Your Genius)

As we discussed during the branding concept, and the discussion preceding that section, in Résumé Purpose, every one of us has a genius about us. This is our *universal* endowment. This genius can be defined as a special gift that differentiates us from others in what we do well, by describing *how* we do it. Putting this in the résumé, gives it the extra element of differentiation early, up-front, and allows to define individual brand, as we discussed earlier. Unique skills are a portfolio of five to seven items listed in rank order of importance—to the employer—that are unique and that differentiate. It is presented typically as a two-word phrase that is intriguing and is followed by a one or two line description of what that phrase means in the context of the target. Crafting the bolded phrases that capture your uniqueness is one of the most creative—and differentiating— elements of writing a résumé. Each phrase, when read, immediately conveys the message of how unique value is created, *without* a need to read the descriptor. Intrigue, pith, crispness, and uniqueness are all at the heart of this phrase.

In thinking and articulating Unique Skills, the focus should be on the *how* and not the *what!* This is difficult for most to appreciate. One reason perhaps, is because our thinking is deeply ingrained in describing the *what* in our communication; *how* that is done is not a natural thing to think about, especially when writing a résumé. One reason why we focus so much on the *what* is, perhaps, because we want to present our accomplishments in a manner that are in a language regarded as currency of the value message. It is easy to see why this became the standard expression, especially in résumé writing: accomplishments presented that describe the *what* tend to be objective in their tone, hence are easier to compare to others' accomplishments.

Let's take an example. If two candidates in sales are writing their accomplishments, the one that states a 12 percent increase in sales is regarded as a "less than" the one who lists a higher number. But, let's take a closer look at their two statements:

Statement #1: *Achieved a 15 percent increase in sales by calling customer more frequently and selling them higher-margin products.*

Statement #2: *Achieved a 12 percent increase in sales by developing closer relationships with existing accounts, which resulted in having to make fewer sales calls. Leveraged each customer visit by collaborating with systems architects to develop business and technology solutions that met customers' long-term business needs.*

On the surface, Statement #1 belongs to a person who achieved higher sales *that year*. But, if you look deeper in the *how*, it is not difficult to agree that this salesperson was mortgaging the future account relationships. Why? He was selling more expensive products to make him look good, perhaps without keeping the customers' interest foremost. Secondly, he was working hard making frequent calls, just pushing products that the customers may not have needed. This is a myopic sales strategy. In this example, salesperson #2 is going to have a time advantage. That person's sales are going to increase geometrically with time. The salesperson #1 is likely to experience an opposite fate!

Thus, focusing merely on the *what* (increased sales 12 percent), does not always tell the right story. Sometimes, it tells the wrong story, as it is illustrated here!

For many, writing this part of the résumé is difficult and frustrating. They invariably end up with statements that do not create differentiation and that lack any excitement. One way to overcome this difficulty is to collaborate with someone who can help you dig out your inner passions and gifts and then help you articulate them in a compelling way. This also requires trial and error and command of being able to write concisely.

Although these statements are not what describe the Unique Skills, they are the basis for them. Unique Skills are *extracted* from such statements, which provide the proof, as will be presented in the Professional Experience part of the résumé.

For example, someone has a genius for understanding complexity and then breaking it down to its elements, so that it can be analyzed for easy understanding. This Unique Skill could read:

Simplifying Complexity: Quickly analyze complex systems, situations, and environment; reduce them to their most elemental blocks by identifying patterns to show how they interact, so that they can be easily understood and tackled.

More examples of these messages are in the résumé showcase, at the end of this chapter.

These three headings (Career Objective, Experience Summary, and Unique Skills) for a résumé are at the top ("above-the-fold" in newspaper lexicon) to help the reader, in a *few seconds*, know why your résumé should be read in its entirety. The rest of the résumé is "evidence" presented in Professional Experience, your formal education, and other historical background.

Technical Skills

This element is important for those in software, hardware, systems, and any technical area in which they participate. In the case of a software expert, it lists all major platforms (mainframes, Solaris, McIntosh), operating systems (HP-UX, Linux, NT), languages (C++, Java) and applications (Oracle 11.0) in which one is claiming expertise. This is all listed as a string of nouns, separated by commas; there are no verbs.

Technical skills are not limited to only technology professionals, they are relevant to anyone possessing specialized skill as it may be for a lawyer, advertising executive, or a financial analyst. Each profession has its technical specialties and this element of the résumé is where they are presented. These skills can be also be mentioned in the respective accomplishment stories listed in Professional Experience. Writing them in this section highlights their presence, allowing a reader to quickly find what they are looking for.

The remaining parts of the résumé are included below:

Professional Experience

This is the *evidence* to satisfy the résumé reader, on the claims made in the top part of the write-up. If this part of the résumé write-up is provided with accomplishments in a "what" and "so what" format, it can carry weight.

Why?

When listing accomplishments on the résumé, narrating short leadership stories that capture the "what" and the "so-what" with relevant facts is far more compelling than merely lacing a statement with statistics in a dry, matter-of-fact style, as is done with listings in a telephone directory. Most write this part of their résumés in the traditional Tasks/Responsibilities format with statistics to make their point. Merely stating facts in a task/responsibility format is not enough. There is a *better* way!

Past work experience written in a Task/Responsibilities or even Task/Accomplishment format can create a limitation in a reader's mind about the scope of the writer's leadership capacity. Sticking to what was at hand and how the writer succeeded in accomplishing the objective is good, but not enough, especially when the market is tough. If, instead, the writer tells a leadership story about how the accomplishments were achieved, then the story can present them in a broader and more compelling light. The illustration presented here (in Before-After format) clarifies this point. Writing past experiences as a story that presents the caliber of one's leadership can create a broader appeal for the résumé, than just narrating the same experience in a traditional Task/Accomplishment format. This is especially important if one is going outside their past area of the job search, or making a career change; for example from high-tech to biotech.

Having entries in the Professional Experience section with just factually accurate information also does not make for good reading or creating intrigue! Using powerful verbs, crafting a concise story, and then weaving facts to present a case, can vivify an otherwise dull résumé, as does a well-written narrative. Only a few bullets, strategically placed early in the résumé—page one, and early page two—that capture recent-vintage stories that are well written, can punch up a résumé. Leaving the remaining accomplishment bullets as one-liners, can give the reader a sense of the writer's leadership quality that supplement and complement the earlier, more detailed bulletized text. *All* Experience span does not have to be in this detailed story-telling format. That can be both time *and* space consuming! Showcasing the most compelling leadership stories (on page one and first part of page two) and then mentioning the rest (not all) in a single-line-bullet format can provide the necessary intrigue and breadth to fill the two pages that make a résumé.

Another consideration for how these stories are told and where they are placed on a résumé, is based on how the Unique Skills are presented. The Unique Skills are presented in ranked order (to the employer) of importance. The stories that are narrated in the résumé are based on how these skills are presented, and are tied to these Skills in an unambiguous way!

An example of a well-written story for a software data architect follows, in a Before-After format.

Before

Delivered a project with Legacy migration application on time and on budget. This was an enterprise-wide success.

After

Led, single-handedly, a critical initiative involving data source migration for a well-entrenched legacy system application that supported sensitive business performance data. This involved transforming a batch-driven operation (two-three per day), to one involving several thousand real-time transactions, which required having to become an expert in a totally unfamiliar technical area within weeks. Result was a successful launch of an entire major geography ahead of schedule, delighting all involved. This success, which became a model, set the stage for the entire migration project, saving countless resources.
Key Skills: Oracle, Kshell, Perl, XML/SAX parser, and XSLT.

Note: This "After" statement looks nothing like the "Before" version. Why? This "After" statement resulted from having read the original one as written, and then engaging with the client in a discovery dialog for about 15 minutes to extract the details, which the client was eager to give. Upon reading the rewritten version, she could not believe that she had accomplished this feat during those challenging times. When I asked her why she did not write this statement originally, which carries so much power, her response was, " I was going to explain it face-to-face in an interview." Most do not realize that résumés not written compellingly do not always result in an interview! Granted, this statement, as it appears, takes more space. With accomplishment statements of this caliber you need only a few; the rest could be more compact or even cryptic one-liners to complete the résumé!

The approach to writing leadership stories, as presented here, shows the impact of moving from telling the "facts" to showing the "truth" about your leadership capability. What is the difference? Facts are dry, uninteresting, and do not move a reader to act. Truth, on the other hand, is self-evident and creates an "aahaah!"

Education

List only *formal* degrees and leave professional development out of this paragraph. If you do not have a formal degree, see Common Résumé Challenges, later in the chapter.

Other Accomplishments

List special awards, patents, publications, and presentations at major conferences.

Professional Development

This part of the résumé contains company-sponsored training and education without giving too much detail.

*Key Words

In this environment of automatically scanned résumés, it is important to ensure that your résumé contains all the words that are critical to your job opportunities for which it is targeted. Most résumé scanning software is programmed to look for certain key words in each job family. It is not always possible to incorporate all key words that are expressly used in different jobs within the same job family. However, different companies use different nouns for the same description. For example MBA, M.B.A., and Master of Business Administration, Masters in Business, and Master's in Business are one and the same thing to a human. But, to a computer they have to be spelled out so that it can recognize them. One way to achieve this is to have a Key Words paragraph at the end of the résumé and list a string of nouns separated by commas. If you then highlight that paragraph and use white text, they remain invisible to the human eye. Since all words in this paragraph are invisible to the human eye, they can be in a small font to save space.

Optional Tagline/Headline

This element is optional because it takes confidence, ability to capture your main gift in a simple, powerful phrase, and good marketing sense to pull it off with impact. When you are hurrying to do your résumé, you'll probably come up with a trite headline that can detract from a résumé.

The placement of the tagline is important because if a résumé is scanned and the tagline is on the top, the scanner may interpret this as a name. Make sure that the tagline is placed appropriately for maximum impact and minimum confusion.

Résumé Editing

Everyone has some input on a résumé! Before you get frustrated with all the inputs that are provided, gratuitously or otherwise, be mindful that there are three types of editing:

- Story Editing
- Copyediting
- Layout Editing

Most do not differentiate between the three. Most are good at the second and the third categories. Story editing, on the other hand requires subject matter expertise, market knowledge, and how to position a résumé with the right *story* to get the message across to the right reader so that it *is* compelling, coherent, and concise. All the elements of a résumé mentioned above have to be integrated and then crafted to present this story. It is one of the most challenging tasks of résumé writing and editing.

Copyediting entails checking errors such as grammar, correct usage, spelling, run-on sentences, and other such copy elements. Good English majors and other professionals, as career counselors, usually provide this service. Some career counselors can also provide aspects of story editing, based on their own depth of a particular subject matter. Layout editing entails making a résumé consistent and pleasing to the eye in terms of its overall look, feel, and presentation. In this day of scanned résumés, this is perhaps less important in most cases. However, if a résumé is presented for a visual review, it must be edited for proper layout as well.

♠ Common Résumé Challenges

Résumé writing can present many challenges. Some of these common challenges are listed and described below:

- ✓ Not having a formal degree
- ✓ Not having an uninterrupted chronology
- ✓ At a single employer for more than 10 years
- ✓ A career history that is not progressive, with increasing responsibilities
- ✓ Having a period when you were sidelined
- ✓ No bottom-line data
- ✓ Previous employer out of business or acquired
- ✓ Temptation to lie or misrepresnt

We will briefly discuss each one below to provide some guidance.

Formal Degree

In many professions, it is not uncommon to have never completed the requirements for a formal degree, and yet have a great career track record. In such cases it is best to emphasize accomplishments and showcase them in a way that conveys to the résumé reader, that not having a degree is not an impediment to your creating value. If you are missing a few requirements for completing your degree, then check to see if you can still fulfill these requirements and obtain the degree in a reasonable time. In such cases, it is appropriate to state in the résumé, the expected date of your degree.

If you have not gone to college or have not completed any formal coursework towards a degree or certification, it is best to leave *out* the Education section in your résumé and, instead, complete the Professional Development section, listing all your development accomplishments, as seminars, certifications, and course completions. If the topic does not come up during the selection process, do not volunteer.

Never lie about your education or academic degrees. Surveys have shown that nearly 41 percent lie on their résumés. Formal education is the single biggest area where most feel tempted to lie. When you deliberately lie, in addition to the potential of being exposed, you may feel disempowered throughout the interview or selection process, always wondering how you are going to address the issue if confronted. This apprehension can seriously compromise your ability to deliver an otherwise great interview. There is yet another factor that comes into play for some professionals who have titles that imply a degree.

Often, people have job titles that imply a formal degree. In such cases if you do not have a formal degree, continue to use that title to promote yourself in that profession. For example, if your title was design engineer, but you do not have a degree in engineering, your career objective could still state "A position as a Design Engineer...." If you are responding to a position that states a certain degree as required, your résumé many not even go past the key-words filters and will be rejected at the outset.

One cardinal rule of job search: never lie, never misrepresent. Once a client, who lacked a Ph.D., got into the selection process for a job for which Ph.D. was a requirement. So, in the Education paragraph, he truthfully wrote: MS Mechanical Engineering; no Ph.D. The computer saw the word and kicked up the résumé for an interview. The candidate made through two rounds before being rejected for an *entirely* different reason: he did not qualify for a security clearance required for the job!

Interrupted Chronology

In some cases a career is interrupted. The reasons could be varied: maternity leave and then deciding to raise a family for several years; a long illness; a jobless period that extends beyond six months; taking time off to earn a degree and so on. In such cases, it is best to include this period in the sequential chronology, so that the chronology is continuous and then state a brief reason for that period so that it does not raise questions in a reader's mind. Some are tempted to resort to a functional format if there are interruptions in their chronology. This is not a good idea because it raises questions and may result in your résumé being rejected from further consideration.

If you have been presently out of work for an extended period, stating this fact on your résumé may interfere with your getting a job. It is best to list this as duration, from the time you lost your job to "Current," stating any work that you may have done to engage yourself. For example, if you have done some consulting opportunistically, even if it were just a few hours, it is still appropriate to list the entire period as being engaged as a consultant. Do not list this period as "looking for suitable employment." Even if you engage as a volunteer, it is appropriate to list this as a part of the current chronology.

Single Employer

If your employment is with a single employer for an extended period of time, break it down into sections that describe your career progression at that employer, year by year. For example, if you were at a single company for 20 years, in a variety of positions, then it is appropriate to list your positions with their respective durations subordinate to the entire duration at that company. An example of this presentation is shown in Résumé Showcase for Cheri Waxman in this chapter.

Stagnant Career History

It is not uncommon to have stayed in one position at a company for a long period of time. To showcase this chronology, it is best to break down the entire career in periods where there was some change in responsibilities, duties, or title. Even if the change in title was not formally done, it is appropriate to list the periods as having different assignment titles, even though the job title my have remained unchanged. For example, if you were employed as *marketing coordinator,* your job title for 15 years, it is to your advantage to list that period in segments that show a variety of *assignments*: Three years as a Project Coordinator, International promotions; four years as Events Administrator, New Product Launches; four years as a Pricing Support Analyst, and so on. If you can justify these assignments during your interview, then presenting them on the résumé will make you more marketable.

Demotions

For a variety of reasons a career can take a detour, resulting in positions that appear as demotions from a previous title. This is not uncommon. If a division is suddenly closed or merged with another entity of a company, certain positions are consolidated. In addition, political pressures can result in your being reassigned to positions that can appear as demotions.

It is a good idea to present these transitions on your resume by being honest and accurate, without giving the reason for such demotions. As long as you are able to show accomplishments during these periods of transitions, these career digressions do not mean much in an otherwise clean career.

No Bottom-line Data

To present evidence of leadership in the Professional Experience section of a résumé, merely showing bullets in the Task/Responsibilities format is not enough. Most write their bullets this way and it fails to create a differentiated message. The key to making a compelling résumé is to have an impactful message, starting with the Career Objective or the value statement, Unique Skills—your genius—at the head of the résumé. This must be followed by the evidence that fortifies this part and corroborates it. If this part is written as a story, and not as a factual statement, the résumé becomes far more compelling. Using the SIMPLE tool, soon to be presented, is an effective way to achieve this.

One of the key elements of this narrative is the ability to state the final impact, the So What or the "E" in the SIMPLE tool, in measurable quantities: dollars, headcount, time saved, customer loyalty numbers, market share, among other metrics. Presenting this data completes the story and makes the entire narrative credible.

Most have problems with this aspect of writing the bulleted stories. The source of their problem is their *perceived* inability to state numbers that result directly from their role in making things better. This perception is amplified if the position is removed from "action" as they see it. This means that if a job does not relate directly to any of the metrics just mentioned, most are unable to tie their accomplishments to these measurable outcomes.

This is a limiting belief and one that greatly vitiates writing a compelling résumé based on not just the facts, but what is true. A fact is what is obvious: did the initiative you proposed, increase sales? If the answer is a no, then it is difficult to tie a fact to your claim. But, the truth is another matter. Looking at the truth takes into account the whole chain of causality that results in a measurable outcome.

Let us take an example to illustrate this point: Suppose that you are an administrative assistant responsible for taking customer orders over the phone. The order-taking process is driven by the telephone system queue handling mechanism, how the sales information is available on the computer screen, and how the order is confirmed to you when a customer calls in. Because of a variety of system-related problems, the order taking process is chaotic. This often results in nearly 20 percent of the customers either abandoning their call in the middle of an order taking process, or they cancel the order after placing it, as a result of this bad experience.

You figure out a way to make a simple change to the ordering process and as a result, this problem is eliminated. For the sake of this example, let us assume that the telephone orders amount to $20 million annually in sales and that you have four other such assistants working alongside to handle the workload.

Let us look at the factual way versus the truthful way of writing this accomplishment story:

Factual

Recommended an improvement to the existing-order entry system, which resulted in eliminating 20 percent of the incoming order calls that were abandoned due to customer frustration.

True

The chaotic order-entry system prevented many orders from being taken correctly and in a professional manner, causing one in every five customers abandoning the order call or canceling an already placed order. Investigated and then suggested a simple change to the process, which resulted in entirely eliminating order-entry problems. The proposed change increased sales by $4 million; 100 percent of the incoming calls resulted in sales orders.

As is obvious, the second statement is much more impactful. It required more knowledge of the job and how it impacts the customer, sales, and the bottom line. This data is not difficult to get or infer.

In yet another example of an administrative position, the two statements are presented below to further illustrate this point:

Factual

Suggested a meeting planning system, which resulted in reducing the time to schedule a meeting facility from typically two hours to 15 minutes.

True

Devised a new system for keeping track of schedules in real time, creating a streamlined boss-availability calendar. Also developed a process where staff could access boss's calendar and schedule their own meetings. Similarly reduced time to schedule a meeting facility from typically taking up to two hours to 15 minutes. Estimated annual savings: $130,000.

How does one come up with the impressive dollar savings in the True version of the narrative? This is an actual résumé in the Showcase at the end of this chapter (Cheri Waxman). Cheri looked after 30 engineers. If there are five meetings every week, three (out of 30) calling the meetings, and each one costs the company $100 per hour, over a 50-week year, the savings amount to over $130,000 annually.

It is not that the numbers alone are impressive, because they are, but the perspective you provide with this narrative is that of a businessperson who thinks in business terms, a compelling quality to getting hired!

Previous Employer Out of Business or Acquired

In this climate of economic uncertainty and rampant mergers and acquisitions, it is not uncommon to have an employer disappear from view. Many wonder if they should mention this in their chronology, or even bother to write that stint on their résumé, since the employer is not verifiable.

This should not be a concern while writing a résumé. All entries within the period that you chose to present must be accurately and completely presented and showcased. If a name has changed as a result of an acquisition, this can be stated in the entry.

The other side of this issue is that some take advantage of the non-existence of the employer and misrepresent their engagement with that employer. Overstating the position, or accomplishments or even the salary that was paid is typically how many exploit this situation. This is wrong! Being truthful and honest about any employer is the cardinal rule while writing a résumé. A company may be out of business or its records inaccessible, but those who worked there with you are always sources of information in this Internet era. Do not be tempted to overstate your employment for this or any other reason.

Temptation to Lie

When a candidate's current qualification do not meet the requirements for an open position the temptation to misrepresent credentials is great. In fact, studies show that nearly 41 percent lie on their résumés, as we presented in the educational qualifications section earlier, in the way they present their credentials. Common areas in ranked order are: academic degrees, years of experience, job titles, responsibilities, publications, affiliations, and level of skills (keyboarding at 90 WPM!).

As mentioned before, the temptation to misrepresent a fact must be avoided at all costs. It is, at once, disempowering. If you lack a certain attribute required in a job, the best approach is to make that attribute irrelevant to that job, by highlighting something else that you bring that has a greater value in the context of the job. This is not as hard as most imagine. See how this is done effectively in *The 7 Keys to a Dream Job: A Career Nirvana Playbook!*, Key-3: Presenting Yourself, specifically Playing golf with Tiger Woods ("How to beat Tiger Woods by not playing golf with him!").

* Multiple-Position Résumés

In a tough job market, it is a good idea to present messages in a variety of ways, to be able to apply to jobs that require different skills mix. Positioning this way offers increased chances for jobs that may not be apparent within the original target-search criteria. This positioning can be done at all levels, including hands-on jobs, as software developer, financial analyst, or IT administrator, among others. As a person's experience gets richer and seniority of their job title shows higher levels of responsibility, multiple positioning is almost a requirement for a successful job search, which allows creating options in ways that are not possible otherwise. One can also carry this too far, creating confusion and stress in an otherwise sound campaign.

So, what is an ideal number of ways in which positioning is possible?

There is no hard and fast rule here. But depending on the previous job level one can easily determine how many ways they can effectively market themselves. For example: someone in software development can position themselves as a software developer, as a software team lead, as a software project manager, or even as a product development or systems development specialist, depending on the level of experience they bring to the campaign. As mentioned earlier, a résumé is about tomorrow, not yesterday. This implies that with enough experience to claim a certain allied position based on one's understanding of that job, it is worth considering doing this early in the campaign. How does one determine what the *allied* jobs are?

One way to see different flavors within a core job family is to research the job openings in a particular area of search. A job family is a group of jobs that share competencies and requires skills that are similar. Targeting different job boards and then researching job families that fall within reach of a given background capability is a good start. How many types of jobs within a family are worth targeting? Although that depends on the job level, three or four types within a job family are typical. More than this number can create confusion, not just in a campaign, but also within the job seeker's mind as well, vitiating the overall effectiveness of the process. Too few can limit target job search and companies.

The following list is a small sampling of how a particular résumé can be flavored for a more effective campaign:

Circuit Designer:
  -Product Designer
  -System Developer
  -Team Lead
  -Project Manager

Financial Analyst:
  -Business Analyst
  -IT Support Specialist
  -Business Process Specialist

Marketing Manager
  -Business Alliance Specialist
  -Business Development Lead
  -Channel Development Lead

The actual titles are, of course, determined by the job categories that populate the job board for any particular position type.

Once the "flavors" are determined, the next step is to assess which of the flavors are most credible within a particular expertise and background, and which ones will get the most action in the job-search campaign. Once this determination is made, specific résumés can be prepared to campaign for those jobs. Spinning off résumés for these flavors does not entail complete rewriting of the résumé; rather it entails flavoring the main résumé to reflect the language from the job descriptions for which each flavor is targeted.

The best way to achieve multiple positioning is by having different résumés so that a career objective clearly states the offered value proposition in that segment of the job market. Of course, the Career Objective is only one, albeit a headlining, element of the résumé. The remaining elements of the résumé, then, need to be in harmony with that headline, so that the entire message is consistent on how the "product" is packaged! An example of how to have two different Career Objectives is shown here:

I. Career Objective: A position as a **software lead,** responsible for developing product requirements, working with customers, and then leading teams to deliver those products to meet customer needs.

II. Career Objective: A position as a **project manager** responsible for: working with customers to develop software and system product requirements and then organizing and leading teams to deliver these products on time and within budgets; managing the overall product life-cycle to generate profitable revenues throughout the life of the products.

The other element that fortifies the different Career Objectives is the way Unique Skills in each flavor are presented. The portfolio of skills that go in this element will be different for each flavor of the Career Objective. For example for the software lead, hands-on development, rapid prototyping, early validation of requirements can be important parts of the Unique Skills portfolio. For the second flavor, project manager, cross-functional teaming, project management savvy, customer knowledge will be the driving skills. For more details on how to develop Unique Skills for each flavor of a résumé, see Genius Extraction Tool and Genius Discovery Exercise, later in this Chapter.

"Bridging" with the Unique Skills

Often, once a particular flavor of a résumé is ready, an opportunity may be presented that almost matches the message in it, but for some specific requirements or skill that job will spell out. In such a case, the best approach is to evaluate if changing the Unique Skills to fit the opportunity can be crafted without changing other elements of the résumé. This is often easier than most realize.

One approach is to identify which Unique Skills need changing ("tweaking) and then change them to suit the job. Making sure that the stories that already exist, support the new cluster of Unique Skills is critical. Otherwise, the connection between the Unique Skills the stories that link to them would be lost. See how SIMPLE tool accomplishes this in the following section.

With a small additional effort, one can generate a highly tailored résumé using an existing flavor and create a high-impact message.

As mentioned before, Unique Skills provide a bridge between "Yesterday" and "Tomorrow" as well as a bridge between "employer needs" and "what you offer." This is a powerful approach to customize a résumé without having to rewrite an entire résumé.

Customized Résumés

Customized résumés are individualized résumés created for each *important* job opportunity. Taking the one that generically comes closest to the opportunity being targeted, and then changing the language to reflect the one in the job description for the posted opening, results in a customized résumé. Although this may seem like a good idea, it can create problems in keeping track of multitudinous versions and making sure that each is sent with no errors: each résumé has to be perfect. This can pose a challenge for a person who is not well organized or is not good at spotting errors in written text. Even with another pair of vigilant eyes looking over each customized version, this approach can be problematic.

A preferred approach is having a few flavors (three typical, five maximum) that address the job families of interest, and then bridging the gap with a compelling cover letter. This is more work, but it is the only way one can ensure that the outgoing presentation has the ability to differentiate the candidate. As presented in Chapter-7: Write to the Point with Letters. Any opportunity to make a mark deserves a cover letter!

Executive Résumés

Executive résumés can have certain variations in their presentations from what is discussed in previous sections. One element that can be different is the Career Objective; here replaced with a Summary in its place. Why? Many senior managers and executives, approach their search differently. Often, they are presented through recruiters or search firms handling their case who dictate how they are positioned. These intermediaries know client company's needs, and have a good sense of how to communicate these needs to the clients. For this approach, a Summary Statement at the header can represent a better alternative to a Career Objective.

The other factor that is different is their length. Many senior executives believe that their accomplishments and track records justify longer résumés. Although this is true, and some experts suggest this approach, the key here is not its length, but how a résumé is presented. Although the material provided, as a part of Résumé Showcase, suggests a two-page layout, more pages can be accommodated for a compelling cause.

However, more is not necessarily better. As we said earlier, a résumé is not a chronological listing of assignments, tasks, and responsibilities. It is a carefully compiled script of the main value proposition that is dripping with acts of leadership and creative force that creates differentiation. If there is a leadership story in an experience narrated on a résumé, and if that story repeats in another assignment, then there is nothing new in it. A single bullet summarizing the stint is enough the subsequent time around. Each citation of an assignment mentioned in the résumé should cover different aspects of a leadership dimension, and should not be a confirmation of leadership qualities already stated. Also, leaving some intrigue can result in a phone call. This is one reason why a résumé should contain just enough information to create intrigue; it is not a document for full personal disclosure!

Résumés of senior executives should also reflect a highly polished, precise, and impactful language. A sample résumé is shown in Résumé Showcase (Résumé #16: William Pearl).

♠ Résumé Tools

The following tools are presented to help craft stories that are an integral part of the Professional Experience section in a résumé. The first tool—**The SIMPLE Tool**—helps story telling. These stories are at the heart of what constitutes the evidence part of the Unique Skills in the résumé. They provide the evidence of how Unique Skills translate into measurable benefits. Most have difficulties writing this part of their résumé.

The second tool is the **Genius Extraction Tool**. Although the Unique Skills (based on your genius) appear first in the résumé presentation, from a résumé development viewpoint, they are the *result* of the stories that are worth telling. So, as a process for developing a résumé, it is best to start with the SIMPLE stories and then use the Genius Extraction Tool to develop the cluster of Unique Skills that are presented in the top part of the résumé.

Of the many labels that can be attributed to this tool, why was the Genius Extraction Tool chosen as its name? The operative word here is *extraction*. Those who remember their visit to the dentist will know the metaphor. The process is painful but you feel better afterwards. Pulling out our own genius is somewhat akin to this process. Once the genius gets identified, the process of giving it life in words is fun and exciting.

Immediately after presenting these two tools, central to the development of a résumé, a genius discovery exercise is presented to make concrete the application of these two tools.

Notes:

♠The SIMPLE Tool (Tool-6)

This tool is designed to help write leadership stories in a résumé's Professional Experience part. **Understanding this tool is central to delving into your genius,** as shown on the following page.

Instead of writing each bullet as a typical Task/Responsibility format, the SIMPLE format allows for a better presentation of the leadership story, showcased as evidence of Unique Skills, one at a time. Keep this write-up to refer back to prior to an interview.

SIMPLE is an acronym that stands for:

Symptom	State what was going on. (Don't confuse symptom with root cause)
Impediment	What was getting in the way?
Measurement	What specific parameters were measured from this impediment?
Plan	What was the Plan of action? (This eliminates the root cause)
Leverage	What was leveraged that showcased your leadership?
Effect	What outcome did you create and how do they measure? Connect this to any claim you want to make during a career transition for a credible leadership story. See Making the SIMPLE Connection.

Illustrative example:

Symptom	At El Camino Hospital, the nursing staff was taking too long to get patients to change their hygiene habits. Patients were coming back with repeat illnesses related to poor hygiene and its fallout.
Impediment	Hospital's refusal to provide authoritative training materials and Internet resources to patients and nurses on how to educate clients to research their needs
Measurement	Repeat client visits costs $1.3 M annually because they revisit the hospital every two months. With properly trained patients they should stop after the second visit.
Plan	Proposed a comprehensive plan that involved using existing Internet resources within El Camino Hospital with others, on a time-shared basis.

Leverage   First trained nurses on how to use this resource and then equipped them so that they, in turn, could train their clients. Prepared a simple tracking log, where clients could record what they researched and how it helped their needs.

Effect   Within three months, 150 nurses were fully trained on how to look up resources and train their clients. Within six months, clients came for two visits and were then self-sufficient to manage their own hygiene. An informal survey indicated that their overall wellness had increased substantially within one year. As a result of this initiative, freeing nursing time saved $1.3M annually. In addition the client quality of life increasing substantially

Reducing to a résumé bullet:

✓ Led a major initiative to change patient habits resulting from poor hygiene. Discovered that lack of coordination resulted in nurses' wasting time treating repeat-visit patients. Proposed a comprehensive plan, freeing up available Internet resources to train nurses, who, in turn trained their clients. Within one year, repeat visits virtually eliminated, saving $1.3M in nursing wages. (This is the *After* version)

✓ Helped clients change their habits by implementing training using Internet resources. This cut down on repeat visits, reducing nursing workload. (This is the *Before* version)

It is easy to see the impact a well-written statement makes using the SIMPLE tool.

The space provided below is for use in crafting your own SIMPLE stories. Using the template below create a few of your own SIMPLE stories that can be transferred into the Professional Experience part of your résumé.

Story #1:

Symptom

Impediment

Measurement

Plan

Leverage

Effect

Reducing to a résumé bullet:

Story #2:

Symptom

Impediment

Measurement

Plan

Leverage

Effect

Reducing to a résumé bullet:

Note: For an impactful résumé, only a few stories are needed. Because they are space consuming, the remaining stories can be one sentence, telegraphic accomplishments, typically seen in any conventional write-up. See examples in the Showcase.

♠Genius Extraction Tool

The effectiveness of correctly discovering and then articulating your genius depends on the power of the stories that result from using the SIMPLE tool. Each story must be carefully prepared in the SIMPLE format and the impact of the story must be clear to someone who is not familiar with it, by reading it. Five-to-seven related Unique Skills make a presentable portfolio. The stories that prompted the Unique Skills are now the evidence to be presented in the Professional Experience part of the résumé. So, as a *process*, this is backwards: first the stories, then the Unique Skills—your genius.

#	Story Theme	"Genius" Phrase (Unique Skill)	Uniqueness Scale (1-10)	Comments
1	Identify repeat problems and discover the root cause. Collaborate to marshal resources. Develop win-win solutions	**Strategic Focus**	9	Strategic focus provides leveraged solutions that go beyond blindly applying problem solving to getting rid of an obstacle.
2	If same symptoms persist across a broad client base, there must be a deeper reason for the problem. Identifying this deeper reason and solving problem across broad client base is central to this story.	**Holistic Perspective**	10 (High)	Since this Unique Skill rates a 10, it is listed at the top of the other Unique Skills. See actual résumé in the Showcase.
3	Translate practical ideas into winning proposals/grants.	**Winning Ideas**	5	This is a skill that many claim, hence, rated low.
4	Collaborate with others to make things happen in a team	**Team Approach**	1 (Low)	This is *not* a unique trait. Not many will claim that they don't work in teams.

LEGEND:

Story Theme: Each story should be developed in the SIMPLE format. A pith of that story is in this column to aid the process. They can be in any order.

"Genius" Phrase: The story is captured through a phrase (two words, typical). Crafting this phrase is difficult, so much effort is needed to make this stand out. Keep working at it relentlessly.

Uniqueness Scale: This is a judgment call on how unique the Genius Phrase sounds and how unique your particular story will appear to someone reading the résumé. Does it have an "aha" factor?

Comments: This is where you note comments about the judgment you make to incorporate this Unique Skill in the résumé. List the Unique Skills in rank order based on the scores in descending order.

Table-10: Unique Skills Development

The example in the tool in Table-2 is from an actual résumé makeover, showcased in this chapter (Catherine Wilson). See the SIMPLE tool example above. The content of this example is used in the tool below for simplicity. The word *Extraction* is purposely used to connote the process that must be employed to discover one's true genius, the basis for the Unique Skills portfolio listed in the résumé (Remember what dentists do).

*Genius Discovery Exercise

Using the template and instructions already given, use this blank to create your own Unique Skills for your resume.

#	Story Theme	Genius Phrase	Uniqueness Scale (1-10)	Comments
1				
2				
3				
4				
5				
6				

Use this space below, to explain one or two of the Unique Skills you have discovered to create a complete write-up. This consists of the Unique Skills phrase in column three and a short description of it in a sentence of two. See Résumé Makeover Showcase for examples.

Unique Skills: (Set #1)
1)

2)

3)

4)

5)

Unique Skills: (Set #2)
1)

2)

3)

4)

5)

Unique Skills: (Set #3)
1)

2)

3)

4)

5)

The reason for showing three sets of Unique Skills is because many venture out with multiple résumés for multiple positions. If the multiple flavors are different, which they are in most cases, each one needs a set of Unique Skills that define the particular flavor. This does *not* mean that for three different flavors, there need to be 15 Unique Skills. It merely means that the three sets be specific to the three flavors with ranking of the Unique Skills specific to each flavor. There may be some variation in the way they are phrased in each flavor, so that each is credible and shows why each flavor is worthy of a résumé.

SIMPLE Tool for Career Transition

One of the major challenges during a career transition is the ability to connect, in a meaningful way, the past experience with the skills needed for the next career. The same holds true when switching jobs that are not a mere extension of the past assignments. Such discontinuous transitions not only require imagination but also the ability to clearly demonstrate the value to the employer, where bringing you on board outweighs the risk by the benefits that come with it. What tool is effective in making such discontinuous transitions?

The SIMPLE tool has proven to be most helpful in this process. How? Using the tool as illustrated in the previous example and then specifically focusing on the final *E* for effect can do the trick. This is illustrated below.

Making the SIMPLE Connection

The power of a message lies in the ability of a job seeker to connect their inner talent with the potential needs of a target opportunity. Without this ability to integrate the two, the message remains disjointed. A résumé reader is not going to expend the effort to make this connection or to see the synergy between the Unique Skills, the presented experience, and the opportunity for which the résumé is being considered. This connection has to be expressly showcased in the message.

This is often difficult for most, who are trying to leverage their past experience to target a new opportunity. In most such cases the Career Objective and the Professional Experience remain disconnected. When this hurdle cannot be overcome, the opportunity continues to elude the job seeker.

Making this connection, however, is not as difficult as most fear. Using the SIMPLE tool just presented makes this not just simple, but even easy. Doing so merely requires some insights, imagination, and an ability to present a leadership story that allows the decision maker to see, what may otherwise be difficult, causing you to potentially miss the intended opportunity. In the explanation of the acronym, *E* was for Effect. In addition to using this element to communicate the impact of the change that was led, it can also be used as a bridge during a career transition. A real example may help make this point:

A fresh graduate with a degree in psychology, with three years as a retail sales clerk and floor manager can connect her experience managing others, to an opportunity as an HR Coordinator. To a casual observer this connection may be tenuous or even non existent.

Pulling out her conflict resolution-, collaborative teaming-, and customer-focus talents and showcasing them as her Unique Skills and then presenting stories to support these claims can substantially change the message of the original résumé (presented in its Before version). These stories remained dormant or even untold in the formulation of the résumé's Before version, but were pulled out to make a strong résumé, as is shown in the After version (see the author's *Reinvention through Messaging: The Write Message for the Right Job!*, pages 298–307).

Résumé Makeovers Showcase

In this showcase résumés are presented in a Before-After format. These are actual client résumés that have gone through a certain rigorous review and transformation as a result of client engagements. The process for a complete makeover was as follows:

> ➢ Client submits résumé for a review
> ➢ Target job families are reviewed to determine if the message generally fits
> ➢ Client and coach collaborate to engage in a dialog to pull out critical messages from the past experience to transform the original résumé message. Client uses the SIMPLE and the Genius Extraction tool to help in crafting the résumé.
> ➢ Client reviews the message and sends the résumé, together with a cover letter
> ➢ If the response is positive the résumé is chosen as a sample winning résumé for the showcase

As we present these samples it is perhaps instructive to see a testimonial a client sent that shows the impact of a résumé makeover in the proposed format. Many *Before* samples have messaging, grammatical, and usage problems. They are presented verbatim to show how such a message can be detracting in addition to being weak. The original layouts are preserved. Clients had responded to job openings with these résumés and letters!

Formatting Note

All résumés in the Showcase are formatted from their original 8-1/2"x11" size. The original or the *Before* versions were of varying lengths. All *After* versions were reduced to two pages, with one inch margin from each edge. In this book's format, the final versions go to three-plus pages. The *Before* versions were cleaned up merely for formatting consistency, with little or no change to the copy.

Author's Note

The résumés in the showcase are sufficiently disguised to make their author unrecognizable, but their messages are real. They resulted following a discovery and collaboration with the client. The Unique Skills are representative of the genius that was manifest during these sessions. The clients took the trouble of applying the SIMPLE and the Genius Extraction tool in the process.

It may be tempting to merely copy these phrases to save time and effort. Please use these samples as guidelines in the discovery of your own genius. Wouldn't you rather really know what it is, through discovery and by using the Genius Extraction Tool provided? The SIMPLE tool and the Genius Extraction Tool provide a process that is fun, robust, and straightforward. Learn how to do this on your own to really own every word in your résumé!

Good luck!

An unedited email testimonial is below, together with the sample résumé and cover letter. (Personal details are disguised about the client who emailed the grateful response!)

Hi Dilip,

This is Cheri. I attended your Two-day workshop last week with other people. I know that you thought that we were not "engaging" in your class, but I was actually picking up on things ☺!

I finally sat down yesterday morning and re-configured my résumé and cover letter using your method. Took me about five hours. Did a bit of detective work to find out "who" was the hiring manager and recruiter contact. Sent off my cover email, with résumé about noon yesterday. Six hours later, I got a call from the HR person from the company! I fully believe that it was your "style" of cover letter and résumé that got me the call. I am now trying on suits to interview in!!!! Thought I would share this with you, because I think it was your method of presenting what I "could do" for them that caught their eye. Sure didn't get any calls with my method and I really thought that I had a nice cover letter and résumé before!

I have attached a copy of my résumé, as well as the cover letter that I used so that you can share it with others that come through your way. I used the sample résumé that you shared with me to help me configure mine for this position.

Thanks again, hopefully the next email you get from me is with the new company's letterhead?

Cheers,

Cheri Waxman

(000) 555-4592 home
(000) 555-4855 cell
~Ride safe through life~

Do you Yahoo!?
Protect your identity with Yahoo! Mail AddressGuard

Author's Note: Cheri sent the original email spontaneously. After a few months, as the idea for this book crystallized, I emailed Cheri, asking for her permission to use her testimonial (disguised) in the book. Cheri's grateful email response follows:
Hi Dilip,

It's so nice to hear from you. How neat, I now know someone that has written a book! I will go out and get it when it comes out.

You can use anything from my experience with your service that you want. I don't care how disguised or not it would be. Everything in my life is an open book! No pun intended!

I'm doing fantastic. I told you about the amazing results that changing my resume per your instructions did. Seriously, I had at least three different interviews where they commented on it and asked about it. I ended up getting a position with a Stanford Cardiac Surgeon, managing his office. I'm a "Stanford University" staff member now, who would have guessed I would end up there?

In any case, I love my new position, I love all of the new areas that I have to learn about and I'm very very happy being out of the corporate world!

A big "thank you" goes to you, I don't think I would have gotten all of the interviews had it not been for my revised resume.

You take care, and if you remember, send me an email when your book comes out so that I can go out and pick up a copy!

Cheers, Cheri
(000) 555-4592 home
(000) 555-4855 cell
Ride safe through life
Do you Yahoo?
Get better spam protection with Yahoo! Mail.
http://antispam.yahoo.com/tools

Rationale

This section is organized to show the original résumé as the client presented it, followed by the transformed version. In almost all cases the client worked collaboratively to transform the message and the process invariably involved dialog and a few iterations to get the message down right, so that it accurately captured the client's soul (their *Dharma*—the basic principle of individual cosmic existence, divine law; our purpose). In almost all cases, it was not the message that was transformed but the *client*. How? In the process of pulling out soulful messages to put on the résumés (and letters), clients went through a deep discovery process. This process forced them to reach deep within themselves and find out—discover—for themselves something they had not ventured before: finding their own genius! Once the dialog allowed to collaboratively explore that space, finding answers and then articulating those in pithy language was relatively easy—actually fun! So, the real transformation happened first within the client and then to their articulated message.

The original résumés (*Before* versions) are presented here as the clients had them ready for their campaigns. In terms of the formatting, language, organization, consistency of appearance, and many other elements that make a résumé presentable, they were in various stages of readiness. Despite this, clients were using these versions in their job search. Not all résumés deserve this rebuke, but some are egregious; and are presented here much the same way that they were used as a starting point. Some original versions had to be "cleaned up" to allow publication in this book form. It is these examples that make their transformation even more worthwhile to see!

Once the presentation challenge was overcome, the next, and the more important step, was looking at the message itself. The common theme was that the message lacked focus and power. One reason central to this basic deficiency was perhaps that the clients themselves did not have a focus. They did not know what their value proposition was. Their resorting to starting their résumé with the traditional career summary exacerbated this. Perhaps this is why most start their résumés this way; hoping that the reader or the decision maker will figure out for them what they are good at! Once this was brought into focus, much of the clutter in a résumé suddenly vanished. Building a coherent message to draft a résumé, from then on, was a straightforward process; not easy, but straightforward!

Résumés: Selection Criteria

The résumés presented here are selected to show the following transformations:

➢ The overall message

➢ Client's value proposition

➢ Visual presentation

This Showcase represents a sampling of résumés that reflect different professionals and professions: from hands-on engineers to senior technical managers; from administrative assistants to accounting professionals. Clearly the list is not exhaustive, but it represents a broad enough cross section of job families that the reader should be able to find the one that comes closest to their needs and work to transform theirs. Not all formats are identical. Some were presented well enough in their original presentation that only the message was surgically transplanted and transformed. Each *Before* version has a notation at the end of the résumé to show where the work had to be focused to achieve the transformation. This is presented so that the reader has some guidance as they start comparing this with the *After* version that immediately follows.

To help readers understand the reason for transforming the original message, each *Before* resume is annotated at the end to show where it could be improved, with specific comments about the areas of concern and deficiencies. The extent of these comments is based on space available at the end of each résumé. To show the impact of presenting the *Before* version, all the formatting, writing, and messaging is left without much edits. Some changes are made to conform to the production standards of this book.

In all cases, the client owns the final presentation, so any inconsistencies across different résumés are because of this overriding factor; client is king!

Comments Note:

Each *Before* version of the résumé is annotated with comments presented at the end of the résumé. These comments appear below a double line drawn across the page, so that this section is visually easy to identify, as shown here:

Comments:

Notes:

Showcase Listing (For convenience each résumé is numbered at the top)

1. Executive administrator: Cheri Waxman

2. A fresh graduate: software: Karlo Mennig

3. Sales/Marketing executive: wealth management firm: Sally Hammer

4. Manufacturing test engineer: John Smith

5. Process improvement consultant: Samuel Jones

6. Strategic global operations manager: David Hunter

7. Leadership effectiveness consultant: Tame Yamasaki

8. Marketing/Branding professional: Lacy Rums

9. Hi-tech product development director: Naomi Wang

10. Product development specialist: high-tech: John Muir

11. Customer loyalty advocate/executive: Sally Gilford

12. Product integrity test engineer (EMI/EMC): James Bower

13. Strategic marketing manager: Telecom: Mary Volt

14. Customer accounts manager: Robert Mylo

15. Finance director/controller: Ram Ratan

16. Hi-tech executive: William Pearl

17. Tax Manager/Legal: Martin Thompson

18. Manufacturing planner: Cameron Blakesdale

19. General counsel for a retail chain: Palmer Shoens

20. Health education coordinator: Catherine Wilson

21. A retired airline pilot going after an HR opening: James Smith ("After" version only)

Cheri Waxman   (000) 555-0000   email123@email.com

BEFORE #1

Qualifications Over 15 year's Administrative process experience, with emphasis in marketing and manufacturing environments. Proficient on computers, operating both PC and Mac's. I am comfortable using all software and calendaring systems. I have strong organizational and communication skills. I am able to work with minimum supervision and I am a very proactive admin. I am comfortable supporting an executive level person, as well as general group support in a team.

Professional experience

2000–present: Hewlett-Packard Company, Cupertino CA
1. **Executive Admin to Managers of the Partner Marketing Group.**
   Support two Senior managers and marketing group of over 50 people with general administrative duties. Calendaring, travel, special mailings, customer meetings and project cost tracking. I am responsible for generation of all purchases orders, check requests, facility needs, supplies and new hire setups. Required to interface with internally & externally.

Education:

1977–2000: National Semiconductor, Santa Clara CA

- **Senior Admin to Director of Design & Applications Group, Interface Products** Support Director and Senior managers in Design & Applications Group of 50+ people with all administrative needs. Responsible for updating dept. web site and generation of sample customer product packs. Support 1 Director and 4 managers, calendars, schedules and all generic administrative needs of the 50+ group.

- **Senior Admin to Director of ASIP Product Development Group and Director of Human Resources, CORE technologies Group**
  Admin to Director of new product development and HR Director with reporting mangers. Responsible for helping to develop infrastructure of SAP Database and populate the software with divisional information. General HR

admin functions including processing of all personal requisitions, offers, new hire/termination processes, while working in a confidential environment. SAP data entry, employee payroll problems.

Other positions held at National include:

- **Systems Scheduler**/Product Definition System (PDS) co-coordinator in charge of developing and controlling all product line build sheets/specs sent out to manufacturing sites and maintained documentation Library of above.
- **Component Scheduler,** in charge of forecast spreadsheets, pulling corporate data for Product Line Managers and producing monthly financial reports for Marketing Engineers, using FOCUS programs to obtain data.
- **Sr. Masking/Diffusion Fabrication Operator,** trained in all masking operations, diffusion, thin films and final inspect areas. Material handler/expediter for fab area.

Graduated from Cupertino High School, Cupertino CA

CPS Certified, International Association Of Administrative Professionals, 9/98

Certificate of completion: Management & Supervision, Mission College

Certificate of completion: Purchasing & Material Control, DeAnza College

Comments: This résumé is too self-focused. Accomplishments are not presented in a format that allows for differentiation. For this position, the presentation and format need to be compelling.

EXECUTIVE ADMINISTRATOR

An Executive's Right Hand
Cheri Waxman
Old Santa Cruz Way
Los Gatos, CA 95033
(000) 555-0000: email@email.com

CAREER OBJECTIVE:

An **administrative assistant or office manager** with overall responsibilities for an entire department, its executives, and their teams

AFTER #1

EXPERIENCE SUMMARY:

Three years at a Fortune-500 high-tech, as a Partner Marketing Assistant to two senior Directors and their 50-plus reporting team members. Handled all administrative and customer service responsibilities in complete support of these teams. Previously, at major semiconductor manufacturing facilities, with extensive manufacturing and engineering support experience.

UNIQUE SKILLS:

- **Autonomous Administrator:** Manage all office and administrative functions for large and small groups effectively with little supervision

- **Mastering Priorities:** Set priorities in a very busy office to manage overall executive effectiveness related to calendar and schedules

- **Budget Driver:** Organize internal and external customer events and off-site activities

- **Hassle-free Habits:** Maintain and generate presentations, reports, update Web site and internal databases for teams and supervisors for a hassle-free routine

- **Anticipate Needs:** Proactively monitor and supply needs of busy executives and offices

- **Fiduciary Champion:** Ensure and maintain complete confidentiality of sensitive matters related to all company information and direct reports of the executive

COMPUTER SKILLS SUMMARY:

MS Word, Power Point, Excel, Outlook, Lotus Notes, Rapid, SAP, Best Buy, Flagship

PROFESSIONAL EXPERIENCE:

Hewlett-Packard Company, Cupertino CA, Executive Assistant

2000–Present

- Devised a new system for keeping track of schedules in real time, creating a streamlined boss-availability calendar. Also developed a process where staff could access boss's calendar and schedule their own meetings. Similarly, reduced time to schedule a meeting facility from typically taking up to two hours, to 15 minutes. Estimated annual savings: $130,000.
- Streamlined a process for small purchase orders (under $1,000), thus eliminating both long delays (from one-week plus, to one day) and multiple signatures on urgent items.
- Implemented a new customer-call escalation system, where incoming calls were screened for urgency and customer ranking, before boss got involved. Increased customer satisfaction (from 56 to 78 percent, in six months). Freed-up engineers from these calls.
- Automated travel for routine destinations, eliminating manual work of about two hours daily.

National Semiconductor, Santa Clara CA   **1977–2000**

Senior Admin to Director of Design & Applications Group, Interface Products

1997–2000

- Support Director and Senior managers in Design/Applications Group (50+) with all administrative needs
- Identified need for updating department Website, resulting in eliminating call taking and manual handling of customer sample shipments. Sample shipment turnaround was reduced from three days to two hours, increasing customer satisfaction. Freed up two hours of administrator's time daily as a result.
- Posted department calendar on the intranet, eliminating manual queries. Automated meeting facilities scheduling function by identifying, purchasing, installing, and implementing state-of-the-art software. This process became an enterprise-wide model.
- Supported all generic administrative needs and posted communications of section heads to all employees via the intranet. This was previously done word-of-mouth with "drive-by" communications.

Sr. Admin to Product Group and HR Director, CORE technologies Group
1991–1997

- Senior Assistant responsible for developing SAP Database infrastructure, populating it with divisional information and maintaining confidential environment

- Handled all general HR admin functions including processing of all personal requisitions, offers, new hire/termination processes, while working in a confidential environment.

- Carried out SAP data entry, handled field and employee payroll administration and problems.

- Helped organize large yearly technology offsite meeting (150 attendees) for technologies Director. Within three years reduced costs 20 percent annually; increased meeting effectiveness.

Other positions held at National: 1977–1991

- Systems Scheduler/Product Definition System (PDS) Coordinator.

- Component Scheduler, forecast spreadsheets, pulling corporate data for product line.

EDUCATION:

- Graduated, Cupertino High School, Cupertino, CA
- CPS Certified, International Association of Administrative Professionals, 1998
- Coursework:
  - Management & Supervision; Purchasing & Material Control, De Anza College, Cupertino CA
  - FOCUS Language, Script, XEDIT, Negotiation & Time Management, National Semiconductor

OTHER ACCOMPLISHMENTS:

- Officer of the Santa Clara women executive support staff
- Headed United Way fundraiser events at the county level for the past three years
- Worked with United Way staff to develop novel fundraising approaches in a tough economy
- President, Toastmasters Club in Los Gatos, CA for two years
- Certified Meeting Planner (CMP)

KARLO MENNIG
Adriana Avenue
Cupertino, CA 95014
(000) 555-0000: email@email.com

Education:
BSCS, University of California, Berkeley, 2001, 4.0 GPA

BEFORE #2

Work Experience:
Hewlett-Packard, Research Labs, Palo Alto, CA
R&D Software Engineer   June–August 2001

- Served as the top Linux expert in the NetServer Division, resulting in a highly focused and forward-looking business outlook for Linux services.

- Performed research and collaborated with internal and external partners to change the direction of support for Linux for NetServer platforms.

- Integrated IA-64 Linux operating system pre-releases with NetServer platforms.

- Made recommendations to other internal groups regarding the utility of Linux and its suitable applications for their projects, resulting in an improved development platform for next-generation products.

- Qualified as an ANSI Certified HP Server Engineer.

Other Experience: Worked as a summer intern for over 8 summers in different companies engaged in electronic design work.
Foreign Languages: Speak German

PROFESSIONAL DEVELOPMENT:
Coursework and experience in a variety of computer and science-related topics include:

Machine structures	Data structures
Computer networks	Operating systems
Efficient algorithms	Intractable problems
Compilers and programming languages	Computer graphics
Database systems	Fractals, chaos, and complexity
User interfaces	Human-computer interaction

References: Available upon request.

Hobbies: Computer programming, circuit design. Skiing.

Comments: This résumé screams *I am fresh out of college, very smart, but don't know much. Don't hire me!* It can also give an impression of laziness for not making the effort to present the material in a well-designed format.

DELIVERING BULLETPROOF SOFTWARE

KARLO MENNIG
Adriana Avenue
Cupertino, CA 95014
(000) 555-0000: email@email.com

PROFESSIONAL OBJECTIVE

A position as a **software design engineer** responsible for design, development, testing, and documentation of technology products, including identifying and defining product features as well as implementing designs to deliver functional products

AFTER #2

EXPERIENCE SUMMARY

Eight years in a variety of companies and industries, including a Fortune-50 high-tech leader, as well as a start-up. Responsibilities included coding solutions, developing product specifications, identifying user requirements, system administration, and delivering industry-defining results, while also beating deadlines. Versed in project management methodology for rapid cycle times.

UNIQUE SKILLS

- **Identify** user needs and then translate them into product specifications
- **Develop** and implement efficient algorithms
- **Communicate** exceptionally well: written and verbal
- **Write bulletproof** code to implement new features or version-one products
- **Troubleshoot** mission-critical bugs, and then incorporate enhancements
- **Collaborate** with others as part of a team as well as with internal and external partners

PROFESSIONAL EXPERIENCE

Hewlett-Packard Company, R&D Software Engineer   **2001**

- Served as the top Linux expert in the NetServer Division, resulting in a highly focused and forward-looking business outlook for Linux services. Developed plans for new offerings.

- Performed research and collaborated with internal and external partners to change the direction of support for Linux for NetServer platforms.
- Integrated IA-64 Linux operating system pre-releases with NetServer platforms.
- Made recommendations to other groups for utility of Linux and its suitable applications for their projects, resulting in an improved development platform for next-generation products.

Elusive Entertainment, Software Design Engineer (Consultant) **2001–present**

- Wrote an optimized 3-D collision detection module for complex object interaction.
- Mentored and supported other engineers, delegated responsibility, and met deadlines.
- Identified key goals and characteristics of the "Urban Jungle" project.

Minerva Networks, Software Engineer (Internship)   **2000**

- Developed alpha-blending and text anti-aliasing engines for most successful DVD authoring.
- Used MFC and ActiveX controls to embed video from the company's presentation product into Web pages to drastically expand the customer base for the product.
- Planned and wrote foundation library for spline-based object representation and manipulation for an MPEG-4 authoring tool. Assisted in defining goals and characteristics of the tool.
- Implemented automatic generation of HTML menus, incorporating JavaScript, to remotely control the playback of video server content through set-top boxes.

Compression Technologies, Contract Programmer (Consultant)   **1998–present**

- Coded a Java port of the Cinepak Pro video compression codec.
- Developed applications to order products online and monitor demo product downloads.
- Consulted with company members to identify appropriate budget, needs, and timeframes.

KARLO MENNIG   (000) 555-0000: email@email.com   Page 3/4

Pinnacle Systems, Software Developer (Internship)   1997

- Developed a windows-based program to run diagnostic tests on video products using C++.
- Defined and implemented an extensible, general plug-in model for the diagnostic tests.

Micro Computer Products, Software Engineer   1996–1997

- Coded "Story Tools," a digital video application that captures, edits, and publishes content.
- Managed source code control system for a project with an approved budget of over $1.2M.
- Administered/maintained many servers and workstations running various operating systems.

Sun Microsystems, Web Programmer (Consultant)   1995–1996

- Identified goals, guidelines, and appropriate tools for the Disneyland project.
- Wrote and tested professional HTML code for the Disneyland Website.

NASA Ames Research Center, Computer Engineer (Consultant)   1994–1995

- Managed NASA's Quest UNIX server and provided support to users of the system.
- Served as a student instructor for Internet classes with over 30 students each.
- Designed HTML and graphics for NASA's K-12 Initiative Web servers.

COMPUTER SKILLS
Comprehensive knowledge of C, C++, Java, Scheme, Pascal, HTML, and Perl languages; experience with MIPS, OpenGL, and Matlab. Experienced with UNIX (Solaris, SunOS, Linux, SCO), Windows (9X and NT), MacOS. Server/network administration/support Windows/Unix

EDUCATION
BSEE and Computer Science, University of California at Berkeley, Berkeley, CA

PROFESSIONAL DEVELOPMENT:
Coursework and experience in a variety of computer and science-related topics include:

Machine structures	Data structures
Computer networks	Operating systems
Efficient algorithms	Intractable problems
Compilers and languages	Computer graphics
Database systems	Fractals, chaos, and complexity

Sally Hammer
Altman Way, Mill Valley, CA 94941
(000) 555-0000:
email@email.com

Professional Experience:

Hamilton & Associates   10/99–present
Regional Managing Director
Market $6.0 Billion money management portfolios in California, Washington, Oregon, & Colorado to Institutional Clients, Private Banking, and Consulting firms.

♦ Raise $150 million per year in new assets

♦ Top Salesperson for 2001, 2002

♦ Speak professionally across the country on Investment Topics

Charles Schwab, Inc.   3/96–10/99
Vice President   (8/98–10/99)
San Francisco, CA

♦ Sales Manager of the San Francisco Branch, a 55 broker office, which generates $20 million in annual revenues.

♦ Exceeded all personal sales goals and San Francisco Branch sales goals for 1998.

♦ Responsible for weekly sales meetings, daily sales ideas, client appreciation events, compliance, public relations, marketing, community relations.

♦ Managed a strategic project with US Bancorp to create a new investment delivery channel, Private Financial Services (PFS) in the California Region.

Assistant Vice President   (4/97–8/98)
Minneapolis, MN

♦ Created national training program for Charles Schwab's developing brokers. Trained 300 developing brokers per year on new program. Highlights: Increased assets under management by 50% in the first year; increased average account size to $100,000; increased gross production by 25% for first year brokers.

♦ Exceeded all personal sales goals, generating $150,000 in revenue.

♦ Wrote a two-day training program on IRA Rollovers (estate and tax laws) and trained 200 top sales people nationally. Highlights: Increased IRA rollover assets by 70% per salesperson.

♦ Created a Pacesetter's Conference for top salespeople in their third, fourth, and fifth years in production.

Investment Executive   (3/96–4/97)
San Francisco, CA

♦ Generated $200,000 in revenue annually by gathering $10 million annually in assets under management. Exceeded all sales goals.

♦ Taught monthly investment courses for women: Estate Planning, Basic Investing for Women, Advanced Investing Strategies for Women, International Investing, Planning for Retirement.

PaineWebber   (5/94–3/96)
Investment Executive
San Francisco, CA

♦ Generated $120,000 in revenue in first year of production and gathered $12 million annually in assets under management. Named Top 5 rookie in class for exceeding all sales benchmarks. Started monthly investing seminars in partnership with national retail chains. (Ex. Neiman Marcus, Gumps, etc.)

Education:
University of California at Davis BA, Rhetoric and Communications, 1991. Minor, Organizational Studies, 1991.
Wharton Business School, University of Pennsylvania, Certified Investment Management Analyst Designation, July 1998.
Licenses: Series 7, 8, 63, 65 and California Insurance.

Comments: This message does not do justice to the accomplishments of the job seeker. The forward-looking objective lacks focus. All experience is presented in a task/responsibilities format, with no stories of leadership that can create differentiation.

Sally Hammer (000) 555-0000: email@email.com

AFTER #3

Career Objective:
A marketing director/sales position in a premier money management firm, responsible for: Penetrating National or West Coast geography in the broker-dealer, wealth management, and private banking channels; attracting major new investments to create strategic and long-term opportunities with sustaining power; and elevating company image using a differentiated style.

EXPERIENCE SUMMARY:
Over 10 years in a variety of sales leadership positions at three premier wealth management institutions. Continually drove investment sales to record highs and led in existing assets and accounts retention, with unparalleled closing success. Trained over 300 new brokers, immediately resulting in superior results; also advanced their sales efforts as an ABOM in a premier wealth management organization, generating over $20 million annually. Developed and delivered a simplified and highly effective financial analysis training to senior—executives at Fortune-50 corporations, immediately catalyzing shareholder wealth.

UNIQUE SKILLS:

- **Outstanding Communication:** Present complex financials and processes in simple, clear, and actionable sales ideas at all affluence levels, leveraging transaction volume.

- **Inspiring Leadership:** Provide consistent thought leadership to sales teams for marketing, launching new initiatives and campaigns, deliver novel concepts to current financial advisors. Guide senior management on strategic/long-term growth.

- **Building Relationships:** Build strategic relationships; nurture existing ones with bellwether clients, broker-dealers, top sales professionals, and community and thought leaders.

- **Trusted Advisorship:** Articulate a consistent message of professionalism, trust, and confidence to familiarize clients in making critical financial decisions.

- **Sales-skills Mentorship:** Consistently provide value-added closing skills to top producers to help them attract and retain business. Mentor sales professionals by creating a learning culture, driving for superior outcomes through effective and consistent communication.

- **Elevating Brand Image:** Strengthen brand image and identity, through consistent delivery of unparalleled professionalism, product/service/sales expertise, and intellectual capacity demanded by select clients driving major investment decisions.

PROFESSIONAL EXPERIENCE:

Hamilton & Associates   99–present
Regional Managing Director

Market $3.0 Billion money management firm in the West in separate account/mutual fund channels to Private Banks, Broker Dealers, Regional Broker Dealers and RIA's.

- ◆ Identified under-penetrated markets in Western States. Initiated new strategic relationships with individual brokers and leveraged existing ones resulting in $300 million in *new* annual sales. Recognized as top salesperson '01 and 02 in a group of ten Regional Directors.

- ◆ Raised over $600 million in total assets between 1999 and 2003.

- ◆ Delivered over 1000 investment seminars on asset allocation and diversification to over 10,000 professionals and clients, nationwide.

- ◆ Established 1000+ relationships with *new* Financial Professionals within three years.

- ◆ Continually surpassed benchmarks, setting standards for other Regional Directors.

Charles Schwab, Inc.   96–99
Vice President San Francisco, CA   98–99

- ◆ Sales Manager, 55-broker SF Branch, generating over $20 million in annual revenues

- ◆ Exceeded all personal sales goals and SF Branch sales goals for 1998

- ◆ Revamped and revitalized branch's weekly sales meetings, daily sales ideas, client appreciation events, compliance, public relations, marketing, community relations.

- ◆ Facilitated and managed development of a new and innovative pilot project between Private Banking and Charles Schwab's Wealth Management efforts to create a new investment delivery channel, Private Financial Services (PFS) in the California Region.

Sally Hammer   (000) 555-0000: email@email.com   Page 3/3

Assistant Vice President Minneapolis, MN   97–98

♦ Initiated a new national program for developing brokers, then trained 300 annually. Increased assets u by 50 percent; account to $100K and gross production by 25 percent for first-year brokers.

♦ Exceeded all personal sales goals, generating $150K in revenue

♦ Designed and authored two-day sales training program on IRA Rollovers (estate and tax laws) and trained 200 top nationally. Increased rollover assets by a record 70 percent per person.

♦ Structured a new Pacesetter's Conference designed to recognize top salespeople in their third, fourth, and fifth years in production, which has continued to operate and grow nonstop.

Investment Executive San Francisco, CA   96–97

♦ Generated $200 K in annual revenue by gathering $10 M annually in assets under management.

♦ Delivered monthly investment courses for affluent women in Estate Planning, Investing Strategies, International Investing, Planning for Retirement, increasing women participation

Paine-Webber   94–96
Investment Executive, San Francisco, CA

♦ Generated $120 K in revenue in first year and gathered $12 M annually in assets under management. Named Top five rookie for exceeding all sales. Started collaborative monthly investing seminars.

Consultant   1999
Consulted with BTS, an innovative and strategic management consulting firm specializing in profitability and shareholder equity initiatives for Fortune-50 firms. Creatively designed training for its sales force and then delivered it to 1000 executives at Intel, TI, and Applied Materials.

EDUCATION:

• UC Davis BA, Rhetoric and Communications; Minor, Organizational Studies

• Wharton Business School, University of Pennsylvania, Cert. Investment Management Analyst Designation, July 1998

• Licenses: Series 7, 8, 63, 65 and California Insurance

John Smith

Sport Plaza Fremont, CA 94539   (000) 555-0000: email@email.com

OBJECTIVE: Manufacturing Engineer

Manufacturing engineer

SUMMARY Test and Development engineer with extensive experience in systems integration, electronics test and new product introduction for RF and microwave markets. Knowledgeable in component selection, product assembly, and signal interfacing for RF and optical fiber. Design team experience as well as an independent troubleshooter. Resourceful in production solutions and solving daily manufacturing problems. Effective in teaching skills and interfacing.

TECHNICAL SKILLS

Test Development	Root Cause Investigations
New Product Introduction	RF Interfacing-coax, waveguide, fiber
Vendor Interfacing	Approval agency testing
RF Instrumentation & Measurements	LabView experience

PROFESSIONAL EXPERIENCE

Lightwave Electronics, Mountain View, CA   Jun 2001–Oct 2003
Manufacturing Engineer

- Teamed with Engineering to develop an optical microwave system with modulation range greater than 100 GHz. Designed RF interface section to handle the 0.05 to 12 GHz control band. Designed and built test multi-functional fixtures with control via LabView interface.

- Coordinated release of all electrical assemblies for the latest bio-medical laser on schedule. Influenced designers to improve manufacturability with production expertise. Reduced cost of power supply 20% by re-structuring assembly for turn-key manufacturing. Created assembly drawings, wrote Manufacturing plan, and created capacity model for production.

- Specified replacement parts for older designs, saving redesign cost. Performed root cause investigations to resolved customer issues and eliminated future issues. Negotiated with component vendors to obtain specific options at no extra cost. Coordinated and resolved issues with approval agency to achieve UL rating for product.

Resume of John Smith   (000) 555-0000: email@email.com   **Page 2 of 3**

Netro Corporation, San Jose, CA (now SR Telecom)   Dec 1998–Apr 2001
RF Test Engineer
- Designed and implemented functional and environmental tests on 26 and 39 GHz broadband radios for wireless ATM networking. Qualified hybrid microwave amplifiers for flatness and compression. Diagnosed distortion problems down to component level, and implemented new test methods to eliminate future problems. Transferred knowledge to contract manufacturer and raised production yields 30%. Set up ESD protection in factory and taught awareness class.

Digital Microwave Corporation, San Jose, CA (now Stratex)
                                                          Feb 1998–Nov 1998
Modem Test Engineer
- Designed and implemented test plans, procedures, and fixtures for the 128QAM digital modem section of a wireless transmission system. Supervised assembly and initial testing of the next generation Automated Modem board Tester. Assisted in the development of the test software done in HP-Vee.

Ericsson Fiber Access, Menlo Park, CA (formerly Raynet)   Apr 1991–Jan 1998

RF Design Engineer   **1996–1998**
- Designed and built the Pilot Inserter headend distribution amplifier in a fiber optic CATV system. Provided 60 dB of spurious-free range over 40–860 MHz. Design included a fixed pilot synthesized VHF tone, and ALC loop to control pilot level to within 0.2 dB over temperature.

Senior Test Engineer   **1991–1996**
- Designed and built RF test stations for fiber based cable TV system. Integrated test operator selections with automated instrument control via a LabView platform. Reduced test times 40% by judicious use of LabView (Virtual Instrument) test modules.

ADDITIONAL RELEVANT EXPERIENCE:

GTE Government Systems, Mountain View, CA (now General Dynamics)

Systems Engineer   9 years

Resume of John Smith   (000) 555-0000: email@email.com   **Page 3 of 3**

- Provided test and systems integration expertise for signal collection systems (HF thru Ku band) for sea and airborne platforms. Supplied test data for white paper studies, technical proposals, and product improvements. Ran environmental tests on system units, and wrote report for customer. Obtained security clearance and installed systems on Navy submarines.

EDUCATION
California Polytechnic State University, San Luis Obispo, California
Communications Systems, 4 years Electronic Engineering Program

UC Berkeley Extension Courses: Mathematics for Communications Engineering, Statistics and Probability, Digital Filtering, Programming in C

Comments: Despite John's excellent track record in RF, microwave, test equipment, and manufacturing methods of electronic equipment and systems, the current market is not hiring in these areas. Since manufacturing function itself is disappearing rapidly in this outsourced age, his headlined objective may get in the way of someone reading his résumé. The areas of interest now are wireless telephony, communications, and military systems. The revised résumé must highlight these areas for John to find targets where he can get reasonable attention to his value message. In addition, the presentation of the message in formatting, esthetics, and consistency is lacking.

JOHN SMITH

Sport Plaza. Fremont, CA 94539   (000) 555-0000: <u>email@email.com</u>

AFTER #4

CAREER OBJECTIVE: **Test Engineer** at a wireless-products company or systems manufacturer responsible for developing and implementing new products testing

EXPERIENCE SUMMARY: Two-and-half years in manufacturing, responsible for release of new laser products, and support of RF and controls. Equal duration as Test Engineer testing digital wireless systems for a start-up, one-plus year as a Design Engineer for a global telephony company, preceded by more than five years developing RF test stations for fiber based CATV modules. Previous experience was as a systems engineer in signal collection for the military.

UNIQUE SKILLS:

- *Early Collaboration:* Team up with system developers early in design to preemptively identify test challenges and minimize test failures and surprises well before release.

- *Anticipate Surprises:* Design with forethought to accommodate future upgrades and/or product revisions with contingency path that allows for longer life-cycle

- *Test Orchestration:* Develop techniques, equipment and processes for emerging products to give the most information, using fewest resources

- *Team Resource:* Exceptional at finding new and replacement parts, vendor services, and materials for all levels of product development

- *Cross-functional Savvy:* A blend of practical hands-on mechanical and analytical skills, broadened through experience on both ends—Systems to Field Installations

PROFESSIONAL EXPERIENCE:

ProNet Professional Networking Group, Fremont, CA   2003–present
Workshop Facilitator
Lead presenter on three of four advanced job search workshops given weekly.

Lightwave Electronics, Mountain View, CA   2001–2003
Manufacturing Engineer
Guided and mentored designers to improve manufacturability of solid-state lasers; fixed electrical sub-assembly problems; implemented quality improvements on existing products

- Teamed up to develop an optical heterodyning test instrument for characterizing the output response of fiber photo-receivers over an extremely wide bandwidth. Set up new product structure, established design standards, and provided the design of microwave pre-scalar section for instrument to meet scheduled debut at OFC 2002.

- Resolved production issues to develop a low cost UV research laser for a demanding customer. Restructured initial parts list to reduce assembly costs 30 percent. Arranged with new vendor special packaging requirements, and delivery time for first shipment

- Authored manufacturing plan for each new product. Created production capacity models to identify process time, equipment and personnel. Solved document storage problem to allow release of newer design documents on company's older legacy file system

- Designed and implemented power supply burn-in fixture to monitor RF output of four units with one Power meter, increasing equipment utilization four fold. Retrofitted standard oven with controller to automate temperature cycling, saving over $2K/oven.

Netro Corporation, San Jose, CA (now SR Telecom)   1998–2001
RF Test Engineer
Designed and implemented test plans, procedures, and fixtures for wireless ATM radios at 10, 26 and 39 GHz. Evaluated hybrid microwave amplifiers for spectral purity and compression

- Set up troubleshooting station, diagnosed, and provided steps to eliminate distortion effecting 40 percent of units. Taught ESD protection to class of 16 techs on the test floor

- Set precedent for robust and dependable test fixtures allowing easy troubleshooting and updating to next product revision. Efficient design duplicated for Taiwan factory

- Specified and assisted in development of an automated IF module tester at 3 GHz by an outside vendor. Ran pre-evaluation tests, and resolved vendor's assembly problems

John Smith   (000) 555-0000: email@email.com   Page 3/3

Ericsson Fiber Access, Menlo Park, CA (formerly Raynet)   1991–1998
RF Design Engineer   1996–1998
Designed and implemented plug-in amplifier modules and associated circuitry as part of a fiber based voice and video transmission system.
Utilized latest surface mount GaAs amplifier to design the headend amplifier module for an optical CATV system. Improved module's RF detector range to allow use as spectrum power monitor as well as RF fault alarm. No significant problems noted during Systems integration.

Senior Test Engineer   1991–1996
Designed and built automated parametric tests on optical receivers and RF amplifier modules up to 900 MHz. Integrated test instruction with automated measurement via a LabView platform.

- Designed and built three generations of RF test stations. Developed optical calibration method to eliminate errors and guarantee accuracy using less-expensive, stock devices.

- Specified algorithm for automated band pass measurements to provide test margin in gain slope and return loss measurements. Improved test times 40 percent by proper sequence and split of data operations between test instrument and station computer

PRIOR PROFESSIONAL EXPERIENCE:

GTE Government Systems, Mountain View, CA (now General Dynamics)
Member of Technical Staff
Integrated and tested advanced signal collection systems (HF through Ku band) for sea and airborne platforms. Provided technical support and data for white paper studies, and proposals.

EDUCATION:
California Polytechnic State University, San Luis Obispo, California
Communications Systems, 4 years Electronic Engineering Program
UC Berkeley Extension Courses: Mathematics for Communications Engineering, Statistics and Probability, Digital Filtering, Programming in C

Certificates and Computer Skills: LabView Basics I; MRP System
MS W, Word, Excel, Visio Drawing, MathCad, AutoCAD, Protel schematic capture, gile, and JD Edwards MRP system.

SAMUEL JONES
(000) 555-0000: email@email.com

BEFORE #5

SUMMARY
Project Manager specialized in leading cross-functional teams implementing enterprise management solutions in both client-server and web environments. Consistently successful implementing systems that streamline business processes, reduce costs, and increase customer satisfaction. Significant experience managing multiple concurrent projects

PROFESSIONAL EXPERIENCE

CORNISH & CAREY, Oakland, CA   2002–2003

Broker Associate: Sold residential real estate in the San Francisco Bay Area.

PEREGRINE SYSTEMS, Concord, CA   1998–2002

Senior Technical Consultant/Project Manager
Determined customer needs and related application software, customization and interface requirements, prepared project plans and budgets, assembled teams, managed hardware and relational database setup, managed data mapping and migration, application software installation and testing, prepared user documentation, trained users, and managed transition to new system. Clients included Hewlett Packard, Vivendi Universal, and Wells Fargo Bank.

- Consolidated four legacy real estate management data sources into a single new real estate portfolio management system eliminating data redundancy, simplifying budget creation and administration and significantly boosting property managers' productivity.

- Implemented new facilities management help desk, providing customers with web-based work request and feedback capability accessible through their desktop PC's.

- Managed the integration of customer's real estate and asset management systems into a new relational database system providing a single source for both functions.

BUSINESS IMPROVEMENT SPECIALTIES (BIS), Danville, CA   1996–1997
Senior Business Process Consultant
Developed, marketed, sold and delivered business process services and BIS Process Manager (BPM) software solutions. Clients were Pacific Bell and AirTouch Communications.

- Led telecom management team in designing and implementing a new process that provided customer service technicians a complete set of on-line procedures and tools to assist commercial customers. Success of this project contributed to the customer's selection of BPM as its primary business process development and deployment tool.
- Developed BPM training course for on-site client training. Became standard training course for a major customer generating substantial revenue for BIS.

ZACSON CORPORATION, Pleasanton, CA   1994–1995
Process Consultant
Managed process design and improvement projects for this telecommunications services company and its customers. Customers were Wells Fargo Bank, IBM and Siemens ROLM.

- Led client team developing customer support processes for a new PC-based banking channel, providing a complete set of on-line processes for customer service agents.
- Designed and implemented Zacson internal call center business processes significantly boosting service quality and customer satisfaction.
- Wrote proposal that won $250,000 process design program for a major banking customer.

INDEPENDENT CONSULTANT, San Ramon, CA   1994
Independent consultant leading projects improving customers' operational performance.

- Developed an operational blueprint for a client's gateway manufacturing processes providing them a plan to significantly increase productivity in this key area. I did a great job!

COLTEC INDUSTRIES, West Hartford, CT   1992–1993
Manager, Productivity Engineering
Set up and managed a new department responsible for improving the manufacturing performance of the Chandler Evans Division of this $1.3 billion manufacturer. Developed, implemented, and led a program to reduce overhead, material and labor costs, shorten lead times, and improve quality.

- Authored and won management and United Auto Workers approval for 3-year operations improvement program designed to yield $2,500,000 in annual savings.

- Launched program by hiring engineering staff, selecting, purchasing, and implementing process analysis software and hardware, and leading mixed staff and union steward teams in operations improvement projects. First year savings exceeded target by 18%.

H.B. MAYNARD & COMPANY, INC., New York, NY   1986–1992
Consultant
Led programs to implement H.B. Maynard's PC-based operations analysis and improvement systems. Managed the installation of Maynard's PC-based process analysis and improvement systems at client sites, including interfaces with existing client systems. Trained teams to use these systems. Acted as on-site program manager, developing and implementing operations improvement program plans. Clients were LTV-Sierra Research, Citibank, Hexcel Corp., Hamilton Scientific, Fibre-Metal Products Co., and the New York Times Company

- Set up a manufacturing operations improvement program for a safety equipment manufacturer that yielded over $2,000,000 in savings.

- Directed an operations improvement program a laboratory equipment manufacturer that realized $1,600,000 in savings.

- Determined crewing requirements for key operations in a new newspaper printing plant. Findings resulted in substantial reductions in contractual crewing guidelines in use for over 40 years.

COOPERS & LYBRAND, New York, New York   1985–1986
Staff Consultant
Undertook two projects with AT&T.

SAMUEL JONES   (000) 555-0000: email@email.com   **Page 4 of 4**

- Helped develop and conduct tests to certify to the U.S. Department of Justice that ATT's commercial customer database correctly registered switches in long distance carrier preference.
- Helped create a workforce management system for branch offices located in the eastern U.S.. This project included installing the system at the office sites.

EDUCATION

MBA, Management, Pace University, New York, NY
BA, Economics, Rutgers University, Newark, NJ

AFFILIATIONS

Member, American Society for Quality
Member, Institute of Industrial Engineers
Certified Management Consultant (CMA), Institute of Management Consultants

---

Comments: This résumé for a process development engineer can be made stronger by rewriting the accomplishment stories to show leadership qualities in a diverse environment. The overall message could be made more focused. Statements as, I did a great job, in one of the accomplishments, impair the message.

Samuel Jones   (000) 555-0000:   email@email.com

CAREER OBJECTIVE: A **project lead position** in consulting focused to improve clients' computer systems, software, and business processes; helping clients achieve superior business performance.

EXPERIENCE SUMMARY: Led cross-functional teams implementing enterprise management solutions for mid-sized and Fortune 500 organizations to streamline critical processes, reduce costs, and enhance customer experience; develop innovative, practical solutions; build high-performance teams; conduct end-user training; lead projects to successful implementation; maintain strong client-firm relationships.

UNIQUE SKILLS

> **Success Catalyst:** Implement solutions that meet clients' expectations, support their success, and provide firm with a rich source of references, referrals and follow-on business

> **Knowledge Assimilation:** Clarify and assimilate articulated and unarticulated needs; represent them to the firm and to third-party contributors. Align clients' needs with firm's service capabilities

> **Implementation Roadmaps:** Create clearly defined project plans with sufficient flexibility to adjust to unanticipated changes, and minimize their impact on objectives, timelines, and costs

> **Operational Blueprints:** Develop vivid blueprints that clearly represent the operational end-state of successful implementation and the benefits that will accrue to the clients' organization

> Change Agent: Win support for change by apprising client management and end-users of new system benefits, addressing their concerns, and incorporating their suggestions

PROFESSIONAL EXPERIENCE
ProNet, Fremont, CA   2003–Present
Marketing Process Consultant
As member of Marketing Department of professional career search networking organization, discovered ad hoc and discontinuous employer outreach processes. Currently developing end-to-end, repeatable processes to improve department productivity and simplify transferability to incoming members.

CORNISH & CAREY, Oakland, CA   2002–2003
Broker Associate
Applied consulting, project management and communication expertise to help buyers secure financing and homes in a historically tight housing market, and allow them to take advantage of unprecedented price appreciation to quickly build home equity.

PEREGRINE SYSTEMS, Concord, CA   1998–2002
Senior Technical Consultant/Project Manager
Led cross-functional teams to consolidate legacy real estate portfolio management systems into single-source solutions allowing property managers to track and maintain property assets, budgets, and leases

- Determined that client's four separate real property management systems were causing data gaps and errors, and significant financial penalties due to missed dates. Overcame political, logistical, and technical challenges associated with departmental systems; implemented a single-source solution that reduced errors and costs, and significantly boosted property managers' effectiveness.

- Implemented a new web-based help desk to replace client's paper-based system. Result was real-time work request and feedback through employees' PC's, greatly improving response time.

- Client's building preventive maintenance program suffered from inefficiencies caused by maintaining separate real property and building asset databases. Managed the merging of the two into a single system that simplified the program and greatly enhanced its effectiveness.

BUSINESS IMPROVEMENT SPECIALTIES (BIS), Danville, CA   1996–1997
Senior Business Process Consultant
Developed business process services and BIS Process Manager (BPM) software solutions.

- A major telecom client was experiencing low commercial customer service ratings. Led a management team to design new processes that provided a complete set of on-line help desk procedures and tools. Customer service was significantly improved, causing the client to select BPM as its primary business process development and deployment tool.

- Client had need of a fast-track BPM training course to replace the existing five-day course. Developed a one-day program that significantly accelerated the client's training program and provided a continuous revenue stream for BIS.

ZACSON CORPORATION, Pleasanton, CA   1994–1995
Process Consultant
Managed process design and improvement projects for this telecommunications services company and its clients, Wells Fargo Bank, IBM, and Siemens ROLM.

- Client was behind schedule developing help-desk processes for a new PC-based banking channel. Led client team to develop complete on-line processes for customer service agents.

- Zacson's internal call center business processes were ad hoc or informal. Designed and implemented new ones that significantly boosted service quality and customer satisfaction.

- Wrote proposal that won $250,000 process design program for a major banking client.

INDEPENDENT CONSULTANT, San Ramon, CA   1994
Developed a blueprint to significantly increase productivity in client's gateway manufacturing operations.

COLTEC INDUSTRIES, West Hartford, CT   1992–1993
Manager, Productivity Engineering
Set up/managed a new department for this $1.3 billion manufacturer to dramatically improve operations.

- Authored and won management and United Auto Workers approval for 3-year operations improvement program designed to yield $2,500,000 in annual savings.

- Launched program by hiring engineering staff, selecting, purchasing, and implementing process analysis software and hardware, and leading mixed staff and union steward teams in operations improvement projects. First year savings of $448,000 exceeded target by 18%.

H.B. MAYNARD & COMPANY, INC., New York, NY   1986–1992
Consultant
Led programs to implement PC-based operations analysis and improvement
systems. Clients included Citibank, LTV, Hexcel Corp., Hamilton Scientific,
and the New York Times Co.

- Saved over $2 M for a manufacturer by revamping safety program in the
  first year alone.
- Directed improvements for a laboratory equipment manufacturer realizing a $1.6 M in savings.
- Determined crewing requirements for key operations in a new newspaper printing plant. Findings resulted in substantial reductions in crewing guidelines in use for over 40 years.

EDUCATION

- MBA, Management, Pace University, New York, NY
- BA, Economics, Rutgers University, Newark, NJ

David Hunter
Alter Drive
Cupertino, CA 95014

(000) 555-0000:   EMAIL@EMAIL.COM   BEFORE #6

Objective:
International product manager for global Internet or financial services company

Summary:

- Global web marketing (**Sun Microsystems**), managing programs in 40 countries
- Web internationalization and localization expert
- APAC regional project management (**Walt Disney**), 9 years expatriate in China
- International organizational development and management
- Major account marketing (**IBM**)
- On-line credit card payments product management (Magnum Resources)
- Speak, read, write Mandarin Chinese, Cantonese, Japanese, French, English

Highlights:

Internationalization and localization

As **e-Commerce Globalization Program Manager** at **Sun Microsystems**, managed corporate website internationalization and localization for 40 locals. Totally revised the global architecture from one of *country* control to one of *central* control, reasserting control over the brand, which had become fragmented and no longer in sync with corporate objectives. Leveraging readily available technologies, developed a new architecture composed of:

- Presentation-independent XML content stored in centralized global content management system
- Dynamic rendering of country web sites, including regional as well as local content
- Translation automated process routing

Result is globally-focused brand management, immediate global web publishing permitting more effective global marketing rollout, new regional synergies and enhanced customer satisfaction.

Asia product management

As **Asia Pacific Information Technology Director** for **Walt Disney**, launched and directed 20-engineer team based in 11 East Asian countries. In collaboration with senior executives from movie, home entertainment, and television business units, integrated product development and distribution processes with IT; for example in television programming and broadcast, animation, movie distribution, manufacturing, systems for international settlements and repatriation of regional revenue. Set technical direction; established consistent specifications, configurations, procedures and policies across the region. Justified and controlled $4.5 million regional budget for all Asia Pacific IT resources and expenditures across three business units, dozens of locations, and in multiple currencies. Negotiated service contracts, regional discounts, and licensing.

On-line credit card payment product management

As **Product Manager** for internet startup, **Magnum Resources**, developed the first (1995) product providing seamless integration of secure on-line credit card payment to web stores. Created business plan, product specifications, and merchant banking relationships; managed product development, marketing and sales. An early customer was Win Zip, and customer base grew to several hundred before company was acquired by Digital River.

Career history:

Sun Microsystems—Menlo Park, CA
E-commerce Globalization Program Manager, 2000–2001

Simultrans—Mountain View, CA
Director—I18n and l10n Project Management, 1998–2000

Walt Disney—Hong Kong
Asia Pacific Regional IT Director, 1996–1998

China Western Management Services—Zhuhai, Guangdong, PRC
Consultant, 1992–1995

Qingdao University—Qingdao, Shandong, PRC
Researcher in Chinese language, 1990–1991

IBM—Hartford, CT
Major Account Marketing Engineer, 1980–1990

Education:

Connecticut State University—New Brittain, CT
M.S., Asian Studies

Quinnipiac University—Hamden, CT
B.A., Mathematics

Defense Language Institute—Montery, CA
Chinese Translation Certification

Skills:
Double byte encoding, Unicode, UTF-8; Object oriented design, design patterns UML, Use Cases, Extreme methodology; J2EE, JSP, Global templates, XML

Comments: The biggest impediment to getting a positive response to this résumé is that it is presented in a functional format, instead of the more conventional chronological one (the client was trying to hide is unemployment period). Additionally, the message lacks focus and does not exploit the candidate's rich experience in a global geography and culturally diverse environment. The résumé also suffers from formatting and messaging problems.

DAVID HUNTER (000) 555-0000: <u>email@email.com</u>

AFTER #6

Career Objective

Operations leader in a technology manufacturing company responsible for developing off-shoring capabilities in Asian countries; leading teams to develop and deliver software and technology products, collaboratively working with domestic and off-shored teams; and working with customers to deliver products, services, and capabilities in an integrated way.

Experience Summary

Extensive experience with global multinationals leading critical initiatives, including:

➢ Nine years in Asia Pacific with manufacturing, consulting, and service delivery

➢ Seven years in various locations improving business and manufacturing processes

➢ Concurrent 10 years working overseas helping streamline businesses/operations

➢ Five years in technology product management, including streamlining global presence of a major multinational Fortune-500 company.

Unique skills:

- **Global Business Models:** Understand how businesses need to organize and execute to succeed in today's global economy and develop and install practices to achieve competitive advantage. Fluent in five languages/cultures: **Chinese, French, German and Japanese.**

- **Seamless Internationality:** Leverage the in-depth knowledge of five languages and Asian cultures to achieve the best possible resource availability for client companies.

- **Unified Messaging:** Review various messaging channels for a global company and define the best strategy to consolidate the process to multiply messaging effectiveness.

- **Technology Champion:** Develop technology options to identify best and most economical solutions to delight the customer in a fiercely competitive environment.

- **Customer Advocate:** Collaborate with key customers to define the best roadmaps for their success and then deliver products and solutions to make them successful.
- **Resource Optimization:** For a global enterprise develop simple decision models to optimize resources and deliver highly effective solutions to beat out the competition.

Professional experience:

DRH Enterprises, Cupertino CA   2003–Current
  Vice President
Develop unique business models to collaborate with manufacturing companies in China and identify opportunities to expand presence in emerging business areas. Collaborate with domestic counterparts.

Industrial/Cultural Exchange Syndicate (Taiwan ROC)   2001–2003
  Liaison
Collaborate with a number of Taiwanese industrial and cultural organizations to develop enhanced relationships with U.S. counterparts to promote trade, commerce, and exchange. Within two years played a key role in expanding the charter to include a variety to businesses that could support the mission, increasing overall membership and trade 50 percent.

Sun Microsystems—Menlo Park, CA   2000–2001
  Global Web Marketing Program Manager
Identified and resolved global organizational issue, enabling Sun to more effectively market its message: Upon taking responsibility for worldwide multilingual web marketing content, immediately identified serious inconsistencies between corporate and in-country online marketing messages. Through unmonitored country delegation of local web content, Sun had undermined its worldwide brand and lost potential regional synergies. Developed a new architecture based on centralized global content and virtual country sites which enabled corporate marketing to centrally control its global online marketing, leverage regional services and events, and eliminate redundant costs.

Simultrans—Mountain View, CA   1996–2000
Director Project Management,   1998–2000
Developed customer loyalty by listening and responding to customer needs:

Simultrans had a history of poor customer satisfaction. Visits with major accounts revealed dissatisfaction stemmed from poor quality and slipped schedules. Established alliances with global vendors offering greater scalability and willing to guarantee quantifiable quality standards, while raising customer satisfaction as a top metric for project engineer's performance evaluations. Results: Within nine months all metrics showed reversed trends, which continued.

Walt Disney—Hong Kong   1996–1998
Asia Pacific Regional Information Technology Director
Put technology at the service of business, rather than business at the service of technology: Responsible for regional technology support of three competing Disney companies, studied business objectives and processes of each, determining the basic model was distribution of services. In partnership with senior executives of each company, made technology an integral part of their business plan. This trusted information was not shared with executives at competing Disney companies. From the perspective of having a detailed understanding of three companies, then offered economies of scale with common solutions, without internecine competition.

China Western Management Services—Zhuhai, Guangdong, PRC **1992–1995**
Consultant
Reasserted corporate interests of a runaway Chinese division through hands-on general management: Under local management, the division was unaccountable, town officials reneging on agreements, and a domestic competitor had planted internal operatives. Within six months, identified and terminated staff working against the company's interests and developed relationships with town officials. Established daily production, quality, and finance reports to company headquarters. The company was finally able to regain control of their investment.

Prior professional experience: Includes working for GE, IBM and Alcoa in a variety of positions.

Education:

- **M.S., Asian Studies,** Connecticut State University—New Britain, CT
- **B.A., Mathematics,** Quinnipiac University—Hamden, CT
- **One-year China studies sabbatical,** Qingdao University—Qingdao, Shandong, PRC

Chinese translation certification, Defense Language Institute—Monterey, CA

BEFORE #7

Tame Yamasaki
South Court
Redwood City, CA 94061
(000) 555-0000: email@email.com

Summary

More than 20 years of professional consulting experience in comprehensive human resource management and organizational development. Bilingual fluency in Japanese and English. Extensive cross-cultural experience in Asia-Pacific, Europe and U.S.. Highly skilled in organizational needs analysis and development through cultural assessment and leadership skills development. Proven track record of balancing people—and results-orientation in leading the search for alternative solutions to human capital development.

Proven success in professional assignments and projects in major global markets in the U.S., Japan, China, Korea, Hong Kong, Indonesia, Thailand, Malaysia, Singapore, Australia, New Zealand, Norway, Sweden, and the UK.
Strategic consulting and OD projects for companies in many industries, including Acuson, Agilent, Bayer, Bristol-Myers Squibb, EKC Technologies, Eli Lilly, Goldman Sachs, Hewlett-Packard, Hoffman La Roche, Lucent, Medtronic, Mochida, Morgan Stanley, Motorola, NCR, Nomura Research Institute, Nortel, Northwest Airlines, Palm, Pfizer, Reuters, Saison, San Jose Arena, Texas Instruments, 3Com, TRW Space and Electronics, United Tractors, Wallenius-Wilhelmsen, and others.
Proven ability to communicate, lead, and relate effectively to executives, managers, individual contributors, cross-functional teams, and multi-national organizations of different cultures.
Extensive experiences in 360 feedback & coaching for executives and managers Strong instructional and training skills in small- to large-group settings in cultural diversity and leadership development.
Formally educated in both Japan (Law) and the U.S. (Psychology).

Experience   Director of Organizational Development, Virtues Technology (Sunny Valley, CA), 2001 to the present

Design, develop and implement million-dollar project for global companies in defining and aligning corporate values principles.

Conduct cultural analyses for organizational alignment and development for merged and/or acquired organizations of more than 10,000 employees.

Provide executives and managers with strategic consultation for virtues-based human resources development.

Train, coach and mentor global executives and managers in leadership development. Develop business through organizational interventions.

Show intense customer focus in developing and managing clients and enhancing strategic business alliances.

Serve as advisor for the owner of Virtues Technology.

Senior Consultant, Employee Decisions Incorporated (San Francisco, CA), 1998–2001

Provided leadership and direction in the assessment solutions practice area for approximately $2 million annual revenues.

Delivered consulting services worth $0.5 million per year in billable hours.

Performed individual assessments for managers and executives for personnel selection and leadership development

Extensively worked with key organizational decision-makers to plan, develop, and manage organizational talent pools and leadership succession.

Provided global executives and managers with individual coaching to enhance their leadership effectiveness in working with local employees.

Director, Employee Decisions Incorporated, Japan (Tokyo, Japan), 1995–1998

Made substantial contributions to the growth and development of SDI Japan, helping it to become firmly established in the Japanese market.

Served a wide variety of global organizations in leading industries, particularly high-tech, pharmaceutical, and financial institutions in Asia.

Consulted with multi-national companies to find or design solutions for their organizational and human resources development.
Directed and delivered individual assessment solutions for multi-national companies hiring and developing local executives and managers in Asia.

Vice President for Professional Development, Baxter Consulting International (New York, NY), 1984–1995
Provided multi-national organizations with consultation for organizational and leadership development.
Conducted globally intensive, experiential executive development programs, primarily in the U.S. and Norway.
Consulted with internal professionals on program development, assessment, and psychometric data interpretation.

Education	Clinical Director, Gateway Communities, Inc. (St. Paul, MN), 1978–1984 Directed inpatient and outpatient clinical services.
License	PhD Counseling Psychology, Kansas State University, Manhattan, Kansas, 1977 MS Counselor Education, University of Michigan, Ann Arbor, Michigan, 1967 LLB (Law), Osaka University, Tokyo, Japan, 1968
Membership	Psychologist by MI State Committee of Psychologists American Psychological Association

Comments: Because of the diverse experience, this client is better off presenting this résumé in a functional format. The accomplishment stories are not compelling; they appear more in a task/responsibility format. The résumé for this level of seniority must show compelling value proposition, it fails in this area.

TAME YAMASAKI SOUTH COURT REDWOOD CITY, CA (000) 555-0000: email@email.com

AFTER #7

CAREER OBJECTIVE:

A position in a global consulting organization responsible for developing business and delivering services, including collaborating with clients to: Define, measure, and develop leadership capabilities; Identify and select the best fit leaders and managers for employment, succession planning, or workforce-reduction initiatives; Coach and mentor executives and managers.

EXPERIENCE SUMMARY:

A bilingual human resource management and organizational development consultant with over 20 years in executive- and management-skills assessment, coaching and mentoring, organizational change through values identification, definition, and alignment; design, development, and delivery of virtues-based team development initiatives; develop, nurture, and manage client relationships and develop business.

SKILLS SUMMARY:

- **Executive and Management Assessment:** Design and conduct assessments in employment selection, leadership development, selection for succession planning, or de-selection for reorganization and organizational effectiveness. Provide clients with critical decision-making recommendations with immediate feedback.

- **Coaching and Mentoring:** Collaborate with highly diverse clients on developing leadership development action plans, and act as a change catalyst. Develop coaching and mentoring agenda for specific skill development, including career reinvention.

- **Virtues-based Change:** Identify and align individuals and corporate values, as well as those of different organizations in mergers and acquisitions, with organization-wide initiatives for large-scale change. Collaborate across broad range of key-decision makers to deliver measurable results, and to develop organizational intervention strategies.

- **Organizational Learning:** Design, develop, and deliver value-based leadership and team development initiatives. Collaborate with regional management to implement.

- **Business Development:** Identify organizational needs, and translate them to solutions to new business-value-capture opportunities, develop marketing plans, and then create profitable revenue streams. Initiate cross- and up-selling initiatives throughout.

PROFESSIONAL ACCOMPLISHMENTS:

EXECUTIVE AND MANAGEMENT ASSESSMENT
Assessed executives and managers of many different nationalities as a lead assessor for leadership development, employment selection, succession planning, de-selection for reorganization, mergers, and/or acquisitions. Helped the hiring global organizations save or create millions of dollars, with high accuracy of success prediction rates in selection procedures. Intra-organizationally provided leadership and direction in the assessment solutions practice area for approximately $2 million annual revenues. Delivered personal services worth of more than 0.5 million per year in billable hours. Mentored others to excel in these endeavors.

COACHING AND MENTORING
Personal growth: collaboratively develop action plans for leadership enhancement, and guided in their accomplishment. In addition, provided with coaching, in a wide range of coaching agenda from explicit identification and alignment of values, belief systems, and organizational culture to skills development, behavioral changes, and career re-orientation. Delivered personal coaching services worth at least $100K in billable hours per year, several years running.

VIRTUES-BASED ORGANIZATIONAL CHANGE
Played a major role as a project manager to design, develop, and implement a $1 M project for identifying and measuring corporate value principles for a global organization. Analyzed the comprehensive cultural survey results, designed solutions and conducted "learning seminars" in Europe, Australia, New Zealand, and Japan. Collaborated with key decision makers of the central office and regional executive directors to implement virtues-based organizational change initiative. Delivered $500 K of billable services annually.

ORGANIZATIONAL LEARNING
Designed, developed, and conducted executive and management development seminars and workshops at various parts of the world, including Indonesia, China, Malaysia, U.S., UK, Norway, and Sweden. Made major contributions for transforming regional and local organizations of Fortune100 companies to collaborative—leadership style and culture.

BUSINESS DEVELOPMENT
Played a major role to establish in Japan, an operating branch office of a major U.S. company-owned consulting firm. Hired, trained, and coached new consultants to transform the organization from inexperienced individual performers to a team of highly skilled and sought-after professionals with reputation, resulting in successful business development. It is now established as one of the most prestigious consulting organizations in Japan, with annual revenue of approximately $20 million.

SIGNIFICANT ACHIEVEMENTS:
Established and directed core businesses of management consultancy in Japan
Pioneered client development and business in Indonesia, Malaysia, China, and Japan
Proven success in client management in a global scale
Service deliveries in different cultures with bilingual capabilities
Jointly established a U.S.-owned consulting organization in Norway with immediate revenues
Educated both in Japan (Law) and the U.S. (Psychology)
Licensed Psychologist, Certified Virtues Consultant

CLIENT ROSTER:

- Wallenius-Wilhelmsen • Goldman Sachs • Hewlett-Packard • Eli Lilly
- Clarica/Sun Life   • Nomura   • United Tractors • Bristol-Myers
- Motorola   • Mochida   • EKC Technology • Nortel

EMPLOYER CHRONOLOGY:

- Virtues Technology, Sunny Valley, CA (2001 to Present), Director, of OD
- Employee Decisions International, San Francisco, CA (1998–2001), Senior Consultant
- Employee Decisions Incorporated Japan, Tokyo, Japan (1995–1998), Director
- Baxter Consulting International, New York, NY, (1984–1995), Vice President

EDUCATION:
Ph.D. (Psychology), Kansas State University, Manhattan, Kansas
M.S. Counselor Education, University of Michigan, Ann Arbor, Michigan
L.L.B. (Law), Osaka University, Tokyo, Japan

Lacy Rums
McKenzie Street
Cupertino, CA 95014

(000) 555-0000:   email@email.com
BEFORE #8

Marketing professional with a background in education and training in the high-technology industry. Experience managing all components of a marketing program including customer satisfaction and survey research, email and website communications, vendor management, content and collateral development, and promotions. Strong communications skills refined in corporate, state government, and volunteer organizations. Passionate about creating a marketing program that clearly articulates the importance of my company's products and services.

Employment: HEWLETT-PACKARD, Cupertino, CA   1998–2003
Product Marketing Specialist

- Managed content and brand compliance of the NonStop Enterprise Division's external Education website, reduced update cycle from days to minutes and personnel required by 50%

- Developed marketing campaigns and associated online, email, and print collateral for internal and external audiences

- Managed customer satisfaction initiatives including market segmentation, survey development, and implementation

- Wrote and published monthly email newsletter that grew to be the largest internal NonStop focused newsletter with a subscriber base of over 2,500

- Created and maintained portfolio of 75 technical course datasheets, improved datasheet content

- Managed customer marketing database of approximately 9,000 customers, updated and improved quality of database content, added opt-in and subscription preference capabilities

- Worked with international and regional user groups in support of NonStop server and education-specific initiatives and grew attendance at regional education sessions by 200%

- Managed print, creative, and promotional vendors, reduced expenses 40%

COMPAQ COMPUTERS (TANDEM COMPUTERS), Cupertino, CA
1996–1998

Sales Training Coordinator

- Coordinated all internal and vendor-led Tandem sales training classes
- Prepared internal billing and departmental cross-charges
- Maintained database for training CD series (approximately 1500 orders annually)

Provided assistance to customer education coordinators

UNIVERSITY OF MARYLAND, College Park, MD   1995–1996

Data Processing and Office Automation Specialist

- Developed and implemented Lotus Notes database for telecommunications service call resolution procedures
- Produced informational mailings for distribution to student body
- Maintained and audited multiple databases for telecommunications automation
- Trained new student personnel

- **Volunteer: WMUC RADIO, UNIVERSITY OF MARYLAND**, College Park, MD1993–1994
- General Manager/Operations Manager
- Managed staff of 200 students, graduates, and volunteers
- Responsible for all on-air programming, station policies, and guidelines
- Interviewed and appointed WMUC executive staff members
- Served as liaison between station and university administration. Handled FCC related and sensitive public reaction situations

Education: Master of Business Administration, Santa Clara University (March 2004)

- Concentration in Marketing Management

Concentration in Finance

Bachelor of Arts,	Criminology and Criminal Justice, University of Maryland
Honors:	Omicron Delta Kappa National Leadership Honor Society
Special skills:	Microsoft Word, Excel, PowerPoint, Access, FileMaker Pro, HTML, basic UNIX, and French

Comments: For marketing professional interested in pursuing branding and marcom, this résumé does not reflect what the person stands for. For this person to be professionally credible, the résumé must reflect her talents in a way that the hiring manager can quickly relate to as creating immediate value. In additional to expressing poorly what this person can do, the experience does not narrate compelling stories of marketing leadership. For someone in marketing, the format and presentation must also reflect better professionalism.

GUERILLA MARKETER

Lacy E. Rums

McKenzie Street   (000) 555-0000
Cupertino, CA 95014   email@email.com

AFTER #8

Career Objective:
A position in **Marketing** responsible for: architecting and delivering a complete marketing program; marketing strategy, brand development, customer experience, and managing channels, including their communications.

Experience Summary:
Seven years working with all elements of a marketing program including customer satisfaction, survey research, and communications, marketing content and collateral development, vendor management, and promotions. Extensive experience with cross-functional and virtual teams; strong web and print communications skills

Unique Skills:

- **Strategic Leader:** Develop marketing strategy based on a comprehensive view. Integrate marketing plans to spark customer interest
- **Brand Management:** Serve, as the voice of the consumer with a focus on user needs, expectations, and buying behavior; recognize that consumers own the brand
- **Relationship Builder:** Develop strong, productive relationships with employees, customers, and vendors to achieve marketing goals
- **Strong Communicator:** Develop effective messages for a broad audience and create excitement.
- **Collaborative approach:** Discover and manage interrelations of marketing activities as they relate to product design, manufacturing, and sales
- **Cause Focus:** Separate cause from symptom when assessing the need for change in the marketing mix resulting in efficient allocation of marketing resources
- **Results Driven:** Define success at the start and drive activities until goals are met

Lacy E. Rums   (000) 555-0000:

Professional Experience:

Hewlett-Packard Co., Cupertino, CA   1998–2003
Product Marketing Specialist

- Drastically reduced product website update cycle from several days to minutes and cut personnel required by half. This was achieved by requiring product change orders to include feature changes right at their release, eliminating having to go back later. Managed content and brand compliance of the NonStop Enterprise Division's external Education website

- Developed marketing campaigns and associated online, email, and print collateral for internal and external audiences

- Managed customer satisfaction initiatives including market segmentation, survey development, and implementation

- Wrote and published monthly email newsletter that grew to be the largest internal NonStop focused newsletter inside of HP with a subscriber base of over 2,500

- Created and maintained portfolio of 75 technical course datasheets, reduced datasheet development time from three weeks to one by routinizing the process.

- Managed customer marketing database of approximately 9,000 customers; updated and improved quality of database content including addition of opt-in and subscription preference capabilities

- Worked with international and regional user groups in support of NonStop server and education-specific initiatives resulting in *tripling* of attendance at regional education sessions

- Managed print, creative, and promotional vendors, reduced expenses by 40 percent

Compaq Computer Corp. (Tandem Computers Inc.), Cupertino, CA 1996–1998
Sales Training Coordinator

- Coordinated all internal and vendor-led Tandem sales training classes; streamlined enrollment procedures with end user feedback

- Prepared internal billing and departmental cross-charges

Lacy E. Rums   (000) 555-0000:   email@email.com   Page 3/3

- Maintained database for training CD series (approximately 1500 orders annually)
- Provided assistance to coordinators in customer education

University Of Maryland, College Park, MD   1995–1996
Data Processing and Office Automation Specialist

- Developed and implemented Lotus Notes database for telecommunications service call resolution procedures, led to reduction in problem resolution time
- Produced informational mailings for distribution to student body
- Maintained and audited multiple databases for telecommunications automation
- Trained new student personnel

Volunteer:
WMUC Radio, University Of Maryland, College Park, MD   1993–1994
General Manager and Operations Manager

- Managed staff of 200 students, graduates, and volunteers; mediated staff conflicts
- Responsible for all on-air programming, station policies, and guidelines; increased public affairs programming by 50 percent.
- Interviewed and appointed WMUC executive staff members
- Served as liaison between station and university administration; handled FCC-related and sensitive public reaction situations

Education:
Master of Business Administration, Santa Clara University (2004)

- Concentration in Marketing Management
- Concentration in Finance

Bachelor of Arts, Criminology and Criminal Justice, University of Maryland

Special Skills: Microsoft Word, Excel, PowerPoint, Access, FileMaker Pro, HTML, basic UNIX, and French

NAOMI WANG
(000) 555-0000:   email@email.com
Bilingual Technologist

BEFORE #9

Objective: Director of Technology

Summary of Qualifications:
Director with over 15 years online systems strategic initiatives development experience excelled in leading products life cycle architecture design, on time deployment within budget constraints, achieving operational and fiscal excellence, skilled in outsourcing management. Startup CIO experience to establish technology organization from ground up, serving cross-function business objectives.

Major Accomplishments:

- Built high performance teams accountable for timely response to engineering, QA, and IT-business initiatives.
- Established and maintained effective working relationships with other divisions, corporate and community.
- Technology breakthrough with awards for e-Bonding and Nationwide Internet Yellow Pages products engineering.
- Streamlined product development processes to meet quality metrics and saved $14M for a $2B e-payment system.
- Secured $2M funding from e-Business client by turning around programs and under-running budget limit.
- Reconciled $20M revenue through e-Commerce and backend systems integration effort.
- Reduced 3 years backlog of Change Requests into 2 months within 6 months of resource management effort.

Skills

- Online transactions products architecture and design, concurrent projects life cycle planning and execution.
- Sales and marketing partnership in developing product strategies and revenue opportunities discovery process.

- Project scope, functional spec, risk, priority, resource allocation, problem resolutions, and time management.
- Forward-looking team-oriented leadership, excellent communication; deliver results on target to global customers.
- Strategic alliance with ASP, ISP, and systems integrators. Outsource contract negotiation, P&L accountability.

Experience

Principal Consultant
EBizsw Consulting, Palo Alto, CA   2002–Present

- Web publishing products roadmap strategy, products releases, scope of changes planning and execution.
- Technology blueprints, budgets/staff planning, Pre-Sales/Post-Sales support, resources/priority management.
- Funding strategy formulation, presentation to the top tier investors resulting $5M funding commitment.
- Consulted small to mid-sized businesses to penetrate Internet sales channels and gained market shares by 200%.

Director, Online Technology
Electronic Arts, Redwood Shores, CA   2000–2002

- Directed business intelligent systems life cycle with personnel, budgetary, and global customers responsibilities.
- Managed web platform development and integration with business partners—AOL and MSN.
- Directed a 200+ web server farm infrastructure with 30+ interactive on-line engineering capabilities (applications).
- End-to-end construction of EAWorld to consolidate software platforms from 200–300 studios with Oracle ERP, EDI, B2B & B2C, DataWarehouse, LDAP, North American Sales Account Management, and PeopleSoft—HRMS.

Technologies utilized—WebLogic, J2EE, COBRA, Sun Solaris, BroadVision, PeopleSoft, Oracle ERP, PlumTree portal, Verity, E-piphany, IIS, DCOM, MS Transaction Server, ASP, XML, JavaScript, VBScript, SQL, ADO, OLE DB, Oracle middleware, BusinessObject (OLAP), WebTrends, Remedy, ClearCase, ClearQuest (RUP).

Chief Information Officer
Kalyan Networks, San Jose, CA   2000

- Architect complex enterprise systems and its network strategy with directors in a 200+ staff fiber optics start-up.
- Built redundant and failure-proof IT infrastructure in compliance with Mayan Networks strategic growth plan for engineering offices located in Sunnyvale, San Jose, Phoenix, and Dallas.
- Strategic alliance with Uunet, GlobalCrossing, Polycom, and AristaSoft.
- Influenced layers of management team in synchronizing business processes for sales automation, account management, billing, finance, CRM, HRMS, and engineering systems platform development.

Technologies utilized—Selectica (product config), Webridge (WebPlatform), Clarify (CRM), JDEdwards (ERP), WebMethods, Active (middleware), Agile (MRP & ERP integration), Solectron/Celetrica (SCM & MRP interface).

Senior Engineering Management Staff
Qwest Communications (USWest), Denver, CO.   1993–1995,1996–1999

- Directed 20+ systems with 50+ engineering staff (offshore included) and 6+ managers across Network Center of Excellence and Customer Experience of Excellence. Large scaled business AI systems life cycle management.
- Led cross-carriers e-Bonding platform development to trim down systems turn-around time within nanosecond.
- Directed technology consortium effort among baby-bells for Nationwide Internet Yellow Pages development.
- Led Internet Yellow Pages knowledge search engine end-to-end product engineering and conversion to NSAPI.
- Directed Ariba systems integration for a $2B procurement org to streamline products engineering processes.
- Evaluated WebLogic and WebSphere for the next generation of EAI platform.

Technologies utilized—WebLogic, WebSphere, DCE, Sybase Replication server, Oracle, AI engine, Java, C/C++, CORBA, MQSeries, Retix, Enterprise Access protocol, gateway servers, Ariba, XML, Tuxedo, BlueStone, Crystal, Actuate, S-Designer, RogueWave, Jaguar, PowerBuilder, HP OpenView, LoadRunner, Purify, Rational Dev Suite.

Senior Product & QA Management Consultant
Microsoft EBPP (First Data Corporation), Denver, CO.   1995–1996

End-to-end product development life cycle management from ground zero to meet IRS deadline and quality metrics.
Microsoft EBPP—Electronic Bill Presentment and Payment acquired this $2B corporate tax-dial-in system.

Technologies utilized—EDI, SmallTalk VisualAge, VB, IVR, DB2 replication server and StorageTech Iceberg.

Software Engineering & QA Management Staff
IBM Informix (UniData), Denver, CO.   1991–1993

Developed API library and quality programs for the next generation of Objective Database distributed systems. Instituted a repeatable and predicable product release process for the consistency of software quality.

Technologies utilized—Transaction engine & ODBMS/RDBMS API (in C/C++) development

Software Consultant—Wireless Products Suite
McKesson (Clinicom), Boulder, CO.   1989–1991

Large-scale touch screen real time ICU CliniCare medical device and RF embedded systems development. Applications included Electronic Patient Charting and Notification of Vital Signs using wireless technology.

Technologies utilized—Oracle/C, IBM RS6000, TouchScreen firmware, RF embedded device, real time systems

Other Experience
Many years experience as business technology consultant across industries.

Education

Master of Science—Information Systems, University of Colorado. This degree consists of 30 semester hours in Computer Science and 21 in MBA. Earned the Graduate Dean's Scholarship Award.

Bachelor of Arts, National Central University, Taiwan.

Oracle Certified Professional
Java Certificate

Awards

- Earned a Certificate of Recognition from the president of Qwest **Client Management** for the team effort to **establish Electronic Bonding** between Qwest and long distance carriers (ATT, MCI, Sprint) via. MEDIACC project.
- Earned recognition from Executive Senior Director of **E-Business** by quickly **turning around multiple projects**, which were in jeopardy, and transforming them to become **corporate Revenue Assurance program** for Qwest.
- Earned recognition from VP of Internet Group in establishing AtHand.com National Internet Yellow Pages site, the **technology consortium effort** among SBC, AmeriTech, BellSouth and Qwest. This technology was licensed to Boeing and partnership with MSNBC.
- Earned *Halcyon* group award for establishing the fastest, most **robust search engine** and obtaining the most traffic (3 million hits per week), the highest award any team could receive from a customer.

Earned recognition from VP of **Direct Payment Systems** from First Data Corp by delivering IRS-IVR project **on time and meeting quality metrics.**

Comments: For someone pursuing a director's position, this very long résumé must show a higher degree of business savvy. It is dripping with technical gobbledygook that makes this person look more as a hands-on professional than as someone who can lead teams and marshal business vision. It also does not show stories of how collaborating with customers and those in marketing, this person can mobilize her technology savvy to generate exciting new products. The long résumé is full of assignments, with no specific thread of leadership capabilities.

Naomi Wang   (000) 555-0000:   email@email.com

AFTER #9

CAREER OBJECTIVE:

A position in a high-tech company responsible for **leading strategic technology initiatives** and providing overall vision to take the organization to new levels of performance in markets, customer loyalty, and team energy

EXPERIENCE SUMMARY:

Four years most recently in a variety of leadership positions shepherding new products, technologies and service concepts; previous five years heading an R&D organization of crack technologists delivering cutting-edge consumer and industrial products in the communications and information domains; additional experience includes collaborating with strategic customers and marketing teams to identify how emerging technologies can help customers to increase their overall experience and value creation.

UNIQUE SKILLS:

- **Technology Breadth:** Develop highly creative solutions that integrate diverse technologies with flexible capabilities. Maintain balance between technology risks and mature functionalities.

- **Customer Ally:** Collaborate with key customers and develop insights about their emerging needs. Anticipate functionality and capability and integrate them into emerging products.

- **Effective Teaming:** Organize teams both in real and virtual forms and lead them across cultural and functional boundaries. Identify issues that can hamper development and deliver exceptional results.

- **Masterminding Innovation:** Identify the crux and mobilize resources to generate innovative solutions that transcend technology and process limitations. Quickly achieve practicable solutions.

- **Systems Perspective:** Contextualize presented problems with broad solution possibilities and develop the most effective systems solution. Continually improve solutions with innovative thinking.

PROFESSIONAL EXPERIENCE

eBiz Systems Solutions, Santa Clara, CA   2002–Current
Principal Architect
Overall responsibilities for developing innovative software solutions to enhance business infrastructure

- Identified key technology infrastructure needs for medium-to-small businesses and developed a five-year product roadmap.

- Developed funding strategy for this start-up and organized an overall plan to make the $5 million second round funding viable. Presented to VCs and other decision makers resulting in full funding.

- Identified key product features for the first generation products and verified functionality with potential customers and bets sites. Improved features through innovative prototyping methodology.

- Collaborated with potential customer and client businesses and developed a plan for selling current offerings. Immediate interest from Innovators and Early Adopters resulted in 200% jump in demand.

Electronic Arts, Redwood Shores, CA   2000–2002
Director, Technology
Work with creative studios and clients to deliver state-of-the art products and define technology direction.

- Led web platform development and integration with alliances and partners with specific focus on their technology needs in the 3–5 year timeframe. Developed collaborative visions for exciting future.

- Organized business intelligent systems to project first-rate capability predicting future platforms.

Kalyan Networks, San Jose, CA   2000
Chief Information Officer
Responsible for overall technology direction of this 200 people start-up

- Architected and led implementation complex enterprise and network platform that defined future of Internetworking. Shepherded entire platform development from inception to beta delivery for five target customer sites on time within one year.

- Developed strategic technology alliances with five key partners who shared development resources and commitment to implement first prototypes.

Quest Communications, Denver CO   1993–1996
Engineering Director
Responsible for overall technical direction of a group that involved 75 highly technical personnel, including off shoring resources; developed AI systems for life cycle costs of complex infrastructure

- Pioneered an effort to develop a novel platform that resulted in system turnaround time using an e-bonding concept from microseconds to nanoseconds for cross-carrier use. An industry first.
- Led a technology consortium initiative among baby bells for Nationwide Internet Yellow pages
- Evaluated new and emerging tools and technologies for the next generation of EAI platforms, which resulted in Quest being seen as the industry leader in a fiercely competitive market.

First Data Corporation (Acquired by Microsoft)   1995
Staff Consultant
As a technical expert oversaw entire technical architecture for this IRS-facing Tax collection and electronic bill presentment service, an IRS first

- Collaborated with IRS experts to define the most rigorous standards for a bill presentment and payment interface. Identified vulnerabilities that even IRS had not foreseen and defined strategies to overcome system challenges. The standard was accepted as the de facto interface for all IRS transactions.
- Developed product life-cycle guidelines and implemented quality and functional standards for all future product families.
- Developed a state version of the federal interface and got it through five different state agencies.

IBM   Prior–1995
Denver Mining Technologies, Inc.
Worked as technical staff at these companies to develop, architect, test, QA and deliver a variety of software-based systems solutions for business use.

EDUCATION
MS Information Systems and Computer Science, University of Colorado, Denver, CO

CERTIFICATIONS/AWARDS
- A variety of certifications, including Oracle, Java, OOP, C++
- Over a dozen awards for outstanding contributions to various employers throughout the career

John Muir
Alexander Ct.
Santa Clara, CA 95051
(000) 555-0000:   email@email.com

BEFORE #10

"ONE MAN WRECKING TEAM"

Multitalented engineer with R&D background seeking leadership position as a consultant or within a consultant company to manage dream of changing the computer industry increasing the serviceability of computer products.

SUMMARY OF QUALIFICATIONS

Highly visionary individual with electrical and mechanical background rooted deeply in product development. Eye for improving products. Ear for customer needs. Passion to succeed. Have a patent for verifying products in warranty reducing time from 3 months or more to 5 days and saving $1.4M. Delivered a well-written report detailing the cost savings by reducing product design complexity. Strong communication, interpersonal and presentation skills. Never afraid to learn, enjoy people.

- Pragmatic approach to problem solving
- Analyze problems quickly and efficiently
- Crave ripping apart products
- Reliable, accountable and responsible

PROFESSIONAL EXPERIENCE

Hewlett-Packard Company, Cupertino, CA   1998 to Present
Customer Support R&D—Hardware Design Engineer
Assigned to notebook product division with goal to reduce in-warranty support costs and improve product quality. Developed and maintained ongoing 12-month product supportability project roadmap aligned with product roadmaps. Analyzed product failures improving diagnostic releases. Evaluated released notebook products recommending new product design improvements. Effectively managed global diagnostics project team. Delivered analysis and evaluation presentations

- Successfully influenced from concept to manufacturing release "hidden partition diagnostics" shipped on the fixed disk drive of every notebook since 1999 realizing a 25% reduction in the No Trouble Found (NTF) rate, increasing access for repair personnel and customers by 100%, and setting the standard for future products in other product divisions.

- Effectively released to manufacturing an on-board warranty tracking mechanism—the now de facto-standard for tracking warranty start date—thereby improving accuracy of verifying products in warranty from 3 months to 5 days saving $1.4M and decreasing the reliance on the corporate data base.

- Delivered a very detailed product case study, called by R&D managers "deep, detailed and thorough" raising awareness by showing that products with lower complexity and higher serviceability reduce post release warranty costs.

- Improved efficiency of the product evaluation process by designing and implementing Visual Basic for Applications forms thereby reducing complexity and saving time to complete.

- Setup a process to convinced R&D that using the product evaluations measuring released products could model and predict the product serviceability during design predicting support costs. Used predictive modeling in product definition documentation for product design vendors. Set precedence for use of product evaluation process.

SIEMENS COMMUNICATIONS (formerly ROLM), Santa Clara, CA
1981–1998

Development-Firmware Engineer/Hardware Engineer/Team Leader
Hardware design engineer, strong technical skills and a long history in Development with experiences ranging from hardware and software design—including embedded firmware—hardware sustaining and circuit design simulation; Possess strong sustaining and debugging skills with released hardware and software as well as drafting Engineering Change Orders and releasing bug fixes for engineering releases, as well as provided training to second level service personnel. Experienced using In-Circuit Emulators, logic analyzers, oscilloscopes and all styles of analog and digital meters.

- Created, managed and delivered project schedule. Team lead for project team driving project status, updates and schedule changes. Adapted development environment for embedded design. Implemented memory-map modifications per Hardware External Reference Specification. Completed code modifications required. Managed junior engineer Delivered completed module to alpha and beta test then to manufacturing. Represented Development in Product Release and Business Team meetings as the Release Engineer. Successfully released hardware diagnostics, communications protocol stack and applications modules meeting scheduled product ship dates.

John Muir (000) 555-3456 Page 3

- Wrote functional, architectural and design specifications. Updated and finalized ISO 9000 suite of documents. Co-designed, -implemented, -simulated and -tested diagnostics and communications modules in C and assembly language for embedded-based boards. Persisted through alpha, beta and manufacturing release process, tracking and fixing reported bugs and managing releases to entities thereof. Released to manufacturing with no bugs on time.

- Participated in document review meetings held up to three times per week while adhering to current project schedule commitment. Worked abnormal hours to maintain current project schedules. Found ways to debug and verify failures quicker than usual. Proficiently modified code base, recompiled and released new firmware for hardware quickly.

- Delivered multi-layered printed circuit cards plans on time. Provided plans for hardware design engineers to deliver per committed schedule.

- Improved quality of OEM devices through collaboration with vendors. Qualified OEM assemblies by testing OEM devices connected to in-house equipment.

EDUCATION/TRAINING

- **University of California Santa Cruz Extension**—C Programming I, C Programming II.

- **Stanford University**—CS110—Microcomputer Architecture & assembly language programming, CS106A—Programming Abstractions.

- **San Jose State University**—Engineering and General Education courses toward BSEE major

- **West Valley College**—Electronic Technician Certificate

AWARDS AND RECOGNITION

- Service ID Patent for HP Notebooks

- ROLM PhoneMail 10th Anniversary Recognition

- Save ROLM 1 Million Dollars Award

- 3270 CTPA (Coax to Twisted-Pair Adapter)/TMS320C31 Firmware Diagnostics Award

---

Comments: This wordy résumé fails to show how this individual can think differently and create designs that are highly differentiated. Despite its extensive write-up it fails to focus on specific stories of how this individual accomplished the extraordinary results that he implies. Overall, this is a weak résumé.

MASTERMINDING INNOVATION
John Muir Alexander Ct. Santa Clara CA 95051 (000) 555-0000: email@email.com

AFTER #10

CAREER OBJECTIVE:
Consulting Engineer responsibility for new product designs, which decrease complexity, increase overall intuitiveness, including serviceability, and setting a standard for greater customer value impact and manufacturing ease.

EXPERIENCE SUMMARY:
Over four years in product development incorporating ongoing enhancements based on continuous customer and user feedback, including service failure patterns. Manage complex product and project roadmaps to synchronize release portfolios and capture enhanced revenue streams. Concurrently managed product life cycles to enhance market presence/competitiveness of critical technology products.

UNIQUE SKILLS:

- **Innovate, Influence, And Implement:** Lead innovations on products to create competitive advantage and deliver greater value to existing and potential users, incorporating ongoing learning from failure patterns and customer feedback. Collaborate with customer and other constituencies to realize a continuously enhanced design.

- **Serviceability Predictions:** Develop models to embody serviceability of emerging products based on existing field data on deployed products. Use this model to define innovative avenues to capture service contracts with potential customers.

- **Process Improvements:** Identify and then standardize critical processes that drive business metrics and customer perceptions and define ways to implement these in a streamlined way.

- **Customer Voice:** Collect customer and support personnel feedback in face-to-face meetings and teleconferences. Deliver feedback to new product generation teams and ascertain learning is implemented.

- Leading Teams: Lead global cross-functional teams to successfully complete products that define new market space in a highly competitive environment with aggressive project goals.

John Muir Santa Clara CA 95051   (000) 555-0000: email@email.com Page 2/4

PROFESSIONAL EXPERIENCE:
Hewlett-Packard Company, Cupertino, CA 1998 to Present
CUSTOMER SUPPORT R&D—HARDWARE DESIGN ENGINEER

Deployed within notebook computer product division in order to contribute to reduced warranty and support cost, and improve product quality using co-developed out-of-box diagnostic service tools and design influence to address emerging products and installed base.

- **Start-of-Life Indicator**—Eliminated uncertainty and confusion on product warranty claims stemming from lack of verifiable "start of life" data. Invented and patented a unique "start-of-life indicator, which recorded the first instance of actual customer use, without regard to how long the product was in transit and storage prior to customer delivery. This fail-safe innovation resulted in eliminating subjective guesswork as to warranty duration, narrowing the "start-of-life to within five days (a 19-fold decrease); estimated savings in warranty costs were over $1.4M in the first year alone for this product, in addition to decreased reliance on corporate database by 50%.

- **Serviceability Predictor**—Introduced a unique predictive modeling value measuring the intrinsic serviceability of emerging designs. Integrated into the product design cycle affecting product design documents, driving business metrics, changing customer perceptions.

- **Team Leader**—Led an effort to integrate different teams across global boundaries resulting in a coherent diagnostic package for emerging products. Formalized the overall diagnostic functionality package resulting in a consistent and highly effective final product, which reduced No-Trouble-Found rate by half within the first year.

- **Disk-Resident Diagnostics**—Lead innovation engineer delivering fixed disk drive resident diagnostics creating competitive advantage and greater value through product differentiation, causing 25 percent reduction for repaired products, increasing diagnostics availability by 100 percent, eliminating need for external media, established standard for delivered diagnostics on products saving over $3M in repair costs.

- **Process Improvements**—Identified need to capture and then communicate to product design teams serviceability data to help them understand the impact of serviceability on product life-cycle costs and eventual warranty liability. As a result, the new product requirements documents began incorporating serviceability parameters, which simplified ongoing designs and greatly reduced warranty costs. Projected savings for one million annual unit sales with $1B in revenues estimated savings: over $6M in reduced service costs.

- **Product Failure Reporting**—Proposed and pioneered an experiment to test actual use of automated diagnostic suite and discovered that fewer than 25% of shipped product is exercised at customer sites when failure occurred. This low rate impacted overall repair cycle, customer satisfaction, and service costs. Identified reasons and data to categorize opportunities for increasing diagnostic run rates. Final report presented to operating divisions clearly identified opportunities for improved penetration of diagnostics and methods for implementing increased customer participation in on-site troubleshooting.

- **Intuitive Products**—Established a process and implemented specific innovations resulting in product designs, which were highly user friendly and easy to maintain. These concepts were then reduced to practical designs, which then were filed as patent disclosures.

Siemens Communications (formerly ROLM), Santa Clara, CA   1981–1998
Development—Firmware Engineer/Hardware Engineer/Team Leader
Hardware Design Engineer, Team Leader and technician with strong analytical technical skills and a long experience in a development organization

- Led and participated on firmware teams for embedded design, involved in full development cycles by defining and implementing communications protocol stack and hardware diagnostics for a voice mail system interface card. While involved with company-wide document review process meetings affecting normal commitments and scheduling and with zero errors or defects successfully released firmware package remaining on schedule for product ship dates.

John Muir   Santa Clara CA 95051   (000) 555-0000:   email@email.com   Page 4/4

EDUCATION/TRAINING:
University of California Santa Cruz Extension—C Programming I and C Programming II
Stanford University: A variety of courses on computer architecture and data structures
San Jose State University—Engineering and General Education courses toward BSEE
West Valley College—Electronic Technician Certificate

AWARDS AND RECOGNITION:

- Service ID Patent for HP Notebooks
- TMS320C31 Firmware Diagnostics Award
- *"Saved ROLM One Million Dollars"* Award

Sally Gilford

Amber Ave, N., Sunnyvale CA 94086 (000) 555-0000:   email@email.com

SUMMARY

BEFORE #11

- Successful entrepreneur and President
- Proven ability to build organizations, attract and manage talent
- Track record of packaging services and market-driven needs
- Developed and implemented effective solutions for managing customer relationships, sales effectiveness, organization development.

PROFESSIONAL EXPERIENCE

1998–2002   Staffing Decisions International, Inc. (SDI)
A global consulting firm specializing in developing, leading, measuring and managing talent

Senior vice president and practice area leader—Organizational Solutions Group (1998–2001)

- Established new division by merging four practice areas into one, using new business model for SDI. Services included organizational effectiveness, customer-centered solutions, human capital strategy, sales effectiveness, and performance management.
- Led new leadership team responsible for developing intellectual property, training consultants, and achieving growth objectives.
- Implemented new consulting process and new business development process.
- Developed new business with clients and prospects.
- Consulted with clients on customer loyalty, organization diagnosis, and strategic account management.
- Key player on SDI's Operations Leadership Team, with responsibility for budgeting, strategic planning, marketing, growth planning. Consulted with SDI's executive committee on strategy issues.
- Identified and developed successor to assume leadership of the Organizational Solutions Group.

Senior vice president—Intellectual Property (IP) Management
(2001–2002)
- Established the firm's IP management function. Developed IP strategies in collaboration with practice area leaders. Prepared the firm's intellectual property for due diligence. Negotiated potential partnerships and examined new distribution channels. Designed a process to guide the firm's future investment in IP. Defined and documented the key points-of-view that differentiate the firm in the marketplace.

1990–1998 RI International, Inc. *(Acquired by Staffing Decisions International)*
Consulting firms dedicated to improving the way organizations manage business relationships with customers, employees, and other stakeholders.

President and co-founder
- Developed intellectual property including consulting models, diagnostic tools, training programs, measurement instruments; packaged services for client use.
- Developed new business with key clients; grew company to $4.3m annual revenue and 50 employees; hired, trained and developed consultants; established client services group to support consultants and clients; established international alliances.
- Established business systems, forecasting, financial reporting, marketing plans, and collateral.
- Positioned the company for sale; approached potential buyers, managed due diligence, participated in negotiation resulting in successful sale of the business to SDI in February, 1998.
- Integrated the company into SDI, retaining key employees.
- Co-authored <u>Management on trial: Bringing bottom-line accountability to business leadership</u>. McGraw-Hill (1994).

1986–1990 Global Information Services, a division of Global Computer Systems
Director of survey research
- Managed 40 client accounts, selling survey research services to executive-level clients.

- Developed methods for employee and customer surveys and market research programs; designed survey instruments with management steering committees; presented results and recommendations to executive teams.

EDUCATION

1986 Ph.D. Psychology, University of California, San Francisco, CA
1977 B.A. Psychology, Kansas State University, Manhattan, KS

CURRENT AFFILIATIONS

- Chair, Baxter College (KS) Board of Directors; Manhattan, KS past chair of presidential search committee; member of enrollment committee and investment committee.
- Bay Area Entrepreneur Award Panel, 2002.
- Outreach Board, Plymouth Congregational Church; Habitat for Humanity liaison.
- Board of Directors, New Foundations, Inc.
- EEAT, Volunteer of the Year (2000).
- Clinical assistant professor, Department of Psychology, University of California.

Comments: For someone who has such an impressive array of accomplishments, this résumé could be more focused on one specific area—customer loyalty creation—that this person claims. It is presented more as a past of the writer's career, than as a message of value creation in a specific area.

Sally Gilford Amber Ave, Sunnyvale, CA 94086 * (000) 555-0000: email@email.com

AFTER #11

CAREER OBJECTIVE: **A strategic position in a customer-centric organization** responsible for championing, driving, and delivering initiatives to transform and sustain **customer loyalty**

EXPERIENCE SUMMARY: Nearly ten years heading a major consulting practice in a pioneering organization that defined new paradigms in customer experience, customer-focused initiatives, and metrics that propel a customer-aligned business. Ten years in a variety of positions focused on market research, surveys, and customer satisfaction initiatives. Concurrent three years as a practice head of Intellectual Property management service in a global consulting organization.

UNIQUE SKILLS

- **Listening to Customers:** Identify ingenious approaches to discover customer experiences and methodize process to create organization-wide learning to capture this as a discipline.

- **Mobilizing Action:** Translate customer discovery into actions that transform customer experience. Develop organizational discipline to make customer experience a top priority.

- **Championing Initiatives:** Identify new initiatives that will transform organizational culture driven by market forces. Define simple and actionable practices that become habits.

- **Business Development:** Translate new ideas and concepts into bankable practices that can be marketed for revenues. Manage service life cycle by introducing derivatives.

- **Nurture Talent:** Recruit top talent and provide an environment for creativity, originality, and success. Mentor high-potential talent for aggressive development; challenge individuals

PROFESSIONAL EXPERIENCE

Chair Baxter College Board of Directors, Manhattan, KS   **2002–Current**
Provide overall leadership to the institution in general management, specifically to enrollment committee and the investment committee. During the past three years enrollment has risen steadily 12 percent each year (previous record was 3 percent); investment return with a radically revamped portfolio has yielded an annual net return of 9.4 percent, despite tanking economy and poor stock market performance.

Sally Gilford   (000) 555-0000:   <u>email@email.com</u>

Staffing Decisions International   2001–2002
Senior Vice President Intellectual Property (IP) Management
Established a formal process for SDI's IP, despite its rich history of pioneering work in seminal areas of human capital effectiveness in Industrial Psychology.

Established formal procedures for IP management and developed a structured process for identifying, controlling, managing, and exploiting intellectual property. Within one year unforeseen revenues due to IP licensing increased from nothing to over $2 million in just two areas (for annual revenues of $100 million and profits of $3 million, thus contributing nearly 100 percent of profits in the first year alone.
Designed a process for SDI's future investment in IP. Defined and documented the key point-of-view that differentiate SDI in the marketplace.

Senior Vice President, Practice Area Leader, Business Solutions Group 1998–2001

- Led a group of 30 professionals and support staff responsible for customer-centric solutions to enhance customer experience in a business and organization.

Established a new division after the RI/SDI merger by consolidating four distinct groups with diverse functional allegiances into a coherent services provider powerhouse. Within the first year of its full operation the new practice area exceeded projected billing rates by 23 percent by exploiting synergies, competitive blind spots, and aggressive business development.

- Penetrated new markets by aggressively promoting new practice area synergistically with existing marketing and sales efforts already in place. Without adding to sales overhead or marketing expenses, captured $2.5 million in additional billings that were over and above budgeted projections in the first year alone.

- Evangelized the customer centric culture, the sine qua non of the original RI business into the merged entity, resulting in steady increase in overall customer satisfaction scores and loyalty measures, not previously possible.

Sally Gilford   (000) 555-0000:   <u>email@email.com</u>

RI International, Inc.   **1990–1998**
President/Co-founder
- Overall leadership of a consulting organization that included recruiting, growing business into unpenetrated space, developing new offerings, and ensuring self-funded and aggressive growth.
- Co-authored and published (McGraw Hill) a major book that formed the basis of consulting practice and then expanded the concept to other areas of applicability. Developed and championed a concurrent platform that enabled organizations to build relationship-based culture inside out. Clients disillusioned with conventionality embraced this pioneering concept rapidly.
- Within five years grew company to 50 employees with 12 consultants located in five geographies, including overseas, and developed a business model that created self-sustained growth. Flexible service delivery model based on consultant capabilities provided for client engagements far deeper and broader than would have been possible with merely delivering the original concept.
- Established growth and control mechanisms that attracted top talent and fueled self-sustained growth, attracting many takeover attempts. Within five years reached $5M in annual billings.
- Prepared company for sale during its unprecedented growth rate, performed due diligence and negotiated, with other co-founders, final sale.
- Integrated company into parent (SDI), retaining key employees

Global Information Services (Div. of Global Computer Systems)   1986–1990
Director of Survey Research
- Overall responsibilities for developing survey instruments, managing client accounts, delivering result, and providing consulting inputs to clients
- Developed and managed 40 client accounts, selling survey research services to executives and then delivering results and action plans.
- Developed methods for employee and customer surveys and market research programs.
- Developed new methodology and framework, which was the foundation for RI International

Sally Gilford   (000) 555-0000:   email@email.com

EDUCATION
- B. A., Psychology, Kansas State University, Manhattan Kansas
- Ph.D., Psychology, University of California, Berkeley, CA

AFFILIATIONS/HONORS

Numerous volunteer and honorary positions in civic, political, and charitable organizations

Awarded honors and kudos for consistent contribution and service excellence

James Bower   (000) 555-0000:   email@email.com

Career Objective:

A **technical leadership position** in an entrepreneurial organization responsible for: Identifying customer needs to translate them into product requirements and work hard with cross-functional teams to meet customer-driven initiatives to achieve specific business goals. This would allow me to combine my ethics, and strong technical expertise with my MBA knowledge and skills.

Experience Summary:

Over fifteen years of progressive engineering experience with strong EMI/EMC/SI capability in all phases of design, mitigation, and testing with nearly two years of diversified management. Extensive experience with PCB and system design including schematic review, placement, route reviews, and signal integrity.

Professional Experience:

EMC Compliance Engineer: 1998–Present
Cisco Systems Inc., San Jose, California

- Design networking product from concept to final qualification to meet the EMC compliance requirements worldwide standards including NEBS certification.

- Responsible for Signal Integrity of the design. This includes IBIS validation, pre-layout, post-layout and Static Timing Analysis (STA).

- Led and mentor test engineers to provide quality testing and quality technical reports.

- Manage overall product from design, testing, verification, mitigation and qualification to provide better quality product and meet customer needs way before the FCS date.

- Cross-functional team collaboration with NPIE, ME, CE, and HWE to deliver high quality product with cost control.

- Received several Team Achievement Awards.

EMC Consultant: 1995–1998

EMC International Consulting, Phoenix, AZ

Engineering consulting in EMI/EMC design, mitigation, modification, and training for local companies.

Facility Manager: 1993–1995
DCX Engineering Inc., SLC, Utah
Managed Chalk Creek EMC facility in Coalville Utah. These duties consisted of site management, marketing, assisting customers with design problems and liaison with home office in California.

Senior EMC Engineer: 1993–1979
Unisys Corporation, Ann Arbor, MI
Designed and redesigned product development so they met EMC and ESD specifications. Created and updated the diagnostic software and other programs for test equipment. Maintained close liaison with design, manufacturing, product safety, production control, and purchasing
Recognized as employee of the month for completing a product on an extremely tight schedule.
Received special commendation work on a PC product line on time-release required "personal sacrifice."
Voluntarily wrote and updated software for automated test equipment in addition to regular duties. Created interactive software for testing that eliminated frustrations and reduced hours required by 40%.

Education:
MBA/Master of Business Administration, Pepperdine University, Malibu, CA
BSEE Santa Clara University, Santa Clara, CA, graduate coursework

Certificates of Completion:

- **MegaTest Lab.,** San Jose, California, completed three classes of High Speed, Signal Integrity and High Bandwidth Models.
- **NEBS Training Seminar,** San Jose, California, completed two days class by ITS.
- **University of Wisconsin,** Oshkosh, WI, Grounding & Shielding Electronic Systems Design.
- **University of California,** Berkeley, California, completed High Speed PCB and System Design.
- **R&B Enterprises,** Washington D.C., completed Microwave and Electromagnetic hazards course.
- **George Washington University,** Washington D.C., completed hazard RF and Electromagnetic radiation course.
- **Jim Smith Consulting,** San Jose, California, Grounding and Shielding.

Professional Development:
Leadership and team building skills, project management, communicating for results,
Visula, Alegro, Intercomm, Valor, Hyperlynx, Hotstage and FLOEMC software tools.

Comments: Looking at the Objective, the writer is trying to accomplish both business results (MBA) and technology leading. This can be a problem with the record of his accomplishments, which are all focused on testing and validation of complex systems. The experience does not show clear stories of leadership because they are presented in a task/responsibilities format.

PRODUCT INTEGRITY WIZ

James Bower   (000) 555-0000:   email@email.com

CAREER OBJECTIVE

A hands-on technical lead responsible for: overall **PCB and system design integrity,** including EMC/EMI, vendor qualification, manufacturability, regulatory and international compliance, component-, subsystem-, and system-level qualification; collaborating with technical development teams and outside partners to achieve time-to-market and cost goals.

AFTER #12

EXPERIENCE SUMMARY

Over fifteen years of progressive engineering experience with strong EMI/EMC capability in all phases of design, mitigation, and testing. Extensive experience, from PCB to systems designs, schematic review, placement, critical nets, routing rules, and signal integrity including pre-layout, post-layout and static timing analysis (STA); Collaborate with vendors on a variety of issues. Develop new alliances.

UNIQUE SKILLS

- **Early Collaboration:** Team-up with development engineers to identify early risk in EMC, test failures, manufacturability, and cost; develop strategies to minimize impact.

- **Practical Focus:** Develop quick means to verify design integrity without resorting to expensive testing/analysis to validate a concept before finalizing a major design.

- **Systems Thinking:** Approach all complex designs with systemic thinking to prevent downstream surprises and provide systems perspective to all component development.

- **Rapid Troubleshooting:** Rapidly converge on root causes of system failures and provide quick fixes/design improvements for tests completion and customers delight.

- **Meeting Commitments:** Plan to develop best means to achieve final deadlines, despite test and equipment failures, design surprises, and finger pointing. Provide leadership in.

- **Broad Perspective:** Go beyond immediate problems to see what can be done to improve outcomes with minimum resources and time. Devise ingenious solutions.

PROFESSIONAL EXPERIENCE

EMC Compliance Engineer: Cisco Systems Inc., San Jose California

1998–Present

Designing/managing Router line from concept to final EMC compliance

- During the introduction of the current Router (UBR 10012) EMC/EMI compliance testing revealed a failure in radiation testing. Preliminary analysis and course of action indicated possible board redesign, which would have required several weeks or new work and several months delay in product release. Using various diagnosing and sniffing techniques identified culprit and was able to continue testing with a simple shielded-cable modification, releasing product on time.

- Identified various deficiencies during testing and protected test and release schedule by devising simple yet permanent fixes to the Router.

Key words: Product management, cross-functional team efforts with NPIE, ME, CE, HWE, analysis, design, mitigation and qualification, technical reports to worldwide standards, NEBS, signal Integrity, IBIS validation, pre- & post-layout and Static Timing Analysis (STA).

EMC Consultant: EMC International Consulting Salt Lake City, Utah

1995–1998

Engineering consulting in EMI/EMC design, mitigation, compliance, modification/training

Successfully led entire test program that entailed initial marketing, collaborating with clients, understanding their products, and then devising appropriate tests to certify domestic and international compliance. Units tested were as diverse as commercial, medical, and industrial products, each with their own compliance requirements.

Facility Manager: DNB Engineering Inc., Salt Lake City, Utah   1993–1995

- Managed Chalk Creek EMC facility in Coalville Utah: Site management, marketing, assisting customers with design problems and liaison with home office in California.

- Marketed testing facility, designed tests, delivered final certification and reports to customers and clients with products ranging from commercial, medical, to industrial. Teamed-up with clients design teams to identify potential vulnerabilities of products and defining strategies for a "first-test-pass." This strategy resulted in many clients dropping DNB competitors.

- Increased within two years, overall business by over 40 percent, by first educating potential clients about preventive qualification testing and then collaborating with them to create a forward-looking roadmap for their emerging products.

Senior EMC Engineer: Unisys Corporation, Salt Lake City, Utah   Prior–1993
Designed products to meet EMC/ESD specifications in first pass; redesigned established and upgraded products for compliance. Created diagnostic software for test equipment.

- During FCC compliance testing of a new model PC, which was to be released for a major customer, one test failure caused entire PC design to be questioned. Modifications would have entailed time-consuming redesign and getting back in the FCC test queue, which was months. Quickly devised a change while still in test, resulting in full certification and with no loss of delivery date. Product sale (several million dollars) was protected, beating competitors.

EDUCATION:
MBA/Master of Business Administration, Santa Clara University, Santa Clara, CA
BS/EE Electrical Engineering, University of California, Berkeley, CA

PROFESSIONAL DEVELOPMENT: (CERTIFICATES)
James Test Lab., CA, High Speed, Signal Integrity and High Bandwidth Models
NEBS Training Seminar, San Jose, California, Completed two days class by ITS.
University of Missouri-Rolla, CA, Grounding & Shielding Electronic Systems/PCB Design
University of California, Berkeley California Completed High Speed PCB and System Design
R&B Enterprises, Washington D.C. Completed Microwave & Electromagnetic hazards course.
Chicago University, Chicago, IL Hazard RF and Electromagnetic radiation

SOFTWARE TOOLS: Visula, Aleegro, Intercomm, Valor, Hyperlynx and Hotstage software tools.

AWARDS/ACHIEVEMEMTS:
Several awards for outstanding performance, team work and for going "Above and Beyond" on most projects.
- Two citations from clients on delivery of project on time in demanding circumstances.
- Three published papers on EMC compliance in professional journals, one winning the "Best Paper Award."

Mary Volt

Hamilton Place• San Francisco, California 94114 •(000) 555-0000: email@email.com

BEFORE #13

OBJECTIVE

Sr. Marketing Manager position with a high tech or communications company responsible for: Identifying new market drivers and advanced technology offerings based on evolving customer needs, development of the business and marketing plans including, product positioning, pricing, promotional offerings and the tactical implementation of strategic marketing programs and value propositions to generate profitable revenue growth.

SUMMARY

17 years Experience in marketing, technical sales and business development for global telecommunication providers. Seasoned expertise in strategic market planning, research and financial analyses, new product introductions and program/offer management. Solid history of identifying new business opportunities, growing revenue and market shares. Concurrent 5 years experience converting customer requirements into product specifications, managing complex projects and aligning cross functional implementation plans. Fluent in French, Dutch, conversant in German

PROFESSIONAL EXPERIENCE

SBC COMMUNICATIONS, San Francisco, CA, 2003–2003
Sales Support Manager, 2003–2003 (contract)
Collaborated with sales teams on special projects, lead lists and data validation. Streamlined provisioning/billing and implementation of voice and data LD packages, ensuring booked sales translated into to billed revenue.
LUCENT TECHNOLOGIES, Milpitas, CA, 1998–2003
Business Development Manager, 2002–2003
Developed strategies and tactics to guide sales, marketing and business developments efforts for Lucent Messaging and new technology services. Led initiatives to secure profitable revenue generating opportunities with emerging Service Providers and company distribution channels. Established Web site, negotiated distribution contracts, facilitated technical product-training sessions and extended consultative support for optimal performance by distributors. Researched industry and market trends and monitored competitor's activities.

- Launched messaging products in partnership with distributors, generating $2.5 million dollars in revenues and volume purchase agreements of $3.5 million.

- Championed creative promotions and incentive programs to drive product penetration and revenue growth.

- Spearheaded successful negotiations of million-dollar multi-year maintenance agreement with key wireless account.

- Initiated new hardware and software proposals and process improvements, generating $3 million in existing expansions and new system growth.

Product Marketing Manager, 2000–2002
Directed revenue generation for the emerging Wireless Carrier Market. Oversaw business and market planning, developed and implemented marketing and training programs, and conceived pricing strategies to gain competitive advantage. Prepared sales forecasts and cost analysis. Led cross-functional teams in support of channels, new product development, proposals and bids. Completed financial, strategic and business case analyses to network configurations and customer market and technical specifications. Successfully managed P&L.

- Exceeded revenue expectations by spearheading implementation of innovative pricing strategy; displaced 16 competitors and generated over $11 million; $5 million over anticipated revenue target of $6.7 million.

- Boosted messaging-product revenues 74% in 2000 and 20% in 2001

- Closed deals with four new customers to generate additional $2.5 million in sales.

- Successfully introduced new hardware and software products through industry tradeshows and events as well as sales presentations and demonstrations with user groups, key decision makers and customers

- Planned and executed quarterly marketing campaigns, product roadmaps, value propositions and training programs for Lucent customers and sales teams; assessed programs for effectiveness and budget compliance.

Marketing Manager, Canadian Markets, 1998–1999

Drove market penetration by targeting previously untapped markets. Developed and implemented marketing strategies and related plans, established sales and marketing objectives, and prepared regional sales forecasts. Provided sales support, technical expertise and developed pricing proposals to successfully close deals. Increased revenue performance by creating customer specific product roadmaps and business cases.

- Implemented marketing initiatives to capture new accounts; exceeded annual revenue by 25%.

- Increased market penetration, positioning and sales through lucrative packaging strategies, product evolution and enhancements, and strategic market trials with major Canadian Service Providers.

- Secured first Unified Messaging beta with Bell Canada by maintaining competitive advantage.

PACIFIC BELL, San Francisco, CA,   1982–1996
Manager Sales Support, 1988–1996
Spearheaded all aspects of sales and marketing operations as well as project implementation of voice and data services for Financial Services and Major Business accounts across Northern California. Collaborated with customers to identify needs based on business environment, objectives and expectations. Developed customized, solution-based plans tailored to identified needs. Grew sales by solidifying relationships with key decision makers and providing responsive pre-and post-sales support to customers. Directed multi-functional teams comprised of engineers, technical and sales, including allocating resources and facilitating vendor negotiations, to coordinate project installation.

- Implemented sales plans and tactics resulting in $6 million in annual revenues.

- Exceeded revenue goals 25% annually by gaining confidence of customer base to further penetrate existing accounts while serving as Sales Support Manager.

- Promoted to **Market Segment Planner,** 1984; directed in-depth market research and industry analysis as well as created strategic market plans leading to 20% increase in market penetration within financial services and insurance industries.

- Initially hired as **Marketing Manager,** International Residence Market, 1982; integrated results of competitor and market analysis to develop marketing communications plans and tactics as well as revamping marketing/brand management programs to attain 23% revenue increase.

Education and Credentials:
   MBA Degree in Marketing, University of San Francisco, San Francisco, CA
   BS Degree in Business Administration—University of Brussels, Brussels, Belgium

Professional Development Coursework:
Certificate: Internet Marketing, DCI Sales Force Automation Conference, 1997
Courses: On-line Marketing, Strategic Thinking, U.C. Berkeley, Berkeley, CA, 1997

Professional Associations
Silicon Valley American Marketing Association; Woman in Telecommunications, SVC Wireless Association

---

Comments: This résumé's author has much to crow about. And yet, the résumé lacks focus, presentation, and impact. One reason for this weakness is the presentation that strays away from the writer's strategic focus and an ability to capture new customers through her unique skills to marshal synergies. The experience is presented in a task/responsibilities format, making it difficult for the reader to understand the dept her leadership abilities. It goes back to far without adding any value to her cause, making it difficult for someone to dismiss her for being "too experienced." For someone in marketing, even just the format needs to be more compelling!

Mary Volt Hamilton Place• San Francisco, CA 94114 •(000) 555-0000: email@email.com

AFTER #13

CAREER OBJECTIVE

A position in **strategic marketing** in a high-tech or telecommunications company responsible for developing imaginative initiatives to capture new market space, brand growth, and then providing leadership to execute these initiatives and achieve unparalleled results. Pilot new initiatives, develop penetration strategies and expand in European geographies.

EXPERIENCE SUMMARY

Over 15 years in marketing, consultative sales, and business development for global telecommunication leaders. Demonstrated expertise in strategic market planning, research, and financial analyses, new product introductions and program/offer management. Unparalleled track record of marketing innovation, strategically identifying opportunities, preempting and displacing competitors to capture market share and presence. Over five years developing strategic customers and forging new alliances

UNIQUE SKILLS:

➢ **Customer Discovery:** Collaborate with customers and identify their articulated and unarticulated needs to strategically translate them into revenue streams. Develop forward-looking plans.

➢ **Technology Roadmaps:** Team-up with key internal resources and architect novel solutions to address customers' long-term business needs. Develop cost of ownership models based on deep insights.

➢ **Collaborative teaming:** Forge alliances with inside resources, suppliers, service providers, and customers to identify creative integrated solutions for emerging needs. Cement alliances.

➢ **Strategic Initiatives:** Devise innovative approaches to identify non-obvious opportunities. Pursue instinctive insights to quickly drive from contact to contract, often displacing incumbents.

➢ **Ideas translation:** Translate visionary ideas into practicable initiatives, generating revenues, loyal customer base, and market leadership. Constantly innovate to preempt competitive forays.

Mary Volt   (000) 555-0000:   email@email.com   Page 2/4

PROFESSIONAL EXPERIENCE:

Silicon Valley Marketing Association,   2003–Present
Provide leadership to expand presence, develop communication campaigns
for brand reach.

SBC Communications, San Francisco, CA,   2003
Sales Support Manager,
Collaborated with sales teams on projects, lead lists and data validation.
Streamlined provisioning/billing and implementation of voice and data LD
packages, ensuring booked sales translated into to billed revenue. Within
months, eliminated billing backlog.

Lucent Technologies, Milpitas, CA,   1998–2003
Business Development Manager,   2002–2003
  Strategically guided sales, marketing and business development for messaging and new technology services during a difficult economy. Led critical and
novel initiatives to secure profitable revenue-generating opportunities with
emerging Service Providers and channels.

- During the difficult period of drastic cutbacks and nose-diving revenues,
  championed a novel initiative to boost sales. Identified a new revenue
  source through existing channels to tap into small businesses. In addition
  to capturing defected customers, captured $2.5 M in revenues and $3.5
  M in service agreements within six months, displacing incumbents.

- Segmenting existing market, championed creative promotions and
  incentive programs to drive product penetration, resulting in 15%
  immediate revenue growth. Initiative was a Lucent first.

- A major account was dissatisfied because of poor service response.
  Investigated total cost to client, recommending an alternate service
  package. Client signed up for a $3 M contract for an
  SLA. Resulting experience substantially boosted client satisfaction scores.

- Initiated new hardware and software proposals and process improvements, generating $3 M in existing expansions and new system growth
  across multiple accounts, despite cutbacks.

Product Marketing Manager,   2000–2002
Directed revenue generation for the emerging Wireless Carrier Market. Spearheaded initiatives.

- Exceeded revenue expectations by spearheading innovative pricing strategy; displaced 16 competitors, including a low-cost leader, and generated over $11 M; $5 M in excess of budget.
- Boosted messaging-product revenues 74% in 2000 alone, through innovative product bundling.

Marketing Manager, Canadian Markets,   1998–1999
Drove market penetration by strategically targeting untapped markets. Developed product roadmaps.

- Implemented marketing initiatives to capture new accounts; exceeded revenue target by 25%.
- Increased market penetration, positioning and sales through lucrative packaging strategies, product evolution and enhancements, and strategic market trials with major Canadian ISPs.
- Secured first Unified Messaging beta with Bell Canada by maintaining competitive advantage.

PACIFIC BELL, San Francisco, CA,   1989 and Prior
Manager Sales Support,
Spearheaded sales and marketing operations and project implementation of voice and data services.

- Transformed company's image from a stodgy telephony service provider to an agile and savvy data services provider by aggressively campaigning across a broad constituency and media. Within a year boosted sales 25% to $40M with ongoing increase. Extended brand reach and expanded brand perception as verified through focus groups.
- Exceeded revenue goals 25% annually by gaining confidence of customer base to further penetrate existing accounts while serving as Sales Support Manager.
- As a market segment planner, led an initiative to research and analyze financial and insurance industries. Developed strategic plan, resulting in 20% increase in penetration with first year.

Mary Volt   (000) 555-0000:   email@email.com   Page 4/4

TECHNOLOGY SKILLS:
VoIP, Packet Services, Voice and Data, Unified messaging servers (SS7), Location-based services,

EDUCATION/PROFESSIONAL DEVELOPMENT

- **MBA in Marketing,** University of San Francisco, San Francisco, CA
- **BS in Business Administration**—University of Brussels, Brussels, Belgium
- **Certificate:** Internet Marketing, DCI Sales Force Automation Conference, 1997
- **Courses:** On-line Marketing, Strategic Thinking, U.C. Berkeley, CA, 1997

PROFESSIONAL ASSOCIATIONS
Silicon Valley American Marketing Association; Woman in Telecommunications, SVC Wireless Assn.

LANGUAGES:
French, German, Dutch

ROBERT MYLO

Ness Road	(952)555-0000 Office
Bloomington, MN 55437	(952) 555-0001 Cell

email@email.com

PROFILE

Innovative **Customer Focused Leader** with extensive experience in healthcare, consulting and manufacturing industries. Has the proven ability to deliver results that exceed expectations while increasing the quality and timeliness of processes and adding customer value. Strengths include:

- Relationship building
- Facilitation of change
- Coordination of interaction between multiple functions with differing objectives
- Creating an environment of follow through, accountability and action taking
- Identifying and implementing people/process improvements
- "Hands on" style

CAREER HIGHLIGHTS

Relationship Building

- Identified key decision makers within an account and quickly determined their specific needs to ensure exceeding their expectations.
- Transformed transactional business relationships into "trusted advisor" status.
- Nurtured relationships with each account to insure account control and customer satisfaction.
- Partnered with other organizations to insure customer satisfaction with contracted service delivery.
- Customized relationship management processes to meet specific client needs. Trained clients to administer the processes and presented results to key executives.
- Generated a network of sources for prospects and market input.

Customer Service/Sales Orientation

- Improved client effectiveness in business development, relationship management, and organizational activities.

- Prospected and built new client relationships resulting in an additional $3 M in revenue.

- Involved clients in action planning for organizational improvement that focused on creating committed customers and employees.

- Established and executed the original business plan for an emerging business

- Transformed a languishing start up business by creatively increasing revenue from $2,000/month to $75,000/month.

- Increased revenue and client retention by developing and supporting major accounts for Employee Assistance and Health Promotion Services.

- Enhanced customer satisfaction through timely and complete contract implementation.

- Developed and administered quality and customer satisfaction standards for the entire company.

Leadership/Management

- Led a group of 26 professionals to higher levels of effectiveness by clarifying processes, improving systems, engaging employees and improving accountability. Quickly changed that organization into a responsive group that embraced quality and follow through.

- Mentored a team of biz-dev consultants that focused on acquiring and retaining clients.

- Coached and developed seven account managers and four Client Services department managers.

- Created a new organization to support sales and marketing efforts of a division "spun off" from a large corporation.

Change Facilitation

- Led the transition from an independent operating company to a support function serving a larger organization during the SDI acquisition.

- Contributed to product development of SDI/RI's product line.

- Enhanced the Contracts Department's overall operating efficiency though process improvements.

- Reduced project costs through organizational and process improvements.

- Developed and implemented processes and procedures for order management.

WORK HISTORY

STAFFING DECISIONS INTERNATIONAL, (SDI) St. Paul, MN 1999–2004
(Formerly RI International)
Director of Client Services and National Accounts

RI INTERNATIONAL, St. Paul, MN (Currently an SDI company) 1995–1999
Senior Consultant

NATIONAL HEALTHCLAIMS CORPORATION, Minneapolis, MN 1990–1994
Vice President, Sales & Marketing

HAZMAT SERVICES, INC., Minneapolis, MN   1989–1990
Program Manager

ETA SYSTEMS, INC, St. Paul, MN   1985–1989
Director, Customer Support (1987–1989)
Manager, Sales Operations (1985–1987)

UNIVERSAL DATA CORPORATION, Minneapolis, MN   1977–1984
Regional Manager of Administration & Contracts   1980–1984
Manager Marketing Sales Administration   1977–1979

EDUCATION

Kansas State University-Manhattan, KS
Bachelor of Arts in Economics and Political Science

Comments: To a casual reader, the writer's customer-relationship-development talent appears secondary to his selling, and operational skills, thus creating confusion in reader's mind. The experiences are narrated in a transactional format of task/responsibilities, making it difficult for the reader to interpret the writer's talents in customer development areas.

ROBERT MYLO

Ness Road   (952) 555-0000 Office
Bloomington, MN 55437   (952) 555-0001 Cell
                    robertmylo@mn.rr.com
                                              AFTER #14

PROFILE

An innovative, hands-on **Customer Advocate,** who has transformed businesses by how customers are managed. Extensive experience in healthcare, consulting and manufacturing industries. Proven ability delivering results that
consistently exceed expectations, while increasing process quality and timeliness and adding unprecedented customer value. Strengths include:

- Identifying key relationships, alliances, and business partnerships
- Nurturing strategic relationships and translating them into highly prof-
  itable revenue streams
- Championing Strategic change and its facilitation
- Catalyzing interactions between multiple functions to create alignment.
- Creating and establishing an environment of accountability and cus-
  tomer-centric action
- Identifying and implementing relentless people/process improvements

CAREER HIGHLIGHTS

RELATIONSHIP BUILDING

- For an established account that was steadily declining, identified key
  decision makers and quickly determined their specific experiences to
  identify changes, increasing revenues within months.
- For a client, a financial institution, transformed a languishing relationship into a major account, vaulting the relationship into a Trusted
  Advisor status. Within a year client increased its major-account participation by 24 percent (previously no growth) as a result
- Transformed relationships with tier-one and tier-two accounts by
  implementing disciplined segmentation and differentiation. Nurtured
  relationship to insure account control and customer satisfaction, even
  for tier-three accounts. Results: Overall billings increased 21% annually.
- Identified partnerships that helped increase penetration in existing
  accounts and insured client business growth with contracted service
  delivery. Result: Increased penetration in existing clients.

ROBERT MYLO (952) 555-0000 (952) 555-0001 Cell; email@email.com Page 2/3

- Extended applicability of existing consulting processes to meet specific client needs. Resulting engagement transformed client's business, significantly increasing its revenues. New process became model for tier-one clients throughout the company.

CUSTOMER SERVICE/SALES FOCUS

- For a $5M annual business, identified that its clients were not contacted routinely to uncover their ongoing needs. Reenergized languishing accounts with new offerings. Mobilized the account and product development teams to capture new business and within two years increases sales 30% and customer loyalty 23 points (from 64 to 87), overall, in a down economy.
- Prospected/built new client relationships, resulting in $3 M in revenues within first two years.
- Involved clients in action planning, which went well beyond the scope of original engagements. This resulted in client-wide organizational improvement that focused on creating committed customers and employees. Result: Established clients routinely engaged services beyond originally envisioned, resulting in 15% growth beyond what was originally possible.
- Transformed a languishing start up by increasing revenue from $2,000 to $75,000/month by creative marketing, promotions, and incentives.
- Increased revenue and client retention by developing and supporting major accounts for Employee Assistance and Health Promotion Services.
- Developed and administered quality and customer satisfaction standards for the entire company.

LEADERSHIP/MANAGEMENT

- Led a staff of 26 to higher levels of effectiveness by clarifying processes, improving systems, engaging employees and establishing accountabilities. Quickly changed that organization into a responsive group that embraced quality and follow-up. Customer loyalty increased 21 percent.
- Mentored business development consultant team focused on acquiring and retaining clients.

ROBERT MYLO (952) 555-0000 (952) 555-0001 Cell; email@email.com Page 3/3

- Coached and mentored seven account managers and four department managers
- Created a new organization to support "spun-off "division's sales/marketing

CHANGE FACILITATION

- Led the transition from an independent operating company to a support function serving a larger organization during the RI/SDI acquisition, without impacting client services, and seamlessly
- Contributed to product development of SDI/RI's product line, enhancing and expanding offerings.
- Enhanced the Contracts Department's overall operating efficiency though process improvements
- Reduced project costs through process improvements, 15% annually three years running

EMPLOYER CHRONOLOGY

Staffing Decisions International, St. Paul, MN (Formerly RI International) **Director of Client Services and National Accounts**	1999–2004
RI INTERNATIONAL, St. Paul, MN (Currently a SDI company) Senior Consultant	1995–1999
NATIONAL HEALTHCLAIMS CORPORATION, Minneapolis, MN Vice President, Sales & Marketing	1990–1994
HAZMAT SERVICES, INC., Minneapolis, MN Program Manager	1989–1990
ETA SYSTEMS, INC, St. Paul, MN Director, Customer Support	1985–1989
UNIVERSAL DATA CORPORATION, Minneapolis, MN Regional Manager of Administration & Contracts	1977–1984 1980–1984

EDUCATION

Kansas State University, Manhattan, KS
Bachelor of Arts in Economics and Political Science

Ram Ratan
Shicks Drive
Fremont, CA 94555
(000) 555-0000:   email@email.com

BEFORE #15

Objective: Financial management position that utilizes my skills in developing the financial planning, cost controlling, compliance with statutory reporting and to be a strategic advisor and team member.

Experience Summary: Over ten years of progressive and diversified financial management experience, including controllership experience in high performing financial driven and competitive manufacturing environment. Performed strategic analysis to determine core competencies of company and provided recommendation to the division president, and corporate controller. Managed finance department and oversee all financial transactions for integrity and compliance. Trained management personnel in financial policy and procedure to ensure operation compliance with statutory regulations, corporate guidelines and meeting operating objectives.

Professional Experience:

Signal Technology Corporation, California Operation
Crane Aerospace & Electronics Division

Director of Finance/Division Controller   1999–March 2004

- In conjunction with the division president, developed and presented the strategic and annual operating plan, rolling forecast and division's monthly operating reviews to corporate executives.
- Anticipated financial challenges and prepared contingency plan.
- Optimized profit, cash flow and achieved corporate goals and motivated management to reduce costs, and took the action necessary to achieve the business plan.
- Performed due diligence support and provided accounting guidance in merger and consolidation of business unit.
- Oversee all of the division's financial transactions ensuring its integrity and compliance to corporate guidelines and GAAP
- Reviewed major pricing proposals and provided investment recommendations.

- Interfaced with external auditor to identify, review and resolve audit issues.
- Prepared and presented financial performance reports to senior management. Supplemented the corporate 10-Q and 10-K filing regarding division performance.
- Developed, implemented and monitored internal controls to safeguard company assets.
- Participated in implementing Kaizen, Lean initiatives and OpEx metrics.
- Developed a loyal, effective finance and IT staff of six and keep them motivated and productive
- Worked with corporate staff to develop standards and adopt them for local business
- Prepared responses for "Defective Pricing" queries form DOD and DCAS

Cost Accounting Manager   1997–1999

Developed and maintained cost accounting systems, ensure the integrity of cost reports, prepared all month end cost entries, maintained WIP inventory ledger, reconciled perpetual

- inventory to general ledger accounts, analyzed excess and obsolete inventory and made provisions for inventory, contracts and warranty reserve.
- Prepared Operational-reporting package—Product line performance, major program review, Inventory turns, burden rates, rework and warranty schedules.
- Reviewed and evaluated variance to cost, schedule, estimated cost at completion.
- Prepared proposal, actual and forward pricing burden rates and progress payment request.
- Established Inventory cycle count procedure.
- Supervised and trained cost accounting personnel.

General Accounting Manager   1995–1997

- Prepared and analyzed financial statements.
- Assisted controller's preparing annual budget, rolling forecast and annual audit.

- Interact regularly with management for operational and financial issues, and gave recommendation for profit and cash flow improvements.
- Reviewed journal entries and ensured that all financial transactions are recorded in accordance with GAAP.
- Managed Cost, GL, A/P, A/R and payroll personnel.

Financial Analyst　　　　　　　　　　　　　　　　　　1993–1995

- Assisted in the preparation of annual budget, rolling forecast and break-even analysis.
- Preformed detailed analysis of actual operating results versus forecast and budget.
- Prepared financial analysis related to product lines and profitability.
- Identified profit and loss cost savings opportunities with functional managers to achieve target.

Education:

- Bachelor of Science in Accounting and Business Administration—India
- Courses in USA: Production and Inventory management, Cost Accounting I & II, Taxation, Financial Management and Pricing of Government contracts, Cost Accounting for Government contracts.

Professional Affiliations

- Member of Institute of Management Accountants (IMA)

Software Skills:

- Excel, MS Word, Power Point
- WDS, Hyperion Enterprise

Comments: For someone at the controller-, CFO-level person, this résumé does not present well; it looks as though the person operates at a much lower level. The leadership stories do not come through as they are all presented in a task/responsibilities format, besides lacking a theme. In reality, this candidate has exercised much leadership in improving his company's fortunes, but the résumé does not present that story, shortchanging him!

Ram Ratan
337 Shicks Drive
Fremont, CA 94555
(000) 555-0000:   email@email.com

AFTER #15

OBJECTIVE: A position responsible for leading, managing, and conducting hands-on activities in all aspects of **Financial Management** in a growing business, including financial planning, cost accounting, analyzing operations, and developing strategic initiatives to progressively improve company performance.

EXPERIENCE SUMMARY: Ten-plus years in progressive and diversified financial management, including controllership of a manufacturing operation. Performed strategic analysis to determine core competencies and recommendations to division president, and corporate controller. Managed department and oversaw all financials for integrity and compliance. Conducted Training to ensure statutory compliance for management. Developed guidelines for meeting operating objectives; coached and mentored staff.

UNIQUE SKILLS:

- **Lead Initiatives:** Identify major initiatives to improve business performance and develop specific plans to make them a reality.—Achieve financial goals with contingency plans.

- **Strategic Perspective:** Develop strategic insights to define and articulate how leveraged actions can be implemented to make the business more effective and competitive.

- **Lead Teams:** Build productive teams through effective leadership, motivation, accountability and recognition. Develop an environment of trust, respect, and high ethical standards.

- **DoD Protocols:** Leverage extensive DoD project experience into commercial and Homeland security initiatives in governmental contracts and projects. Thorough knowledge of protocols.

- **Operational Excellence:** Implement business performance metrics/continuous improvement.

- **Regulatory Compliance:** Familiar with Sarbanes-Oxley compliance and SEC filing requirements. Act (Section 404) to keep company on compliance track.

PROFESSIONAL EXPERIENCE:

Signal Technology Corp., CA Operation (subsidiary of Crane Co.)
Director of Finance/Division Controller   1999–2004

- Led an aggressive cost-cutting initiative to undertake self-funded product development projects to position for immediate new business. Within six months catalyzed organization-wide initiatives resulting in annual savings of over $2.2M, which were directed to new products. Within the first six months alone, consolidated floor space and subleased 20% area, which paid for the entire facility, saving over $500 K in rent. Improved budgetary controls resulting in additional savings. Reduced write-offs with just-in-time systems and regularly performed major contract reviews. Increased productivity from $120 K to $150 K per employee within two years.

- Cash Flow: Generated positive cash flow by increasing inventory turns from three to six within two years. Improved payable and receivable cycles.

- Led the due diligence effort prior to company acquisition and provided financial guidance in merger and consolidation of business units.

- Implemented and monitored internal control and oversaw all financials for integrity and compliance, which resulted in reasonable and reliable assurance for financial records to auditors. Audit deficiencies were eliminated within two years.

- Recruited, organized, and developed a loyal finance and IT staff of six, making them increasingly productive. Improved monthly closing cycle from five days to three. Significantly improved financial reporting systems to make them more responsive to business needs through discipline.

- Trained management in financial policy and procedure to ensure statutory compliance and aid it in the use of financial concepts of decision-making.

Cost Accounting Manager   1995–1997

- Developed and maintained cost accounting systems, ensured the integrity of cost reports, prepared all month end cost entries, maintained WIP inventory ledger, reconciled perpetual inventory to general ledger accounts, analyzed excess and obsolete inventory and made provisions for inventory, contracts and warranty reserve.

- Prepared Operational-reporting package, product line performance, major program review, Inventory turns, burden rates, rework and warranty schedules.
- Reviewed and evaluated variance to cost, schedule, estimated cost at completion.
- Prepared proposal, actual and forward pricing burden rates and progress payment request.
- Effected considerable savings and accuracy by changing annual physical inventory audit to cycle count procedure. Result: Variance down 30%, with a savings of $230 K and no plant shutdowns.

General Accounting Manager   1995–1997
- Prepared and analyzed financial statements.
- Assisted controller in preparing annual budget, rolling forecast and annual audit.
- Interacted regularly with management for operational and financial issues, and gave recommendation for profit and cash flow improvements.
- Reviewed journal entries and ensured that all financial transactions are recorded in accordance with GAAP.
- Managed Cost, GL, A/P, A/R and payroll personnel.

Financial Analyst   1993–1995
- Assisted in the preparation of annual budget, rolling forecast and break-even analysis.
- Preformed detailed analysis of actual operating results versus forecast and budget.
- Prepared financial analysis related to product lines and profitability.
- Identified profit and loss cost savings opportunities with functional managers to achieve target.

Education:
- **Bachelor of Science** in Accounting and Business Administration, India

- Courses in USA: Production and Inventory management, Cost Accounting I and II, Taxation, Financial Management and Pricing of Government contracts, Cost Accounting for Government contracts.

Professional Affiliations

- Member of Institute of Management Accountants (IMA)
- ProNet—Fremont, Lead weekly meetings

Software Skills:

Excel, MS Word, Power Point; WDS, Hyperion Enterprise

WINSTON PEARL
Sparrow Ct., Saratoga, CA. 95070
(000) 555-0000:   email@email.com

HEWLETT-PACKARD COMPANY, Palo Alto, California

2000–2003 **Vice President, Strategy and Planning, Enterprise Systems Group**
BEFORE #16
Responsible for strategy development and long range planning for this $15B group. Led integration planning team during HP-Compaq merger for solutions and marketing. Created 3 year plan for ESG, hitting profitability targets on schedule in first 18 months of merged operations. Drove restructuring of ESG's $500M equity portfolio to gain alignment.

1998–2000 **General Manager, Strategy & Investments, Business Customer Organization**
Created and managed strategic investment process for BCO, one of 5 HP business units. Reporting to HP Controller Jon Flaxman and business unit President Ann Livermore. Led strategy and process for all acquisitions, divestitures, minority equity investments and major alliances for the business unit. Managed equity fund of $200M.

1996–1998 **Director, Corporate Development**
Managed department responsible for acquisitions, equity investments, joint ventures, divestitures, and corporate alliances for business units of HP on a world wide basis. Responsible for leading HP's acquisition strategy for Storage Systems, Networking, and Professional Service. Closed 8 major deals, including acquisitions, minority equity investment, Joint Venture, and divestitures.

1992–1996 **Channels Marketing Manager** for HP's UNIX Server Division
Managed department responsible for all channels of distribution and ISV partner relationships for HP's UNIX server business. Developed and successfully implemented division's 5 year channel strategy. Moved HP's position from being 4th tier vendor to being #1 UNIX platform for 8 to top 10 world leading ISVs. Increased indirect channels business 10 fold in four years to $1B+.

1989–1992   **R&D and Channels Section Manager** for HP's Industry Marketing organization.
Managed a section responsible for HP's marketing and business relationship with strategic software suppliers in the manufacturing marketplace.

1987–1989   **Product Line Manager** for industry targeted solutions (Aerospace & Electronics).

1986   **Anderson Consulting, San Francisco, California**
Senior Consultant in the firm's Management Consulting Services practice.

1982–1984   **EASTMAN KODAK COMPANY, Kingsport, Tennessee**
Mechanical Engineer in Chemicals and Fibers Manufacturing Research group.

1980, 1981   **GENERAL MOTORS ASSEMBLY DIVISION, Doraville, Georgia**
Mechanical Engineer in the Plant Engineering department, GM Scholar

EDUCATION:
1984–1986   **STANFORD GRADUATE SCHOOL OF BUSINESS, Stanford, California**
MBA, 1986 Course concentration in Finance and Strategic Management

1978–1982   **CALIFORNIA INSTITUTE OF TECHNOLOGY, Pasadena, CA**

Comments: For somone at this high a level, the presentation does not tell enough to pique the reader interest. It must be presented with enough detail to project the stories of leadership.

Winston Pearl
Sparrow Ct., Saratoga, CA. 95070;   (000) 555-0000:   email@email.com

SUMMARY OF QUALIFICATIONS: AFTER #16

Action oriented executive with expertise in corporate development and business restructuring. Identify winning strategies and drive those strategies to successful implementation. Demonstrated track record of seeing through conventional wisdom and then crafting a winning approach endorsed by top management.

UNIQUE SKILLS:

- **Inspirational leadership:** Talent for achieving results through an infectious positive attitude.

- **Business transformation:** Expert in leading successful merger, strategic alliance, joint venture and equity ownership activities ranging from $1M to $10B. Skilled in complex negotiations.

- **Execution excellence:** Successful in translating strategy into reality to deliver bottom line results.

- **Merger integration:** Hands on experience making complex integration and business restructuring successful. Executive leader in the successful HP-Compaq merger.

- **Operational improvement:** Intuitive ability to identify business drivers most critical for success and drive relentlessly for improvement. Strong financial and operational capabilities.

PROFESSIONAL EXPERIENCE:

Hewlett-Packard Company, Palo Alto, California
Vice President, Strategy and Planning. Enterprise Systems Group (2002–2004)
Directed post-merger (HP/Compaq) business planning and strategy for this $15B organization reporting to the Senior VP of Marketing. Managed team of 20 planning and operations managers.

- Championed development of entire first post-merger business plan, obtaining support from HP CEO and executive council. Transformed mindset by developing a disciplined process and then creating accountabilities for all. Achieved critical targets within 16 months as committed.

- Immediately upon merger discovered that prevailing model was untenable in emerging business environment. Identified potential to significantly reduce R&D costs while increasing revenues through more effective global sourcing strategy. Concurrently, repositioned R&D resources in India to go beyond their original mission to include, customer-facing activities, resulting in over $250M in increased revenues within one year. This was spring boarded to other HP entities.

- Determined after the merger that combined organization's $500M equity portfolio was strategically scattered and ineffective at supporting forward-looking goals. Developed a set of focused investment strategies and rebalanced the portfolio accordingly. Developed ongoing review process to dynamically align portfolio to changing business environment.

General Manager, Merger Integration. Enterprise Systems Group (2001–2002)
Led pre-merger integration program for Server, Storage, and Software businesses (30 senior staff).

- Soon after merger announcement, reviewed customer segments of combined businesses to verify projected opportunity for revenue growth. Discovered that initial projections were overly optimistic and needing revisions. Lead charge to define revised business model and sold it to top management.. Resulting plan was better aligned with realities of the emerging market forces and the year-end performance was thus realized.

- Architected a three-month blueprint for the operational needs the new Enterprise Systems Group, which routinized all critical operations down to the most mundane. Result: ESG was recognized as a post-merger success showcase.

General Manager, Strategy and Investments. Business Customer Organization
(1998–2001)
Drove business expansion activities for HP's $16B Business Customer Organization, with focus on merger and acquisition programs.

- Led expansion strategy for the professional services business units, successfully completing six equity transactions and joint ventures to support growth plan.

- Led business team during due diligence for a planned $14B acquisition of a major service provider. Uncovered and diligently pursued key issues impacting value of the target business in spite of leadership's reluctance to push the matter. Results of due diligence contributed to HP's eventual decision to terminate deal.

- Managed corporate equity portfolio representing 75 percent of HP's corporate equity activities.

Director, Corporate Development   *(1996–1998)*

Led M&A, new business ventures and corporate alliances for storage, networking, and service businesses

- Championed a critical review of HP's track record on equity activities to date, leading to a restructuring of HP's processes and organization. This achieved better alignment with business goals and improved accountability.

- Drove successful close of eight major transactions to support HP's growth goals, including acquisitions, minority equity investment, joint ventures, and divestitures.

Manager, Channels Marketing, HP UNIX Server Division   (1993–1996)

Directed department responsible for all channels of distribution and software partner relationships for HP's UNIX server business. Developed and successfully implemented division's five year channel strategy. Moved HP from being a second tier vendor to being the #1 UNIX platform for leading ISVs. Increased HP's indirect channels business tenfold in four years to over $1B.

Manager, Marketing and R&D   *(1986–1993)*

Held various positions of increasing responsibility including Product Line Manager, R&D team leader and Marketing Manager. Created new business model which integrated marketing and R&D support for independent software vendors (ISVs) whose software ran on HP's computer systems. Manage team of 40 marketing and R&D employees. Developed a highly successful business model working with the software vendors, doubling HP's market share in 18 months.

Anderson Consulting, San Francisco, California
Senior Consultant, Management Consulting Services   (1986)
Provided engagement leadership for business strategy projects. Project lead for profit analysis of a mid sized food company. Identified opportunity to better track manufacturing costs and steer production towards higher margin goods. Led second engagement with customer to implement changes, succeeding in gaining 2 points of increased profit for the customer. Developed very strong rapport with client and was requested to stay on after conclusion of project to provide additional consulting.

EDUCATION:
MBA Stanford Graduate School of Business, Stanford, CA (International Business).
BSME California Institute of Technology, Pasadena, CA, Graduated summa cum laude.

MARTY THOMAS
San Jose, CA 95119
(000) 555-0000: email@email.com

BEFORE #17

OBJECTIVE: Accountant with a specialty in Tax compliance and Contract analysis

QUALIFICATIONS:
Juris Doctorate, member of the State Bar of California, with strong accounting background, specializing in tax. Proven track record of reducing liability and public exposure through application of expertise, research and appropriate decision-making. Analytical, diplomatic problem solver who works well independently and as part of a team. Key accomplishments are:

- Prepared audit responses for Federal and State audits leading to significant reductions in late filing fees, penalties and additional tax assessments.
- Drafted standardized software licensing agreements resulting in fewer negotiated licensing terms and conditions.
- Broadened access to new products and sales regions by reviewing product license agreements, identifying terms and conditions that severely limited access to new products and sales regions and renegotiating new agreements.
- Prepared required statutory documentation for foreign entities and subsidiaries.
- Designed and implemented new accounting software resulting in reductions in reporting turnaround times.
- Developed and implemented new accounting internal controls, producing streamlined accounting systems.

EXPERIENCE:

Tax Specialist 2001–2004
H&R Block

- Productivity increased 18% due to increased experienced and continuing education classes.
- Successfully prepared Informational Requests for audits through extensive research and culling of internal documents.
- Reductions of up to 75% of proposed tax assessments resulted from IRS mediation agreements .

Tax Specialist   **1999–2000**
Qronus
A savings of $5,250 in external accounting and audit fees resulted from managing all general accounting functions .

- Renegotiated a new agreement that broadened access to new products and sales regions by reviewing product license agreement, identifying terms and conditions that severely limited access to new products and sales regions .

- Eliminated risk of penalties, fees and additional assessments by the timely filing of all tax compliance documents.

Contracts Analyst   1998–1999
Mercury Interactive

- Saved the company $25,000 annually in external legal research and review fees annually by the internal administration of contracts in compliance with corporate terms and conditions.

- Ensured that the final licensing agreements were in compliance with corporate terms and conditions.

- Reduced the review time for corporate for corporate licensing agreements.

Senior Tax Analyst   1996–1998

- Reduced cost in the range of $10,500 annually by the internal coordination of all statutory Federal and State tax returns in conjunction with the external auditors

- Led audits for Federal and State Income tax, sales and use tax and property tax resulting in significant reductions in fines, penalties and additional tax assessments.

Legal Studies   1991–1995
San Jose State University

- Successfully completed credit requirements thus resulting in graduation from San Jose University School of Law

- Researched various aspects of tax, enhancing my ability to manage tax audits

- Successfully passed the California State Bar Exam thus allowing me to practice law in the State of California

Other Experience:
Intel Corporation
General Electric Corporation

EDUCATION:
Member of the State Bar of California
Member of Santa Clara County Bar Association
Juris Doctorate   San Jose University School of Law
MBA   San Jose State University
BS   San Jose State University

Comments: This résumé looks fragmented with a variety of messages: accounting, tax, legal, corporate, and office management. The accomplishment stories are weak and lack focus as well. There is no connection made between this person's tax, accounting, and legal experience. The message fails to show how the tax, accounting, and business experience can be leveraged to create synergistic value to the employer.

Marty Thomas
Don Way San Jose, CA 95119
(000) 555-0000:   email@email.com

CAREER OBJECTIVE: AFTER #17

A position as **Senior Tax Manager** responsible for: the overall management, planning, compliance, preparation and analysis of all tax matters as they relate to the successful operation of a growing business. Tax matters include income tax, property tax, sales tax and their impact on a successful business.

EXPERIENCE SUMMARY:

Three years as a tax specialist working with private and corporate clients preparing and filing their income tax returns; Two years as corporate tax lead and office manager in a growing high-tech company; two years as a corporate tax specialist at a Fortune-100 company. Previous experience also includes accounting responsibilities and legal matters in a large corporation.

UNIQUE SKILLS

- **Establish Systems:** In a rapidly changing tax code and business environment set up systems that are friendly for those inside to comply with complex tax codes and unburden employees with unnecessary tasks. Eliminate repeat tasks and resulting errors.

- **Audit Compliance:** Organize tax preparation in a highly streamlined manner to field ongoing audits and provide audit trails to protect further tax liabilities and resource drain.

- **Reporting Mechanisms:** Set up automated reporting mechanisms to management so that up-to-date tax status is visible across all tax obligations and their impact on business.

- **Income Recognition:** Delve into business operations to accurately capture income so that tax liability vis-à-vis business picture is accurately presented. Minimize tax liability.

- **Build Teams:** Organize teams and communicate member roles and goals. Communicate clear objectives and inspire team members.

TECHNICAL SKILLS:

Proficient in: Microsoft Excel, Word, PowerPoint, Turbotax, Quicken, and Quickbooks

Marty Thompson   (000) 555-0000:   email@email.com   Page 2/3

PROFESSIONAL EXPERIENCE:
Tax Specialist   2001–2004
Independent Contractor

- Worked with individuals to prepare their income taxes, helping many to simplify their tax returns and decrease their tax outlay by creatively structuring their affairs and educating them on the emerging tax codes.

- Successfully prepared Informational Requests for audits through extensive research and culling of internal documents. In most cases audits resulted in no additional tax liability.

- Mediated effectively with the IRS, helping clients reduce proposed tax assessments by as much as by 75 percent

- Worked with corporate clients in preparation of their income taxes and helped them organize their tax matters for minimum tax impact. Set up and organize systems for easy tax compliance.

Tax Specialist   1999–2000
Qronus (software installation and support, A subsidiary of Mercury Interactive)

- Recommended to the CEO that creating operations independent of the parent, Mercury Interactive, would help overall business and improve morale. Recommendation resulted in physically separate operations within three months, achieving unprecedented operational effectiveness and increased sales and profitability within nine months.

- Streamlined operations and consolidate administrative and accounting functions, saving over $100,000 in personnel, contract, and services costs during the first year.

- Renegotiated service agreements that broadened access to new products and sales regions by reviewing product licenses. Created uniform terms and conditions across all clients resulting in greatly reducing contract variations and accelerating client on boarding.

- Eliminated risk of penalties, fees and additional assessments by the timely filing of all tax compliance documents.

Contracts Analyst   1998–1999
Mercury Interactive (A 500-plus strong software business in infrastructure support)

- Eliminated need for external legal services in contract reviews and saved $25,000 annually in external legal research and reviews. Established legal protocols to make it easy for employees to carry out their roles with minimal threat of lawsuits and court actions.

- Reduced myriad contracts, which resulted in time-consuming reviews of each agreement to a single boilerplate document. This approach eliminated individual review and helped clients identify unique requirements, thus allowing streamlined contract support.

Senior Tax Analyst   1996–1998
INTEL CORPORATION: CORPORATE TAX DEPT. (A FORTUNE-100 HIGH-TECH COMPANY)

- Pioneered a tax calendar across all tax filings and liabilities, and prepared a timeline of events and accountabilities for individuals. This single initiative alone eliminated all late filings and attendant penalties; an Intel first.

- Led all audit queries and developed a systematic approach to audit compliance, resulting in no additional tax liabilities and streamlining audit process. Overall savings in millions of dollars as a result of additional taxes, interest, and penalties.

Senior Accountant   1995–1996
General Electric, Corporate Tax Group
Provided accounting and administrative support to a $21B operation that included nuclear power and jet engines divisions.

EDUCATION AND CREDENTIALS:

- Juris Doctorate   San Jose State University

- MBA   San Jose State University

- BS   San Jose State University

Member of the State Bar, State of California
Member of the Santa Clara County Bar Association

CAMERON BLAKESDALE
Park Ave.
San Jose, CA 95128
(000) 555-0000
Email: email@email.com

Objective: BEFORE #18
A position as a **product manager and/or production planner**

Summary:
Over four years at Hewlett-Packard responsible from product flow, leading new product introduction teams, guiding cross-functional teams to support the overall product introduction. Previous ten years managing safety testing and certification at UL.

Professional Experience
Hewlett-Packard Company, Sunnyvale, CA 1997–2001
Planner/Scheduler 1999–2001
Coordinated the production of color laser jet printers, memory kits and paper handling products at dual coast third-party manufacturing sites, based on shipment forecasts and customer demand. Evaluated production line capacity, and prioritized planned production based on customer demand and delivery deadlines. Negotiated production schedules with other Planners and third-party suppliers to fill backlog orders. Input shipment forecast in SAP to drive product builds and procurement of materials by OEM Buyers within lead-times. Developed and implemented production strategies to increase profits.
Initiated a production line capacity analysis by engineering and third-party suppliers, which resulted in an increase of monthly output of memory-kit products by 5200 units.

Product Manager/Project Lead 1997–1999
Managed family of color laser jet printers, and approximately 15–20 accessory products simultaneously through product lifecycle. Maximized shipments to a business delivery plan, and to customer expectations. Tracked and monitored aggregate levels of inventory at two distribution centers daily and prepared weekly reports for evaluation of overall product performance by a cross-functional team and management. Assisted in the shutdown of HP's 240,000 sq. ft. distribution center in San Jose, CA and helped launch a third-party distribution center in Ontario, CA. Successfully managed the move of over 200 truckloads of remaining inventory to a third-party distribution center in Ontario, CA.

Underwriter's Laboratories, Santa Clara, CA 1986–1997
Engineering Assistant
Interpreted UL Safety Standards and evaluated customer safety test results in accordance with established guidelines and regulations. Offered alternative test solutions to customers to resolve non-compliance discrepancies. Reviewed and revised safety requirements in technical documents used to conduct inspections and on-site testing by field staff.

Comments: Having a one-page résumé makes it difficult for its writer to do justice to her value proposition. Each stint lists the overall assignment in somewhat generic terms, without any stories of leadership or accomplishments that can differentiate this person. In an economy that is shedding anyone engaged in manufacturing, this résumé must focus on a diverse range of value-creating talents that differentiate this job seeker from others.

CAMERON BLAKESDALE
Park Ave., San Jose, CA 95128
(000) 555-0000: Email: email@email.com

CAREER OBJECTIVE: AFTER#18

A position as a **product manager/production planner** in a technology company responsible for the management of products through their lifecycle, and the overall planning, delivery, and logistics for product family through its supply chain

EXPERIENCE SUMMARY:

Over four years at a Fortune 50 high-tech company with overall responsibilities for the product availability and shipments of a family of computer peripheral consumer products. Additional responsibilities included leading new product introduction teams, guiding cross-functional teams to support the overall product introduction, and maintaining them within critical cost schedule constraints. Previous ten years managing projects for safety testing and UL certification.

UNIQUE SKILLS:

- **ERP Savvy:** Drive production builds and material procurement to insure product availability for customer orders, and reduce material-driven production downtime.

- **Strategy to Ships:** Analyze/understand business strategies and translate requirements into executable shipment plans/deliverables to protect shipment commitments, workaround savvy

- **Catalyzing Tools:** Develop custom tools to track finished inventory; support business plans for back-end supply/demand match and reduce monthly inventory; eliminate backorders

- **Collaborative Teaming:** Form alliances within and outside functional areas to ensure no surprises in supply/demand, parts, resources. Manage products through their lifecycles

- **Synchronizing Supply:** Coordinate timings of all events across diverse supply-chain elements and achieve near JIT performance. Train alliances and channels on streamlining.

- **Effective Communication:** Leverage communication to achieve near flawless team performance and on-time, defect-free shipments.

PROFESSIONAL EXPERIENCE
Hewlett-Packard Company, Sunnyvale, CA   1997–2001
Planner/Scheduler
Drive JIT production of $4.5 B annually of color laser jet printers, memory kits and paper-handling products

- Initiated capacity review and realized that greater delivery rates and more stable flow were possible. Initiated a production line capacity analysis, resulting in an increase of monthly output of memory-kit products by 12%, 5200 units, increasing margins, stabilizing backlogs.

- Organized meeting with marketing, procurement, third-party suppliers and engineering to investigate a rework strategy for the excess inventory. Rework resulted in additional shipments that generated revenue of $280 K annually.

- Championed weekly collaboration meetings with third-party suppliers to evaluate potential production issues, create production contingency plans and to *eliminate* missed shipments. Reduced missed shipments by 68% within nine months with continuing improvements.

- Identified resources within the chain, allowing additional capacity when new products created surge demands. Resulting arrangement increased new-product sales by nearly 14% on a $2.2 B product line. It also increased leverage with channels in negotiating terms.

Product Manager/Project Lead
Managed family of color laser jet printers, and 20 accessories through product lifecycle.

- Streamlined and consolidated distribution points by creating a continuous delivery stream of products based on demand, eliminating excess inventory. Eliminated a local 240, 000 Sq. ft warehouse as a result, replaced by a third-party distribution center in LA area. Developed transition strategy to fill customer orders from San Jose, rather than incur costs to shuttle inventory to LA. This strategy resulted in a cost savings of $75 million.

- Coordinated and completed move of remaining 200 truckloads of inventory from San Jose to Ontario in 26 days (target was 60 days). Shipments to customers were without interruption.

- I achieved increased profits by 41% on high-cost, color laser jet printers by accurate forecast and sales reports allowing build-and-ship above forecast.
- Minimized finished goods inventory storage costs (nearly 28%) by adjusting the build-plan to meet five-day delivery, without having to build to forecast.

Underwriter's Laboratories, Santa Clara, CA   1986–1997
Engineering Assistant
Evaluated products by interpreting UL Safety Standards and test results in. Offered alternative test solutions to customers to resolve non-compliance discrepancies.

- Initiated review and update of technical documents to ascertain that standards were current and relevant. Result helped field staff conduct thorough inspections at factories and insuring that only products in compliance with safety regulations were submitted for certification and sold. This initiative increased UL's reach in enforcing safe product to consumers. Re-tests to bring products into compliance generated revenue of up to $2,000 per project (10% increase).

Technical Correspondent
Provided written and/or oral responses to customer inquiries.

- Championed and organized UL's participation in one local high-visibility technology tradeshow, and two international tradeshows intended to promote UL services, which resulted in increased queries and business. Developed documents for tradeshows including, *Introduction to UL Services* letters, and *Follow-up* letters, ordered materials to be distributed at tradeshows and scheduled UL representatives in booth over a two-day period.
- UL's attendance at the tradeshows resulted in an expansion of its customer base by 10%.
- Direct customer interface helped maintain good customer relations.

EDUCATION
BA in Public Relations with Marketing emphasis, California State University, San Louis Obispo

COMPUTER SKILLS
Knowledge of Excel 97, Office 97, Outlook, SAP, Visio32, Netmeeting, BRIO, and MS Project.

PALMER SHOENS
Aspen Court
San Jose, CA
(000) 555-0000 (work)
(000) 555-0001 (messages)
email@email.com

EMPLOYMENT HISTORY   BEFORE #19
FEDERATED DEPARTMENT STORES New York, NY **General Counsel Macy's West** (1998–present); **Director of Legal/Macy's West** (1992–1998); Senior **Attorney, Macy's West** (1989–1992)

PREMIUM MORTGAGE INSURANCE COMPANY San Francisco, CA **Senior Attorney** (1986–1989)

BADER, BERNSTEIN & TITEROTH San Francisco, CA **Litigation Attorney** (1984–1986)

CASTLE, KELL & KAMP Hayward, CA **Law Clerk and Litigation Associate** (1980–1984)

MEMBERSHIPS AND AFFILIATIONS
Licensed to practice: **California** and **Minnesota State Bars** (inactive in MN); **U.S. Court of Appeals, 9th Circuit; U.S.. District Courts** for Minnesota and Northern District of California

EDUCATION
Undergraduate Work:

- **BS** Communications (Hons), Benedict College, Benedict, SC (1970–1973 and 1974–1975)

BS with honors in Communications and Philosophy and graduate work in Communications.

While at BSU I taught radio and television broadcasting and hosted my own radio show and exhibited at the national collegiate juried photo exhibit, Refocus, in Iowa

Graduate Work:
Southern Illinois University, Carbondale, IL (School of Journalism) (1973–1974)

While at SIU I directed the Office of External Support, which assisted graduate students in writing grants and proposals for philanthropic funding

Law School:
Yale School of Law, Yale University, New Haven, CT, (1975–1979)
Worked full time during law school for the General Counsel's office of Title Insurance Company of Connecticut.

Publications and Presentations

"Making Peace" (use of mediation as a dispute resolution device) <u>Los Angeles Daily Review</u>, Feb. 16, 1995

Preventive Law "Marketing Tips" for Corporate Counsel, <u>Preventive Law Reporter</u>, Fall, 1995.

Co-author, <u>**ABA Model Electronic Payments Agreement and Commentary (For Domestic Credit Transfers)**</u> (American Bar Association, 1992)

Controlling Legal Costs Seminar, 1995 (**Effective Retention Guidelines**)

Women Corporate Counsel, 1995 (Controlling Outside Legal Costs)

1995 Woman Advocate Conference (**In-House Views of Outside Counsel**)

ABA Annual Meeting, 1994 (Presentation of **ABA Model Electronic Payments Agreements**)

Contract Negotiation and Transactional Work

Drafted and negotiated all types of contracts; IS licensing, (software, hardware, R&D) and maintenance agreements; construction; real estate (purchase, sale, leaseholds and reciprocal easement agreements for shopping center development); transportation, communications, purchasing, and marketing agreements.

Reviewed marketing and pricing programs for legal compliance. Initiated internal contract review procedures for IS, merchandise, building services and construction contracting.

Negotiated and prepared exclusive and nonexclusive overseas (Hong Kong) buying agency contracts representing business totaling $255 million annually. Study of negotiation techniques including attendance at the Harvard, Pepperdine, and Karras negotiation courses. Study of international business transactions including week-long course at Stanford, and ICC International Arbitration Course.

Litigation Management

Managed claims and complex commercial, and personal injury litigation as well as administrative enforcement actions and class actions; responsible for selecting and supervising outside litigation counsel.

Successfully managed litigation and mediation of complex and high profile matters, including, wrongful death, regulatory violations, sweatshop labor, false arrest, and wrongful discharge cases. Successfully reduced media exposure, capped risk, and diminished erosion of corporate goodwill in high exposure cases.

Created litigation retention guidelines, budget forms, and internal tracking mechanism for litigation matters, including development of mediator and counsel evaluation file on line to assist in more efficient management of litigation. Introduced fixed and capped fee deals in litigation.

Employment Law

Developed internal ADR program for contested employee terminations at Macy's West that directly decreased the number of administrative agency claims and suits filed. Counseled corporation on employment issues. Coordinated several reductions in force.

Co-authored Violence in the Workplace policy and referral protocol, and participated in developing non-violent workplace training. Helped form Macy's West Crisis Management Committee for handling dozens of threat episodes without incident. Developed emergency stand-by network.

Assisted in developing store closing strategy involving coordination of building services, HR, Public Affairs and Finance functions to minimize distraction of staff layoffs and community backlash.

Preventive Law

Handled investigations for and responses to corporate compliance hotline and participated on federal sentencing guidelines/corporate governance and compliance committee.

Trained and counseled clients on advertising compliance issues, antitrust compliance, trademark protection, sexual harassment prevention, asset protection techniques, importing, Prop 65 and weights and measures compliance, and other subjects directly related to retail business operations

Developed construction and IS contracting processes; conducted Asset Protection intervention program for spotting and resolving potential litigation early; trained Merchants and Sales Promotion clients on flammability issues, intellectual property rights and trademark enforcement.

Regulatory Compliance/Commercial Disputes/Government Affairs/E-Commerce Developed vendor ethics training program designed to combat sweatshop labor exposure. Formulated press responses to Wall Street Journal, 60 Minutes and other national media regarding this and other issues.

Negotiated successful resolutions with DAs and AG on price verification dispute, gift receipt and refurbished jewelry programs. Negotiated favorable joint press releases. Participated on Total Quality Team (the Price is Right) to resolve pricing accuracy issues on a cross-departmental basis.
Developed company wide privacy policy for web sites anticipating new regulations under Children's Online Privacy Protection Act
Provided input and educational assistance on proposed legislative measures being responded to by state retailer and business associations and the National Retail Federation, including rewrite of weights and measures regulations, efforts to reform private attorneys general standing, scanner law, used goods treatment, tort reform and other issues related to ad copy, and security officer licensing.
Active participant on California Retailers' committees on pricing accuracy, sweatshop legislation, Prop 65 reform, tort reform and general retail issues. Assisted in redrafting proposed legislation and developing lobbying strategies.

MERGERS AND ACQUISITIONS
Participated in due diligence fact gathering and review during acquisition of Macy's by Federated Department Stores, after Macy's bankruptcy filing.

Assisted in drafting and editing of stock purchase agreement and transition services agreement.

Comments: This résumé presents factual chronology without telling a story or leadership focus of this talented attorney. The message lacks direction, although it accurately captures the writer's past track record.

PALMER SHOENS
Aspen Court, San Jose, CA
(000) 555-0000   email@email.com

CAREER OBJECTIVE   AFTER #19

A hands-on **Counsel** responsible for: providing leadership in all legal aspects of running a consumer-oriented retail or technology business; seamlessly integrating legal and business units with forward-looking processes to create a competitive advantage.

EXPERIENCE SUMMARY

General Counsel for Macy's West for most recent five years responsible for a variety of initiatives and overseeing legal function across geographies and functional areas; Director of Legal Services for previous seven years responsible for catalyzing a major reorganization of the legal function; preceding three years as Senior Attorney; previous experience also includes litigation work at defense oriented law firms.

UNIQUE SKILLS

- **Leveraging Foresights:** Anticipate trends of events and patterns of activities to forge an action plan to proactively position a business for competitive advantage.

- **Creative Collaboration:** Collaborate with functional teams and partners to develop practicable outcomes to otherwise untenable situations for win-wins.

- **Precedent Strategies:** Develop strategies that define precedent-setting outcomes favoring client positions for long-term success.

- **Empower Clients:** Plan and develop seamless infrastructure to enable clients easy access to legal resources in their domains, eliminating defensive posturing.

- **Regulatory Compliance:** Develop methods, procedures, and policies to prevent reactive audits and to demonstrate compliance. Integrate compliance operationally.

- **Integrate Vision:** Translate corporate vision into easily implemented and legally transparent initiatives to help across client constituencies. Set up controls

PROFESSIONAL EXPERIENCE

General Counsel, Macy's West   **1998–Current**

- During the economic slump, starting late 2000, competitive retail pricing practices severely impacted sales performance. Identified creative marketing strategies to allow for aggressive pricing vis-à-vis key competitors without provoking significant legal challenges. Results: Despite general retail slump, entire chain showed 3.5% growth.

- In a continuing litigious environment, managed significant, high-exposure litigation including class actions, wrongful death and regulatory enforcement actions, including disputed-coverage matters with minimal disruption to executives engaged in the ongoing business and to the brand image. Result: Minimal involvement of executives in time-consuming and disruptive litigation and negotiated results that were economically advantageous and that minimized negative media coverage of controversy.

- In an unfair business practices class action, negotiated a structured settlement making use of pre-existing corporate charitable giving and consumer coupon programs to minimize financial impact of penalties that would otherwise have amounted to over $200,000 K.

- Property Development and Technology groups were hampered by long closing cycles in making critical decisions in a dynamic retail environment. Identified tardy areas and evolved processes to speed transaction time and empower clients to issue spot and self-initiate deal documentation. Closing times were shortened to two days (from seven). .

- Media coverage on controversial issues such as sweatshop labor and jewelry pricing were distracting management focus on core business and were creating a negative customer image. Formulated position statements for national media inquiries designed to assuage negative customer impact. Result: media negative coverage of Macy's West significantly slowed down, despite continued coverage of similar stories for competitors' brands.

Director, Legal Svcs Target   **1994–1998**
Responsible for the overall leadership of the legal aspects of business.

- Anticipating increased litigation, developed internal employment dispute appeal process with significant (30%) decrease in EEOC claims as a result of terminations, est. at $3.4M

- Faced with serial products litigation over CA's Prop 65, extrapolated existing consent decree precedents to develop preventive protocols teaming with QA. Result: avoided litigation other retailers had already settled and minimized potential product litigation.

- Streamlined royalty payment process across multiple clients, resulting in elimination of complex and distracting audits and more favorable royalty terms.

Legal Counsel, Target   **1988–1998**
Responsible for hands-on legal function supporting the overall operation of a $16B retail chain

- Identified safety concerns and co-authored Violence in the Workplace policy. Calm and orderly handling of multiple threat incidents without physical violence.

- Originated knowledge management initiative within Legal to capture organizational learning, capturing master forms and processes and attorneys' learnings. Created ready resource, maximizing operational efficiency, flattening learning curve for new hires.

- Championed an initiative for legislative reform efforts teaming with retail trade groups to minimize new law fallout, directly resulting in million dollar plus savings.

- Initiated cross-training model for paralegals in Real Estate and Litigation for flexible workforce. Eliminated contract hires with a stable headcount despite workload increase.

- Championed a corporate-level response system for weights and measures, which resulted commendation by coalition on pricing accuracy efforts; a Federated first.

EDUCATION
- JD, Yale School of Law, New Haven, CT.
- BS Communications (Hons), Benedict College, Benedict, SC

MEMBERSHIPS AND **PUBLICATIONS**

Licensed to practice: CA (active) and MN State Bars; U.S. Court of Appeals, 9th Circuit Author, coauthor and presenter on mediation and dispute resolution, marketing the in-house legal function, controlling outside legal costs and the ABA Model Electronic Payments Agreement

Catharine Wilson   (000).555.0000
E. Marquez Avenue   Sunnyvale, CA 94085

Health Education Coordinator

BEFORE #20

Objective: To design and implement a cutting-edge prevention and wellness department taking responsibility to train peer counselors, track longitudinal studies, and successful grant writing.

Summary:
Expertise in multi-disciplinary educational approaches to health, psychology and learning. Wellness, prevention and alternative approaches are the foundation of my work. Trained in curriculum design and numerous teaching modalities. Combination of linear thinking combined with intuition and common sense. Multi-disciplinary using a broad range of principles applied with philosophy and worldwide, multi-cultural perspective.

Skills:
- *Multi-tasking*/organizational skills
- *Organized presentations* in a linear, understandable fashion resulting in clarity and understanding
- *Learning style adaptation* for a broad range of ages from 8-82
- *Detail organization* for dissemination of information & testing purposes
- *Independent* and capable of team efforts
- *Persuasive* resulting in funded programs

Professional Experience:
Ferguson Consulting, Sunnyvale, CA. 1995–Present
- **Design, develop, and implement educational programs using technology** for Health Education Departments, Behavioral Medicine Departments and Pain Management Units in hospitals and clinics in the area of alternative medicine/health and wellness
- **Use of the Internet** in Research and Design of materials.
- **Demonstration of the NET** for hospital clientele in the area of health/wellness
- **Inspire creation of wellness and prevention department** within hospital as a direct result of the overwhelming participation in presentation

Las Positas College, Livermore, CA. 1996–2001

- **Research, design and implement curriculum** for Health Psychology I. Involves the use of the Internet, CD-ROM. Field trips, research demonstration w/the NET in areas of personal growth, health and psychology. Class: 107 students/year
- **Human Sexuality.** Design and implementation of curriculum in the area of human sexuality, staying safe, birth control, panel of speakers w/broad range of sexual preferences and perspectives.

Chabot College, Hayward, CA. 2000

- **Developed and implemented curriculum.** Designed panels, invited guest speakers, used the Internet, and designed testing modalities for the students [pre and post testing]. Encouraged class participation and empowerment of the individual participants.

Prior Professional Experience:

AMES RESEARCH CENTER, MOUNTAIN VIEW, CA 1998–99

- Contract with Ames to provide job search training, stress management, and counseling during down-sizing. Created presentations using job search engines [i.e. Monster Board], role-playing, panels, entrepreneurship. Created camaraderie, bolstered self-esteem and developed a peer-to-peer alliance

CONSULTANT, TRW, SUNNYVALE, CA

- **Designed and executed a "Woman's Health" seminar** for the Women's Professional Group. Created a reference guide with further readings resulting in awareness of alternatives and prevention thus empowering participants in their own health issues.

Health Education Instructor, San Jose State University, Women's Health Issues.
- **Developed curriculum and taught** Women's Health: Prevention and Wellness

Instructor, West Valley Community College, Understanding Addictive Behavior
- Diffused the concept of "addiction." **Curriculum design included: guest speakers, panels, outside resources.** Encouraged the exchange of experiences within group creating a cohesive class. [Over 300 students]

Facilitation Experience

- Team building seminar for a unit of the Federal Government (GSA) that: **encouraged individual risk taking** in a creative, supportive and problem solving environment through the establishment and setting of goals. Promoting cohesiveness and encouraging personal integrity. Resulted in each individual demonstrating maximum effectiveness toward attainment of common goals

- Consultant—Navy Supply Command: effective team planning using creativity and intuition; **encouraged participants to take risks** which increased the flow and **interchange of ideas; strengthened camaraderie of the various ranks** [Captains, Rear Admirals and civilians] resulting in enhanced productivity and communication

- Stress management to the General Products Division of IBM that: **measurable increase in effectiveness** of planning process through stress and conflict reduction.

Education:
Ph.Dc Studied at Institute of Transpersonal Psychology, CIIS, Summit University of Louisiana
Certificate: Organization Development, California Institute of Integral Studies
M.A. Health Education/Counseling, JFK University, Orinda, CA
BS Health Education, Eastern Illinois University, Charleston Illinois

---

Comments: This résumé lacks coherency, a foundational message, and underpinnings of core skills on which the message of value is based. For a casual reader these nuggets are going to be difficult, if not impossible, to extract from this résumé. The career history is not presented as a progressive track, making it difficult to see the evolution of the career into a meaningful theme.

CATHERINE WILSON
Arques Avenue
Sunnyvale, CA 94085
(000) 555-0000: email@email.com

AFTER #20

Career Objective: A leadership role in planning, developing, implementing, coordinating, and evaluating innovative prevention-based health/counseling program to significantly improve student health/wellness quality. Collaborate with university leadership to innovate continually.

Experience Summary: A highly diverse mix of experience in academic, healthcare, health management, and public health domains designing, delivering, monitoring and coordinating initiatives that transformed the concept of preventive health management. Over 20 years in designing, delivering, and coordinating educational programs for high-impact outcomes

Unique Skills:

➢ **Holistic Perspective:** Look beyond symptoms; identify repeat behaviors that cause health/wellness issues in younger clients. Identify change patterns to transform mindsets

➢ **Strategic Focus:** Look for points of leverage in behavioral insights and identify messages that transform clients' perspectives. Create ownership for individual wellness

➢ **Innovative Programs:** Define constituency and identify key stakeholders. Create accountability for roles, goals, and deliverables. Educate, communicate, and shift perspectives

➢ **Intuitive Insights:** Use experience and intuition to quickly converge on issues and develop win-win solutions with minimal outlays and expeditious outcomes

➢ **Winning Ideas:** Quickly translate practicable ideas into winnable grant and proposal efforts. Lead winning teams for authoring grant awards competitively

Professional Experience:
Ferguson Consulting, Sunnyvale, CA Consulting with Hospitals/Individuals
1995–Present

➤ Transformed the leadership mindset at Mills Hospital that involved using the Internet and technology to educate clients and staff in pain management, alternative and behavioral medicine. Increased hospital's awareness of return on investment on time and energy in training staff. Proposed a staff training session for training patients. Intervention freed up staff for other projects and empowered patients, creating a positive environment.

➤ Championed integrative approaches at Valley Care Medical Center, Pleasanton. Over-reliance on pharmaceuticals and lack of comprehensive education on alternatives resulted in "medication-only" mentality compounded by rapid staff turnover. Initiative resulted in hospital and patient commitment to on-site meditation group combined with progressive preventative medicine education for staff and patients. Increase in referrals to massage and short-term therapy, thus shifting focus from reliance on drugs to healing therapy.

Las Positas College, Livermore, CA   **1996–2001**

➤ A college survey highlighted endemic alcohol-consumption was becoming an epidemic, resulting in accidents, fatalities, speeding tickets, and unsafe environment, further exacerbated by fewer insured drivers. Despite peer pressure and prevailing attitudes, identified an approach that involved open, mock AA meetings. Coupled with education, interventions, and collaborative efforts, successfully reduced weekend student drinking by 75 percent within one year, making campus much safer.

Human Sexuality.

• Led a major initiative resulting in students practicing safe sex, despite refusal and denial of consequences of pregnancy, sexual transmitted diseases. Designed tracking journal for students acknowledging behaviors and consequences. Within four months, over 60 percent began using preventative measures and educating their peers.

Chabot College, Hayward, CA.   **2000**

- Implemented a cultural approach to healing methodologies pioneering the concept of "Open Space". Empowered students to participate, make decisions, and implement.

Prior Professional Experience:

Ames Research Center, Mountain View, CA   **1998–99**

- Contracted with Ames to provide job search training, stress management, and counseling during downsizing. Resulted in making downsizing process less stressful

Consultant, TRW, Sunnyvale, CA

- Designed and executed a "Woman's Health" seminar for a Professional Group.
  Health Education Instructor, San Jose State University, Women's Health Issues

- Developed curriculum and taught Women's Health: Prevention and Wellness.
  Instructor, West Valley Community College, Understanding Addictive Behavior

- Diffused the concept of "addiction," leading to open discussions and sharing of personal solutions, which resulted in implementation of college campus NA, AA, OA meetings facilitated by students themselves, a campus first!

- Established outside support groups for participants. Frenetic workplace prohibited nurses from sharing solutions, combined with lack of self-care. Within four weeks, participants designed format for sharing knowledge and met for weekly professional support.

Facilitation Experience:

- Federal Government (GSA)-Designed and delivered a Team building seminar for a unit of GSA to encourage individual risk taking in a creative, supportive and problem-solving environment through goal setting, promoting cohesiveness, and encouraging personal integrity. Result: each individual demonstrated maximum effectiveness toward attainment of common goals and teams started reaching for aggressive goals.

- Consultant-Navy Supply Command: Designed effective team planning using creativity and intuition; encouraged participants to take risks, which increased the flow and ideas interchange; strengthened camaraderie across ranks [Captains, Rear Admirals and civilians] resulting in enhanced productivity and communication

- Consultant—IBM General Products Division: designed steps that resulted in conflict resolution skills, reducing stress and increasing program planning process effectiveness.

Education:

- Ph.Dc., Studied at Institute of Transpersonal Psychology, CIIS, Summit Univ., Louisiana

- Certificate: Organization Development, California Institute of Integral Studies

- M.A., Holistic Health Education, JFK University, Orinda, CA

- BS Health Education, Eastern Illinois University, Charleston Illinois

James Smith (#21)
Belmont, CA
000-555-8979 (H); 000-555-1250 (Cell) email: jsmith89@yahoo.com

CAREER OBJECTIVE:
Labor and Employee Relations Manager in a government agency responsible for providing leadership for effective management of labor and employee resources in a complex organizational environment that includes diverse geographic and bargaining units.

EXPERIENCE SUMMARY
Six years as a chief union executive responsible for all aspects of Airline Pilot's Association, Int'l (ALPA) functions at *American Airlines* and two years on its board of directors and member of the high-stakes negotiating committee responsible for the most significant airline acquisition and its eventual viability because of innovative and most radical labor redeployment; championed the reengineering of employee relations at the airlines before and after the acquisition. The entire process positioned AA for its current business success. Continued leadership role in airline's affairs; ongoing advisorship to ALPA at the airline in a key executive capacity. Pioneered many innovations in employee and labor force effectiveness

UNIQUE SKILLS

- **Strategic Perspective:** Develop strategic direction for overall human resource management by looking at trends, identifying needs, and organizational effectiveness

- **Implement Solutions:** Analyze problems in a complex and dynamic environment and devise cost-effective solutions that create a win-win for all involved

- **Anticipate Needs:** Collaborate with client organizations, their human resource leaders, and alliances to identify needs in training, development, and resources. Establish plans.

- **Employee Empowerment:** Identify roadblocks to employee decision-making and develop an environment of trust where decisions are made at the lowest possible levels.

- **Dispute Resolution:** Identify root cause of discontent and develop strategies that bring rival factions to the table. Facilitate dispute resolution process for a win-win outcome.

PROFESSIONAL ACCOMPLISHMENTS

Strategic Perspective:
As American Airlines was battered by huge and ongoing losses in the mid 90s, management chose and finalized the "only" option: liquidation of much of the long-range aircraft fleet, layoff employees and shrink to profitability. Management informed union executives of the board-approved decision just hours before going public. Within hours mobilized an innovative solution of aircraft redeployment, pursuing an entirely new and viable venture. Within days management reversed its decision, redeployed assets in new direction, with no loss of employees, making airline profitable again. Adopted strategy resulted in a highly effective operation of AA since.

Implement Solution:
- When the pilot's union and the airline management agreed on a new approach to developing a streamlined method for scheduling personnel, based on an union initiative, there were many impediments posed by the existing systems, labor and employee work policies and FAA regulations. Working within the framework and developing a collaborative relationships with all involved with the change process, implemented a radically new approach to scheduling pilot routines. The new method brought much sought predictability to pilot routines and made the schedule itself more efficient, serving it as a model for other airlines to follow.

- As AA continued its business in the mid 90s, its operating costs became a growing factor in profitability. Recommended to management a major initiative that dealt with the flight profiles and how they affect fuel consumption. After careful study management accepted critical recommendations and went on to implement many changes. Helped catalyze new procedures to institute fuel efficiency management initiative, which resulted in comprehensive revisions to operations with substantial ongoing cost savings.

Anticipate Needs
When the airline adopted a new dedicating their long-range aircraft fleet for commercial and military charter operations to save itself, anticipated that locating pilots at the major hubs and operating centers would greatly streamline flight planning and crew scheduling for quick response. Suggested to management a radical new idea of creating pilot domiciles on the eastern seaboard and in Europe. Within months a new personnel deployment plan was in place. This multi-site plan enhanced scheduling capabilities, personnel commitment, and profits.

Employee Empowerment
During routine flight operations discovered that the existing boarding schedule and procedures were resulting in flight delays, which were costing money, eroding on-time record, and employee morale. Suggested a new boarding plan and initiated comprehensive logistics revisions to make it work by collaborating with various employee segments. Within months plan was adopted, resulting in greatly increased passenger satisfaction and vaulting the airline to top-ranked on-time performance for two years running, realizing substantial cost savings and increased sales.

Dispute Resolution
Led a major initiative to change pilot workload, which was causing morale erosion and dissent among ranks. Although management realized its responsibility, no consideration was forthcoming. Championed a major initiative to hold airline accountable, and despite limited finances, negotiated a win-win package for all. Airline savings was in the millions of dollars.

SIGNIFICANT CHRONOLOGY

Pilot American Airlines	1980–Current
Chairman, Official Committee of Unsecured Creditors	2003–2004
Chairman ALPA Article VIII Committee	2001–2003
Director American Airlines Board of Directors	1994–1996
Litigation Trustee	1998–2001
Master Chairman, Master Executive Council American Airlines	1988–1994

Summary Chapter-6: Building Your Platform

This chapter describes an effective template for writing a résumé. A résumé is about tomorrow, not yesterday, and it is not about you (it is about the employer!).

Central to the résumé's message is the genius that defines what differentiates the writer from everyone else. This chapter shows two tools that help explore the genius dimension in a structured way. The SIMPLE Tool allows developing leadership stories of accomplishments that set the writer apart from others. The second, The Genius Extraction Tool, facilitates taking these stories in a structured way to extract the genius and then develop language around its description, to make it ready for incorporation into a résumé. Actual examples are shown. The writer's genius is represented by the Unique Skills, which is central to the message of a résumé.

A typical résumé template has the following elements:

- Career Objective
- Experience Summary
- Unique Skills (Your Genius)
- Technical Skills
- Professional Experience
- Educational Background
- Professional Development
- Other Accomplishments
- Key Words
- An Optional Headline or Tagline

Examples of 21 real-life résumé makeovers are shown for the three most common formats in the Résumé Makeovers Showcase: chronological, functional, and hybrid. Not all résumés conform to the suggested template, yet their makeovers are presentable in a compelling way.

In making over a résumé, the following elements must be central to the process:

- ✓ A forward-looking Career Objective or the value proposition
- ✓ An Experience Summary that fortifies the claims of the Career Objective
- ✓ Unique Skills presented so that your genius is showcased in a ranked order (to the target)
- ✓ Professional Experience presented in a story-telling format, so that your leadership qualities are showcased to highlight your accomplishments.

Common résumé challenges, as not having a formal degree, gaps in chronology, are presented to overcome apprehensions around how to make a message compelling, despite these "limitations."

Chapter-7: Write to the Point with Letters

"A Targeted Letter is an intimate way of communicating to its reader that you know them and that you can help them with what they need."

—Dilip Saraf, career and life coach (1942–)

Introduction

Letters serve a dual purpose during a transition. One is to bridge the messaging gap between the résumé and the intended job opportunity. When sent without a résumé, it serves its other purpose as your proxy, to entice its targeted reader to take the intended next step.

Many think that letters are a waste of time when pursuing job opportunities! This view is shared on both sides: those on the receiving end find most letters redundant, those on the sending end find it an unnecessary step that is more a burden than help. This is probably because it takes an effort to write a compelling letter, cover or otherwise. Most take the easy way out and cobble together something that is copied from an existing template. Worse yet, many cut and paste what is already in their résumé with what is worthy of plagiarizing from the posting itself and create a message that clearly shows its pedigree. With each of these approaches, the job seeker is sending a message: Don't bother reading mine, I am too lazy! If everyone is taking this easy route, it provides an opportunity for those, who take the time and effort to write a good letter to differentiate themselves in a campaign!

Another rationale advanced by poor letter writers—or by those who write well, but are lazy—is that, in a tough market, there are many opportunities to which responses need to be sent. In order to get maximum coverage of targets, it is difficult to write all these customized letters. So, they take the shotgun approach and send many mediocre letters. As a result, none of them create any impact. If, on the other hand, job seekers selected just a few choice targets, researched the opportunities and then send select few letters, their chances of success are greatly increased. Remember, one needs only one job!

In a tough job market a *good* cover letter is a must. It further differentiates those that send it from those who do not. If the letter is well written and goes beyond what is in the job description, it commands attention and action. In the previous chapter on résumés, we emphasized that a résumé is not about you; it is about them—the employer. In the case of the letter, it is even more so. Typically, cover letters are an intimate and personal way to draw the decision-maker into *your* world by talking about *theirs*. Done this way, it resonates with their needs. A good cover letter should grab the target reader by their shoulders, look them in the eye and convey to them, I know you!

How does one do this?

Some Letter-writing Basics: Process

A letter sent in pursuit of a job opportunity is an exercise in business writing. This applies to both the cover letters that normally accompany a résumé as well as those sent to pique the interest of the target decision maker, typically called prospecting letters, enough for them to want to talk to you. Prospecting letters are sent without a résumé attached. Just as a résumé must follow some messaging guidelines as presented in the previous chapter, so, too, must cover letters. There are many good references on this topic, so the discussion here is limited to the basics of writing good business letters.

The following checklist will help in formulating a good letter:

- Plan
- Draft
- Edit
- Follow-up

Plan

Planning is critical before any letter is written. Typically, a well-laid plan should take nearly 50 percent of the total time it takes to execute an effective letter. Planning precedes plan. In other words, planning is a process that results in a plan that can be executed. This plan includes knowing:

- Who is the target reader and who is the actionee? Sometimes these two entities are different and the way the letter is created and presented must reflect this knowledge.

- What information you plan to present in the letter that will grab their attention ("grab them by their shoulders") and give them the message, "I know you!"?
- How do you get this information?
- How do you translate this information into an effective message?

Draft

Once the planning is done and the necessary research is completed (the time to do the research is a separate budget, but how to do it is part of the planning process), a draft is prepared. This draft should typically be about — page. The draft stage of the process should take about 20 percent of the allotted time.

Edit

Once the draft is done, editing and polishing the message take over. This step takes about 30 percent of the total time budget. Editing is critical to tighten the message and increase its impact by arranging the logical flow of the message, using the correct words, and style. Editing typically should take 50 percent more time than drafting the letter, because it is the editing that sets the final tone of the letter.

Send

After the letter is ready, it must be sent by an appropriate means. There are a variety of avenues available to send a letter and how it is sent dictates how the follow-up is carried out. Some of the common avenues are:

✓ Email
✓ Fax (use only as an exception)
✓ Mail (U.S. Mail)
✓ Courier
✓ Hand delivery

How a letter is sent should be driven by its content, the import of the content, and to whom it is targeted. For important messages using more than one mode is common. For example, if an open posting requires a email response, sending a response on the company's Website in addition to sending a mailed or courier response is appropriate. Using this approach can allow an easier way for follow-up.

As mentioned before, the person to whom the letter is addressed can be different from the one who takes action. How? Sometimes, to get attention of a high-level manager, it a good idea to address the letter at least two levels above the potential hiring manager. If the letter makes an impact, the recipient is going to send it "down" for action. The action now comes from the hiring manager or from the person above them.

♠ Follow-up

Following-up is the weakest link in the chain of the letter-writing process. Job seekers spend much effort writing an impactful letter and sending it to a well-researched recipient. But, only about 10 percent of the letters sent get followed up with any diligence! After spending much effort and time writing a good letter, it is lamentable that job seekers do not expend the final five percent of their effort diligently following-up on their own letters!

Writing good letters can be time-consuming. Letters of the caliber shown in the showcase, with a well-researched target can take as much as one week's time *initially*. Once the learning curve is behind them, most are able to get one out in about a day's time and a few hours' worth of effort!

Follow-up Guidelines

The guidelines below in following up a submittal (open job or otherwise) may help those who procrastinate following up after they have sent a good response. Next to a cold call, a follow-up is the most dreaded undertaking for job seekers:

- Before sending a response make sure that there some way to follow-up with the person to whom the response is addressed.

- If you send a courier pack (FedEx) track to see when the package was delivered and to whom.

- Even if you have sent a great letter (and a résumé), do not assume that the person receiving it is going to call because you believe that they should. These days job seekers routinely send a FedEx (or courier) letter, many of which are not worth the effort and expenditure.

- Start tracking the movement of the package after checking with the initial recipient how the package was routed.

- The best timing is immediately following the delivery to the intended recipient. Do not wait for more than a day to talk to the person or leave a message that you intend to talk with them.

- If you are not able to connect with that person first leave a voice mail with a clear subject line (Dave's résumé response). Use that exact phrasing in the Subject line of the email sent immediately following your voice mail so that the person can connect the two messages.
- In the message leave an option for you to call them back ("If I do not hear from you in a day or so, I plan to call you again.")
- Your follow-up efforts should fall just short of "stalking."

emailed Letters

These days emails are becoming more and more common forms of business communication, even for employment matters. The problem with emails is that a typical manager gets so many of them every day that it is easy to get lost in the sea of emails. The following tips may help increase chances of your email response getting read:

1. Make the subject line impactful. Instead of saying Dave's résumé, say "A must-hire candidate!" See Asmita Page emailed letter in the Showcase.

2. In addition to attaching a Word document insert the same text in the body of the email. Some companies do not allow their employees to open attachments.

3. Another approach is to convert the file into an Adobe Acrobat (PDF) and then to attach it to the email, in addition to pasting the body of the letter in the email.

4. Summarize your letter in one line at the top of the message, with the action you want the reader to take. This is called "Bottom lining at the top."

5. Be clear what you want them to do and be very specific. ("Please give me 15 minutes of your time at your earliest to show what I can do for you!")

6. Make only one point and repeat it in more than one way, but be concise

7. Send the email either at the beginning of the day (7:45 AM) or at 1:30 PM so your message is at the top of the stack, when managers are opening their mailboxes.

8. Since most mail boxes stack and show new messages in the descending order or arrival—most recent at the top—make sure that if you are sending multiple messages consecutively, the one landing at the top is the most critical. Sometimes, this can mean re-ordering your messaging priorities for outgoing mails.

9. When sending an email, state that you are also sending this message by U.S. Mail or a courier so that they can look for it. See Walter Chase letter to Palm in this chapter.

10. Send a voice mail with the same subject heading as the email so that the aural and visual messages are connected. Some cultures are voice mail dominant and others, email. Make an effort to come up with catchy subject lines, both on voice mail and email.

11. Have your complete information in the signature block (including your email address). This includes your full name, telephone number, cell phone, address, fax, and any other information that is relevant to your existence.

12. Be specific what you are going to do to follow-up.

13. Separate the text of the letter from that of the résumé by drawing a two horizontal lines at the end of the letter.

14. At the bottom of each email have your complete identification, including your email address and phone numbers, in the signature block.

Chapter Organization

This chapter is organized by first laying out the ground rules for *cover* letters. These rules describe what must go in a good cover letter vis-à-vis what is attached to it, as well as how to send it. Letters—prospect letters—sent without any attachments, with a specific target in mind that deliver a punch to its targeted reader, are also discussed in this chapter.

A Showcase that features actual letters, sent in various circumstances that got action and results, then follows.

♠Cover Letters

Cover letters are an element of the job-search campaign, in importance at par with the résumé! Why? Simply because a cover letter can enhance the overall message well beyond what a résumé can by itself! As mentioned in the résumé section, a résumé should be tailored to each *category* of jobs. It is not uncommon in a tough market to have up to five different résumés for the same person, depending on the market one is trying to capture (please see résumé examples in the previous chapter). A well-written cover letter complements the résumé message and does not repeat it. If the résumé is not about you—as we emphasized in that chapter—a cover letter is even less so! One concession in cover letters: you can use personal pronouns (I, me, mine) that we railed against using in the résumé. Use this concession to your advantage in the way your letter creates a "I know you" message with the target company.

There are various formats and styles of cover letters. The least effective is the one in which you open it with the job description or job reference, and then start repeating what is in the job posting to show why there is a good match. The other equally prosaic approach is to summarize what is already in the résumé and then urge the decision maker to call you for an interview. Neither of these shortcuts to writing a cover letter adds any value to the message already in the résumé. In fact, it may detract from it. Why? Because of the time constraints, if the cover letter offers a good summary of the résumé, the hiring manager may not even feel the need to read the attachment.

Some compensate for this by making a custom résumé for each job to which they are responding. Taking this approach is even more dangerous because of the sheer volume of jobs to which one needs to respond to in a tough market. Sending customized résumés poses a further problem of keeping track and of the possibility of inadvertently sending résumés with errors. These errors can occur because of time constraints and the lack of convenient "second pair of eyes" required for sending a perfect résumé in each case. The other problem with sending a custom résumé for *each* opportunity is that the recipient does not know that this is one of the many that you spun out for targeting your job search. If the résumé is too specific, it creates suspicion in the readers' minds. A well-written cover letter acts as a third party that introduces your résumé to its reader, intriguing them to peruse it.

A résumé is not something that should be changed casually. It is time consuming to craft and proof a résumé so that it is flawless—every time! Having railed against a custom résumé for each job, it is appropriate to say that *tweaking* a résumé to suit a target is not a bad idea. Here tweaking means emphasizing particulars of a target opportunity that are stated in the job posting, such as specific procedures, operating systems, markets, and so on. This tweaking further fortifies what is in the cover letter, without repeating it.

Recruiters disparage cover letters. Some do so because they keep seeing the same messages recycled. Others simply do not have the time to read letters and then go to the résumé and verify that the two messages are in synch. Many recruiters pride themselves in their ability to spot the flummery just by scanning a résumé. Regardless, a good cover letter is a must as a differentiator if the targeted opportunity is important to pursue.

Use cover letters, therefore, in *all* cases where it is possible. The quality of the cover letter is dependent on the importance of the target opportunity. All things being equal, this element provides the added factor to differentiate. For this reason, it can also be a detractor if not done correctly.

* Cover Letters: Dos and Don'ts

The following is a list of dos and don'ts in cover letters:

Dos:

- Be concise, compelling, and cogent in about a — page
- Present your case so that the letter naturally leads to your résumé
- Make most of the letter about *them*, not about you
- Send it to someone who can be contacted to follow-up
- Send an *impactful* letter in an impactful way, e.g. FedEx

Don'ts:

- Don't repeat what is in your résumé
- If you are proposing an idea, be concise and intriguing; give just enough
- Make more than one major point of argument in the body of the letter
- Avoid "but"; use "and" instead (e.g. I do not have 15 years in sales, but I bring rich field experience. Instead say: I bring sales experience in major geographic theaters of the world and know cultural preferences of markets where most growth is expected)
- Do not send a mediocre letter (or a résumé) using an impactful method (FedEx)

In addition to a compelling cover letter, what is even more important is how the entire package—the résumé and the cover letter—is sent. If a posting requires sending the résumé using a Website, then exploring if the response allows a cover letter with it can be worthwhile. Some Websites allow posting a résumé with a cover letter; they present a disadvantage if that is the only way you can transmit your response.

One approach to making it easy for the reader to look at an electronically sent response is to first cut and paste the text of the cover letter in the window provided for submitting the response. After the cover letter, drawing two lines and then starting the résumé as a continuous text message will allow the recipient to see that there is a cover letter, which is separate from the résumé.

If the target company is important (an "A" company), then ensuring that the résumé and the cover letter go in a differentiated way is critical. Merely relying on the Website, to get your message to its target for such an important opportunity, is chancy.

Why? This is so, because your response will be piled up with all other responses. It will be viewed if the key-word filters used to screen résumés let yours through for action. For priority targets, extra effort is justified to ensure that the cover letter is compelling, allowing you to stand out from the crowd. If your response is delivered using a special method (FedEx), in addition to it being sent electronically, then it stands a better chance of creating action. Taking the extra effort (FedEx Ground or Green Label, costs about $5) to find out who the hiring manager is and then sending a courier pack with a great cover letter and a stellar résumé can win the day. Very few will take this route and *that* is a differentiator. See Figure-3: The Messaging Challenge in Chapter-5.

In addition to making an impact, the courier method allows for easy tracking. Once the package is delivered, you know who signed for it. Calling that person in a few days allows you to find out to whom the package was delivered. Then from there, you can start your follow-up process. Another point that might help you differentiate further in the process: send the response to both the hiring manager and the recruiter for a priority target company. And, once again, make sure that each recipient knows that the other also got the same package. That simple expedient will ensure that if the hiring manager is interested, the recruiter is more than likely to get a "pull" call to bring you in for an interview. It is that effective.

Follow-up after sending a package by a courier is critical. Many feel timid calling to take this extra step. Without this step, your chances of being treated differently are greatly diminished. Once the package gets opened and the contents become part of the clutter on someone's desk, all the impact of a courier delivery goes away. This is why timing of the follow-up is critical.

After sending a courier pack, with a great a résumé and a matching cover letter, many have difficulty following up on their transmittal. A common approach is to track the package from the time it is signed, and then call the next person who is on the tracking log inside the company. Usually, this person is a senior-level person—at least a hiring manager—who needs to know that you bring what others don't. So, when following up with a phone call, merely saying, I am calling to follow-up on my résumé I sent…is going to get an abrupt disconnect. Instead, saying, I am calling to see if you had a chance to look at the FedEx package I sent yesterday, after you confidently introduce yourself by name, is going to be much more effective.

Letter-writing Tool

This tool is provided to help the letter writing process. As presented before, spending 50 percent of the time planning how to write is required for a good letter. This tool demonstrates why this is so. Use this tool to generate your own plan and then write the draft of a winning letter.

Letter-writing Tool

Use this tool to plan for writing your letter—cover or otherwise—and prepare your draft as a first step in the process of creating a winning communication. Feel free to improvise and make this tool your own.

This tool is adapted from Dumaine, Deborah. *Instant Answer Guide to Business Writing: An A-Z Source for Today's Business Writer.* iUniverse, 2003.

1. **Purpose**
   A. Why should I write this letter?
   B. Does it go with my résumé?   Yes   No
   C. Who is going to read it?
   D. What do I know that the reader does not?
   E. What do I want the reader to do?
   F. How am I going to get the reader to see my point of view after I send the letter?
   G. How should I present my view so that the reader looks at it positively?

2. **Bottom Line**
   A. What one point I want the reader to remember?
   B. How does that impact his position at the target company?
   C. How can I make the impact more urgent to the reader?

3. **Strategy**
   A. How should I send it?
   B. When should I send it?
   C. How do I follow-up?
   D. When do I follow-up

4. **Action** (estimate time for each task): Total time: _____ Hrs.
   A. Plan (about 50 percent)
   B. Draft (about 20 percent)
   C. Edit (about 30 percent)
   D. Follow-up (less than five percent): Although this is a small amount of time it is the most leveraged throwaway, as most letter writers practice it! Follow-up is a highly leveraged activity.

Sample Letters

Following examples show how résumés can be sent with these cover letters. Section following the first block of cover letters, which are sent with résumé attachments, is for Non-existent jobs and Contingent Employment opportunities. These letters do not have any attachments; hence they are not cover letters, but prospect letter. Each is numbered and labeled according to the purpose it serves from the listing below. In the showcase, the attachments are not presented.

1. A well-researched letter in response to a posted opening
2. A cover letter in response to a posted opening using insider insights
3. A cover letter leveraging generic industry insights and software processes
4. A cover letter in response to a posted opening, showing itemized compliance
5. An emailed response to a posted opening with insights and industry knowledge
6. A cover letter with résumé, following an informational interview
7. An example of a bad cover letter in response to a posted opening
8. An example of a good cover letter for the same posted opening
9. A cover letter for a posted opening, using a previous tenuous connection
10. A cover letter to a posted opening using an unconventional approach
11. A letter for a non-existent job that embodies a new idea
12. A letter showing how to switch industries (high-tech to biotech): non-existent job
13. A prospect letter from a hands-on engineer to a CEO
14. An idea letter for a non-existent job
15. A letter in response to a closed position with another perspective
16. A well-researched letter sent to pique interest in an idea: non-existent job
17. A well-researched letter exploiting an opportunity and insight
18. A prospect letter with an insight based on everyday observation/some research
19. A prospect letter to a senior executive with a new idea: non-existent job
20. A prospect letter to a CEO with an idea

33. Asim Kedaur   (000) 555-0000   email@email.com

#1

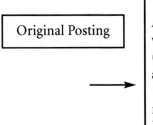

Original Posting

Group Leader Manufacturing
A leading biotech company needs a leader for warehousing operations for the entire business ($4B). The position is based in Santa Clara, CA and reports to VP of operations. Only those with 10+ years in warehousing, logistics, and operations need apply. Biotech a plus. Send your résumé to: Hire@guidingtech.com.

March 30, 2003

Mr. John Mortons
Vice President, Logistics
Guiding Technologies, Inc.
101 Bayshore Way
Oakland, CA 94545

This information was available by researching public databases.

Dear Mr. Mortons,

I am pleased to respond to the open position of Group Leader, Manufacturing (Job # 21058). My résumé is attached.

In addition to meeting or exceeding all of your job requirements, my specific strengths, which will create immediate value for Guiding Technologies are:

Leading initiatives to reduce Guidant's relatively low inventory turnover, to a number, more in line with today's business norms for this industry, or a more acceptable number. I have a proven track record of doing this aggressively in a complex environment, and in a variety of settings, with impressive outcomes.

Looking at the overall logistical flow *systemically,* and then collaborating with other functions, suppliers and alliances to reduce the overall investment, exposure and increase material and cash flow velocity significantly.

Looking at the logistical locations, international tax and tariffs, and then making recommendations for overall improvements in the way they impact the bottom-line. With 30 percent business overseas, this affords an attractive opportunity for globalization of logistics.

I am excited about exploring this opportunity further with you, and am looking forward to hearing from you. If I do not hear from you within about a week, I plan to call you.

Cordially,

Asim Kedaur

> Most of the data was inferred from publicly available sources and finances.

Enclosure: Résumé

All comments are removed to present a clean version of this letter on the next page.

(This letter and résumé got a response within three days.)

Asim Kedaur (000) 555-0000 <u>email@email.com</u>

#1

A RESEARCHED COVER LETTER

March 30, 2003

Mr. John Mortons
Vice President, Logistics
Guiding Technologies, Inc.
101 Bayshore Way
Oakland, CA 94545

Dear Mr. Mortons,

I am pleased to respond to the open position of Group Leader, Manufacturing (Job # 21058). My résumé is attached.

In addition to meeting or exceeding all of your job requirements, my specific strengths, which will create immediate value for Guiding Technologies are:

Leading initiatives to reduce Guiding's relatively low inventory turnover, to a number, more in line with today's business norms for this industry, or a more acceptable number. I have a proven track record of doing this aggressively in a complex environment, and in a variety of settings with impressive outcomes.

Looking at the overall logistical flow *systemically,* and then collaborating with other functions, suppliers and alliances to reduce the overall investment, exposure and increase material and cash flow velocity significantly.

Looking at the logistical locations, international tax and tariffs, and then making recommendations for overall improvements in the way they impact the bottom-line. With 30 percent business overseas, this affords an attractive opportunity for globalization of logistics.

I am excited about exploring this opportunity further with you, and looking forward to hearing form you. If I do not hear from you within about a week, I plan to call you.

Cordially,

Asim Kedaur

Enclosure: Résumé

BEN SMITH

Prospect Street
Fremont, CA 94555
(000) 555-0000   email@email.com

Mr. James Dregmist   May 28, 2003
Chief Technology Officer
Community Hospitals, Inc.
1 City Plaza, Suite 2600
Oakland, CA 94612

USING INSIDER INSIGHTS
#2

Dear Mr. Dregmist,

I am responding to your posting for Manager, IT Project Portfolio Administration.

In addition to meeting or exceeding the job requirements, I bring the following perspectives:

➢ In-depth understanding of strategic IT initiatives, and how to execute these across an enterprise, with culture steeped in siloed thinking. Your current EPIC initiative, for example, would require, a deep understanding of each of the functional areas that it touches, and how to get all these silos to understand, what it takes to embrace change and maintain their identity. I am familiar with this change barrier.

➢ Immediate knowledge of IT industry and emerging trends, enabling me to provide ongoing input to ensure that the *most* effective solutions are planned for implementation. This outlook will provide a flexible, effective, and forward-looking infrastructure so critical to a large organization's long-term and strategic success.

➢ Skilled in project management and cross-functional teams to allow me to manage effectively a broad portfolio of critical projects, and maintain performance, schedule, and budget integrity.

➢ Excellent understanding of leadership needs to oversee, lead, and deliver major initiatives involving large-scale change. Creating a seamless experience in the minds of those who touch an organization, and those who support it, are critical to maintaining the overall vision for the change. I have a good understanding of how to leverage that, and achieve exceptional results under very challenging circumstances.

I look forward to speaking with you to explore this further. I plan to call you in a week.

Cordially,

Ben Smith

Encl: Résumé

> Each of the items above came from researching the target organization using publicly available information. This research took about six hours. The recipient called the candidate the following week for a phone interview, followed by a face-to-face.

MICH APPS

Terrace Ct.
Belmont, CA 95434
(000) 555-0000   email@email.com

#3

Ms. Joan Sanders   August 15, 2003
Recruitment Manager
McAfee Enterprises
3001 Stevens Creek Blvd
Cupertino, CA 95014

LEVERAGING GENERIC INDUSTRY INSIGHTS

Dear Ms. Sanders,

I am responding to your job opening for Software Engineer and I am listing below a brief summary of accomplishments during my five years at Hewlett-Packard and NEC:

I designed and developed several complex software applications with minimal supervision. For example, one business-critical Web application project assigned to me with aggressive deadlines and minimal definition, was delivered ahead of schedule. When QA tests were conducted, this application was found to have *no* errors, and was then integrated with the corporate Website seamlessly. All my development work is delivered error-free.

Working closely with QA, I collaboratively helped them define test strategies and helped minimize test time and test risks. I have an excellent record of promptly correcting any uncovered defects, regardless of who wrote the original code prior to my involvement on the project.

During the critical integration phase, I have on many occasions, volunteered to help facilitate the process and provided innovative solutions to deliver the product on time.

I enjoy working in teams, large and small, and work to deliver final products on aggressive timelines. I have also *led* teams to deliver critical products when the occasion required it.

I am excited about exploring this further and looking forward to discussing with you in person. I'll call you in a week to follow-up.

Cordially,

Mich Apps
Encl: Résumé

JOB AD

Senior Designer Needed!! Reply to: email@email.com
Date: 2003-10-01, 3:27PM

Senior designer needed for extremely busy residential resale property staging business. Looking for a very organized, self-starter with a good design
eye, to quickly set up homes and other properties being marketed for sale.
Must have a trained eye for accessories and furniture. Must be able to manage a team. Lifting and some physical work required. Must have a car, van
preferred. Can be full or part time, some weekends. Must have professional
interior design experience. Window merchandizing experience excellent.
This is interior design emergency ward work! Very fair compensation and
room for advancement. Please do not call, if you are not experienced! Call
Carolyn @ (000) 555-0000.

	Asmita Page
eMailed	# Lost Leaf Ave.
Response	Los Altos Hills, CA 94022
	(000) 555-0000 email@email.com

Subject: TRANSFORMATIONAL DESIGNER:

#4

October 1, 2003
CAROL DeSOTO
email@email.com
Bus. (000) 555-0000

COVER LETTER WITH ITEMIZED COMPLIANCE

Dear Carolyn,

I happened to see your ad on Craig's List and am anxious to find out more!
My background combines staging, interior design, real estate, marketing,
and creative services management. Following is what you're looking for and
why I can help your business:

Carol DeSoto
October 1, 2003
Page 2

Residential Real-estate Staging Business:
I currently work with several peninsula realtors and contractors, preparing their listings for market. This includes meeting with sellers, renting furniture, and re-designing using existing furnishings, shopping for accessories, paint color and finish selection/coordination, hosting broker tours, and open houses to monitor property feedback.

Very Organized:
As a freelancer, I manage multiple projects in a time-driven environment. Earlier this year, my staging experience included work for Jo Ann James Design Group in Menlo Park, CA. I worked on her projects in Atherton, Woodside, San Mateo, and Menlo Park. Listings ranged from $2.5-$20 million.

Self-Starter:
While managing creative services and advertising at Hewlett-Packard, I was named a "Top Marketing Leader Worldwide." In parallel with that successful career, I completed my interior design certification from UC Santa Cruz ext., and remodeled a Los Altos 1930s Spanish style home. I'm an "accredited staging professional" and my Bachelor's Degree is in Design and Advertising.

Keen Design Eye:
I was a *Sunset* Magazine renovation design contest winner. My interiors were featured in *Palo Alto Design & Garden* and the Los Altos town newspaper. Contractors and realtors hire me for my design advice.

Quick Set Ups:
Staging is my life. I spend weekends looking at open houses so I can learn better, faster, easier, newer ways to approach designing property to sell.

Manage Teams:
The HP corporate leadership management-training program was completed and my local direct reports ranged up to 27 employees. Others were geographically dispersed throughout the country. They were given opportunities to learn and grow and enjoyed my collaborative style.

Physical Labor:
I keep in shape by regularly participating in Jazzercise and a community services dance performing group.

Transportation:
My driver's license is current and my vehicle is regularly maintained.

Carol DeSoto
October 1, 2003
Page 3

Professional Experience
Former Madison Avenue designer, Lynn Hollyn, hired me as a freelancer. I also worked for her as an intern. Currently, I work with clients on interior design consulting and direction.

Window Merchandizing:
While attending college, I designed visual displays for merchandising for a retail hardware and house wares outlet.

Flexibility
I can work as much or as little as you like. My freelance schedule is flexible. My passion is seeing the transformation of property and sales results.

So, just call me. That way we can both learn more! Best of luck in finding a good fit.

Regards,

Asmita Page

June 30, 2003   **By email**

INSIGHTS AND INDUSTRY KNOWLEDGE

Subject: A must-hire IT Analyst, Mr. Hillburn!

#5

Dear Mr. James Hillburn,

I am pleased to respond to the position of IT Analyst. In addition to meeting or exceeding all your requirements, I bring to following additional value to the position:

I am intimately familiar with gap analysis that drives change in how IT applications are deployed in business-critical situations. At HP, I conducted such gap analyses for a team of senior business managers on how a new application could successfully replace one that was a part of the Legacy system, and was business critical. This had a user base of over 10,000 globally in the finance and marketing domains. My analysis not only showed a clear implementation strategy, but this work, and the subsequent implementation of it, went on to become a company-wide showcase of how to lead such critical initiatives for successful outcomes.

One of the key challenges in successful execution beyond the gap analysis is management of change. One reason for my success stems from my ability to collaborate with key stakeholders, who are affected by the change, and then communicating with them in ways that shows them clear benefit in their day-to-day work. Shifting from resistance to excitement with those most affected, is at the heart of the change process.

Additionally, I understand that Cisco is currently in the process of migrating its business systems to a different platform. I have delivered on multiple migration projects, where I overcame various challenges, both technical and organizational, to a successful finish.

Additionally, I bring a value-add to this job with my past experience, specifically in the following areas:

➢ Dual Business and IT role, and how to *weld* IT to business to make it successful

➢ Integration of data from various technical platforms as SAP, Legacy as well as business domains as finance, customer, product, and transactions

➢ Design new systems/modify existing ones to quickly adapt to changing business models

I am interested in exploring this opportunity further. I look forward to hearing from you. I can be reached at phone (000) 555-0000 or email@email.com

Cordially,

Anshima Mapp

Encl: Résumé

Sumi Jarvis: (000) 555-0000

Century Wy.
Cupertino, CA 95014   email@email.com

July 5, 2003

FOLLOW-UP ON INFORMATIONAL INTERVIEW

Maura Fox
Manager, Embedded & Personal Systems Div.
Electronic Systems, Inc.
Pruneridge Ave
Cupertino, CA, 95014

#6

Dear Maura,

Thank you for taking the time to chat with me about the open position for Manufacturing Development Engineer. I am enclosing my résumé for your review. I am also summarizing below critical parts of my background for this position:

I bring a unique combination of skills that embody both a deep understanding of basic PC technology as well as the manufacturing processes, and how these processes are a result of successful alliances of diverse supply-chain partners. My experience at Dyno Systems includes taking advanced products through a rapid manufacturing, and delivering a series of successful netservers in a demanding environment. My skills include:

➢ **Technology Roadmaps:** Develop and communicate technology roadmaps to cement alliances and future product success in a competitive setting.

➢ **Alliance Development:** Forge strategic alliances with key providers and maintain ongoing partnerships to ensure high-integrity supply chain.

➢ **Quality Processes:** Set quality standards in both products and processes by aggressively driving continuous improvement and reliable process technology.

➢ **Cross-Functional Teams:** Collaborate across global teams and cross-divisional boundaries to ensure leadership of new products and their manufacture.

> ➤ **R&D/ODM Interplay:** Lead ongoing product transition from R&D to ODM and manage qualifications at ODM sites.

> ➤ **Components/BOMs:** Develop a robust process to manage common component use across, ensuring latest product revisions, compatibility, and lowest costs.

I am looking forward to further exploring this position with you and am excited about the possibilities and opportunities this presents.

Please call me when you would like to explore this further.

Cordially,

Sumi Jarvis
Enclosure: Résumé

Pamela Moon
Grant Road
Mountain View, CA 94040
(000) 555-0000   email@email.com

Imported Stores, Inc   December 2, 2003
20332 4th Street
Oakland, CA 94607   #7

A BAD COVER LETTER

Dear Recruiting Manager,

In response to your posting on your Website for an **IS Network Manager,** I am enclosing my résumé. The following table summarizes my candidacy:

Your Needs	I Bring
Ten years supporting IT in corporate environment	Over seven years solid experience that includes corporate IT environment.
Leading teams of software developers, networking specialists, and business analysts	Hands-on experience with some team-lead assignments. Collaborated with business area managers to identify their IT software needs and then implemented projects.
Skilled at network operations and support	Managed a group of engineers and technicians in a complex networking environment. Maintained 24x7 operations at a major B-B division.
Off-shoring skills and familiarity.	This is a new trend and I am confident that I can learn this quickly.
Certified in Cisco systems	Certified in Cisco systems.
Multi OS familiarity	Have worked in business environment with Windows, Unix, Linux, and Mainframe OS
Develop Helpdesk capability and support	Demonstrated Helpdesk experience.
Customer centric focus	Have always worked closely with customers and kept high level of satisfaction.
Negotiate SLAs and manage outsourcing and vendor activities	Have developed several SLA and vendor contract agreements.
Develop training, mentor teams, create procedures for ongoing success	Mentored teams/coached new hires. Written policies and procedures.

I hope that you will consider me favorably and call me for an interview.

Sincerely,

Pam Moon

Encl: résumé

In a tough job market the résumé is not likely to be read because of the presentation. This letter screams "Don't waste time reading résumé; I've summarized right here!" Avoid this format *even* when there's a perfect match! Instead, see what is on the following page.

Pamela Moon
3321 Grant Road
Mountain View, CA 94040
(000) 555-0000   email@email.com

December 2, 2003

A GOOD COVER LETTER

Imported Stores, Inc
20332 4th Street
Oakland, CA 94607

#8

Dear Recruiting Manager,

In response to your posting on your Website for an **IS Network Manager**, I am enclosing my résumé. Your 23 percent sales growth and the addition of 41 stores over the past year are now behind you. This is, indeed, an impressive achievement in the current economic environment.

As the economy now rebounds, your growth rate for the coming year could be now even more. With this growth rate, however, comes additional challenges particularly in the IT infrastructure and the support necessary to sustain this rate. During my tenure at General Merchandise, I have consistently supported growth stemming from ongoing acquisitions of various businesses, which required having to support a larger client base representing double digit increases. During these times, I provided design, support, and operational procedures to ensure resources and infrastructure did not limit growth.

I have extensive experience in corporate network operations, including several years as a front line network operations manager. Most recently, I conducted contract negotiations for Internet services resulting in a projected $5M annual savings.

I am customer focused and have experience with and developed internal and external SLA agreements, network policies and procedures, security guidelines, and delivered technical training sessions for helpdesk personnel, resulting in increased customer satisfaction. I am proficient in Cisco configurations and have a background in UNIX and Windows system administration.

I look forward to meeting with you to discuss in more detail how my diverse background and qualifications can quickly work for you.

Cordially,

Pam Moon

Encl: résumé

> Using one element of research from Hoover's, this letter ties the potential need of the business to what Pam brings to make it happen. This letter was a winner!

Michael Smith
Hansen Way
Cupertino, CA 95014
(000) 555-0000   email@email.com

Ms. Cindy McCaffrey   June 12, 2004
Vice President, Corporate Marketing
Google Inc.
2400 Bayshore Parkway
Mountain View, CA 94043

LEVERAGING A PREVIOUSLY TENUOUS CONNECTION
Dear Ms. McCaffrey:

#9

Your presentation about a year back to my E-Business class at Santa Clara University inspired me to make Google my employer of choice upon my graduation! My years of prior industry experience make me confident of how I can quickly create value for Google!

As someone deeply interested in marketing messages and how they drive people's behaviors I did some research on messages Google puts out and how they are perceived. For example, when I tapped those who avidly use your Website I was surprised to discover that even they were largely unaware of Google's broader offerings. Your recent open position for Associate Product Marketing Manager; would allow me the opportunity to change some of these perceptions and improve the visibility of Google's services.

In addition to meeting or exceeding *all* of the job requirements (see attached resume), my specific strengths, which will create immediate value for Google are:

- Leading initiatives that broaden business and end-user awareness of Google's advertising and search services portfolio. Catalog Search, AdWords, the Google Toolbar, and Froogle are great applications of Google's technology and they could still use improved visibility among users. I create marketing programs that generate awareness and action.

- Positioning new services to the end user. I've collaborated with all groups involved in creating and marketing new services and bring an objective and creative view to the development process. Clearly defined services can be a key to Google's future.

- Analyzing Google's industry position and developing sound marketing strategy based on competitive evaluation, the consumer, and Google itself, I can creatively apply analysis to develop sustainable competitive advantage beyond what it currently does.

Google is much more than just a search company and I am excited about creating a comprehensive message that delivers that promise. I look forward to hearing from you.

Sincerely
Michael Smith

Enclosure: Resume.

Walter Chase
Echo Lane
Saratoga, CA 95444
(000) 555-0000   email@email.com

BY FEDEX

November 22, 2003

#10

David Davenport   POSTED JOBS "UNCONVENTIONAL APPROACH"
Vice President,
Operations
Palm
300 Dixon Landing Road
Milpitas, CA 94330

Dear Mr. Davenport,

I am pleased to apply for your position of Packaging Engineer, job #2231. My résumé is enclosed.

My research shows that Palm is currently undertaking aggressive initiatives on cost cutting and product yield. To that end, I have done some specific research, about opportunities that exist at Palm, in the areas of product packaging and cost savings. For your current model of the handheld, which is the most used organizer in the market today, as much of 52 percent of the product is considered "rejected" after it enters the channel. This is a high number by any standards. Typical return rate for consumer electronic products is in the low 20s! I also found that nearly 80 percent of these rejects stem from a single cause: the breakage of the liquid crystal display!

I also went and purchased one of your models and took it apart to investigate why such high incidence of breakage and returns can occur. My initial conclusion: the way the liquid crystal is packaged is prone to shock and impact, in the most benign transport environments. By merely inserting a small pad of any of the resilient materials—and I know just the ones right for this application—the breakage incidence can be reduced by half! This will bring down the overall return to a more respectable 25 percent or so. This alone may result in a savings of over $13 million per quarter and almost wipe out the loss you reported in the latest quarter.

I am excited about this possibility and plan to call you in a few days to follow up.

Cordially,

Walt Chase

Enclosure: Résumé

PS: This package was also emailed to you today

By eMail

Subject Header: How would like to turn your loss into profit, Mr. Davenport?!

#10

Dear Mr. Davenport,

I am pleased to apply for your position of Packaging Engineer, job #2231. My résumé is enclosed.

My research shows that Palm is currently undertaking aggressive initiatives on cost cutting and product yield. To that end, I have done some specific research, about opportunities that exist at Palm, in the areas of product packaging and cost savings. For your current model of the handheld, which is the most used organizer in the market today, as much of 52 percent of the product is considered "rejected" after it enters the channel. This is a high number by any standards. Typical return rate for consumer electronic products is in the low 20s! I also found that nearly 80 percent of these rejects stem from a single cause: the breakage of the liquid crystal display!

I also went and purchased one of your models and took it apart to investigate why such high incidence of breakage and returns can occur. My initial conclusion: the way the liquid crystal is packaged is prone to shock and impact, in the most benign transport environments. By merely inserting a small pad of any of the resilient materials—and I know just the ones right for this application—the breakage incidence can be reduced by half! This will bring down the overall return to a more respectable 25 percent or so. This alone may result in a savings of over $13 million per quarter and almost wipe out the loss you reported in the latest quarter.

I am excited about this possibility and plan to call you in a few days to follow up.

Cordially,

Walt Chase

Enclosure: Résumé

PS I have sent the same message by FedEx today.

ALAN BROWN

Smith Lane
Los Gatos, CA 95032.
(000) 555-0000   email@email.com

September 16, 2002

NON-EXISTENT JOBS

Dr. James Smead,
Research and Technology Center,
BMW,
1990 Page Mill Rd,
Palo Alto, CA 94304

#11

Dear Dr. Smead:

I have read a great deal about the Telematics and Smart Vehicles work at the BMW Research Center in Palo Alto, over the past several years. I believe that your work is paving the way for the convergence of automobiles and "smart" technology.

I am a researcher in consumer electronics and mobile computing, who has been following your work. I believe that, like other technology convergences, moving telematic technologies, from early innovators/adopters, to the user majority, will require their creative application to the market. Based on my past research at IBM and Bosch, I believe that by viewing telematics from a different viewpoint, and thus structuring the platform technologies differently, can allow it to move to the user majority. Doing so, would increase user flexibility and platform openness, reduce implementation costs, and improve the user's experience. Giving telematics the potential to be applied to the whole product range and adopted incrementally.

I would like to explain the ideas behind these concepts with you in person and shall call you in a week or so.

Cordially,
Alan Brown

Brim Brene
James Circle
Saratoga, CA 94302
(000) 555-0000   email@email.com

June 9, 2003

SWITCHING INDUSTRIES: NON-EXISTENT JOBS

Mr. Lew Smithson, Jr.
Executive Vice President, CFO
Genentech, Inc.
1 DNA Way
South San Francisco, CA 94080

#12

Dear Mr. Smithson,

As someone deeply involved with Information Technology and how it supports strategic growth and competitive advantage, I have researched your company. Recent successes with the FDA approval of your new drug, favorably poise Genentech for imminent rapid growth.

I worked at Hewlett-Packard during several years when it was growing at 10–20 percent annually. This level of growth posed challenges to infrastructure providers, especially the IT function. I had a leading role in several IT initiatives driven by this rapid growth. I believe that my knowledge and experience can bring significant value to Genentech.

As a biotech leader, Genentech probably spends about four percent of revenues, or $100 million per year, on IT, much of it on infrastructure updates, and related costs. Rapid growth poses unique challenges to an organization and if these challenges are not managed, it can impede its strategic position. Particularly:

- In periods of growth, IT must respond proactively, so as not to impede growth of the core business. The challenge, of course, is to expand capability and maintain profits. I believe it is possible to reduce ongoing IT expenditures by 10 percent or more—an annual savings of at least $10 million. Much of this will come from carefully reviewing capital acquisitions and then focusing on how to make the existing infrastructure more effective, utilized, and available—most are used only about 10 percent. These savings can not only offset expenses necessary for growth, but also provide for a more productive infrastructure.

- I facilitated management and financial planning processes, as HP's infrastructure was transforming itself from a technology focused to a global services organization with customer experience as the driver, delivery of integrated solutions, and profit/loss/growth targets per service. I can leverage that recent experience into Genentech.

I look forward to speaking further with you about this and shall call you in a week.

Cordially,

Brim Bene

Walter Johnson

Alexander Avenue
Santa Clara, CA 95051

(000) 555-0000   email@email.com

December 4, 2002

NON-EXISTENT JOBS

Mr. Stephen P. Jobs
CEO and Director
Apple Computer
1 Infinite Loop
Cupertino, CA 95014

#13

Dear Mr. Jobs,

As someone steeped in technology in the Valley, I have always admired Apple Computer products. I am deeply grateful for your work in transforming Apple back to its product leadership position, as it was originally under your helm.

Looking ahead, I think that there is an opportunity, in an aspect of your product suite that may interest you. This aspect deals with design for service and the overall customer ownership experience, following the initial buyer excitement, as well as how all this affects the bottom line and long-term loyalty. My research shows that there is a movement afoot at Apple, to change *attitudes* about emergent product reliability, maintainability, and serviceability. My long and hands-on experience in this discipline shows that changing mere attitudes into disciplined *habits* is a long and expensive journey.

I am expressing my interest in exploring Apple's future plans to improve products in these areas of design and how, what I bring in this area can be of value to your company. Would you take a moment to forward this to someone with whom I can explore this further?

If I do not hear back from you within a week, I plan to call you soon thereafter. Thank you for your attention!

Cordially,

Walter Johnson

> *Within a week of this letter, sent FedEx, Walt got a call from Mr. Job's office, stating that Steve Jobs would like to see his résumé! Walt is a hands-on individual contributor.*

Jean Soder: (000) 555-0000   email@email.com

February 22, 2003

Mr. D. S. Smith,
Director, Customer Advocacy
Cisco Systems
2323 North First St.
San Jose, CA 94352

Dear Mr. Smith:

I am writing to you, because the role, in which your organization is engaged, intrigues me. Also, I have some proven ideas on how to make your mission more customers focused.

As a customer advocate at HP's Executive Briefing Center, I was leading the charge of ensuring that strategic customers came to the Center, to hear about our new offerings and went away wanting to buy more and keeping loyal relationships. Initially, when I was learning about this process, I discovered that there was a disconnect between what the customers came expecting and what was presented to them. Interestingly, there was no robust process to ascertain this disconnect, until I started a process and took the initiative to approach visiting customers and found a way to get to the core of their issues. This simple process of "structured discovery" entailed researching the customer account history, talking to those who service the account, and then formulating a discovery interview with the customer face-to-face.

This simple dynamic of face-to-face discovery, yielded actionable information that helped HP attend to many inputs in a personal way. The result was immediate change in customer attitude and increased business. Additionally, I made sure that the follow-up with the account teams was diligent and that the customer experienced an outcome that was positive.

This discovery process that inevitably results in immediate improvement in customer loyalty, appears simple initially, but it is *not* easy! There are many details that can make or break the overall impact of what this process can accomplish, and I have now learned of those elements.

As someone who is in charge of customer experience and advocacy, you would be interested in making such an initiative work at CISCO. The results are worth the effort and they are immediate. I would be interested in exploring this with you, and show some of my work at HP that resulted in my getting a Customer Advocacy Award. The improvement, I initiated, went on to become a company-wide best practice, very quickly.

If I do not hear from you, I plan to call you in a few days.

Cordially,

Jean Soder
(000) 555-0000

Sandy Smith
Glorietta Circle,
Santa Clara, CA 95051
(000) 555-0000   email@email.com

January 28, 2004

Sheila Bonet
Human Resources Client Services   #15
Stanford University
Redwood Hall, Rm G-12, MC 4120
243 Panama St.
Stanford, CA 94305-4120

CLOSED POSITION: NON-EXISTENT JOBS

Hello Sheila,

Thank you for your prompt response to my recent query about job #002479. Although this position is no longer open, I would like to express my continued interest in similar positions, which may open up.

Reading from some of your recent job requirements, ITSS appears to need highly effective and energetic matrix managers, with a proven track record, for influencing and working across multiple organizations and serving the needs of diverse user constituencies.

ITSS is probably in the best position to identify and implement high impact change initiatives, across multiple IT organizations, and deliver a differentiated cross-discipline value at the lowest possible cost. However, in a constituency as diverse as Stanford, implementing consistent change across parochialism of individual departments, can sometimes be challenging, particularly when executing in a matrix organization. I have a demonstrated track record of influencing diverse interests to embrace a common cause, develop integrated plans, and execute on established targets. Time and again, in a highly dynamic and rapidly changing environment, I have proactively detected forces of resistance, and then neutralized them effectively to keep the project momentum, creating broad alliances in the process, and always delivering my commitments on schedule!

I am confident that with my extensive experience and proven project management successes in a high-tech environment, I would be an asset to the ITSS team.

If some of your positions are temporarily frozen, due to budgetary constraints, I am more than happy to discuss creative approaches that can lead to a win-win outcome.

I look forward to exploring this further with you.

Cordially,

Sandy Smith

Sandra Jenkins
Hillview Court,
Los Altos Hills, CA 94022
(000) 555-0000   <u>email@email.com</u>

October 23, 2003

NON-EXISTENT JOBS

Mr. Hakim Mashouf
Chief Operating Officer
The Fashion Center
22 Union Square
San Francisco, CA 94101

#16

Dear Mr. Mashouf,

I heard, through a mutual acquaintance, that you recently canceled your plans to search for vice president of IT at Fashion Center. Although I understand the reasons for possibly making this decision, I would like to present the following solutions.

My research into your operating strategy, business growth objectives, and potential risk factors makes me reflect on my own management skills and experience in high-tech, suggesting that at this juncture, I could create unparalleled value for you. Additionally, my passion for fashion and retail would be an asset to your franchise. I can create differentiated value for you in the following ways:

- Your executive team is highly knowledgeable and skilled in fashion and retail. I bring a unique balance to this team with my strong and proven technology leadership and experience, combined with keen business acumen.

- In order to maintain your edge, in a highly competitive fashion industry, you may need a strategy for:

  o End-to-end (design to store-front) value chain integration

  o Chosen technology needs to effectively meet the needs of the target non-technical user: interface must be user-friendly

  o The IT&S solution must enable real-time delivery of quality information to diverse users, ranging from executives to store employees, to enable rapid, quality decision-making across the value chain.

- o IT investment is 'background' to your business: it must produce the best ROI.
- You need a leader who has demonstrated success in managing remote teams, has the ability to recruit and retain the needed technical expertise in a "non-technology" company. Concurrently, the ability to effectively communicate with top executive team, as well as other users of IT&S, are critical for success.

I am confident that my extensive management experience in high-tech, will be an asset to your company. At a more personal level, I am excited about this opportunity for the following reasons:

In addition to my experience managing technology teams, I have a flare for fashion. I have a good understanding of your customer profile. Your business presents me with the unique opportunity to combine the two.

In looking at your current international business reach, I look forward to discussing potentially extending that reach to other countries as India. I am of Indian origin and see strong potential for business opportunities on both, the supply and consumer side.

Being a Stanford alumna, it was heartwarming for me to learn about your active involvement in education of future graduates and business leaders.

I look forward to exploring this further with you.

Cordially,

Sandra Jenkins

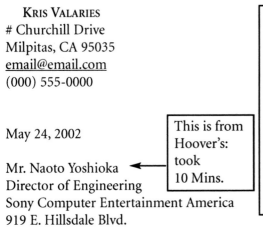

KRIS VALARIES
Churchill Drive
Milpitas, CA 95035
email@email.com
(000) 555-0000

Engineer:
Software Engineer

Sony Computer Entertainment America, Inc. has positions available for software engineers in Foster City, CA. Please send résumés to:
Sony Computer Entertainment
Attn: Staffing Ref. SJIA
919 E. Hillsdale Blvd. 2nd Floor

May 24, 2002

This is from Hoover's: took 10 Mins.

Mr. Naoto Yoshioka
Director of Engineering
Sony Computer Entertainment America
919 E. Hillsdale Blvd.
Foster City, CA 94404-4247

NON-EXISTENT JOBS

#17

Dear Mr. Yoshioka:

The reason for writing you this note is because there is, perhaps, an opportunity for Sony Computer Entertainment to significantly increase the eye appeal and animation quality to its PlayStation 2 platforms through focused firmware and software engineering.

As a seasoned hands-on software architect and someone familiar with the products that originated at Sony Computer Entertainment, I have the following observations: the PlayStation 2 still continues to enjoy good consumer following; it is still the market leader. My research shows, however, that recent advancements by your competitors, have gradually eroded your market position and that trend seems to be on the rise. Sony's new pricing may be a partial acknowledgement of this.

The recent resurgence of your competitors' products, perhaps, stems from their ability to deliver a superior overall game experience to the players. Your competitors' animation is perceived as more dynamic, smooth, and realistic, their colors more vivid. One way to achieve or exceed that level of rendition and effect is to have an experienced software/systems engineer creatively collaborating with the artists, early in the development. By preserving the basic game script, keeping the integrity of animation, and making the motion more real-to-life and smooth, with vivid colors, players can enjoy a more enhanced and thrilling experience. I have done similar work with creative artists and am confident that such an integrated product enhancement can be realized (with some effort).

I would like to explore these ideas with you more in person and shall call you in a week or so.

Cordially,

Kris Valaries

| Called Fry's Electronics: 10 Mins for research. |

| When Chris called Mr. Yoshioka within a few days, he acknowledged the letter and had a conversation about the next steps with him! |

Priti Jain
May Avenue
Cupertino, CA 95014
(000) 555-0000
email@email.com

NON-EXISTENT JOBS

Mr. Stephen James   November 20, 2003
Executive Vice President,
SureSoft Inc.
10 Maguire Road, Suite 332
Lexington, MA 02421

#18

Dear Mr. James:

Congratulations on your recent win at United Nations and continuing inroads in the ASP market share, in the mid-to large-size markets!

SureSoft Inc. can further increase its market share, by insuring dominance in new segments as BPO services in finance and accounting, and off-shoring. My research also shows that for on-demand services, a space in which your competitors are currently outperforming you, there is an opportunity, where I can help you close that gap, and soon, position you to vault them. With these new services, SureSoft can expand their presence in Europe and APAC rapidly.

As Director of Business Development/Sales of HP's Managed Services, I am in discussion with several ASP providers, on ways to aggressively capture outsourcing opportunities. I offer:

- Over10 years in strategic global IT management, primarily focused on building and growing start-up businesses in Offshore and Hosting Services market space.

- Expertise in PeopleSoft Hosting Services, Messaging on Demand (Adaptive Network Infrastructure Services), Business Process Outsourcing (BPO), and Web Hosting Services.

- Experience with small, medium, and large-scale customers ranging from $5M to $25M.

- Leader in designing, structuring, and implementing opportunities with end-to-end solutions.

- Expertise in sales, operations, marketing, engineering, R&D, and customer support/service.

- Competitive intelligence to win opportunities against competitors (primarily technical solutions, costing and pricing in application outsourcing business space).
- Strong experience in managing U.S., Asia-Pacific/Europe. I speak German and Hindi.

I shall call you in a week to discuss this further and follow-up.

Cordially,

Priti Jain

Pam James
Mary Avenue
Cupertino, CA 95014
(000) 555-0000   email@email.com

Ms. Stephanie Charles   November 22, 2003

Vice President   NON-EXISTENT JOBS
Mayfair Mall
39000 Stevens Creek Blvd
Cupertino, CA 95014

#19

Dear Ms. Charles:

As someone who shops at the Mayfair Mall regularly, I am excited about the recent renovations you have done to attract more customers. I think that with your new design, layouts, and the way anchor stores are positioned, your foot traffic should greatly increase and your overall appeal, as a trendy mall, should become a showcase for other malls to follow.

In addition to your current initiatives, to spruce up the physical appeal of the mall, I wonder if you have considered other avenues to reach the community, by sponsoring events that make you more visible in the eyes of those who are within a ten-mile radius of the mall. I have the following ideas:

- Sponsoring specific events that entail student contests at local schools. Awarding winning entrants certificates from merchants who are mall clients will bring students and their parents to the mall, in addition to their regular visits here. There are 23 schools in this area and the student population of about 5,600. If you count parents of students, who come with them, this can substantially increase the flux of customers to the mall. I have worked out details of this program, after talking to my daughter, her classmates (they are all around 13 years of age), and some of their parents and teachers. They thought that this was a workable idea. We can also design this program to make the schools get something out of this, in this era of budget cutbacks.

- There are also 12 playgrounds nearby that hold weekly tournaments and games for kids, ranging in age from nine to 18. Their parents often come to these events. I also have some ideas on how to sponsor events at these playgrounds, on a regular basis, that will tie into increased traffic to the mall. I can show you these ideas in person.

- We have two movie complexes with 12 screens within a block of this mall. I do not see any mall advertising before the main feature. Tying the movie tickets to discounts at mall merchants can be a win-win situation for all, since the movie complex is within walking distance from here. The mall has ample parking and the movie theater, does not.

I have other ideas on how to promote the mall through community outreach. I would like to meet with you to discuss this in person. I plan to call you in a few days to set up a meeting.

Cordially,

Pam James

Charles Smith
Emerson Street
Los Gatos, CA 94556
(000) 555-0000   email@email.com

January 27, 2003

Mr. James Burrows
President and CEO
New Ventures
Enterprise Computers, Inc.
Austin, TX, 78754

#20

Dear Mr. Burrows:

Enterprise Computers has made impressive strides in capturing home and small-business markets. As someone who has followed Enterprise, for the past few years, your new initiatives to aggressively pursue Enterprise space, imaging, and printing are equally impressive.

As yet another area ripe for Enterprise to pursue, I wonder if you have considered total/high availability critical computing systems. For the past sixteen years, I have been steeped in this area and have made seminal technology contributions that have advanced the state-of-the art in this area. Particularly in the past seven years, I was a key player in helping HP NonStop penetrate into taking over NASDAQ. I architected the major part of the transaction software and worked on integrating that with its matching engine. There were many challenges, both in technology and applications. Throughout this period, I collaborated closely with the marketing team and customers, helping each achieve an appreciation of possibilities and then making it a reality. Even after the full deployment, I continued to work to support the customer on enhancing performance to a level where customer felt assured, even on the worst trading days.

I am proposing that you, as someone leading strategic initiatives at Enterprise, take a closer look at what you might be able to do, using the existing and emerging technology, and leverage that to penetrate this promising and high-visibility market space.

What I bring to this initiative is my passion, track record of unparalleled success, and an ability to deliver at every level of the project: technology, business, customer hand-holding, and follow-up support, to provide the kind of assurance both Enterprise and its critical computing customers are going to need in such an endeavor.

I would like to discuss this personally with you and explore how this can be moved forward to achieve success. I plan to call you in about a week to follow-up.

Cordially

Charlie Smith

Carol Lee
Lake Merrit View
Saratoga, CA 94333
(000) 555-0000   email@email.com

James Harbrake   July 23, 2003
Manager, IT Operations   CONTRACT/CONTINGENT EMPLOYMENT
Stanford University
Stanford, CA 94305

Dear Mr. Harbrake:

#21

Thank you for your call yesterday and your explanation why the job opportunity that I was pursuing in your organization, is now put on hold. I was looking forward to concluding the interview process and coming on board quickly, to help you get ready for the flux of events that suddenly start with the Fall Quarter, now just a few weeks away!

During the three rounds of interviews I've had with you, your staff, and higher-level managers, I saw the following challenges that your organization must deal with to make IT infrastructure support the academic and administrative functions:

- Making the student data available to *all* constituencies on the campus, within 24 hours of enrollment, so that services can be made available to the entire student body quickly, efficiently, and without any errors. The current system and processes take up to a week to do this. I have some ideas that we discussed previously that are very practicable.

- The ability of the IT staff to help different office areas with new applications and special software to make them work more efficiently in administrative tasks. With recent cutbacks of administrative personnel, this is now even more urgent.

- Integrating the myriad procedures for handling student needs so that regardless of where students are pursuing their studies—and now this is global for many students—they are able to have a uniform method by which they can do their administrative chores easily and focus more on their studies. I talked to a few students, just to check this for myself, and there is a crying need for this initiative.

In an era of cutbacks and reorganizations, it is tempting to hold off on critical initiatives and let things continue as they have in the past. My view is that these cutbacks can exacerbate the impact of older IT systems on the entire campus and not just the student body.

I am willing to work with you now, to help you get started on these and other IT initiatives. With the Fall Quarter fast approaching, wouldn't you like to be ready when the students start flooding in? I am willing to work on a contract basis, at a rate that you can afford. Once the budget matters are settled and you see what I can do for you, we can go from there.

I plan to call you in a few days to see what you think.

Cordially,

Carol Lee

Soujil Vasques

(000) 555-0000   email@email.com

November 12, 2003

Mr. Tom Cotton   CONTINGENT EMPLOYMENT
eBay, Inc.
2145 First Street
San Jose, CA 95125

#22

Dear Tom,

It was a pleasure meeting you yesterday. Thank you for giving me the opportunity to introduce my new idea about customer events to eBay.

After our meeting, you expressed interest in the speaker program that I developed at Cisco. In reviewing your eBay Web site and having attended an eBay University seminar in San Jose, four items immediately came to my mind.

- **Session Class Offering** could use a stronger framework

- **Session Content:** How do participants know what to attend? At eBay Live! There were 75 classes offered. Some classes had similar-sounding titles. How can you indicate progressive presentations to leverage attendee learning and have attendees using eBay more productively?

- **Customer Data:** What type of data collection devices do you use on-site for customer breakout session entry and why would you need this customer data?

- **Session and Evaluation Processing:** I noticed that speakers presented their class more than once. How can speakers access feedback from their presentation on-site and make adjustments or improve the content for their next session?

The thrust of my approach in suggesting improved design for your eBay Live! Event is differentiation, segmentation, customer friendly offerings, and actionable outcomes. These actionable outcomes are natural fallout of the design eBay can easily adopt. The benefit to eBay, of course, is dramatically improved customer mind share, loyalty, and increased business volume. I am confident that I can help achieve this with ease!

I have mapped out some details and would like to meet with you to share this. I'll call you early next week to see when you're available. If we agree on this, I would like a short engagement to prove my value to eBay.

Best regards,

Soujil Vasques

LINDA S. BRONSON

123 Lake Merrit Avenue 000-555-1234
San Jose, CA 95124 email@email.com

A WELL-RESEARCHED COVER LETTER

January 20, 2005
Mr. Jeff Vijungco
Staffing Manager
Executive Search & Corporate Functions
Adobe Systems
345 Park Avenue
San Jose, CA 95110-2704

#23

Dear Mr. Vijungco,

Your recently posted position for the Director of Enterprise Relationship Marketing to build and sustain client relationships intrigues me.

The Adobe Intelligent Document Platform certainly is a breakthrough answer to overcoming the enterprise document-data divide and could be of immense value to businesses and government agencies worldwide. Its application spans disciplines, industries, and geographies, and outdistances much of what the competition has to offer.

Interestingly, in my research I was struck by the market's lack of awareness of this platform, its technology, and business applicability. In fact, AMR Research reported last year that "barely anyone knows about it (the platform)—at least at the enterprise level." I am sure that this perception is now changing, but is it changing fast enough?

In further researching Adobe's marketing partners and channels, I was also struck by the possibility that Adobe could exploit an additional leverage in penetrating the enterprise market and capture the space for which Microsoft and others are vying. This space is huge and growing and, by aligning itself with more of the right partners, Adobe could accelerate its acceptance and success as an enterprise market incumbent. .

By properly attacking the enterprise market—and with the technological edge Adobe already has—it could easily and rapidly capture significant market share in this space. While Adobe may be already uniquely positioned to differentiate itself from others in the creative and consumer markets, it could be better positioned in the enterprise market to compete and win against companies as Microsoft that are already firmly established in that space. My past experience and first-hand knowledge of how to do this successfully would be invaluable to Adobe.

I am confident that I can help Adobe build enterprise relationships, and develop and articulate a messaging strategy for the enterprise that is seamlessly integrated into communications programs worldwide. I would be interested in pursuing this opportunity further, and I look forward to talking with you about it further. The attached resume and my profile on LinkedIn provide more detail about my past and my accomplishments in these areas.

Cordially,

Linda S. Bronson

LINDA S. BRONSON

123 Lake Merrit Avenue   000-555-1234
San Jose, CA 95124   email@email.com

May 11, 2005

#24

Mr. Bobby R. Johnson
President and Chief Executive Officer
Foundry Networks, Inc.
2100 Gold Street
San Jose, CA 95164

A WELL-RESEARCHED COVER LETTER

Dear Mr. Johnson:

Your company's search for a Marketing Communications Manager has caught my interest and attention, particularly in light of your recent success at Interop Las Vegas. Not only did Foundry capture the Best of Interop award for Network Infrastructure, it also walked away as Best of Interop Grand Prize Winner, no small feat considering the formidable competition you faced. I was particularly impressed when I read that Ron Anderson, the lead judge, said "Foundry emerged as the one product we felt would impact the marketplace most during a time when every IT investment dollar is being scrutinized for maximum return." Wow! What an endorsement!

Clearly, as attested to by Interop and CMP, Foundry switches, routers, and Web traffic management solutions can be of immense value to any enterprise or governmental entity.

In my research, however, the level of awareness of Foundry struck me. While I found that, of course, most markets crown Cisco the undisputed leader in network infrastructure, there is little distinction among Foundry, Extreme, and Force 10 in the minds of enterprise customers, network integrators/resellers, and other influencers. I am sure that Foundry is changing this perception, but is it changing fast enough? In today's high-velocity world, "fast" has a new meaning!

In further researching Foundry marketing partners and channels, I was also struck by the reality that Foundry could exploit additional leverage in penetrating the enterprise and midsize business markets. These spaces are huge and growing (albeit at a more moderate rate than during 2004). By aligning itself with more of the right partners, Foundry could rapidly pull ahead of companies like Extreme and gain valuable ground on Cisco. My past experience and first-hand knowledge of how to do this successfully in the current flux would be invaluable

I am confident that I can help Foundry develop and articulate a messaging strategy that is seamlessly integrated into marketing communications programs worldwide. Your products are impressive, and I am certain that by properly and urgently exploiting the opportunity, Foundry could easily become the next Silicon Valley success story.

I look forward to talking with you, or someone you designate, about this position. The enclosed resume provides more detail about my past and my accomplishments in these areas.

Cordially,

Linda S. Bronson

LINDA S. BRONSON

123 Lake Merrit Avenue   000-555-1234
San Jose, CA 95124   email@email.com

Mr. Andrew Preston   January 14, 2005
Senior Vice President, Marketing
Actelis Networks
6150 Stevenson Boulevard   #25
Fremont, CA 94538

A WELL-RESEARCHED COVER LETTER

Dear Mr. Preston:

Your posted position for a Marketing Communications Manager intrigues me.

Your MetaLIGHT breakthrough certainly seems to be the right technical solution to overcoming the limitations posed by copper infrastructure. Clearly, the Actelis solution could be of immense value to both telecom service providers and the enterprise.

However, as I did some research on Actelis, its strategy, and the current market dynamic, I was struck by the lessons of my past experience working with companies serving these same markets. This may be of interest to you in how you could, perhaps, position Actelis vis-à-vis these two market segments.

In researching your marketing partners and channels, I was also struck by the possibility that Actelis could be missing out on additional leverage in penetrating the enterprise market and exploiting the space that Cisco and others are now conquering. This space is huge and growing and, by aligning itself with the right partners, Actelis could accelerate its acceptance and success as an enterprise market provider.

Looking back, I watched many technology providers focusing their products, messages, and resources on the telecom market and only opportunistically approaching the growing and highly lucrative enterprise market. As markets matured and technologies stabilized, telcos were relegated to competing as commodity vendors, while data enterprise companies flourished.

By properly positioning itself, Actelis—with the technological edge it already has—could capture easily both the telecom and enterprise markets. While Actelis may be uniquely positioned to differentiate itself from telco old-guard competitors like Nortel and Lucent, it could be better positioned to compete and win against networking incumbents like Cisco and Extreme, who are already firmly established in that space. My past experience and first hand knowledge of how to do this successfully in the current flux would be invaluable to Actelis.

I can help Actelis stake its claim to the enterprise market and capture significant additional market share. Your products are impressive, and I am confident that by properly exploiting this opportunity, Actelis could easily become the next Silicon Valley success story.

I would be interested in pursuing this further and look forward to meeting with you and your colleagues. I plan to call you in a few days.

Cordially,

Linda S. Bronson

LINDA S. BRONSON

123 Lake Merrit Avenue   000-555-1234
San Jose, CA 95124   email@email.com

April 26, 2005
Mr. Dan Chu
Director of Global ISV Alliances
VMware, Inc.
3145 Porter Drive
Palo Alto, CA 94304

Dear Mr. Chu:

A WELL-RESEARCHED COVER LETTER

I am pleased to respond to the ISV Alliance Program Manager position, for which my qualifications meet or exceed your requirements. My resume is enclosed.

As VMware competes against Microsoft and continues to improve its ISV ecosystem with moves such as its agreement with Oracle, VMware will need creative and innovative leaders to identify and drive partner channel operations projects and marketing programs worldwide. I have worked with field sales force and technical support organizations, and bring a creative approach that capitalizes on my background in business. I have led virtual teams for the cross-functional development of innovative high-tech products spanning the product lifecycle, from initiation through product release and through its life cycle. As a program manager at Hewlett Packard, I led, organized, and coordinated the comprehensive workflow and implementation of all aspects of worldwide product launches successfully.

My research into the partnering practices of SAP, HP and Microsoft shows that these companies continually assess dynamic partnerships for new and maximized profit opportunities, by providing clear value to partner field organizations and end customers as well as fostering close ties among the high level executives. Instituting innovative partner projects require attention to many aspects, including analysis for strategic planning, strong marketing and sales initiatives, coordination and partnership with stakeholders, and training and support mechanisms. Often, I found that selectively going after strategic partnerships and then nurturing them are far more important than merely on boarding a hoard of partners and then letting them languish. My background in leading projects with stakeholders outside the company provides me with a broad business perspective and a respect for the need for attention to detail, risk management, and contingency planning. My legal background will be useful in contracts and potential issues, ranging from patent rights to service level agreements.

I look forward to the opportunity to explore this further with you.

Cordially,

Mary H. Chay
Encl. Resume

LINDA S. BRONSON

123 Lake Merrit Avenue   000-555-1234
San Jose, CA 95124   email@email.com

#27

April 8, 2005

Mr. James Dragmist
Network Appliances
3435 Java Court
Sunnyvale, CA 94086

A WELL-RESEARCHED COVER LETTER

Dear Mr. Dragmist

I am pleased to respond to the Technical Marketing—Technical Sales/Partner Enablement Program Management position, for which my qualifications meet or exceed your requirements. My resume is attached.

As Network Appliance diversifies its channel strategy with partners such as Avnet, Arrow, and Fujitsu, focusing on small and mid-sized accounts, it will need creative and innovative leadership to expertly support technical sales across organizations. Network Appliance's direct sales force also faces the challenge of promoting more complex SAN solutions. I have experience leading cross-functional development of innovative high-tech products, from initiation through product release and beyond. I bring rich and proven program management experience with product launches, a deep understanding of technical sales needs, and a creative approach to solving problems. As a product manager I have developed sales tools, trained systems engineers and sales representatives, and given cogent customer presentations.

Network Appliance's recent announcement of its manufacturing alliance with IBM is an example of the importance of partnerships in all areas, including channel distribution. Development and smooth implementation of channel partnerships will entail professionals with the ability to align participants to meet ambitious goals and vault competition. I have coordinated, influenced, and motivated geographically and culturally diverse cross-functional stakeholders, both inside and outside the company, to deliver products that delighted customers. Additionally, my legal background will be useful in contracts and potential issues, ranging from patent rights to service level agreements.

Flawless projects that enable partners and generate end user demand require an experienced program manager who can execute a project within tight time and monetary constraints, and who can implement process improvements. I successfully initiated and then managed a program for outsourcing manufacturing functions, which had been behind schedule from the outset and slipping, and then brought back on track. For an important customer site, I significantly reduced delivery time, saving the account by working closely with the stakeholders.

I look forward to the opportunity to explore this further with you.

Cordially,

Linda Bronson
Encl. Resume

LINDA S. BRONSON

123 Lake Merrit Avenue   000-555-1234
San Jose, CA 95124   email@email.com

Don Johnson
iPod Manager
Apple Computer
One Infinite Loop
Cupertino, CA 95014

#28

Dear Mr. Johnson,

A WELL-RESEARCHED COVER LETTER

I am responding to the job posting for the iPod + HP Program Manager and am enclosing my resume for your review. In addition to meeting or exceeding the job requirements, I bring the following specific strengths:

Apple's iPod has created a splash in the marketplace and its tremendous response is apparent in the product shortages that caught many retailers flat-footed during the past holiday season. Its alliance with HP to channel the iPod to retail customers provides an additional avenue to generate sales backed by a recognized powerhouse brand, which will only help further its market penetration.

As the product's novelty surge transitions into a steady demand through various channels and HP garners more and more share of the overall product revenues, managing a steady and predictable flow of iPods to HP and its channels is going to be critical. Additionally, as derivative products at various price points begin to become available the flow of logistics, product demand/supply management, and the oversight of the partnership between Apple and HP are going to become critical in the ultimate success of Apple's star product.

Industry insights suggest that there is going to be a flash memory version of the iPod in the near future for the low-end market and that Apple is planning a strategy to tie that product to some of the future platforms. Since iPod is going to be major player in the product revenue stream for Apple in the near future, managing the overall program with key partners as HP is going to be critical to iPod's ultimate and overall success. Managing both the supply chain upstream and downstream to make sure that product flow is seamless to meet the market demand and expectation is going to be central to this success.

I bring a disciplined approach to program management, including a formal legal background in contracts and working with vendors and channels. My previous experience with HP and high-tech products and systems programs uniquely qualify me for this position and I feel confident that I will be able to deliver exceptional rather than expected results in this position.

I am looking forward to exploring this further. If I do not hear from you in about a week I plan to call you to follow up.

Cordially,

Linda Bronson

LINDA S. BRONSON

123 Lake Merrit Avenue   000-555-1234
San Jose, CA 95124   email@email.com

May 23, 2005

Ms. Edith Johnson
CEO, BankServ
2343 Sansome Street
San Francisco, CA 94111

#29

Dear Ms. Johnson

A WELL-RESEARCHED PROSPECT LETTER

I have watched BankServ grow into a major player in the financial services market. I would like to explore an idea that may benefit its future growth. As a seasoned marketing and public relations professional, I have helped several technology companies in this market expand their businesses and establish leadership positions.

With six successful years in business, the Swift and Inc. 500 awards, and 300 customers in 52 countries, BankServ has moved into a strong position and has the opportunity to generate considerable interest among influencers. I would like to take advantage of the track record and build on its ongoing momentum.

Here's how:

Create US market and customer awareness of BankServ by developing a differentiated message that will enable the company to stand apart from its competition and that highlights the benefits of the company's unique products such as the Check 21 Compliant service, Turboswift and Global Funds Exchange.

Generate press and analysts coverage of the company and its message with a steady stream of in-person visits, press releases, customer stories and opportunities for product reviews targeting the technology and financial market influencers, business and trade reporters, and key market analysts.

Build credibility and recognition by developing a Lighthouse customer program with customers who are willing to talk with press, analyst and potential customers about their product experiences.

Develop a brand image for the company by consistently applying the message across all communication vehicles such as the web site, sales literature and presentations, and public relations materials.

Create company and customer awareness and leads with local seminars in key markets and by exhibiting at select trade shows, which also offer opportunities for public speaking and for leading seminars and other programs.

The enclosed resume shows how I've worked with other companies and achieved results. I will call you next week to explore the opportunity with you.

Cordially,

Linda Bronson

LINDA S. BRONSON

123 Lake Merrit Avenue   000-555-1234
San Jose, CA 95124   email@email.com

Mr. Harold W. Brooks, CEO   April 13, 2005
American Red Cross
85 Second Street, 8th Floor   #30
San Francisco, CA 94105

Re: Director position for Prepare Bay Area Project

Dear Mr. Brooks,

A WELL-RESEARCHED COVER LETTER: NON-PROFIT

Please consider me an enthusiastic applicant for the Director position for the Prepare Bay Area Project. As you'll see in my résumé (attached), I have the expertise needed to get this critically important project off to a quick start and carry it through to meet your goals and exceed your expectations.

As a grant-funded initiative, time and money is limited—so you need a director who will hit the ground running and make an immediate impact. I can do just that, as I proved last year during a six-month contract to produce educational materials for the Easy Voter Guide Project (www.easyvoter.org). Within weeks, I streamlined production systems and improved collaboration among staff, consultants, government agencies and a diverse group of community volunteers spread throughout California and Nevada. The result was an increase in voter turnout, and a dramatic improvement in the quality of service to the Easy Voter Guide audience: new voters, low-level readers, new citizens and ESL readers, and professional staff engaged in voter education projects. I can rapidly deliver similar results for the Prepare Bay Area Project.

To better understand some of the challenges that will arise in implementing the Prepare Bay Area Project, I spoke about it with Albany Vice Mayor, Allan Maris, and City Councilmember Jewel Okawachi—both of whom I currently work with on the Albany Schools Drug and Alcohol Task Force (DATF). They each had a similar reaction: "It sounds great—and of course, it's needed. But the city is already short-staffed. So this project would need to be very well designed to make it easy to participate, or it simply won't happen."

As the founder and coordinator of DATF, a new citywide effort to create drug and alcohol prevention programs and services for youth, I understand their concern. I'm an expert at building community campaigns that make it easy for over-extended and over-stressed stakeholders to work effectively and produce tangible results. By creating sensible organizational structures and providing clear communications, effective agendas, useful reports, facilitated meetings and on-going volunteer management, I've succeeded in bringing together school staff, local government leaders, city and county agencies, community groups, businesses, parents and students. I'm ready to do the same kind of work for the Prepare Bay Area Project.

I've recently wrapped up my freelance practice and am looking for a full-time position with a mission I genuinely support—and I support the mission of the Red Cross wholeheartedly. I look forward to meeting with you to discuss how I can ensure the Prepare Bay Area Project achieves its objectives.

Thank you for your time and consideration.

Cordially,

LINDA S. BRONSON

123 Lake Merrit Avenue   000-555-1234
San Jose, CA 95124   email@email.com

March 22, 2005
Mr. David T. Ching
Senior Vice President & CIO
Safeway
5918 Stoneridge Mall Road
Pleasanton, CA 94588-3229

#31

Dear Mr. Ching,

A WELL-RESEARCHED COVER LETTER

I am pleased to respond to the open position of Director, Application Development, Tracking code #191-05, at Safeway. I meet or exceed all your job requirements.

With the highly competitive markets in the space in which Safeway operates, IT can play a key role in combating inroads by aggressive super chains as Wal-Mart and Costco. Driving costs down is key in successfully establishing a brand and presence for a grocery store chain in the emerging competitive markets and then creating an exceptional customer experience. With Safeway's employee growth at nearly 10 times its revenue growth, there is a great opportunity to increase margins by identifying opportunities for productivity gains and automation. I see the following factors as critical to this goal:

Constantly evaluate how the overall vision for the organization is being implemented through technology initiatives and identify opportunities that remain untapped.

Identify where costs can be driven down through automation and develop an agenda for prioritizing this across the entire value chain

Automate as many of the manual functions as are customer friendly, while continually evaluate customers' preferences to provide an exceptional experience than what is expected.

Develop a community-specific technology implementation plan that provides most productive and cost effective store operations.

Constantly evaluate if the current technology infrastructure provides the best ROI and then recommend appropriate initiatives to make sure that this does take place.

Develop a highly disciplined software development and implementation process that makes businesses drive technology and not the other way around.

My track record will show you how I have used my technology insights and customer/client knowledge to provide the best solutions in a very cost effective and timely way.

I am excited about working for Safeway and looking forward to exploring this opportunity further.

Cordially,

Linda Bronson

LINDA S. BRONSON

123 Lake Merrit Avenue   000-555-1234
San Jose, CA 95124   email@email.com

#32

Bill Miller   May 25, 2005
CEO & President
Valchemy, Inc.
1825 South Grant, Suite 300
San Mateo, CA 94402

A WELL-RESEARCHED PROSPECT LETTER

Dear Mr. Miller,

Congratulations on your company's recent venture capital award. As the business pages of major newspapers and magazines keep reporting, merger and acquisition activity is on the rise. Valchemy will want to take advantage of this trend to introduce and promote its merger and acquisition software, an enterprise solution that streamlines and automates the transactions process. You may be considering developing a strategic communications plan to help educate and raise awareness among key investment and financial groups.

Public relations can help the company build sales and a customer base by building credibility for the product among buyers, potential buyers, competitors, trade and business reporters and market analysts, other key influencers and opinion makers. I see the following factors a critical to this goal:

- Create U.S. financial and investment market awareness of Valchemy merger and acquisition enterprise product by developing a differentiated message that creates a brand name for the product.

- Generate press and analysts' coverage of the company and its message with a steady stream of in-person visits, targeted press releases, customer stories, and opportunities for product reviews, targeting the technology and financial market influencers, thought leaders, business and trade reporters, and key market analysts.

- Build credibility and recognition by developing a Lighthouse customer program with customers who are willing to talk with press, analyst and potential customers about their product experiences. Build a community of evangelists.

- Develop a brand image for the company by consistently applying the message across all communication vehicles such as the Web site, sales literature and presentations, and public relations materials.

- Create high-profile executive presence in the financial and investment community through regular speaking engagements at key conferences and forums. Leverage network serving these professionals through extensive executive participation.

My track record will demonstrate that I have extensive experience working with high technology companies and start-ups, launching companies with emerging technologies into new markets, early market development programs, and helping companies establish a market presence and leadership positions. I also have significant experience with high technology solutions targeting the financial and institutional market.

I look forward to talking with you regarding your plans for public relations and marketing. I can be reached at 000-555-1234 or by email at email@email.com

Cordially,

Linda Bronson

Summary Chapter-7: Write to the Point with Letters

This chapter presents various types of letters that are sent to explore and respond to job opportunities.

Before writing a letter it is worthwhile to review the process of business writing and sending a letter. Remember the following sequence in the process:

✓ Plan. This should take about 50 percent of the total time budget for the letter

✓ Draft. This should take about 20 percent of the total time budget for the letter

✓ Edit. This should take the remaining 30 percent. Editing takes 50 percent more time than drafting a letter!

A letter-writing tool is provided to help craft an impactful message. Sending the letter to the right target is critical. The weakest link in the letter writing process is the follow-up. Only about five percent know how to follow-up a well written letter diligently. A letter may a compelling message for the target company, but it is not a good idea to assume that the recipient will call back to talk to you. You must follow-up!

What the letters should and should not cover are described in details, including a listing of Dos and Don'ts. A showcase of different types of actual letters—32 letter assortments that got positive results—that go with and without the résumé is presented.

Dos:

• Be concise, compelling, and cogent: about a — page (a few showcase samples are little longer)

• Present your case so that the letter naturally leads to your résumé or a phone call

• Make most of the letter about *them*, not about you

• Send it to someone who can be contacted to follow-up

• Send an *impactful* letter in an impactful way e.g. FedEx

Don'ts:

• Don't repeat what is in your résumé

• If you are proposing an idea, be concise and intriguing; give just enough

• Make more than one major point of argument in the body of the letter

- Avoid "but"; use "and" instead (e.g. I do not have 15 years in sales, but I bring rich field experience. Instead say: I bring sales experience in major geographic theaters of the world and know cultural preferences of markets where most growth is expected)
- Do not send a mediocre letter using an impactful method (FedEx)

After reviewing this Chapter, revisit Chapter-5 and review Figure-3: A Typical Messaging Challenge, to fortify your understanding of how messaging amplification works through differentiation.

Chapter-8: Marketing the Product—You!

"Your reach should be greater than your grasp."

—Ralph Waldo Emerson (1803–1882)

The Marketing Campaign

Marketing provides the springboard to launch your message that you have spent your time and energy on so far. In addition, it also entails identifying targets and opportunities where your message needs to go. Your marketing campaign can take on a variety of shapes and forms and often is a mix of different approaches coming together in a coordinated way.

Introduction

Once the résumé is ready, there is a need to go back to the starting point—the market—and shift gears. Why? In the previous chapters, we presented *how* to send the résumé and letters, including cover letters, without discussing *where* to send them! We explore that here.

The résumé was based on market *survey*. The survey provided the boundaries of the job-search perimeter, so that you have a good idea of "what" types of jobs—job families—to address in the résumé. Once it is done, it is time to go to the same well in a different vein. This time the intent is to use the marketplace information to actually create a marketing campaign and launch it with the résumé to answer the "where" question. Now in the same marketplace you are changing your mode from *surveying to researching*; you are gathering intelligence.

Sources of Market Intelligence

Gathering market intelligence entails finding rich sources full of information to leverage, so that there is a solid marketing plan. This plan consists of target companies carefully selected and ranked in order of their potential targeting value and desirability in landing your dream job. Looking at job-board postings that are publicly available and then merely sending résumés to these open positions does not create a differentiated advantage. It *cannot*! Your résumé is one of thousands that are received in response to a posted job. In fact, it is best to expend minimal efforts on such opportunities because the yield on them, typically, is so poor.

The effort invested in a marketing campaign that entails applying for jobs should be targeted to where the action is. For example, spending an hour per day (in a typical eight-hour day) on the Web, sending responses to jobs *already* identified and posted is excessive. As presented in this chapter on networking, most of the action is in working within a network and that is where most of the effort should be invested. You can use the information gathered on the Web to prime your network and leverage it into more direct avenues of getting your candidacy known to the target company. This is how you can justify spending up to two hours (25 percent of your time) daily, on this approach, to do your job searching. Any additional time on the Web should be spent doing company research and sleuthing.

Posted Jobs

There are job postings available through a variety of channels as a first source of market intelligence. Some of the more familiar avenues for this fountainhead of openings are:

- Job boards on the Web: there are dozens of these but some familiar ones are Monster.com, Careerbuilder.com, Careerladder.com, Hotjobs.com, Indeed.com, and Simplyhired.com, among others
- Local areas have their own sites that highlight jobs in specific areas. For example, in the San Francisco Bay Area, in California, Bayareajobs.com is a good site. Similarly, Craigslist.com is also getting growingly popular and getting increasingly wider audience.
- Classified advertisements in print media as newspapers, magazines, and trade publications
- Company Websites
- Special Websites hosted by outplacement and other career-focused companies
- Public bulletin boards
- Employment newsletters and other publications
- Other public sources of information

Any of these sources can be a good starting point for researching jobs of interest. In this chapter, in Target Segmentation, we shall see how to rank-order a target opportunity universe into three categories, so that how to leverage this information to get what you are after will be decided.

Once the job opportunity is identified, the next step is to formulate a response so that it is consistent with the marketing strategy. As we shall see in Target Segmentation, the level of effort in formulating a response will be consistent with this segmentation. Gathering this market intelligence from posted jobs, however, is just one avenue to tapping into the job market and responding to it.

♠Company Sources

Information available from companies of interest can be a veritable source of job knowledge, overt and covert. Overt jobs are the jobs companies are openly seeking to fill. These jobs are on the company Website, job boards, and other sources of public information. Covert jobs, on the other hand, are the openings about which the company does not want just anyone to know. One reason may be that the incumbent may be eased out and it needs someone qualified to replace that person. These covert jobs can be of two categories: one that the company recognizes, and for which it is willing to entertain a candidate for consideration; the other is where the company does not even know or recognize that such a job should exist because its management has not thought about the need.

Quality of Information and Your Time

Information from job boards and company Websites can be found to be disparate. Why? Organizations post jobs and other information on job boards to disseminate openings. Often these openings get cancelled, filled, modified, or even consolidated depending on the flux of factors that change from company to company and economic realities. It is not uncommon to find a posting from a company on a well-regarded job board, which, when you visit the company Website, may not exist. This can be frustrating. What is even more frustrating is to find a posting on a company Website, of a recent vintage, and then find out that the location, where the company posted the opening, does not even exist. Why? One reason may be that the task of posting, managing, and removing job openings takes resources. Since the cost of posting an opening on various job boards is trivial compared to what print media charge, most companies do not bother to diligently keep their posting up-to-date. This is not expected to change any time soon.

One such incident happened to a client, who, after getting frustrated with the integrity of openings posted on job boards, decided to go directly to the company Websites. One such company—a Global Fortune-10—had just posted a job, very much in line with what she was looking for, about a mile from her home!

Having been disappointed with such tantalizing opportunities before, she decided to explore more about the job and find the name of the hiring manager through someone she knew, who worked at another part of the same company. She was crushed when she discovered that the physical location posted for the job did not even exist. They had disbanded that operation, some three years back, and had dispersed it to several different locations in California! It is, therefore, a good idea to check on all opportunities before investing *significant* time in response to them. If you plan to send a mechanized response that takes less than a minute, then it may be worth your while to chance it! But, then do not spend inordinate amounts of time following up on such transmittals; consider them "fire and forget" job-seeking missiles!

Analysts and Industry Experts

Industry and financial analysts can be a source of latent jobs a company may be contemplating. These industry mavens have insight about what direction a company is or should be taking, and are able to influence the company's management on a variety of matters. Typically, these positions are at a higher-level—director and above—so that if you do not have interest in those levels of openings, you do not need to focus on this avenue.

*Customers, Suppliers, and Channels

Every company has customers, suppliers, and channels through which it distributes its wares. Those who are in this category of company's stakeholders have inside knowledge of what its needs are in the current and future terms. These needs may not be openly known to others and certainly are not in the public domain. Tapping these constituencies can be a useful source of knowledge and intelligence on how a company is going to fill certain positions.

Industry Press and Publications

Industry and trade publications can be a veritable source of what is going on inside a company. If these sources are suggesting, in their news coverage, a need for a certain position either openly or insinuatingly, then it is worth pursuing these leads. Your approach based on this intelligence will, again, be driven by what segment of your target the company in question falls.

Recruiters and Search Firms

Even in a down economy, companies find it useful to pursue bringing on potential candidates through retained or even contingent recruiters. Search firms mostly work on a retained basis. A retained search is one where a company contracts a particular search firm to fill a position. The company pays the fee regardless of the outcome of the process. A contingent search, on the other hand, is where the recruiter is paid only when a position is filled through *that* recruiter. A search firm will not divulge the client company's name unless the process is well under way. Talking to recruiters and search firms can be a veritable source of knowledge on where the action is and what kind of talent is getting action. In a tough job market, these resources, however, are stretched thin as their business levels are down and their databanks full of candidates looking for work through these channels. Do not expect much cooperation and openness from recruiters in a tough job market!

For more discussion on this topic, see the section on Working With Third Parties, presented later in this chapter.

♠ Culling your Target List

Your list of targets should be compiled from search criteria that you can assemble based on a number of factors, some obvious, others less so! Some of the more obvious search fields are listed below:

- ✓ Industry
- ✓ Geography
- ✓ Employee count
- ✓ Sales volume
- ✓ *Fortune* ranking
- ✓ Domestic vs. foreign presence
- ✓ Product line
- ✓ Geography/distance to work
- ✓ Company track record
- ✓ Reputation
- ✓ Management
- ✓ Financial performance history
- ✓ Employee treatment/layoff history

   ✓ Minorities/women treatment

   ✓ Growth history

   ✓ Future plans

   ✓ Defense/Non-defense

The lesser known attributes of a company are listed below and should be part of your search equation:

   ✓ How a company treats those over 40 (AARP publishes a company list)

   ✓ How a company treats women in management and promotions

   ✓ How a company provides for working mothers

   ✓ How a company supports special causes (e.g. does not invest in countries having poor human rights records)

Of course, as the job market becomes tighter, the search criteria have to be somewhat broader than when the job market is less so. Even though you may be looking for a job in an employers' market, it does not mean that you should surrender your principles for want of a job where you are not likely to be happy. You can always choose your offers based on your final criteria and judgment.

It is better to start with less restrictive criteria and then limit them, which will make the list smaller. If you are focused on getting what you know you want, you will more than likely get it. If you go after any company that has a job opening, you probably will get into one of them of no particular appeal to you. It helps to be choosy even in a bear market!

One way to tap a list of companies from criteria that you develop is to use one of the more commonly used industry databases. This is discussed under Some Search Tools later in this chapter. The databases will provide a list of companies that match your criteria. This list could be of any length depending upon your criteria and size of the database (number of companies in it).

♠ Target Segmentation

Once the list is available, the next step is to select from this list those companies matching your finer criteria, suggested from one of the lists above. Then segment the companies into three categories:

        "A" or Gold

        "B" or Silver

        "C" or Bronze

Gold companies or those on the "A" list are your dream companies based on criteria you selected. The same goes for the Silver and the Bronze list.

To have a good list for a robust marketing campaign the following mix is suggested:

Gold   10 companies

Silver   25 companies

Bronze 100 companies

At any given time, in a good campaign, you need to ramp up to have a **mix of 135 companies** that are on your radar screen or in your pipeline of activities. We'll use the radar screen metaphor to talk about the *target* companies and the pipeline metaphor to talk about the *activities* on these companies, such as how many résumés, how many letters, how many follow-up calls, etc. in your campaign that you are shepherding.

The list should be a dynamic one; as you remove those that do not pan out, you toss new ones in the mix so that they come in and out on the radar screen. At the start of the campaign you are not expected to have all 135 targets ready to attack with your message! It may take up to one month to ramp up to this level of activity. But once achieved, you need to constantly keep a list of back-up companies, in each category or segment, so that your radar screen has the same number of target companies and the pipeline has the same flux of activity.

It is important to keep your activities at a level high enough, to keep you engaged and visible in the marketplace. Managing this mix of activities takes a full time effort—about 40 hours per week, giving you a reason to get up in the morning if you are out of work and looking! It takes time to ramp up to this level of activity, starting with nothing at the beginning of your campaign. Those looking for a change from their current job can start and work with a smaller number and fewer targets; they perhaps do not need to have any "C" targets.

Opportunistic Targeting

In addition to the targets identified by the segmentation approach, one must also pursue opportunities, as they become available, even when they are not on the radar screen as originally targeted. The 135 targets are identified, as the campaign gets rolling, to give focus, visibility, and priority to those targets that are worthy pursuing. In a tough market, one must also pursue opportunities as they become known and add to the list already in place, even if that goes beyond the 135 targets mentioned in the previous paragraph. That number was the starting point. As more target opportunities become visible, even beyond that pool, they should also be reviewed for their priority: Gold, Silver, and Bronze, and treated accordingly.

The approach described here works in any market. In a difficult job market, this approach provides the discipline and a structure needed to start an aggressive campaign. It forces those seriously looking for jobs to go after selected companies that interest them, rather than reactively applying for anything that appears and then sending a response.

♠ Some Search Tools

There are several search tools and databases available to cull company lists. These databases and lists are maintained on an ongoing basis to keep them current and user friendly. They offer different information to the client and are usually fee based. The following resources are available for doing on-line search.

Reference USA

Reference USA is a good starting point for a broad search for companies within the U.S. This tool is available from most public libraries (hence free) and can be accessed from home on the Internet. It lists over 12 million businesses within the U.S. Once you know what your general boundaries of search are, this tool provides a way to mark these boundaries and find every target within these boundaries. After entering custom search criteria, the database produces a list of companies that meet the criteria. Once this list is printed, names can by highlighted in three colors to identify Gold, Silver, and Bronze target companies.

Hoover's

Hoover's is the next level of research tool where you can get more detailed information on any chosen target from the Reference USA list. For more information visit www.Hoovers.com. This is a subscription service, although a stripped-down version is available for free.

Other Sources

There are a variety of sources available to do search in a specific area. Most of these sources are subscription-based services.

♠ Working with Third Parties

Third parties in a job-search campaign provide an added dimension to a marketing effort. They represent a whole class of professionals who can provide resources, contacts, and help bring the employer and employee together to create a win-win situation. Even in a down economy, third parties can provide value to both sides as discussed here. In this section a brief overview of different types of third parties is provided.

Third-party Basics

Third parties are catalysts who connect employers, who have job opportunities, with those seeking to fill them. They range from highly dispersed organizations with international presence to individuals. Typically, they facilitate connecting the employers with potential employees and vice versa, and include a variety of businesses based on different models. Many job boards and ISPs such as AOL and Yahoo! provide electronic job-search agents that allow job seekers to post specific search criteria for their dream jobs, and have the "agent" notify them of a match. They each play a role in some way to make the connection between the demand and the supply of human resources for organizations. As in every business, economic conditions and the demand and supply equation drive how these providers create and bring value to the process of putting employees on employers' payrolls. What makes this business interesting, from a jobseeker's viewpoint, is that most jobseekers—especially those out of work—get involved with them in an emotional state, and are driven by how they are able to manage these emotions more than any other factor.

This section is an overview of how a third-party can play a role in your placement and how you can leverage that resource to your best advantage. Also, knowing their business model can help you make the right choice. This is critical to avoid getting hurt before getting emotionally and financially involved.

The basic economic rule for third-parties existence is how they are able to generate revenues by helping attain your job-search goal. Some actually place you; some get you ready, so that you can do this yourself; yet others provide some service so that you can decide how you want to go about this process yourself. In some cases—outplacement—the cost is borne by the employers, so that individual clients do not bear any cost of the service for a limited time. Some get it from the government, as is the case of the Employment Development Department (EDD), so that there is no cost to participants. There is no free lunch, however! The quality of what is available is not only driven by the cost to you, but also by the way the business is conducted.

A brief overview of different resources available from third parties is provided here. There are dozens of books written by those who are engaged in this business. There are many books that list the names of these organizations, and these books are kept up-to-date with revisions. Constant, though, are the fundamentals on which each business model is based and the nature of the business in which each one is engaged.

Search Firms

Search firms are organizations that are retained by employers to find the right candidate for a particular position. The company, in which the open position exists, pays the retained firm. This is generally true, although there are contingent search firms that will base their activities on *placing* the right candidate and then invoicing its client organization.

The way a search firm works is that each one has a pool of client organizations that they service. These client organizations place their employment needs in the form of a requisition or job description to these firms. For a retained search, the firm gets paid regardless of its placing a candidate in the client company. Enterprising search firms scour the market for the right candidate, poach its clients' competitors, and pirate talent just to meet its clients' needs. In good times, this is rampant. Search firms are even given the names of particular employees that the client company is interested in poaching from its competitors. In favorable times, this is a good business. Search firms handle candidates at all levels, each firm specializing in a certain talent pool.

Generally, search firms also operate on the practice of specializing within an area and assigning specific recruiters to it. Sometimes, a recruiter is assigned to a client company and sometimes, a recruiter is assigned to a specific job category. If you position yourself as a candidate with a particular specialty, a recruiter may handle your résumé. This recruiter may not even be aware of opportunities that exist within the same search organization for someone with a different flavor (see multiple résumés in Chapter-6), especially if you have not promoted that flavor with someone else in the same organization. This can result in some missed opportunities.

Generally, search firms (and recruiters) do well for themselves, their clients, and those seeking employment. In tough times (high unemployment), things are interesting and are worth some caution. With talent available from the street, tight operating budgets, and employees available from competitors, client companies are unwilling to use search firms as readily. The positions at which these searches take place in tough times move up substantially, and it is rare to see those below a director or a vice president level being pursued by a search firm for placement. The action, too, happens not so much for the unemployed, but more for those already employed. This is why for those who are out of work and looking, this is not as good an avenue as it may seem. Search firms are in the business more to re-employ those who are already employed than those out of work and looking! This is why looking for work through a search firm is much more productive when you are already working.

Recruiters

Recruiters are mostly contingent third-party employment brokers who help those looking for a job—employed or out of work—and keep track of where hiring is going on. They, too, have their client organizations that pay them after a successful employee intake. If a particular recruiter is unable to place a candidate, they do not get paid. This is the contingent part.

In tough times, there is plenty of talent on the street looking for work. The only reason recruiters are brought into the process by a company is because the process of selection can be costly using internal resources, especially for a smaller organization. The recruiters do all the work prior to presenting candidates and qualify them. Some companies use internal recruiters —company employees—to do the same. Some companies outsource this function so the recruiters are hourly contract employees. This is why it is critical for a candidate to be clear who has approached them before getting excited about the prospects. It is a good idea to ask a calling recruiter their way of operating and how they are being compensated.

In times when unemployment is high, recruiters do not do well. Companies are unwilling to pay to bring someone on board if they can get comparable talent from the street. This is why protecting your marketing and how you are marketing yourself are so important. Many desperate recruiters, in tough times, will raid job boards for résumés because they can have access to them and call those, whose résumés they find interesting, with an enticing sales pitch.

If you have not seen much action on the job front, you could be lured in by such calls, and, in an emotional exchange, might hear perhaps what is not even said. After you get in bed with an unscrupulous recruiter, your résumé can go to many employers in the country and even abroad in a very short time. Once a recruiter has a résumé in a company's hands, directly seeking a job there on your own is compromised, even at a later time, because the company now owes this recruiter their fee. This fee becomes a factor even though if that résumé results in filling a different position. Many jobseekers are frustrated by getting blocked from consideration, even for positions in a company for which it sees them as a good fit, because of what a recruiter can do using these tactics.

Companies do not want to pay recruiter fees in a tough economy, so, as a result, you end up getting sidelined.

This is why it is critical to carefully screen all recruiter calls when approached after posting a résumé on a public job board. This, too, is why it pays to be selective in posting a résumé only on reputable job boards, and then staying with just the reputable professionals.

Some Tips on Posting Your Résumé on a Job Board

The following tips are offered to make your job-search campaign more effective, if you want to use public job boards to post your résumé:

1. Make some subtle way in which your résumé, posted on a public job board, is uniquely identifiable to *you*. When your résumé lands on someone's desk through a recruiter, it is competing with the one you might send directly. What also matters is which version reaches a company first. One way to make this differentiation, known only to you, is to change, for example, the address from "Street" to "St." on the two versions, so that you can identify your version. The recruiter may block you from employment in that company by demanding the commission, if you are offered a job there. Having this identifier on the résumé can help if it comes to a showdown on whose résumé got the action.

2. Make sure that only you, the recruiters, and the employer companies have access to your résumé. If anyone—another competing candidate—who logs-in, can access any posted résumé, then you are losing your competitive advantage by someone stealing ideas of differentiation from your résumé. Many career management firms give free access to all clients' résumés, which are posted on their site and are in their database.

3. Periodically revise your posted résumés and purge the older versions.

4. Do not put any information of personal nature as a Social Security number or a complete street address on your résumé; merely the name of your city is enough along with the contact information.

5. Keep track of all versions you have posted and then periodically update and purge as market conditions change.

6. Post résumés only on select job boards, and tag each one discreetly, so that you can identify the source when someone calls you as a result of your postings.

7. Take all your posted résumés off the boards after you have landed a job and started working.

Outplacement Firms

Outplacement firms are third parties engaged by their client organization to facilitate employee termination and their subsequent transition. They help terminated employees manage their transitions so that the client company is perceived as a caring and humane organization in the eyes of those affected by terminations and those who matter to the company. The outplacement service is also seen as a part of a compensation package and is a factor that can make a company a preferred employer. Outplacement firms are also known as career management firms.

Outplacement firms provide a variety of services depending on the agreement with the client organization. The services provided, typically, include the following:

Orientation and Venting: This step helps you deal with your job loss, immediately following your termination. This is where a career counselor from the outplacement firm can provide emotional support and guide you through what services are offered during your transition. It may also provide optional services, you can purchase from them, beyond what is contracted with your ex-employer.

Résumé Workshop: This is a one or two-day workshop in a group setting—typically your company group—that walks you through how to make your résumé and how to market yourself in the particular geography and conditions.

Résumé Service: The service includes some support preparing your résumé, making multiple copies, mailing them to a list of employers, and administrative support, such as computers, copying, faxing, and access to the Internet.

Assessments: This may include a battery of tests and assessments that let you develop some insights about your career preferences. This is usually included in a high-end package as assessments can be expensive. They include Meyer's Briggs Type Indicator, and Strong Inventory, among others.

Career Counseling: These are face-to-face sessions with an experienced counselor. The number of sessions is negotiated as a part of the contract.

Success Teams: These teams meet weekly to discuss their progress searching for jobs. An experienced counselor typically facilitates these sessions.

Roundtables: These are one or two-hour discussion sessions where a trainer presents topical information on a particular subject of general interest to the group.

Special Workshops: These are one-day workshops on topics such as entrepreneurship, consulting, contracting, among others.

Job Consultants: Consultants with specific expertise in job search and connections with employers are available as a part of this service.

Job Fairs: Many firms stage their own job fairs where they invite outside employers who are hiring. This is a good opportunity to participate in a more intimate and non-threatening event for those who are new to this process.

Networking Events: Special events are organized to help those who are shy coming together in a social setting looking for work or sharing their needs with others.

Résumé Bank: Most keep their own databank of résumés of internal clients. Employers and recruiters who pay a certain fee to have this privilege subscribe to this bank.

Job Bank: Employers who have an agreement to post new jobs, post their openings on the job lead link. This link can be part of the Website accessible by clients who are on the service roster at any particular time.

Alumnus List: Past alums of the organization are listed on this page from the Website. This can be a good networking resource.

Company Website: Most have a comprehensive Website to provide research, informational, and support data to its clients. Access to this portal is controlled.

Outplacement services can be expensive and when companies are watching their bottom line in a tight economy, they want to manage these costs. Some employers open up their own outplacement center internally to help those exiting their company. While some employer-run centers are good resources, employees' views on such an arrangement are mixed. One reason is, perhaps, the exiting employees resent having to come back to the company that just let them go. Another reason may also be that having to come back to their place of work—albeit at a different location—and having restrictions on access, facilities, and what they can do, while still at "their" company. Some also find it awkward dealing with their old colleagues. Quality of available services varies.

The typical length of service for outplacement contracts varies from one day to six months or more. In tough times, when companies are cutting costs, they do whatever possible to make sure that their costs are contained while offering outplacement services.

Job-Placement Specialists

Job-placement specialists are professionals who help clients with assessment, coaching, and connecting with employers who have specific openings that are exclusively or non-exclusively known to them. Fees vary.

Career Consultants

Career consultants are specialists who do assessments and help clients interpret these tests in the light of emerging job trends and career choices. They also provide individualized coaching. Fees vary.

Often, career consultants are professional therapists, or those in HR, who have decided to do something on their own. They bring some value to the process as career consultants. Some are focused on the process and are not versed with content. What does this mean? In many cases they will verify to see if a résumé is correctly presented, but may not be able to help in how to repackage it with the knowledge of the job market. Their *content* knowledge is not their forte, their process knowledge is. If you are not clear yourself what you are seeking, the value in such an arrangement could be less than if you sought out someone who understands the job market and has been in such jobs, and who can also be an excellent coach. Before engaging a consultant, check out fees, references, and background.

"Information" Brokers

"Information" Brokers are a somewhat shady bunch of businesses that exploit their clients' fragile emotional state and their desperate situation looking for an opportunity. Often, they represent the ugly underbelly of the employment brokering business. In addition to a variety of more commonly available services of some or marginal value—assessments, emotional support, résumé preparation, etiquette, among others—they claim to have an "inside" track to the "secret jobs" in client companies that no one else knows about. They mostly cater to the immigrant population known to have saved money during good times, whose language skills and cultural knowledge to successfully navigate through a job search are marginal. The sales pitch is based on appealing to clients' perceived inability to network, market, and develop viable leads. A majority of their clientele is frustrated looking for work, using ineffective methods, and are unable to generate action on their own. They are also running out of funds or options in their current situation. These unscrupulous "information" brokers rope in such clients with a promise to generate action on their search front, for an up-front fee that can be as high as $15,000. Some will even promise action to those who are close to losing their visa status and are willing to pay any amount just to stay in the country.

When dealing with such underhanded operators, the watchword is caution. If something sounds too good to be true, it probably is. Never sign any agreement where there is money involved, without making some inquiries and checking references. Some do not even believe in a written contract; just a "trust me" pitch. Those who get sucked into deals with these unscrupulous brokers, are often too embarrassed to admit that they have been duped. They often count on the fact that immigrant clients with Visa-status problems will not be around to sue them to recover their money.

Contract Agencies

Although many are employers, their main business is derived from hiring contract workers and then filling open positions for "temporary" work in their client organizations. Some temporary engagements can last several years, some even resulting in full-time jobs. They have their own recruitment process. Some organizations specialize in connecting temporary consultants with client companies. They help position opportunity seekers with their clients without any cost to them, and derive their income from the fee as a percentage of the billing for the time of engagement.

Employment Development Department

Most states have EDD as a part of the state agency that administers the unemployment benefits and provides help to those looking for some type of retraining, as market conditions change. These agencies also double as clearing houses for job-related information and provide some basic resources critical to all job seekers. Résumé preparation—typically for low-end and union employees—copying facilities, and seminars for the jobless are some of the services provided at these centers. In tough times EDD offices provide resources to professionals by conducting seminars and inviting guest speakers to motivate job seekers and help them.

Job Fairs

There are various types of job fairs. The main two categories are private and commercial.

Private job fairs are organized and hosted by individual employers interested in hiring. They are also hosted by private third parties such as career management firms, who invite employers to participate in an organized event, as well as by those who may organize them and invite employers to come and screen potential hires. For example, many career transition and outplacement companies, and even in-house career centers, routinely hold job fairs as a part of their service to its clients. For more detailed discussion on job fairs see Key-7 in *The 7 Keys to a Dream Job: A Career Nirvana Playbook!*.

Job-search "Agents"

Job-search agents are usually electronic hounds that sniff out the job one is looking for and notify of a find without having to constantly look in a certain domain as a job board. Many job boards, ISPs as AOL, Yahoo!, and others have a simple and user friendly interface on their Websites that allow for job seekers to create job alerts by entering their search criteria into a data bank. When a job that meets the criteria is posted on their data bank, the alert or agent creates a notification, automatically going to those who are looking for that match. This can be a time saver for those who are searching many job boards and have different "flavors" of jobs they are looking for in different markets.

Networking

As the job market tightens up, networking becomes the prime source of landing jobs. In the Internet age, many rules of searching for jobs have changed. This was followed by a sea change in hiring rules, following the dot-com implosion in 2001. Even in a slow economy, millions of jobs are visible with questionable integrity on the job boards. This is perhaps because it is more trouble for companies to review what is on these boards on a regular basis and have someone manage them.

Newspaper job ads and print media are different. Only paid ads get published and stay in the print until someone decides not to pay for them anymore, a much more controlled and reliable way to trust what is in the printed media. Similarly, from the side of those responding to jobs, it takes a few seconds to keystroke and send a ready résumé to a company for a posted position. Millions, thus, respond to posted jobs, even when they know that the match between the posted requirements and the response is marginal at best.

This mode of posting jobs and how applicants respond to them has spawned a new approach to processing incoming responses. Most résumés and incoming responses are scanned electronically, then sorted and organized by key words. Only those that match a certain threshold are passed on to the next level, where someone visually eyeballs them in an electronic format on a computer screen. The whole process has become increasingly more robotic and impersonal. Many smaller companies have simply given up on using their Website for job postings. They cannot handle the avalanche of responses for even esoteric jobs, especially when the unemployment rates are high.

One countermeasure for this impersonal approach to selection process and to leverage information on unposted jobs, is to find someone who has an inside track on an opening. Although people are still hired by a variety of approaches, social networking by far is the most prevalent way by which they land their jobs, because it allows them this inside track on an opportunity. This approach to job search has become a favored mode for employers, since the advent of the Internet over the past decade. This implies that for jobseekers to be productive, they had better start social networking to get what they want. The following list shows how different approaches to job search are ranked based on the *action* they generate in landing a job:

Networking	64%
Search firms/recruiters	12%
Advertisements (Print)	11%
Other (job fairs, etc.	9%
Internet	4%

These statistics were compiled from a variety of sources and have remained indicative of the emphasis of how jobs are found in this Internet age. The percentage of jobs landed by those using the Internet has steadily declined over the years. Additionally, for those making in excess of $60, 000 annually, the percentage of landings, using the Internet, is considerably smaller than those at the lower end of the salary range.

It is, therefore, safe to conclude that networking beats the Net at least 16:1 for *landing* an opportunity, if not for a job search. The Internet still can be a good source for *searching* posted jobs! It is also a good source for *researching* information about companies and the job market as we presented in Chapter-6: Building Your Platform. One should know when to switch from the Net to networking and how to use each one synergistically.

Those who feel lost in the networking maze wonder what a good starting point is for networking activity. The following graphic, Figure-7 (adapted from a model developed by Vivienne Powell, a career counselor) is a good tool to start the process. Networking is often disparaged or even maligned by those who engage in professions where their social skills are not at a premium in the performance of their jobs. Engineers, scientists, and those who engage in highly technical fields as individual contributors share this view, as do shy and timid individuals and Introverts!

Looking at the statistics of what creates action in the job-search arena, networking by far wins hands down. In an economy where jobs are scarce this percentage remains high.

Networking Forums

Those who find themselves suddenly out of work and are not well "networked" find it discouraging to start connecting. They believe that their expertise in the areas of their field and their modicum of connections will get them going. Their next logical action step—after their denial and grieving—is to start their résumé and start sending them out. This can be frustrating. As we just presented, networking is the most productive way to get action in a job search, *even* in a good economy. Those engaged as individual contributors in functions that do not require social connections as a part of their job find it challenging to start socializing with others who can help them. They believe that since they have nothing to give, they have no right asking others for information. This is a misperception!

As a part of getting into gear, looking for opportunities following a job loss, one of the first actions must be to find out where the local networking events are held. For those who are looking for a change while holding a job, this is a bit easier because they live in a working environment, where information and interactions flow. In a job market with fewer jobs, those unemployed can represent a large population. Many enterprising, out-of-work job seekers start their own networking events. Some events grow to become weekly scheduled activities with hundreds attending. Often such groups gather at a restaurant, early in the day, and network, followed by lunch and a guest speaker. Even though several hundred attend such events, the design of the event allows great latitude in the way people come together. As people start to gather, one or two hours before lunch, they start socializing, networking, and exchanging information.

One such successful networking forum, in the heart of Silicon Valley, emerged out of a group of jobseekers coming together to share leads and support each other. This forum, now named C-Six, gathers every Tuesday and boasts an attendance exceeding 200 (during the peak unemployment period in the Valley in 2002) and a membership ten times that. This number of participants allows for a rich exchange of diverse information in current areas of interest and the information is very fresh. Despite its size, the way it is run provides the intimacy of a small group and a way to exchange leads, information, and needs (www.csix.org). It now has chapters around the Bay Area, in many communities.

One good way to break the fear or even shame of networking is for you to force yourself to go to such events early in the jobless state. Those who are working and are looking for outside opportunities, may find this forum awkward, because of the need to keep the search private and its possible conflict with work schedule. Another apprehension many have, is that they believe that they do not have much information to give to others early in their search. The best approach here, is to state the obvious during your introduction at these events and mention that you are new to this process and do not have any leads to share. Even in that case, if you can share information about your employer, that just let you go, it may be of help to some in the group.

As you progress in your search, your networking becomes more effective. If you are turned down for a job, you can now share that information in your group and share the names of the hiring manager and others in the interview chain, so that others can benefit and, in turn, you can get similar information in return. It is not the lack of information that holds people back from networking; it is their shyness and diffidence. Get over it and network!

The other benefit of networking socially is that it provides the much needed support that is an emotional tonic for those who feel isolated, especially in a jobless state. Even for those who have jobs, and are seeking a change, this support is important.

Virtual Networking

Virtual networking is done in cyberspace, not face-to-face! This is a boon to the shy, the timid, and the Introverted. One example of this cyber forum is www.linkedin.com, with an appropriate tag line, "Your network is bigger than you think." For those who prefer to do their "socializing" on the Internet, this resource can be an option. It is designed to connect people and provide degrees of "separation" similar to a social network.

For example, if you want to connect with someone at the second or third degree of separation, you had better get someone in the second degree, to introduce you to the one you are trying to connect with. The etiquette here is not much different from the one in a social networking. This is an emerging concept and its business model is not yet defined, so its success remains to be seen.

LinkedIn provides a great opportunity for informational interviewing or ferreting out information that is not openly known. The contact success rate can be very high. One client, who had amassed 78 contact in his circle, had no trouble getting informational interviews with hiring mangers three degrees away. In one instance, he contacted nine hiring managers, some of whom were 2–3 degrees away and was successful in getting all nine informational interviews! Sometimes, the LinkedIn provides a more effective connecting passage than being an alum of a school and trying to connect with others from the same school.

Networking Universe

Figure-7 shows how a typical networking universe can be modeled. Even for those who believe that their networks are marginal, might be surprised to discover how extensive it is, if they map out their own network as shown in the diagram. Do not underestimate your networking capital! A brief description for each category, within the universe, is given below.

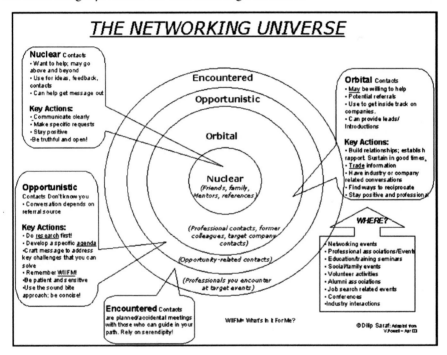

Figure-7: The Networking Universe

Nuclear Contacts: These are your most immediate connections—your social nucleus. Your friends, family, relatives, and even some colleagues fall in this category. "Nuclear" also means that you can take these contacts and "explode" them into a much bigger universe! One criterion by which you can identify contacts in this category is that, if you called them at any time, they will take or return your call.

There is an irony in this most intimate of networking domains. Because those who belong to it are intimate in their connections to each other, assuming that everyone in this domain knows your business and future plans can be presumptuous. Because of this very closeness, many within this category may be embarrassed to ask you about your business and what specifically you do or are looking for. The best way to overcome this apprehension or even misapprehension is to send them your résumé and marketing plan. It is even better if this is personally presented to them and discussed so that there is no confusion about your goal. If this circle of contacts is large, it is normal to segment this circle so that each segment has the correct version of the résumé (if you have multiple flavors of them) and the appropriate marketing plan and target companies. Do not give more than one message to a group within this circle. It can confuse them; keep it simple (see below: Networking Segmentation).

Orbital Contacts: These are contacts that you have developed over your career. The idea is to get people who have target company information, and bring them to this sub-universe. Those in this category will typically return your calls, when called during normal business hours.

Opportunistic Contacts: These are carefully developed connections and your purpose with them is somewhat selfish. They know it. So, you need to expend special efforts to get their attention to serve your cause. Those in this category may not even return your calls. A client tried one clever approach of opportunistic contacts, to expand his strategic network successfully. He was a mountain-bike enthusiast and a runner. Many companies have groups of employees who jog or bike regularly during their lunch breaks. This client waited outside targeted companies and joined the groups that departed for their recreational activities at lunch. During this outing with the group, he connected with a few joggers and found contact information. He tried this at three target companies and two offered him interviews and the third a job!

Encountered Contacts: These are chance encounters. If you keep your social radar turned on and your antennas up, you will run into many such encounters. For these contacts rely on serendipity.

Networking Segmentation

Similar to the market segmentation, a network also needs to be segmented, especially for multiple résumés. If you send every version of a résumé to everyone in your networking contact, confusion can ensue, which may, at best, result in no action, or worse, in confused action. You should make special efforts to segment your network for each version of your campaign and then keep them each separate, and manage that process for most impact. This is why keeping *different* flavors of a résumé should be limited to five.

*Keeping in Touch!

It takes a tremendous effort and time to build a network. This is because most put their focus on this activity only in the time of *their* need. So, if you have not kept in touch with your contacts when times were good, it becomes difficult to reconnect after a long pause. It takes a special effort to overcome this inertia stemming from years of being out of touch and then re-igniting a long-faded relationship. Once the reconnection is made, however, keeping up with the renewed relationship is easier. The Internet makes this possible. Ironically the very source that has made cyber networking easier for staying in touch has also been the reason for having the need for social networking!

One approach to nurturing networked relationships and sustaining them over time is to start your own newsletter. Send this newsletter in times, good and bad, to all those whom you contacted as a result of your job search. Job uncertainties are the wave of the future. Keeping abreast of what is happening in your search, as a part of the newsletter (monthly or so), can be a good way of staying in touch without intruding or imposing. A newsletter could be one or two pages of tidbits or things of interest to the circle of network. These tidbits could typically include family matters, education, finances, humorous anecdotes, and some personal details of general interest. Although a newsletter takes time and effort to pull together, it is a good and effective way to protect your investment and build on it.

If you are out of work and aggressively looking, or if you are working and looking for a change, you must discipline yourself to network two-three times weekly, and make sure that it happens. If you are unable to engage in in-person networking, one of these "events" could be some scheduled time you set aside for yourself on the Internet, and do some serious cyber networking, no *more* than once a week. The remaining interactions must be in person.

Another rule for success in networking is to give more than you take from the network. See Key-7 for networking etiquette in the author's *The 7 Keys to a Dream Job: A Career Nirvana Playbook!*

Cold Calling

Cold calling is a term that is often used in the context of making sales calls to potential buyers. Telemarketing is a cold call, since the caller calls the unsuspecting prospect and explores avenues to make a sale. Cold calling has thus become a dreaded phrase especially for those who are not in the selling business. Even to those who are looking for jobs on their own turf—sales and marketing professionals—cold calls are an anathema. Why? The success rate is very low for telemarketing cold calls (typically about three percent), and in a job search it is probably even less, and it takes an emotional toll on your psyche, because the product is *you*!

However, cold calls can also be *redefined* as a call made after you have been introduced to the called party in some way. When this is already done it is no longer a "cold call" in its classical sense. There are a variety of ways to getting introduced to the person you'd like to call. In the order of increasing impact they are as follows:

- Someone refers you to the person you are trying to contact
- You send an unsolicited letter that piques a person's interest and then call that person to follow-up
- Someone (known) calls the person you want to contact before your call to them
- Someone calls the person while you are on the line, a three-way call, introduces you, and lets you connect, and then you continue on your own
- Someone introduces you to the person you want to contact in a special way, preferably face-to-face

Even if someone refers you to call another person, the best way to get that person's attention is by first sending a letter or email stating who has referred you and why. The letter of introduction should be functional, compelling, and polite, with a reminder that you will be calling this person in a few days to introduce yourself. Now, this is NOT a cold call anymore in its classical sense!

The best antidote for fear and apprehension around a cold call is to send a proxy—a letter, email, a third party call, an introduction—to obviate the awkwardness of a true cold call!

There is another strategy for successful cold calls: once you have sent something ahead to announce your cold calling, make many "cold calls" in a block of time one after another. Making 10–15 calls in one sitting is far more effective than randomly calling. Also, make these calls when you are at your peak alertness and energy. That way those who refuse to take your calls or disregard you in your first encounter with them, will not bring you down as much. Besides, when you are at your best, you are far more likely to make a good impression with the proper tone of your voice and your telephone personality.

Always follow-up a cold call with a thank you note.

*Sending a Differentiated Response

Unless your response to a job opening is differentiated, it is not likely to get a response. This process of differentiation begins at the first contact and continues until the offer is accepted. One way to find a key to keep this differentiation at each step, is to ask yourself this question: what would everyone else do to respond to this opportunity, and how would they respond? Whatever the answer is, do its opposite, so that your message is effective.

A guerilla approach to marketing involves doing unusual things to get what you are after. Typically among these approaches can involve calling a company's customers, suppliers or others who may have some insight and then leveraging that to get attention. One can also take unconventional approaches—as sending a prospect letter by FedEx—to job search. There is a brief discussion of unconventional approaches later in this chapter. The reason for presenting both these approaches is because they each present a different perspective to candidates, each allowing them to think outside the box. Part of the challenge is managing a campaign, so that it employs a variety of creative approaches, to produce an effect that is not possible by just any one of its components. You may decide to emphasize one or more of these approaches in your campaign mix, based on your own learning, and your appetite for taking risk and having fun.

In the space below, various creative ways to marketing are listed in the order of increasing differentiation impact. The easiest is ranked first:

- Sending a well-articulated résumé in response to an opening without a cover letter
- Sending the résumé with a cover letter
- Sending the résumé with a *well-researched* cover letter
- Sending a package through a courier service delivered directly to the hiring manager
- Sending a Point-of-View (POV) letter to a high-level executive *without* a résumé
- Sending an attention-getting letter to an executive and then "cold calling"

A good campaign should use these methods to target companies for a response. This is where the Gold, Silver, and Bronze or "A," "B," and "C" tiers are important in a marketing plan. The above approaches should be used according to the tier, to which the target company belongs. For example a "C" company is not worth much more than a résumé alone, whereas an "A" company would get something at the lower end of this list!

The following tale of success is worth noting:

A Tale of Success

The story in the box below is a true tale shared by an excited and grateful client:

Carolyn's Tale

The following story is a success tale of differentiating yourself by using tactics that are easy and the ones that involve making your own rules:

Carolyn wanted to get into an entirely new area, after some 25 years as a marketing communications manager, at a Fortune-50 company and after taking an early retirement, forced by its recent cutbacks. She wanted to get into interior decorating, as her new career. With no formal training in this field and no experience other than remodeling her own home, and having it showcased in a national magazine, anyone would have called Carolyn a mirage chaser in a tough economy!

Carolyn's original approach was to apply to major building material chains, as Home Depot, which sell interior decorating products and has sales people on the floor with some decorating taste and expertise. If that is what any average person would do, she decided to do the opposite: go after the top name in the field. A Madison Avenue designer Lynn H. immediately struck Carolyn. The decorating diva—Lynn H.—was giving a lecture at a local university, during one of her whirlwind tours. Carolyn attended the lecture. At the end of her talk, Lynn announced that those looking for internships at her new local studio, should forward their résumés to an email address, which she flashed on the screen at the end of her talk.

From the large crowd that had gathered to hear the master, literally hundreds emailed Lynn their résumés to the address that evening. Many respondents had years of professional experience and impeccable credentials in interior decorating. Carolyn did the reverse: she sent a letter, with intent to serve as an intern, personally addressed to the diva by FedEx, *with* her marketing communications résumé. The hundreds of emails remained unopened as the FedEx letter was delivered to the diva herself and she signed for it the next day. She was about to inaugurate her new studio, in a day or so, locally and wanted someone to help her do that right away. Lynn, of course, did not have the time to weed through the hundreds of résumés and then go through the selection process. The FedEx-ed letter made the impact. Imagine Carolyn's surprise and delight when she was personally called by the diva that night asking for help with the new project the next day! The following day, Carolyn was offered the internship purely based on her personality, moxy, and enthusiasm, bypassing the many who were far more qualified than she!

Such is the power of a differentiated response!

Carolyn's letter to Lynn is shown on the following page.

Hi Dilip,

Thanks so much for all your advice and support.

The idea of a targeted cover memo, sent two-day Fed Ex directly to the principal, worked for me. Everyone else I was competing against "followed the rules" and sent their résumé via e-mail to the office manager. Mine arrived hand delivered later in the week.

It stood out from the beginning! Then I was told it was well written and I included comments the principal had said in her lecture. It demonstrated I took her seriously.

I've attached a copy of the actual letter used. As you said in the class, "give it a try—there's nothing to lose and everything to gain."

Carolyn

Carolyn DeSoto
391 Benvenue Avenue
Atherton, CA 94025
Bus. 650 555 6427/Res. 650 555 8483

Lynn xxxx   September 22, 2002
536 Ramona Street
Palo Alto, CA 94301   **By FedEx**

Dear Lynn,

Your presentation, at UCSC Extension yesterday, was spellbinding. I've always been kidded for my affinity for continuity. However, now I've met the "master."

I'm beginning my journey in your field of expertise. In parallel with my successful management career at Hewlett-Packard, I completed the UCSC Interior Design Program and renovated my 1930's home. *Sunset Magazine* photographed my garage conversion to cabana and *Palo Alto Home & Garden Design* is working on my story for publication.

So, if that's about me, how could I help you? Enclosed is my résumé. You'll find that my management and marketing communications background, combined with a designer's eye, can help you and your staff with the many commitments necessary to run a business. I want to help you and your team *and* continue my passion for learning design.

Consider me for your internship program. Or, remember me when you need a hardworking, conscientious, project manager with a design background. And with the upcoming holidays—I'm sure you'll be inundated with requests from clients.

Sincerely,

Carolyn DeSoto

P.S. I'm ready to get it done for you. As you said, "no task is too small." Just call me!

The ensuing Thank you note after Carolyn's first stint at Lynn's boutique, the next day is below:

Hi Lynn,

What an impressive staff you've assembled! They're committed and share a strong work ethic—from Cathy, Joannie and Angela through to Elle, Lilliana and Bob. They're an important asset to your business.

And your gala opening was a success. I chatted with Leslie, Deirdre and Aurora—who all had a good time and were very excited about the cover on "Traditional Home." (Although, I think Leslie's Mom, in New York, may have been more excited). Meeting your confident son, Culin, was a kick, too.

There's no doubt about it, he's going to make it big time!

So, even after meeting the extended "family" and standing "trial by midnight oil," I'm still interested in the internship. When is a good time to discuss it? If I don't hear back this week, I'll give Cathy a call.

Thank you for the opportunity. I look forward to it.

Best regards

Carolyn

Needless to say, Carolyn was offered the internship the following day!

♠ Follow-ups and Actions

Follow-ups for every response are as important, if not more, than the responses and actions themselves. Why? It is easy for a response to get shuffled and lost in an organization. As the market gets tougher, the number of responses and the overall activity, on the job front, increase dramatically inside any organization. As company resources get cut, this becomes increasingly more difficult. Even though you have sent a response that is highly differentiated, you cannot assume that someone has read it and will respond to it. Once again, you need to differentiate yourself by doing follow-ups and making an impact.

How? Just the same way the response was sent in the first place. If the response went by a courier, then calling the person who signed for the delivery is a good starting point. Then, tracking to see to whom the package went next and so on. The person who actually opened the package should be the one with whom you need to follow-up. This person may not be the one to whom the package was originally addressed, based on your best research and guess. Initially leaving a voice mail, and then calling again after a few days works well. The idea is to get this person to invite you for an interview; first telephone and then face-to-face.

If you sent your response on the Web, then the person to follow up with is the one named in the posting. Often such names are not given in a tough job market. Calling the main number and then asking someone in HR or recruiting can work, but this approach is not very fruitful. This is why sending a differentiated response is critical, if the target is a "Gold" or an "A" company for you.

Another approach to follow-up is to use your internal contact or network to present the résumé in person. The electronic submittal can be in addition to this approach. The contact can give the details on how to follow-up and with whom. Here persistence pays and the approach to following-up should be just short of being a pest! One way to manage this is, at any given time, having many activities and targets to follow-up so that you do not fixate on one target.

As we shall see in this section, a bit later, how to manage your pipeline (Managing Your Pipeline), having multiple actions on which to follow-up creates a backlog of activities that need to be checked off daily. This, then, becomes a routine activity.

Those who send a few responses and have no marketing plan, zero in on following-up with the obvious names that are announced in the job postings. Some call them nearly every day and keep leaving messages. At this rate of follow-up, your anxiety is tantamount to stalking, which can turn off the recruiter or hiring manager. There is a thin line between persistence and stalking, so it is a good idea to know what that is. If you have a good marketing plan and you are managing a full or near-full pipeline you should not have to resort to "stalking". For a more detailed discussion, see the author's *The 7 Keys to a Dream Job: A Career Nirvana Playbook!*(Key-5).

Follow-up strategies that work

The most common failing in making sufficient progress in a job search campaign is weak follow up. The following list shows proven strategies that work:

1. If you send a response by FedEx track the package and call the person who received it

2. Ask that person how it was routed and try to get the contact information of that person and call within a day of the receipt. Waiting "ages" the response—especially one sent by courier—and after a day or so the recipient does not even remember that the contents were sent by overnight package.

3. When you find someone who is traced as a recipient through the internal tracking system, keep calling—no messages—until that person answers. If that fails, leave a voice mail that is very brief that allows them to make the connection with the package they just received and then mention that you would be calling again, leaving your contact information.

Unconventional Approaches

Unconventional approaches to job search include adopting methods that are not usually embraced by the masses. This is one sure way of differentiating yourself. Unconventional approaches should be used for all opportunities, including posted jobs for which many respond. There are three categories of jobs presented using this approach: posted jobs, unposted jobs, and non-existent jobs.

Unconventional job searches entail doing things in an out-of-the-ordinary way, to get what you want in your job search. This type of search goes well beyond merely ferreting out the jobs that are not posted; it goes to explore how to present a message so that new jobs are created because of what you present. This approach is suitable for your Gold or "A" companies. Once you make your case, then you become the only candidate for that job!

This section will present a variety of ways of doing an unconventional job search and provides examples of letters and other communications, so that you can pursue this as a *part* of your campaign!

Posted jobs

For posted jobs, the competition is fierce, so there will be a cataract of résumés flooding the employer. Using an unconventional approach, is even more important here, to stand out from the crowd. The following list provides a summary of how to provide unconventional responses for a posted job:

- Research the company to find out more about why the posted job is now being filled and use that knowledge to fortify your résumé and the cover letter; update the résumé to reflect this. This insight should go beyond what is in the posted description. See in the author's The 7 Keys to a Dream Job, an example in Key-3: Sample Cover Letters, particularly, the letters of John Mortons and Catherine Jenkins. See Key-3: Résumé and Researched Letter for a Posted Job.

- Find the name of the hiring manager to whom you send a response—résumé and the cover letter—via a courier.

- During the phone interview, show your knowledge gathered from the company and competitive research you have already done to stand out.

- During the interview, use your research to show that you bring more to the company with your insights than anyone else.

- Talk to the company's customers, suppliers, and channel partners to get nuggets of information, so that you can leverage that information, to show that you know more about the company's dealings with its constituencies than even the hiring team does (see following story)!

- If you have a solution to the problem that the company faces and *acknowledges*, and your research shows what the company is seeking, then take your solution, show it to those whom you meet, and discuss it giving details. Make sure you do not leave anything behind or give copies of your material. Politely refuse or use your best judgment.

- Create intrigue around how you can fill a company's need by doing research and showing confident insight:

One candidate who was being interviewed by a high-tech company, for a position of sales trainer, found out that the company Website had endorsements by its customers, who were identified by name and their affiliations. For a sales training to be effective, the ultimate test of its success is the customer experience, and how the customer feels about the company's sales force. So, this candidate decided to call each of those customers whose names appeared on the company Website. This entailed some research to connect the names with the location of each person. He called each of the six customers listed and represented himself as a potential sales trainer looking for ideas to improve customer experience, through improved sales training. Most customers responded with alacrity because they were intrigued by this idea. They had a selfish motive; to have an enhanced experience through the company's sales force. Although the first four raved about the sales force, the last two gave critical information. The candidate was able to leverage this input in the interviews to show that he knew more about what the training focus needed to be than did the hiring manager. As this story circulated among those who interviewed the candidate, the higher-ups quickly realized that no one else could beat this candidate in his initiative, originality, and customer focus.

He was hired within a week from a crowded field of respondents, on a salary much higher than even he expected!

This approach to talking to a company's customers can also be used in developing a letter to get its attention. Some find it difficult to approach customers directly, as this client did, and in some cases, customers may decline to speak specifically about a company without betraying their relationship, when asked directly. One approach that worked, with yet another client, involved contacting customers who appeared on that company's Website. In this instance, the client felt more comfortable representing himself as someone writing an article or presenting a conference paper about a certain business practice in that industry. He probed to explore how one of its suppliers—a company he was interested in pursuing as his target—was faring in this particular area and got insights that otherwise would not have been possible.

Unposted Jobs

Unconventional approaches for the unposted jobs are similar to the ones for the posted jobs with the *addition* of the following:

- Find some compelling way to get the attention of those who have the knowledge of the unposted jobs. Good networking skills are critical here.

- Look for media coverage of the company, find competitive information, read analyst reports, and infer what the company might need.

- Keep in contact with at least a few search firms, especially those who are in the field of your industry and those who know you so that you can get the scoop of the unposted jobs. More than likely, you will have to work with the search firm to get in. What do you care? The employer pays the fees!

- Talk to the customers, suppliers, and channels to learn about the company and how it is trying to move ahead. This search will give clues about possible opportunities.

Non Existing Jobs in Your Dream Company

This category of jobs stem from your own view of how a company should position itself in the current economy, to move ahead of its competition and achieve things that it has not yet achieved. The following list is a summary of what can be done to discover this knowledge:

- Research company's competitors and discover what they are doing, which your prospect company should be doing, and then make a case for it through a letter written so that some one higher up (at least two levels above the hiring manager) gets to see it.

- Talk to those who sell or service the company's products to discover what the company might benefit from to enhance the overall product or customer experience. If you are in product development, sales, marketing, or customer support, your argument on how to do this better can be compelling and an attention getter.

- Research company's finances and read its SEC filings (10-K/10-Q), publicly available. Use this research, to make a case, for why its management may need someone with your skills to beat out its competitors. This can be done at job levels starting from a hands-on design engineer to a senior VP!

Summary: Chapter-8: Marketing the Product: You!

Marketing yourself is a challenge that goes beyond merely posting résumés on a job board, sending a response to an open position, or responding to "inside" jobs. It takes a systematic approach to identify target companies and then segmenting these targets into a prioritized list. A job search can be far more productive if a systematic campaign is launched that included a process of constantly ferreting out targets, identifying the right strategies for each target segment, and then following a proven protocol to get action from these targets. The available job market can be segmented into three categories of companies:

- "A" or "Gold" (10)
- "B" or "Silver" (25)
- "C" or "Bronze"(100)

The numbers in each category represent the desirable level of companies that must be targeted to have an effective campaign. It can take up to one month to ramp up to this level of activity (135 targets) to fill a marketing pipeline. Typically, for someone out of work and looking for a job, up to 30 hours per week are required to land a *dream* job within a reasonable time. Although a typical dream job belongs to "A" targets, getting an offer from "B" or "C" companies can help leverage an offer from an "A" company.

To get a company's attention, research is required to flesh out information that is not normally available. This information can be available through a variety of sources, including the company's own Website, customers, suppliers, or employees. Other sources are analysts, industry experts, and those who have worked with the company. There are also databases that provide this information with varying degree of quality, currency, and depth. Normally, a synthesis from a variety of sources is required to develop a point of view (POV) for a compelling cover letter. A cover letter must reflect your insight that is not normally presented by others who are going after an opportunity at a particular company.

There are a variety of avenues for you to market yourself through third parties. Recruiters, search firms, counselors, and outplacement firms are some of these avenues. Each avenue is discussed in specific detail, with pros and cons.

Networking is a good way to reach companies of interest and get their attention. Nearly 64 percent of jobs are filled through networking contacts. Sending responses to what is posted on the job boards by blindly forwarding a résumé yields poor results (four percent). A graphical view of the Networking Universe is presented to show how your network can be organized.

The chapter ends with a discussion of using unconventional methods for:

- Posted jobs
- Unposted jobs
- Non existent jobs

Strategies for each type of target are presented so that a high yield campaign can be launched.

Chapter-9: Acing the Interview

"The meeting of two personalities is like a contact of two chemicals; if there is any reaction, both are transformed."

—Carl Jung, psychiatrist (1875–1961)

The Interview

In critical human interactions, many look for the chemistry. Going through the interview process is not leaving to chance the chemistry of one's makeup. This chapter demystifies how such chemistry can be "created" through careful preparation, targeting, and execution. The presentation here is in the sequence in which events occur after a résumé gets someone's attention. It is aimed at showing how to develop a process, to minimize leaving to chance, the matter of one's "chemistry."

The Telephone Call

Many job seekers have the wrong notion about the purpose of their résumé. They expect that a good résumé will get them their job. This is not entirely correct. A good résumé gets the first phone call, which leads to a second, which then can lead to an interview. A first interview then leads to further interviews, which can result in a job offer! A résumé, no matter how great, can only lead to that first phone call.

Getting that phone call from sending a response to an opportunity is the first thing jobseekers yearn for. And yet, it is alarming to see how many are not fully prepared to handle *that* call. This all-important call is a gateway to being invited to a job interview; *all* subsequent actions depend on how this call is handled. It can be a passkey to the world of landing a job and working at a dream company, even though the initial call may be from a lesser company. How? This is because the first call may lead to a job. Even if that job is not ideal, it opens the door for using that success and leveraging it into a company of your choice. What are some of the common roadblocks to the next step after the first call?

The following list delineates the most common impediments, which can block success:

- Making it difficult for people to reach you
- Taking calls on a cell or cordless phone
- Not having ready access to the material sent in response to the opportunity
- Taking the call when unprepared to provide a best response
- Not knowing who is calling, why, and what the next step is
- Not knowing how to close for the next step

*Making it Difficult for People to Reach You

The following checklist is a good reminder to audit telephone habits and make sure that this most critical element, in a successful job search, is not taken for granted because of its familiarity.

1. **Having a single telephone line:** In this world of the Internet, people spend much of their time in cyberspace. Having a single telephone line, on which to do all the activity, including being on-line, can be a problem for those calling you. Many give out their cell phone numbers, as their primary point of contact, on their résumés. It is advisable to give your home phone as the preferred point of contact, with the cell line as an alternate. Cell phones and connections can be unreliable. Not being at a convenient spot can be a problem, too, when such a call comes on the cell phone.

   The best defense against missed or lost calls is to have at least *three* residential lines: one for business and job searching, one for the Internet, and the third one for family and personal calls. If there are teenagers in the house, there may be a need for additional lines depending on one's lifestyle. The line used for job searching must have a warm, personal greeting that is concise and business-like. That line should have a distinctive ringer so that only *authorized* members—preferably only you—of the household answer that line. Additionally, that line should be available at multiple points in the household so that it can be answered conveniently and promptly with an ability to transfer an incoming call to a quiet and well-organized place of choice. At this location a workstation, laptop, or a computer and other resources should be available for easy access. A headset that is integral or connected to this line is helpful for a hands-free conversation. An interview or screening call, taken in a stressful environment, will show that stress to the caller, in addition to the customary nervousness. And, the price paid for this disadvantage, can jeopardize the next step of being invited to the interview! See Chapter-2: Tools and Rules of Transition.

2. **Having caller-ID:** Having caller-ID on the business line is a good idea. It provides the ability to identify and decide if the incoming call is worth the distraction.

3. **Greetings and voice mail:** The business line must have a professional greeting that is short, pleasant, and personal to welcome those calling. Do not have a child singing a ditty as a welcome greeting on a business line! Avoid robotic or canned greetings that come with store-bought machines. Such greetings can convey an impression of laziness to record a personal message. They also fail to identify you to the caller by your name or even by the tone of your voice. If there are time restrictions on the recording device, they should be part of the greetings: "You have 30 seconds for a message." Doing so will warn callers to be aware of this so that they can manage their message. Not being forewarned of this time limit can result in missed calls. Few hiring managers may bother calling back to re-record a cut-off message, if that mishap was not caused at their end, especially in a tough market.

4. **Not ready for the call:** When a screening or interview call comes, being ready for that call is important, otherwise that call should be rolled over to voice mail. Although this is chancy, proper judgment about taking that call can protect the opportunity. Sometimes, when you are not ready to take a call, because of your state of mind or the circumstances in the household, it is best to pass up the call for a possibility of a future reconnection with that caller. It is also a good idea to have call screening. Old-fashioned answering machines allow this feature.

5. **Security screens:** Many install a security screen on their incoming lines, despite the legislated "Do-not-call list," to avoid telemarketers or unwanted callers from intruding their phone space. This feature thwarts random callers by asking them to identify themselves and asking them to wait until someone is willing to take the incoming call. This barrier to calling can be a turnoff, especially if the caller is in a hurry and has other calls to make for the open position. The set up may result in a missed call and the caller may not call back because of the set up. Simpler means

of screening incoming calls, as answering machines that allow listening to the callers' messages, can avoid this possibility.

6. **Quality Check:** Imagine being frustrated because of no action on the phone, even after sending hundreds of résumés! When this happens, checking the telephone number on the résumé is a good start to verify if it is correctly listed! Transposing digits is easy and there are about 10 percent, who have mild dyslexia. Few bother to call themselves by *reading* their number, as they know it by memory. Calling oneself by *looking* up, or asking someone to call from reading what is listed on the résumé is a good practice. This also provides for someone to audit the incoming voice greeting for quality.

7. **Message back:** When responding to someone's call and leaving *them* a message, it is a good idea to be clear. Instead of saying " Hi, Jim this is Dave, and I am returning your call from yesterday. You have my number since you called me, so I'll wait to hear from you." Instead, try "Hi Jim, this is Dave Gifford, three-two-three—five-five-five—zero-zero-one-two (avoid saying *double not* as those from some European and commonwealth countries might say). I am responding to the message you left yesterday about the job for a program manager, your posting # 2342. Thank you for your message and I am looking forward to talking to you. My number, again, is 323-555-0012, the same one you called yesterday. You can also reach my cell at 323-555-1121. Once again, the cell phone is 323-555-1121. Looking forward to hearing from you soon and thank you!" can be much less puzzling to the caller. Speak the numbers S L O W E L Y and C L E A R L Y, as the called party may have trouble writing this fast enough, have a hearing problem, or may be dyslexic themselves.

If in doubt, leave yourself a message and ask someone to hear it!

When answering the incoming call it is a good idea to be situated for an efficient setup (See Chapter-2: Tools and Rules of Transitions: Getting Organized) and having all the materials necessary for a good conversation at your fingertips. A good way to achieve this is the low-tech way of using an old-fashioned three-ring binder, which is discussed in the next section.

The initial call, typically, comes from someone in HR or recruiting. The caller in this position has the task of connecting with a selected group of candidates to make sure that they exist and, if their initial screening goes well, to arrange for an interview. So, if the caller sounds unsophisticated, has an accent, or who speaks English in an unpolished way, treating them with disdain or contempt is ill advised as they have the power to decide if the face-to-face interview is the next step in the process. They typically start out calling with a list of names. If a candidate does not treat them well and dismisses them because of their perceived low status, the caller has the power to either take the name off that list, put it at the top of that list, or at the bottom. Respectful and businesslike response to the caller is recommended, regardless of the level at which they are perceived to be functioning. Being polite and thanking them at the end of the call can help being called for an interview.

Taking the Calls

Taking incoming calls is critical. This is such a familiar task that most underestimate the variety of ways it can go wrong, or at least put you at a disadvantage. Let's look closer:

Cell Phones

Cell phones are everywhere now and people routinely carry them and conduct their business on the move. They are also rapidly overtaking the land lines. By the late summer of 2005, the number of cell phone accounts exceeded the land line accounts for the first time in the U.S. For a job-search, a cell phone should *not* be the primary contact line. Why? For one, it can ring at any time, making it awkward to take the call. Cell phones do not typically have reliable connections and they can drop chunks of messages, when connected. Another factor is that it is unlikely that you have ready access to key information needed to ace the interview if conducted on a cell phone, while on the move.

Cordless Phones

Cordless phones are ubiquitous. In addition to the cell phones, they provide callers and those receiving calls mobility over a range well beyond what was possible with long cords on conventional instruments. Although cordless phones offer the convenience of taking the call in a walk-about mode, they create a disadvantage for an important call such as an interview. Why? It permits the call taker to pace or move about while talking. This can be a distraction. To the calling person this distracted attention may come across negatively. The other disadvantage of a cordless phone is the static noise that can occasionally interfere with the conversation. When the power goes out, too, so does the connection; one can face a suspenseful wait wondering if the caller will then call back! Even if the caller calls back, without a wired land line that you can answer using a standard phone, you cannot even take that call!

The other reason for not taking an incoming call for an interview on a cordless phone, is possibly the voice and how it sounds to the calling party. Taking the call standing or pacing on a cordless phone invariably results in a higher pitched voice than when sitting down. A higher pitch can communicate anxiety. The other disadvantage of the cordless, or any phone, where you have to hold the handset, is that, for an extended conversation, it can be stressful. When you take your call, holding the handset between your cocked head and the shoulder, while talking for any length of time, can be taxing. This is especially true if you are required to use your hands for taking notes or keyboarding. This can further exacerbate the negative "tone" to the caller.

The best arrangement for taking incoming calls for a telephone interview is to be comfortably sitting down with easy access to materials. Ability to be focused and to take notes, to be relaxed and sound confident, can only help graduate you to the next step for an interview. Having a headset is a boon to this set up. Keeping a beverage to sip on during long conversations can help a dry mouth and throat, which can only betray nervousness or anxiety to the caller.

Having Ready Access to Material

During an interview call, having ready access to files and correspondence is critical.

There are, of course, a variety of ways of keeping such information, so that there is ready access during exigent times as an incoming interview call, which can come without any notice. With computers obsolescing the old-fashioned paper files, most keep their important files now on their PCs.

For job-search related matters, here's a low-tech alternative that is more effective:

A three-ring binder, big enough to hold important outgoing responses to job openings and other correspondence, is such an alternative. Thumb tabs organize it, alphabetically, with each target company filed under its respective name. Each stack of papers, under a tab, consists of the cover letter, résumé, any company research, notes, and other materials. All generic responses go under an "Other" tab. Why is this a preferred organization? Simply because it affords the most convenient, reliable, and simple arrangement of files for ready access, regardless of what the PC decides to do at a critical time! Yet, another psychological advantage is that having a stack of papers in a binder creates visibility to what is in the "Pipeline."

When an incoming call comes on the "Red Phone," answering it promptly and then holding the conversation from the designated place, can give an edge to ace the interview. It does not matter now if the PC were on—the three-ring binder should be right next to the PC! Putting on the headset, opening up the three-ring binder to the tab for the company calling and launching into a professional conversation, with a smile in your tone can begin immediately! With your hands free to take notes, a relaxed, poised, and engaged conversation can now take place without any distractions!

The other advantage of having a three-ring binder for all outgoing job responses is that it is available to be taken wherever it is needed, for studying without the technology paraphernalia. Maintaining the discipline, by constantly organizing the materials, to keep it slim and uncluttered with extraneous information that becomes obsolete, is critical as the outgoing responses mount in a long campaign!

Having the PC as a *back up* for files and folders is a good idea. Here, too, keeping the entire system well organized and managing similar sounding file names, especially for résumés, are critical. This naming problem can result, when in a hurry, in sending as an attachment the wrong files. The best antidote for this possibility is to keep all versions of a résumé separate by carefully naming them, so that they are not confusing during harried moments. Anything that has become out of date or obsolete should be periodically purged, regardless of the size of the hard drive! As we discussed in Chapter-6, Building Your Platform, having multiple flavors of your résumé can be a good idea. Each flavor can evolve over time as you learn new ways of presenting your message. Each revision must be tracked carefully by labeling your résumé with the version number, which can be located in the bottom right corner with a size eight font. This simple discipline will allow you to correctly respond to a caller, who may have an old version of your résumé, by simply asking them to check the number printed at the bottom right corner during the conversation, and then clicking open that document on your PC screen.

Taking the Call When You Are Not Ready

Most interview calls come at home, when that is the primary telephone contact on the résumé.

If the call comes as a surprise, then it is a good idea to find some reason to defer it. It is hard to pass up an opportunity for an interview—phone or otherwise—without wondering if it would come back. This is why this judgment should *not* be made casually. But, if your judgment is that the call should be deferred, find some way to dodge the call and politely ask the caller if you can call them back. Otherwise, taking the call is prudent, especially in a tough job market!

Here are some occasions worthy of avoiding taking an interview call:

- You have fallen asleep and the call wakes you up. Let the voice mail take the call. If you are just waking up from a nap or sleep, you will sound groggy to the caller and disoriented. The caller may think that you are under the influence of a drug or alcohol! Not a good first impression.

- You are harried and are in the middle of something critical. You are distracted. Let the voice mail take the call. If you have the ability to screen the call and you hear the caller talking into the machine, you may have enough time to mentally regroup and then pick up as the caller is hanging up, with the message now on the machine. This is a matter of judgment.

- You are enjoying your evening cocktails and the call comes. Do not take the call as your gaiety and inebriation can compromise making a good impression.

- You are angry or frustrated about something personal and are not in a best frame of mind. When the call comes let the machine take the call and hope that you are able to reconnect with the person.

- You are driving and are about to enter a tunnel or a bridge. Your cell phone rings because the hiring manager wants to interview you. In addition to a potential safety problem, the connection can be cut off because of where you are headed. Ask to be called back or pull over to the shoulder and hold the conversation, if it is safe to do so.

- The call comes when you have a definite time pressure. If possible, hold an initial conversation if the time allows and then explain the situation. There is nothing worse if the caller feels rushed and you feel cheated for giving flighty responses to interview questions.

When you do take the call and have to dodge it, be polite, apologetic, and businesslike in handling it. Make sure that the caller feels welcome for having called, despite your exigency!

No matter how you take the screening call, your mission should always be to parlay that into a face-to-face interview. All your energies and focus should be on this outcome! You should learn how to finesse it in a smooth, businesslike, and easy fashion.

If one of the reasons for the call is to schedule an interview, do not jump at the chance by saying "Of course, I am free all week!" A better approach is to say that you need to consult your calendar, and, as you are reading it, convey to the caller that you are genuinely a busy person (mumble the entries)! If you have entered your daily routine on your calendar, you are busy; just leverage that discipline to make yourself more desirable to the caller!

Not Knowing the Caller and the Intent

When the call comes for a telephone interview many job seekers can be flustered, even discomfited, despite following all the tips outlines above. To many it is the surprise element of the call and not knowing who is calling and why. The best approach to overcoming this apprehension is to first ask the person calling to say their name and then ask them to spell it as you write it down. Then ask what their affiliation is and how they got your résumé. This conversation can be an icebreaker and will help in composing yourself for the dialog that is going to ensue.

Having a clear sense of how the caller is a part of the hiring process gives the insight on how to position your messages during this highly leveraged event. It is so because your getting called for an interview as a natural next step is based on how you handle this call.

Often, the first call comes from someone in HR, typically a recruiter, or directly from a hiring manager if you have sent a FedEx package with a great cover letter. The FedEx package may have been sent to someone a level or two above the hiring manger, as is described in Chapter-8: Marketing the Product: You! This is why it is important to take the first few moments to know how this call came about. It is also good to explore if the recruiter is a company employee, a contract hire, or an outside agent. The reason for knowing the organizational affiliation of the caller and their role in the hiring process early in the conversation is that these bits of knowledge allow you to compose your thoughts and prepare your responses that are most likely to result in your being moved up on the list of those who get invited for an interview.

Recruiters, generally, screen you for vetting the facts on the résumé. HR administrators also play this role and are chartered with the responsibility to assess if you are a person they feel can work in the company environment and that you are easy to deal with. So, in such interactions it is best to be pleasant, factual, calm, and personal. Asking questions is also a good idea so that you can get a better sense of where the process is and how many candidates are at this stage of the screening process.

Those calling from the chain of command—typically a hiring manager—are looking for a different perspective. Their focus is on the technical content of the conversation, suitability, flexibility, assessing your level of involvement in what you did—in essence your title—and how you could best fit in within their organization. So, asking incisive questions, throwing some intriguing business ideas, showing knowledge of some recent positive and negative developments in their area of work are some of the topics sure to get your lined up for an invitation to an interview.

The Salary Question

One of the trickier aspects of the initial phone screen is the discussion about compensation. Since most of the telephone screens are conducted by someone from HR, the exploration hinges around getting answers to the most basic of questions of employment.

One of these questions is about your salary. How much you are making now and how much you expect in your new position are the most typical of the questions in this area. Of course, if a hiring manager asks these questions during the initial telephone interview the best response would be to give a *range* of your current salary and leave the expected salary question for a later discussion after you understand the responsibilities a bit better. For a more complete discussion on salary negotiations, please see Chapter-10: Negotiating the Offer.

The following list summarizes responses to the salary questions during the initial telephone interview stage:

- Recruiters: Lowball your salary

- HR callers: Give a range for your current position

- Hiring Managers: Wait until you have a clear idea of your position

When in doubt, you are always better off giving a range than a number.

Sometimes, early in the process, some companies not only ask for your last salary, but also your salary history. This is arrogant. Especially in this market, where career progressions are not linear, such a question can create a problem. The best defense against such insults is to preempt it by stating the range of salary you will accept. Then in the interview explore the responsibilities and agree to a number based on what responsibilities you will discharge.

Not Knowing What's Next:

As the phone interview comes to a close it is not enough to merely sign-off by thanking the caller and hoping that someone would call you for an interview. The best course of action is to ask, as the conversation is winding down, what they see as the next step. *Do not ask how the interview went!* Instead, ask who is going to be calling you and what the call is going to be about. Also, get the contact information of that person and the time or date when they might be calling. Mention that if the person does not call you, you plan to call them back and follow-up and then call the person who was supposed to be calling you.

What this outlined conversation establishes is a clear accountability for the next steps and its timetable. It will also impress the caller that you are a responsible person and that they can rely on you to carry out assignments that are likely to be yours when you work there.

This simple step also puts you in charge of the ensuing events. Otherwise, you are at their mercy and you lose control of the process.

Once the details are nailed down, it is time to thank the caller for their time and to show them how much you appreciated their insights.

This sign-off must be followed by a thank you note (email and a mailed card as appropriate). This is why getting the details about the contact information of the caller during the first few minutes is critical and then repeating what you wrote down as you sign-off on the call

♠ Face-to-Face Interview

A successful phone screening leads to a face-face interview. In a tight market, candidates are screened several times and many of these phone screens can be long conversations. Employers do this to ascertain that there is a good fit, before the in-person interview, to save time and expenses for both sides.

Interviewing face-to-face after the telephone screening, can be the most dreaded event in the job-search process. Why? For one, candidates feel that all their apprehensions and fears will militate against them and gang up to frustrate their efforts to land the job they are after. For another, there is a lot riding on an interview and a rejection can be a crushing blow to the sometimes-fragile self-esteem of the job seeker. All these emotions result in job seekers feeling apprehensive, even fearful about this critical step for which they have waited and prepared for so long! *They* become their worst enemy.

One way to overcome and conquer this feeling is to become fearless—without becoming smug or complacent—during this process. Being ready and prepared is one way. Another is doing some exercises and getting prepared to face this dreaded event. Looking at it as a fun and adventurous opportunity can also help, but to many, this is a stretch! Of course, preparing well for an interview helps, too! See Chapter-2: Tools and Rules of Transition, specifically, Managing Your Fear.

Following the guidelines suggested in the preceding paragraphs, the chances of landing an invitation for a face-to-face interview are good. The mission now is to ace the interview and get the offer. The following discussion is a good guideline for a successful interview *process*:

Before the Interview

Before delving into company-specific information, it is a good idea to get a general sense of the state of the industry. Why? Every company belongs to a certain industry and each industry has its "culture." How this culture drives a company's operational needs is a skill that many do not have and even fewer know how to leverage that into a successful interview.

For example, the biotech industry does product development using its own "best practices." These practices differ from those in high-tech, which are highly evolved over the years. Finding a common theme across many companies in biotech and how their practices, as a class, can be transformed to fashion after those used by the high-tech companies can be an additional piece of insight into the interview process. If this insight is presented during an interview, it may even create a compelling case for someone migrating from, say, high-tech industry to the biotech industry, without the detailed knowledge of that industry!

Yet another example may be taken from IT in *any* industry. The traditional focus of IT has been technology first, how it is integrated into the business operations and its availability, effectiveness, and ease-of-use, second. Even less of concern, historically, has been how the human factor interacts with the technology to create meaningful change that serves—or impedes—a business. So, when going in for an interview as a director of IT services, the preparation focus should be how factors, *outside* of technology, can help make any IT initiative successful inside the target company. These factors may include: managing organizational change as new technology is implemented, leading cross-enterprise integration, socio-technical factors, as, how those using technology embrace it and feel comfortable with it. An IT expert is *expected* to know the technology. But very few would have insights on the other aspects mentioned here. Having some articulate and studied views on any or all of such "adjunct" factors can be a great differentiator in an interview. These insights are not limited to "executive" ranks. Individual contributors and other professionals can frame this perspective in their own context as well.

Once the industry landscape is understood, the following step-by-step company-specific homework can help in the interview:

1. Pull your materials together so that you can review all that has happened so far. This includes your notes, your responses from the binder, all your research about the company and the position for which you are being considered.

2. Research the company and its affairs for the past two years for a good understanding of what it does, its current challenges and outlook. There

are several excellent research tools available: Hoover's, Reference USA, InSite-2, Dunn and Bradstreet, Lexus Nexus, among others. Many of these tools are online and are available from the local library. Subscription is expensive.

3. Visit the company Website for any endorsements posted from its customers, suppliers, and others who are stakeholders in its success. If they are identified by name and affiliation, make a point of calling them. Your call should be for discovering some insights about the company, so that this discovery can help you position yourself more strongly and in a highly differentiated way during the interview process. See related story in Chapter-8: Marketing the Product—You!: Unconventional Approached, Posted Jobs.

4. Find out anything from the company Website that you can use to leverage your interview.

5. Look at the financials, using the annual report, either from the Website or from any of the tools mentioned in #2, above. Infer some information and draw insightful conclusions based on this research. For example, if you are targeting a position in this company as a lead R&D engineer, look at any data about research expenditures during the past two years. If these expenditures are declining, you can suspect that the company is focusing less and less on R&D, which can both be good and bad. The good part is that the company is now more conscious of how it spends its research dollars; and the bad is that you may be expected to deliver a heroic effort. You can use this research to explore more clearly how you will be positioned once you get in and your chances of success. The interviewers will be impressed by your research and insights. They can then provide their own take on this trend. With several interviewers, you have the unique advantage of integrating all inputs and deciding for yourself if there is a common theme and evaluate what is being presented as they are courting you, a definite position of advantage!

6. Look for the track record of the company in the area of your pursuit. If you are in marketing communications, look at the company's recent marketing campaigns and their successes. Talk to customers and those who are affected by them. See if you might do this to create a different impact. Then present this information during the interview and have a discussion on this. The interviewers will be impressed by your impeccable research: a good thing for someone who should be doing the research before putting out a marketing message!

7. Get a résumé updated, again with the latest insights reflecting your research. Pull together your portfolio of materials that you may want to take, to showcase your accomplishments. Make this portfolio a professionally packaged presentation.

8. Line up and prime your references, as you get ready for the interview. Always have about a dozen or so names ready. The reference mix should include: previous bosses, peers, customers, suppliers, and other professionals who have worked with you and who will not betray your confidence by saying something less than stellar about you (this is a 360 degree reference roster). Call them one by one and tell them where you are in the process and what aspects of your past association with them is now important to you during this process.

9. If you have letters of recommendation or references from the past, integrate them in your portfolio (see #7, above). Do not take your past performance reviews!

10. Get out your interview wardrobe. If you are in doubt as to what is appropriate, go and check out the building where you would be interviewed and park outside. Observe who goes in and out of that building and their dress; wearing one cut above what you see; shine your shoes, spruce up your accessories! Thus, if you see most of who come in and out of the building, where you will be interviewed, wearing a tie with no jacket (for men), or a skirt and blouse with a jacket (for women), it is safer to wear a business suit. A jacket and tie might work for men, too, as would a smart fashionable attire that is conservative for women. Do not wear business casual. One thing about interview attire is that you can always remove something if you feel overdressed. If you walk in and suddenly feel underdressed, then you feel bare and that conscious feeling can compromise your confidence at a critical time. This can be an edge that you just lost.

11. The idea behind this attire suggestion is, that when you go for the interview, you should feel special but not conscious! Think conservative. An interview is not a place where you want to make a statement about the fashion world. Don't let your interviewer see what you're wearing before they see you! If you are not in a habit of wearing a suit, buy one and wear it to some occasion prior to the interview so that, socially, you can get used to the idea of being seen in a suit. Do not wear the suit for the first time at the interview. You may feel self-conscious; also something about the suit may surprise you, and make you feel ill at ease. You may end up compromising an important opportunity on account of your unfamiliar attire.

12. Find out who will interview you. Someone organizes all interview logistics, and then notifies you. That person then calls you with confirmation details about the event. If you do not hear about these details, ask that person who they are and what their role is in the interview. Get the correct spelling and functional title of each person you are going to see on that day. Once you have this information, you have a good sense of what kind of information will be part of the interview. You can then research that information and get ready!

13. Make a dozen copies of your résumé on a premium stock paper. Organize your materials in a well-presented briefcase with your business card on it and a supply of them inside. Carry a small, unopened bottle of spring water and a dry snack that does not leave salty or sugary residue on your hands or lips as you munch on it (Never *during* the interview!).

14. If you are on prescription medication, as antidepressants, see if you can avoid taking them as the interview event nighs. Often, such drugs can make you zone out and make it difficult to keep you alert. Consult your physician before changing your regimen.

15. Now you are ready to head on to the interview!

At the Interview

The following tips will help you to ace the interview:

1. Arrive 30 minutes before the appointed time! Why so early? For one, you want to be at your best for the interview. Coming early allows you to check in and make sure that you are in the correct building. Sometimes, the entire interview set up gets changed at the last minute, and everything gets moved to another building clear across campus. Now, you have to rush to find the new building and be on time. Even if this were not the case, coming early can allow you to settle down and get used to the environment and feel relaxed to be ready for the interview.

2. Introduce yourself to the receptionist and smile. Be courteous and pleasant to everyone from now on. Do not demand coffee or any other favor from this person. Get it yourself. Sign in at the register or login device and wear your security badge. Make sure that the host is in the same building where you arrived or that the location is close to the lobby of the building. This is important to ascertain early. In some places, the behavior you display and the attitude you exhibit towards the receptionist are reported as a part of the interview. Do not assume anything from here on!

3. Strike a pleasant conversation with the person at reception. Make small talk. This can be of help on your way out, especially if you connect with this person.

4. Observe what is in the lobby. Any company literature, periodicals, news, or product literature can be great icebreakers. So, too, can the awards on the walls of this lobby. Be observant of the people coming in and out. Take in how the receptionist talks on the phone to others and how those coming in and out of the building interact with the receptionist. You are now sampling the "culture" of the work place! For you to be compatible (one of the three "C's" to be discussed later) this could help.

5. Make sure, as you sign in, to tell the receptionist that you are early and not to announce you yet to the person you are seeing for the interview.

6. Relax, breathe deeply, and think happy thoughts. Visualization can also help you feel relaxed at tense times.

7. Bring some of your own reading material. Some lobbies have nothing to read. This way, although you are sitting there pretending to be reading, you can still look businesslike and engaged in something besides gawking at something or someone. Working on your laptop is also a good way to while away these tense minutes. Do not curse or get angry if your system crashes while you are doing this! Do not play portable video games as someone might get the idea that this is how you while away your time, not a good impression to make!

8. When the appointed time comes, politely ask the receptionist to announce you to the interviewer. If this person is on the phone for a long time or is constantly answering calls, do not cut in or look impatient standing next to the front desk, tapping your fingers. Do not pace. You should observe, as you are sitting and waiting, the call frequency and the talking habits of this person before you decide when to approach them for announcing yourself to the host. If you cannot get their attention, hand them a note stating that you are now late for your interview and you would appreciate their helping you as they continue on their phone—personal call or not!

9. Once you are announced, close your magazine, laptop, or whatever else you were engaged in. Sit comfortably and wait for your host to come and get you.

10. When the host arrives, smile, greet, shake hands, and follow them!

The Handshake

Much has been written and said about shaking hands. Some claim that a handshake is a window into personality; much the same way as others who say the way you write is also a hallmark of your personality. Regardless, some tips on good handshake etiquette are in order here.

A handshake is a good way to convey, during the first moments of apprehension and anxiety when meeting someone important, that you are comfortable, confident, loyal, honest, and eager to prove yourself.. A weak or reluctant handshake gives the impression that you are tentative, diffident, and simply not interested in your surroundings.

There are various ways and styles of shaking hands and they vary from "The Bone Crusher" to the "Cold Dead Fish," with the "Two-Handed Vote For Me" sandwich somewhere in between. A handshake is a social custom to get to know the other person with a human touch in a warm, friendly, and business-like manner. The Dead-Fish handshake stems from your clammy hands, you are nervous and unable to offer a firm hand, it is also cold from the sweating. This is why coming early and doing some relaxation exercises can help overcome the anxiety prior to meeting someone. If you still cannot suppress the sweaty palms prior to a handshake, keep a handkerchief ready (right trouser pocket for men) and before the host comes to greet you, discreetly wipe your palm so that, at least temporarily, it is dry for the handshake.

The following four-step process is what is recommended for a good handshake: engage, pause, observe, and remember. The first step of engagement has to do with how you engage the other person's hands. Grabbing hands in haste can be looked upon as aggressive. While you clasp the other hand, your shoulders should be squared to the person, eye contact should be maintained, with your palm flat with the webbing between the thumb and index finger fully engaged with the other person's. After pumping the hands a couple of times, the next step is pausing, and, it is during this brief time that you make a connection with the person. It is during this pause that the third step also takes place: observing. Here you observe the other person and size the way they connect with you. The fourth step is remembering: this is when you remember if the other person was nervous, tentative, or confident and relaxed.

This entire script can sound intimidating, but is a learned and practiced behavior.

In the Interview

There are three ingredients for a successful interview, or for that matter, any successful interaction with another person: Ethos (*eethas*), Pathos (*paythas*), and Logos (*logas*).

In Greek, ethos means the basic character or essence. In everyday vernacular, it can be equated to personal chemistry. The two other factors also play a part in that dynamic. The second, pathos, means sympathy, or that the two people meeting, harmonize with each other in the way they see their pain. This can be equated in common parlance as compatibility; and finally the third, logos, which means logic or reasoning in everyday use, can be equated to competency or skill that you bring to the position. For a successful interview, all three are critical. This prescription applies to selling something to anyone, or having that person see your point of view. We'll discuss these in more detail on the following page.

It is, therefore, critical to understand this basic dynamic for a successful interview. In the following script, we'll present how to achieve this interview *nirvana* through a tried-and-true method.

Now you have come to the place where the interview is going to take place. During the time you are walking with your host to the interview, you use ice-breakers to connect with the person. If, for example, you saw in the lobby an award—say the Malcolm Baldrige Quality Award—plaque hanging on one of the walls and next to it was a commendation from the CEO stating that your host was instrumental in securing this rare and coveted honor, this is your great chance to show that you read that commendation and to offer your congratulations. Then, if you ask what role the person played in securing the award, you are connecting with this person with a rare and compelling means. This is a much more subtle and personal way to access the host's ethos.

Ethos also means " I am like you." In addition to being "like you," if you can get that person *to like you* as well, that further cements the potential desirability. Liking someone goes beyond just ethos. What that person has attained is appreciated and that is important to you! Talking about the weather, the parking, or last night's ball game are mundane and chancy topics because that person may not share your views, and you have now created a discord, right at the outset on a matter that is impersonal! At this point of your interaction, do not talk politics, religion, or anything that can be controversial—even a movie!

Yet another way to develop ethos is to observe what is on the desk or the wall as you enter the host's office. The reason is because it is important to that person. Ask questions. Let the person get into the discussion on that item of interest to you. Your commenting on it is an acknowledgment that you share that interest. Once again, ethos!

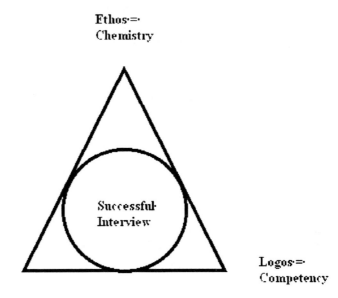

Figure-8:· The·Interview·Success·Trilogy

Sometimes the interview is held in a meeting room or a conference room. In that case, you need to think of some clever way to connect with the person. If anything pops up during your walk with them, use that time to see if you can break the ice and establish ethos.

Once you have arrived at the place for the interview, do not impose by asking for a beverage. If offered, assess if your host is up for it and then decide. Do not take the time to walk down to another building just for a cup of coffee. It is a good idea to carry a small bottle of water in your case, as we presented before. Your throat may be parched, even on a cool day, and your mouth may feel like it has cotton balls. Interviewing in that state definitely puts you in a state of disadvantage!

♠ Individual Interview

The following checklist will help you with the process where it is a 1:1 interview:

1. Once you enter the room where the interview will take place, take charge. When asked, sit comfortably in the designated chair with confidence. Put your briefcase down and not on the table or the desk! Relax. Pull the briefcase in your lap to get things out and place them in front of

you. These things may be your notepad, pen or pencil, your organizer or calendar. Do not clutter the desk or table with more than the essentials. Your résumé should be part of the stack that consists of the writing pad and other material—a *small* stack!

2. Look at your host and smile. Breathe easy. You are naturally anxious. Do not show it by making solicitous, even smarmy comments: "Gee, I am really sorry you are catching cold," if you just saw your host sniffling. He may be allergic to something *you* are wearing and not really catching a cold!

3. Thank your host for taking the time for the interview. Ask politely, how much time is set for the interview, who else might see you, and anything else that is logistically relevant: "Is Tom coming here or I am going to his office?" So that you are clear on the course of the activities planned for your visit.

4. Let this host launch the *formal* part of the interview with the first question—the informal interview began when you first shook hands! Make sure you understand the question. Generally, the first questions are easier. But, do not assume if you do not understand something. The interviewer is nervous, too; use that to your advantage. For example, he may assume that the person who did the phone screening took care of certain preliminaries, as the company's expansion plans, overseas contracts, etc. Politely state the facts and ask for further information. You entire line of response may hinge on this critical information.

5. ♠ There are two things critical to the interview dynamics: the person asking the questions is in charge of the interview; the person doing the talking is doing the selling. You should not automatically assume that your host is in charge of the interview after the first question. They are just in charge of the arrangements for the interview, and that is why they are your host!

6. One way to take charge of the interview without overtly showing that you have now done so, is to first *answer* the question in a leading way. Then ask back a question at the *end* of your response, so that the interviewer has to respond with a thoughtful answer.

   For example, if the interviewer asks why you see yourself as a good fit for the position, the best response is not to assume what the position is, merely after having read the job posting. A good response is to first advert your response to what is already on your résumé, and state what you have done in the immediate past at the company you left or are leaving. This is all factual. Then, at the end of about a minute or so, pause, and ask the following: "Now that you know what I have done at HP as a product manager, and I also have read the job description for this position, what is your perspective, and what do you expect the new hire to do to bring value to you?" This is *not* the same as asking what the job is; you should know that, having come this far in the process! But, everyone has a perspective and expectations on how this position will be filled, and what the new hire is expected to deliver.

7. ♠ Once the interviewer launches into an answer, take brief notes on what is critical in their response. Watch their body language carefully. Do they betray a discord in stating what is being said, or do they really believe what they're saying? Sometimes hiring managers or other interviewers do not buy into all open positions for political reasons. Your knowledge of this is critical. Once the person stops talking or you see a natural opening into what might be a longer answer (after about 60–90 seconds), interrupt politely and say "That is very interesting, John, because that is exactly what I do well." And, then go on to say, "Let me explain!" Now, go on to those parts of your résumé that have supporting material to what was said, and then build on it. Use the very language and the words that were just used to describe their expectations. Now you cannot lose. If you do not follow this simple script, you are shooting in the dark and you have no clue if you hit the mark.

8. Once you have come to this point, you have probably crossed the tipping point in who holds the control of the interview. Now you can bandy questions and answers back and forth, and you both are having a dialog, not an interrogation. Remember, you have to ask about half the questions—starting early—and do half the talking. This way you are both selling each other, a perfect barter!

9. Throughout this exchange, carefully watch the interviewer's body language. See the following section: ♠ Understanding Body Language, and tips for reading body language.

10. Do not make responses to anything based on your assumptions. Do not infer anything from what you know, especially if it puts the company in a negative light. Let the interviewer suggest, rather than your insinuating something to make a point. This can back fire quickly and is very difficult to get out of!

For example, if you have done some digging about how the company deals with its customers, by actually talking to them, before going into the interview, you can leverage that insight. Do not factually state what they said, if it is negative. If it refers to improvement that you can provide; it may sound self-serving coming from you. Wait for the interviewer to bring it up by your leading them that way. For example, rather than saying "your customers think that your sales people do not have adequate technical understanding of the technology, and often end up providing inadequate or wrong solutions, as a result," ask how the company makes sure that during a sales call there is technical representation, so that the solution is sound. Then, if the response comes in the form of something less than stellar, jump in and say: "I actually talked to some of your customers, and what you suspect is shared by some of them, and I know one way to mitigate that…."

This approach to solving a problem, only when it is presented and owned by the interviewer, is far more appropriate, than merely assuming that the interviewer already knows what you see as a major problem, and that they are looking at you for its solution.

➢ **Never provide a solution to a problem that the interviewer does not even know exists or owns!**

Remember Pathos! Also, as we discussed in Chapter-2, Tools and Rules of Transition : Career Transition Styles for Different Types, those with NP types may feel compelled to showing their "insights" to impress the interviewer, if the interviewer happens to be an ST, they may be offended!

11. ♠ If you see the interviewer disengaging from the interview, as suggested by their leaning back, showing distracted gestures, or looking at their watch, quickly recognize it, and back peddle what you just said and see if you can recover. It is good to recognize early a potential derailment before it is about to happen than to wait for complete derailment or even a train wreck. (See ♠ Understanding Body Language, in the following section.)

12. One clue on how the interview is going is to check the elapsed time. This is why asking up-front how long the scheduled interview is—item # 3— can be critical. If the interview is going really well, you both lose sense of time. Good interviews that are really engaging, go well beyond the scheduled time. If you see anything is getting in the way of that, it is your responsibility to make sure that you bring that back on track!

13. Throughout the interview, take notes, if you do not have an answer to any arcane or unexpected question, despite all your preparations, make a note of it, smile, and politely say that you would get back with an answer. In fact, this strategy will help you reconnect with the interview-

er in ways not possible otherwise. Similarly, if you find a natural opening for showing your knowledge on some related topic by having read some relevant material in a journal or publication, state that observation and say that you plan to send that article upon your return. This also gives you one more chance to connect with the interviewer after the interview.

14. If the interview has progressed to a heart-to-heart dialog, then it is safe to assume that you have aced the interview. You are not out of the woods yet. You've got to establish yourself as the only and ideal candidate. The following is one way to achieve *that* goal:

    During the process where you realize that you have now taken control of the interview—without the interviewer knowing it, of course!—asking the following question can give you more insight into how you stand vis-à-vis other candidates. Your mission now is to make you the only candidate by asking: "If you were to bring on board an ideal candidate, what would their performance look like in the first year?"

    The response to this telling question is critical. The interviewer is likely to say something like: "We expect the candidate to do this and that." Once you get a grasp of what that means in terms of what you can do to achieve the same outcome, your immediate but studied response is how you would deliver that performance and how you have already delivered similar performances before. In essence, you have now made it known to the interviewer that you are *that* ideal candidate. When presenting this argument, specific examples will help even further.

    The other advantage this question provides is that now you can leverage this information during the entire interview circuit after this first round. You will not only impress the others with this knowledge and insight, you will plant in their mind, too, that you are *it*!

15. Since this is the first interview, do not bring up any salary or similar information into the discussion if the interviewer does not ask you. If you are asked, politely say that this is your first interview and you would like to explore more by talking to others about this job and then decide how it is scoped. If you show haste in this step, you are likely to come across as too anxious!

16. As the interview is winding down, be mindful of the time and make sure to ask questions so that, not only you get answers to these, but also, more importantly, make the interviewer think of the significance of *your* questions. If you have done thorough research before the interview and know

what the hot buttons are, you should be able to pose some trenchant questions that will differentiate you. Often, the most obvious questions can stump an interviewer and show that you are not a run-of-the-mill thinker. Also, learn to leverage one question in an interview into another one!

17. Throughout the interview maintain eye contact and smile in a relaxed way. Feel empowered by what is happening in front of you; your body language should project this state. You should radiate confidence, control, and calm! The interviewer will be impressed by your aplomb.

18. ♠ As the interview comes to a close and you see things are winding down—you will sense the energy—ask, at an appropriate time, what the next step is. This is a telling question on how well you have done and what the interviewer thinks of you, and how you did. *Never* ask about how the interview went. These questions show insecurity and put the other person in a position of power. The unspoken word says much more here than most realize.

If the interviewer says that you should know in a couple of weeks, as there are other candidates, you should quickly pull out your pocket calendar—the throwaway, plastic variety—and say something like: "Two weeks from today would be November 21, which is a Friday. Why don't I call you on Monday, November 24, if I do not hear from you? What is a good time?" By this exchange, you have ascertained that if you do not get that call on November 21, you are free to call on Monday to follow-up. This also puts you in charge of the follow-up process.

In most cases, you will not get that call on the 21st as promised! This exchange also shows that you are good at holding people accountable for actions; a good attribute if you are seeking a program manager, sales, or similar position, where accountability is central to your success!

19. At the end, once again thank the interviewer for their time and express how much you learned from this exchange! Also, express that you are now even more excited about this position than before and would look forward to working for this manager.

20. On the way out make sure you pick up all your trash, put all your papers away in your case, and leave everything behind as you found it when you entered the room. The interviewer will probably escort you to the lobby or to the next spot for the interview.

Interviewing in a Group Setting

This mode of interview has now become more and more common, as resources and time available to process a candidate through a series of interviews become more and more critical. The following rules are worth reading before going to an interview that may be conducted by a group:

1. Know before hand if you are going to be interviewed in front of a group. Understand how many and who will be in the group. Also, understand what the affiliation of each person is, so that you can anticipate the focus of the questions from each of the interviewers. Ask how long the whole process and the interview itself may take.

2. Take at least as many copies of your résumé as the number of people in the room and take some additional ones for safety. Also take extra copies of other materials and make sure you keep track of what remains behind and what does not. Do not make more than one copy, of what you consider proprietary or your own intellectual property that anyone can plagiarize. Just having one makes it easy to retrieve and keep track. Mark this document *Proprietary.*

3. As you enter the room, smile and look at every person by scanning the room. You do not need to shake each person's hand. Just introduce yourself and take a seat, if you are asked to sit down. Say "Thank you!"

4. In front of a group, you are likely to be even more nervous than with just one person. So, do not hesitate to pull out your bottle of water and place it next to you.

5. If you are asked a question, listen carefully and then pause before answering it. This shows a studied response, instead of a hasty one, even if you already know the answer. This approach will help you when you do not have a ready answer. Here, you can use the same pause to dig for an answer.

6. First, look at the person who posed the question. Then scan the other participants, keeping brief eye contact with each one, and then moving on to the next pair of eyes. Smile as you contact each person with your eyes. Watch each expression, as they listen to your response. If you see any apprehension in their expressions, see if you need to rephrase your answer or back peddle your idea.

7. Using your notepad, draw a diagram of the seating arrangement in the room and write each name as they are introduced. This way you can

refer to people by name, as you look at them in response to a question. This approach will make you look poised and professional.

8. Ignore any person who is engaged in an activity outside paying attention to the interview or to you. Some may talk among themselves, or do some other activities that may be distracting (and rude)!

9. When the interview is over, get up with alacrity, and thank every member as a group and organize your stuff before putting it back in the briefcase and leave the room.

10. Do not ask how you did in front of every one!

11. Do not ask the whole group, as you leave, what the next step is. Save this question to the one who hosted you and see that person on your way out.

♠ Understanding Body Language

During a job interview, your focus is mostly on what is asked and how you *verbally* respond to those queries. Ironically, only 10 percent or less of what we communicate is verbal; the rest is body language and tone. With 90 percent riding on the invisible, the unknown, and the unmanaged, it is no wonder that we are often surprised at the outcome of an otherwise "good" interview. Some pointers below (mostly summarized from what was already presented before):

1. Dress code: always dress up and not down; you should feel special but relaxed.

2. The handshake: relaxed firm, not clammy; smile. Ask to be seated; take charge.

3. Seating erect and confident, 10–15 degrees forward and alert. Men/women knees together. Do not cross legs.

4. Practice some easy icebreakers: observe the office or comment on the lobby.

5. Legs relaxed, but no spreading or bopping up and down of a leg.

6. Breathing with the others, deep and quiet. Smile often. Know nervous habits.

7. Look at the interviewers (in a group interview) without looking through them or staring at just ONE person; this can mean you are ignoring the others.

8. Engage in a *dialog* early; do not surrender to an interrogation. Ask to clarify as needed.

9. Always remember: the one who's talking is doing the selling; make them talk.

10. Speak deliberately, articulate well, and watch the body language response of others.

11. Call on body language. Flicking off imagined lint signals disagreement, as does finger on nose or face, or scratching face.

12. Take manual notes (avoid gadgets) and maintain eye contact, smile, nod, and agree.

13. Do not use *but;* try using *and* instead.

14. Do not engage in an argument, even when you know that the interviewer is wrong.

15. Be prepared to take on invidious or sarcastic comments: respond kindly, with a smile!

16. Stay in charge of the interview, always.

17. Ask not what the job can do for you; state what you can do to/for the job.

18. Don't betray anxiety or desperation by jumping ahead, instead be calm and deliberate.

19. Drop seeds for easy follow-ups later on. Mention articles you've read that support your discussion. Mention articles by name and publication.

20. ♠ Avoid steepling fingers upright (arrogance). An interviewer doing this portends difficulty. If you see an interviewer leaning back, looking away from you, and then steepling (a typical sequence), you are in increasing difficulty over what you might have said. Back peddle early, if you detect this sequence, as the interviewer starts leaning back! (Note: steepling is when you bring your two hands with extended fingers together as a steeple, pointing upwards.)

21. Don't lie, ever, or misrepresent. This is disempowering! Don't volunteer adverse information; we all have it.

22. ♠ Throughout the interview, observe interviewer's facial expressions. Expressions on a face are a good indicator of inside emotions. If you observe a reaction to what you said on the interviewer's face, quickly recognize it and regroup. A typical emotion is displayed on a face in less than a second and can last for up to two or three seconds.

23. Focus on your value and not on your shortcomings.

24. Show enthusiasm, excitement, and positive energy. Attitude is more important than intelligence.

25. As you depart, shake hands, create accountability for the next steps; stay in charge.

Fortifying Your Position

An interview is the best opportunity to get first hand insight into the company that you have researching from the outside. If all the preparations and discipline on how to do a great interview presented so far have not convinced you to present yourself as an intriguing yet compelling candidate here is the final place to get it. What is presented so far will help in preparing you to put the best foot forward. But, not all interviewers are easy to deal with during an interview. Some will sit across from you and fire away questions from an Excel spread sheet and check your responses robotically. Some, even engage in an interrogation that will put a skilled defense attorney to shame, asking you to simply answer a "yes" or a "no" to their list of questions. To many, these encounters are unnerving and discouraging on an otherwise good interview circuit. Remember, a person who conducts such an interview gives the same treatment to all candidates, so you are not at any particular disadvantage. The only disadvantage you put yourself perhaps is if you did not play by *their* rules.

Regardless, when you are done with all the interviews during one round, you must take stock and assess where you did well and where you did not. Then write notes to each one specifically addressing where you have come up short and then fortifying with responses that show that you have the openness and the savvy to come back with a better answer.

As you walk away from an interview, you must make mental notes of how each interview went and have a good sense of come back answers—almost staircase wit—that will further ingratiate you with each interviewer. As is described under the following heading, you must include this comeback in your Thank you note.

♠After the Interview

After the interview you are probably back in the lobby checking out and handing over the badge to the person who greeted you upon arrival and signed you in. Thank that person and tell them that you really enjoyed the experience. Remember the discussion about making friends with this person at the beginning: use this connection to get from the person, anything you might need to close the loop after the interview. If you shook hands with someone during the interview, but failed to record or register the name, this person is likely to give that information. Simply describe the person or say the name in any way that you remember; this person will look up and give you the details you need, so that you get what you came looking for.

Also, get this person's contact information, so when you return and you have something that you need in your follow-up, this is now your inside contact!

Upon your return from the interview, compose your notes into a coherent informational resource. Reflect on the interview; does anything stand out as having gaps or holes that needed a stronger answer? This must all be done in the first 24 hours following the interview.

Compose a thank you note for electronic transmittal. This note should be brief and should make one or two points about what could have been done better. Without an apology, state your afterthoughts so that the interviewer appreciates your diligence in following up with a stronger answer. This further cements your candidacy! Repeat the timeline that you agreed at the end of the interview, so that who calls whom and when are clear from this note.

A sample emailed and mailed thank you note follow. For an important target ("Gold",) send a short thank-you card in the mail instead of a note. The message here is brief and personal.

♠Thank you note

Dear Jim,   **Via email**

Thank you for your time yesterday, meeting with me, and explaining the initiative to improve customer retention and loyalty at Global Enterprises. I know how valuable your time is and appreciate your spending more time than what we had originally scheduled for our meeting.

After our discussion, I am now even more excited about working with you.

I am summarizing my reflections, since our meeting, to help us move this process along:

- I am impressed that you have started a new initiative to improve customer retention and it is already paying off in less than three months. This is great! Now that we know what works, I would like to share with you my success from similar initiatives.

- Working with sales and customer support, identify customer accounts that are placing undue burden on Global's resources. Using the 80:20 rule I was able to identify which accounts were causing similar disproportionate drain on resources at International Electronics. We used the same rule to identify which accounts were giving us the most revenues and profits. We were then able to identify how to leverage that information in to multiplying that effect.

- Starting a customer loyalty initiative: Provide customers reason to come back to Global and buy more. By creating a tiered incentive plan, I was able to get many customers to shift their business from our competitors to us.

- Customer habits: I did some research on my own in your customers' buying habits. Some of them also buy your products from direct channels and other sources. Have you thought of creating a price incentive model that benefits the customer if they make the sales call a one-stop shop? I have done this in two other companies with great results.

- Not just surveys: I have some ideas on how to go beyond the customer surveys you currently do. Surveys are a good source of sensing the overall mood, but they do not create actionable outcomes. I suggest doing a face-to-face customer discovery. I found this to be a source of actionable input and have developed a simple model.

- Involving the customer: Have you thought of involving the customer during early design phases? You mentioned a disconnect between the customers and product features. This simple process will not only make designs more customer centric, it will also accelerate time-to market. I have some data to show you.

I am excited about the possibilities at Global. I am looking forward to seeing you again!

As we discussed, I plan to call you on November 19, if I do not hear from you on the 17th.

Once again, thank you for your time and thoughts!

Cordially
Sally Jones

Mailed "Thank You!" Note

A Thank You! Note is sent in the mail in *addition* to the email. This is done for effect and impact! A sample follows:

Dear Jim,

Thank you for your time yesterday. Spending nearly two hours, when you had only one on your busy calendar, is appreciated. After listening to you, I am now even more excited about the Global opportunity!

Since our interview, I have reflected on many things you said and what we talked about. I have summarized my thoughts in an email I sent you today. I am writing this note to express my special appreciation for sharing with me your most passionate thoughts about customers and how they need to be treated.

I am excited about the possibilities at Global. I am looking forward to your calling me on November 17. I shall call you if you are unable to call me then on the 19th!

Cordially,
Sally Jones, 11/9/03

♠Staying in Touch

Despite your best efforts and ways to keep the interviewer accountable, you may feel that you have lost touch. Your call on the promised date does not come, so you call the next day as agreed and the person is not available or gone out of town. You leave a message and even get a hold of the administrator, only to encounter silence and no action. Not knowing what is going on and why no one is calling or responding, can be nerve wracking, especially with a great interview and unspoken signals that told you otherwise.

This is not uncommon, even in the most promising of circumstances. In absence of the expected call, the following course of action is suggested:

1. Find out if the person expected to call you is available. If the person has suddenly gone out of town—a common happenstance—wait till you have some idea when the person would be back in the office. Wait one or two days *after* that to reinitiate your calling.

2. Send an email to the person, after their return, and state that you plan to call, in a day or so, to reconnect as you had agreed after the interview. This time leave a voice mail.

3. If this does not create any action, just wait for a week or two and call someone else. Your HR recruiter may be a good option. State your circumstances and ask if you can get help on this follow-up. If the person knows what is going on, you will know.

4. After one or two weeks, mail something you discussed in the interview. See item # 19 in the "Understanding Body Language" list. The cover note should state the context and that you plan to call the person in a few days. The idea is not to harass the person with persistent messages. The idea is to give this person a reason to call you or for you to call them.

5. After sending the material, send an email stating what you have sent and mention that you plan to call in a few days. Mailed letters and packages can sit in the boxes for days and weeks, as most important exchanges take place electronically. Sending an email to convey what you have sent is polite and not redundant. Do the same if you faxed the material. Fax numbers can be shared and the material can sit on the machine. In your companion email message, write the fax number where you sent the material so that they can go an retrieve it.

6. Yet another approach to keeping the mind share of the hiring manager is to send some interesting article or publication that supports your point of view during the interview. This is one of the easier ways to get back in the running. Use such an article to get their attention and then follow-up with a message to see if there is any reaction. Do this, however, once or twice, or else move on!

7. Make sure that in all this effort you stay politely non-obtrusive and respectful of the person's space. Often people get busy and distracted by unforeseen or personal events and it makes it hard to keep commitments. Just staying in their mind in a non-obtrusive way is the best method of leveraging your past success. If the person sees you as too

anxious, even though they have been remiss, you might not again hear from them.

8. Make sure that you do not obsess on this episode—non-responsiveness—and keep yourself occupied with other pursuits.

9. When the person eventually gets in touch with you, do not act annoyed or do not sulk! Pleasantly pick up and move forward as if nothing has bothered you about this long silence! For all you know, this person may be testing your patience and see how you behave in a situation quite likely to occur in real life—especially if you are in sales or marketing!

10. If after all these attempts you still do not succeed in connecting with the person, just wait for them to initiate the call.

11. If you have an internal connection in the company, see if you can discretely find out what is going on. Do not contact any one officially as HR or someone in the chain of command. If this fails, too, move on!

♠ Navigating Through the Process

Once you have started the process of connecting with the hiring manager, you are on your way to getting the offer. In tough times, hiring managers have limited time for something that is not their immediate concern: managing their functional areas and departments. As cutbacks continue, fewer and fewer end up doing more and more. This includes the hiring manager. This is why so much time is spent on the telephone interviews and initial screening.

Because of this early screening, there is an opportunity to continue to solidify your position in the process and increasingly make you the only candidate left at the end! How? As competition gets more and more intense, fewer and fewer are able to withstand the grueling march of the process. As we discussed in the last section, every step is an opportunity to differentiate yourself and making a mark. As the number of steps increases, so do the chances of making a mistake or doing something inadvertent, which can help eliminate others in a lengthy process. In tough times, the hiring process can take on marathon proportions and only those who can sustain the scrutiny, become worthy front-runners. The following list is aimed at helping you manage this arduous and seemingly endless journey:

1. When something does not happen as expected or planned, think of a way to get back into the race by salvaging what is still within your control. For example, answering a question in an interview, it is possible to have made an oversight. In such a case, it is never too late to correct that

answer. How? In the follow-up thank you note, give a thoughtful and memorable answer that is concise and intriguing. No guarantee here, but how you recover from a setback says much about you.

2. Always think of how one of your competitors would deal with the follow-up process. Know what a normal response and expectations are from one of the competing candidates. This means that if two messages do not get you a call back, do not leave a third message or get angry and show it, as most of your competitors would. This simply means that you need to follow another route to get their attention. Most of your competitors are likely to follow the expected route and alienate the hiring manager in the process. This makes you now a stronger contender, too! Send something, as an article in the mail, as discussed in the previous section, and wait to reconnect. In tough times everyone is stretched thin. You are out of a job and are looking for one, and this can make you edgy. Step back, and be rational. Do not compromise all the time and effort you have already invested in the process, by doing something rash or being impetuous.

3. Instead of fretting over the delays and lack of response from just one target, focus on other opportunities. Make sure that other targets in your pipeline are not being ignored while you focus on any one possibility.

4. In uncertain times, even job openings can be precarious. Budgets are suddenly frozen, jobs restructured, projects de-scoped, and managers reassigned. This does not mean that you are not going to succeed in what you started. It just means that higher priority items are interfering with what you are looking for to accomplish. Just be patient and use some of the ideas from the previous section to keep yourself in the running.

5. If you do get a call, perhaps because of reasons described in #4 above, explore if the hiring manager is willing to bring you on board as a consultant or temporary employee until the uncertainty goes away. See Chapter-8: Write to the Point with Letters: Sample Letters (Contingent Employment, letter #22).

6. If you get the subsequent rounds of interviews, always keep the hiring manager in the loop. Do not assume that the hiring manager is fully aware of what is going on. Sometimes HR, or recruiters, will keep the others involved, without the hiring manager's awareness, and it is your duty to keep the hiring manager manager apprised, just in case. Keep sending those thank you notes with the copy to the hiring manager and

the recruiter. Unless it is an important interview, just email thank you notes are sufficient.

7. Use what you learned in the earlier interviews to leverage a better outcome from the subsequent ones. For example, the question suggested about the "ideal candidate" in the initial interview can be an excellent springboard for acing the subsequent interviews.

8. Always stay in charge of what is happening and where you are in the process by constantly apprising the hiring manager and the recruiter. Often helping them along the way can be your competitive advantage and your ticket to the final step of the process.

*References

References are usually the final step in the selection process. This being the case, however, the references should be readied well before the interview process begins. In fact, as soon as you decide how you want to package your message, through your résumé, the references should be stroked to see if the message is consistent with how they can reference you! This also means that you need to cull your reference list, based on the overall message you present in your résumé. The résumé is about tomorrow, references are about yesterday, so there can be a big disconnect between the two. Once you have your marketing campaign ready and the positions you are seeking are clearly known, you should begin your dialog with your references. This ensures that your references will not surprise you at the last minute.

One way to ensure proper and supportive references is to write a reference letter yourself, and send it for a review and signature. This does two things that will help you in the long run: you will know if the particular reference sees you the way as you perceive; secondly, if there are any differences in the two perceptions, there is time to correct the record, or drop the reference all together. This should not be left to chance. Your drafting your own reference letter may strike some as odd. This is common and a matter of courtesy to the reference, because this way all they have to do is to edit what you wrote and sign it. Your script helps them remember you in the context of the job. They may have no clue, what that is, other than what they generally know about your association with them. You cannot leave that to chance!

Another effective strategy you can use, once the interview process gets serious, is to have a reference make a call to the hiring manager. They can provide an input without being asked. On many occasions, this has made enough difference to push the candidate to a front position. The final references can be done at the proper moment.

It is also proper to carry the reference letters that you have already prepared, and signed by your star references, in your portfolio so that you can show them to the interviewers when appropriate. This is also a good way to show that you are prepared with the right ammunition to ace the hiring process.

When references are requested, give a list of names and contact information, so that they are easy to reach for the person calling. Call the references ahead of time, to brief them on what to expect and who might be calling. Also remind them what to emphasize, perhaps once again, so that they are armed with the right and fresh information to make the overall process smooth, swift, and effective. Request, too, that you would appreciate being informed upon completion of the reference check. This is one way you know that the process is underway and that the only remaining step left is the final offer!

When the job market is tight, some companies request the reference list early in the process. Many do this to ensure that the candidate has nothing to hide and that the process does not take up time which may be wasted if the reference check results in rejecting an otherwise promising candidate.

From your perspective you have a dilemma: if you do not give references you may deselected from the process. If you give the names and contact information then you risk "using up" your references as they get imposed by many people calling them from various companies.

One approach that has worked in some cases is to have a list of references ready and primed as you start your campaign. If a company asks for references early in the process (first interview or after the initial phone screening), giving the list without details of contact information is acceptable. Explaining that you are interviewing at other places and you consider that calling your references would be an imposition if every one called them so early in the process. But, you are willing to provide all the other details about the reference as to the relationship and the role they played working with you and so on. Your further saying that you would furnish the contact information after the process converges for a decision, should be viewed as a gesture in good faith.

Notes:

Summary Chapter-9: Acing the Interview

This chapter deals with the process that begins with a response from the potential employer as to how you presented yourself. Usually this response is a phone call from the interested party. This summary is broken down into each important step of this process.

The phone call:

This everyday routine can be an opportunity killer. If you do not take care of simple matters as making sure your phone number on your transmittals is correct. Details of all suggestions offered for an effective connection and messaging are listed in The Telephone Call. Please use this entire section as a checklist so that you leave *nothing* to chance. Once you get the exploratory call, you must finesse it into getting yourself a face-to-face interview. See how by revisiting this section!

Face-to-face interview:

Protocols for before, at, and during the interview are detailed in Face-to-Face Interview. Study these protocols, internalize them, and make them your habit, even if you need just one interview and one job offer. These protocols—especially the one on body language—can give you the edge you need in this important step.

Staying in touch:

Post-interview jitters make candidates antsy about follow-up. Too many, too soon, too anxious! All these apprehensions make it difficult for job seekers to be effective in this important step. Many lose out because they did not manage this process effectively, despite their stellar interview. Read the details in Staying in Touch.

References:

When the process gets to the point of asking you for references, you can be certain that the employer is serious. Handling this process, from the needs of the employer as well as managing the expectation of the references, is presented in this section.

Chapter-10: Negotiating the Offer

"In negotiating, the one who speaks first gets the short end of the stick."

—Anonymous

Employment Offer

An offer is a culmination of the job-search campaign, though it is not the culmination of the overall process. An offer is received with a great sense of anticipation and relief. At the same time, it is full of open and unresolved issues. For many, the anxiety around an offer is palpable. It even gets worse *after* an offer is tendered! Why? Despite the unmistakable relief that comes from "I am in," there is this unmistakable apprehension: "Can I get what I really want?"

The following process defines how to get the offer and what to do with it, once presented.

Getting the Offer

Once you have navigated through the interviewing process and gone past the reference stage, the only remaining step is being offered the job you are after! Sometimes, it can take several weeks before the final offer comes because the referencing can take time. This is why your ability to persuade your references to call in on their own can accelerate this process. Ask first, so that the right person is called, and, that it is acceptable to do this step your way, and not the way it is traditionally done. As mentioned before, having your references get back to you after each check is a positive way of staying in control, but this is not always possible, especially if you have references at high levels.

There are various ways an offer can be made. The following list is typical in most situations:

- During one of the later interviews by the hiring manager
- Over the phone by the hiring manager

- During one of the interviews by the HR representative in person
- Over the phone by the HR representative after the reference checks

How one deals with what is offered has much to do with *how* it is offered. Of course, you want to get the best offer, and if it is not what you expected, you want to make sure that it is the best that you can get, based on how the entire hiring process has gone to this point. This is why making an end run on an offer is not a good idea; one has to position correctly right from the start, as we discussed before.

Depending on the nature of the job market, company practices, and your own candidacy, the length of the hiring process can vary. But, after a sequence of interviews that ratchet up in their importance, an offer is presented. If the hiring manager is offering the position, the following dialog is useful in protecting your (you are John, in this hypothetical dialog) options to get the best offer possible:

> Hiring manager: "So, John, looks like things have gone well, and you seem to be a good fit for us, what kind of salary are you looking for?"
>
> John: " Thank you, Sally, I really enjoyed the exploration! Does this mean you are offering me the job?"
>
> Hiring manager: " Yes, John, I am!"

(Note: If, at this point, you are *not* being offered the job, issue a look, without saying a word, which conveys to the hiring manager "what kind of fool do you think I am?" If you had already given out a number in response to the salary question earlier, even to another person, you can no longer do this. This is the power of learning how to do this right! If this happens over the phone, responding by saying: "why don't we wait until you are ready with one?" can work.)

> John: "Thank you, Sally! What position am I being offered?"

(Note: Do not assume that the position being offered is the one for which you were originally considered. This can change as a result of how you presented yourself, and how the company perceived you throughout the process!)

> Sally: "We're offering you the position of Marketing Manager, Consumer Products Group."

(Note: this is the position you were pursuing)

> John: "This is exciting! Thank you, Sally! What is the salary range for this position?"

(Note: the Hiring Manager must know this; she cannot feign ignorance on this point. If she does not know, ask her to please look it up!)

> Sally: "Well, John, this position is scoped at $95 K-$135 K with benefits and bonuses."

> John: "Well, Sally, this is within my range of expectations and within the range I made at IBM. As I mentioned to you before, I consider myself a top performer, and I expect to be compensated accordingly! I know that you will not disappoint me here!"

(Note: Neither one knows what this dialog exactly means; however, each person is thinking a different number now. Hopefully, Sally is thinking the higher of the two!)

> Sally: "John, we understand that and that is why I am willing to offer you $117K base."

(Note: This number puts you on the right side of the midpoint of the range. At IBM you were at $107, but Sally, hopefully, does not know that!)

> John: "That is an interesting number, Sally, may I see that in an offer so that I can look at the whole package and reflect on it before making a decision. When may I pick up the offer?"

(Note: Never betray your emotional reaction to what you just heard (voila')! Be calm, and coolly have the discussion as if you were expecting something like this. If the number is disappointing and is below what you had in mind, and the person wants to know if you would accept that salary before they put it in a written offer, feel out if you can negotiate right there. Read on.)

> Sally: "Let me see what I can do here."

> John: "If I can pick up the offer tomorrow, I would like to look it over and then get back to you with an answer in a week or so, is that O.K with you, Sally? And, thank you, again!"

By doing what John just did he has put Sally on the spot to rush the offer and have it ready for him in a day or so. If this is not possible, she will probably tell him that the offer would be sent FedEx in a few days.

The thing to remember here is that no matter what the offer is, the numbers have to come from the hiring manager (or someone making the offer). It is better that way, and is in your favor. If you came up with a number, then you cannot negotiate that because it is what you wanted. Also, generally, with the dialog we just showed, the offer comes at a number higher than what you might have secured otherwise!

Not all dialogs go like what is just scripted here. The point of this script, however, is that there is a way to stay in control if you have managed the process thus far. Remember the quote at the head of this Key!

Coming to this point of getting the best offer is not something that should be left to the last minute. You have to have positioned yourself from the start to be considered the tops and everything that you did throughout the process should reflect that level of confidence. You also should defer discussing any numbers till you come to this point.

The following table shows how the total compensation can be looked at as interplay of different elements of the package. Depending on the position and priorities you have at any particular point in your life and your career, focusing on one of these elements can help you navigate through the negotiating process!

Compensation Package

A typical compensation package is shown in a matrix form below:

Compensation	Benefits	Stock
-Salary -Bonus -Sales Commission -Other Incentives	-Insurance -Vacation -Sick Leave -Retirement -Sabbatical -Company Products -Free Refreshments	-Options -ESSPP -Profit-Sharing
Development	**Perquisites ("Perks")**	**Relocation**
-Education/Tuition -Training Programs -Management Dev. -Career Counseling	-Company Car -Expense Account -Facilities Access -Company Access (upon termination)	-House-hunting Trip -Moving Costs -Temporary Housing -Low-cost Mortgage
Severance Provision	**Employee Services**	**Life Style**
-Outplacement -Severance Package	-Child Care -Onsite Services -Fitness Centers -Valet Service	-Memberships

Table-10: Compensation Matrix

Not all companies offer this comprehensive a package and not all positions in a company qualify for a package this comprehensive.

Multiple Offers

If the campaign is executed well on multiple fronts and you have diligently managed the pipeline (see Chapter-8), it is not unusual to get more than one offer in a short period. Although getting the first offer itself may take a while, the subsequent offers can come more or less on top of each other! In fact, the whole purpose behind organizing a campaign as outlined in Chapter-8 is for this to be a reality. If you have leveraged the momentum of each interview and carefully orchestrated the progression of events, multiple offers are inevitable. In fact, when one offer is imminent and you have progressed in the interview process well at other targets, it is your duty to make sure that you get multiple offers by leveraging one with the other.

One way to do this is to not wait for an employer to actually make an offer before you call the one that is dragging their feet. You can shake an offer loose by calling them and saying that an offer from another employer is imminent and that they are expecting a rapid turnaround. This will mobilize the actions at the place that is slow in moving and result in their offer coming at about the same time as the one that is imminent. Always remember never to lie about impending offers! Somehow, people at the other end have an uncanny ability to spot a lie! If this happens, you have compromised that opportunity.

Once you have multiple offers, even oral ones, it is time to decide which one is most to your advantage. Not every employer has to know the details of each one to be able to give you the parameter that you seek from them. For example, if one has given you a higher title and another, a higher salary, you can decide which parameter is important to you and then call the one that needs to up the ante to get what you want. Doing this with care, discretion, and without giving an air of exploitation is critical, otherwise offers may be withdrawn.

Doing this part of the selection process well, gives you the opportunity to regain your confidence in your worth, and, for that reason alone, this is a good place to seek and do well at it.

See Accepting an Offer and The Ethics of a Job Offer at the end of this chapter.

♠Win-Win Negotiations

Now that you have the offer(s), you must consider if you want to take it as it is being presented or if there are areas where you need to negotiate. Regardless of the economic conditions and job market, an offer is considered worth negotiating if you are not happy with some aspects of it. This is why it is best to not react or respond to an oral offer until you have seen the entire offer, including your job title, reporting relationship, and other details in a *written* form.

Once you have carefully reviewed the employment contract, make sure that you can live with it, and identify areas where you need some changes. This does not mean you are going to be able to even negotiate them, it simply means that you are carefully assessing the pros and cons of the offer. Once you have done this, the next step is to write the pros and cons down, perhaps in a columnar format for an easy visual review and then decide where you need to look for opportunities to negotiate. Salary is not the first and the only thing that is worth negotiating, although it is so, for many.

Some underestimate the benefits of parameters that are not on the employment offer. A partial list of items that are not on the table above appears below:

1. **Telecommuting:** If you are living far away and like to work from home a few days, this could be important.

2. **Job sharing:** If you are a working mother, or have some obligations, some companies allow job sharing, so that you work only part of the week, enough to get the medical benefits for you and the family. See Key-2 Job sharing. If you have not already brought this up during your interviews, this is not the time to bring it up for a solution, because for job sharing, you need to have identified and qualified someone before getting to this point. But you can bring it up as a future possibility.

3. **Travel:** Some jobs necessitate travel far beyond what is considered normal. Although this is not negotiable at this late a stage of the process, if you have special needs that are acute—someone ill at home and needs caring for the next six months, pregnancy, among other exigencies.

4. **On-Call Duties:** How you are scheduled for a 24x7 call, when this applies, and how you can structure that assignment based on your own needs and preferences. This is the best time to bring it up.

5. **Overseas Assignments:** How you would be compensated for an overseas assignment, if that is not spelled out and if that is a major part of your job. This can have serious consequences on your taxes, expenses, and living arrangements.

You should discuss these items during the interview process. None of these should be a surprise to you or to the hiring manager when an offer is being made. The reason they are listed here is because, sometimes in the rush and excitement to get the offer accepted, you can forget what factors can have an impact later. Once you have accepted the job, and have started working, it becomes too late to effectively change something that is otherwise much easi-er, before accepting the terms of employment!

The other reason for this list is that people too often focus on the salary. There are many other factors that can increase their retained wages *and* the quality of the work life, as well as work-life balance, if they look at the entire contract in a thoughtful and studied way.

Once you have decided what part of the package you want to negotiate, pick just *one* from the list that is most important to you. Then list the second most important and so on. This is a good strategy to allow some latitude if the first item of negotiation does not result in a favorable response.

Remember, you should negotiate *only* one major component of the package. Do not stickle over other details after you have exhausted this component and concluded either way. Do not move on to another one thinking that you should now get some consideration because you were shortchanged on the first!

Let us say that you want to explore negotiating a higher base salary—a com-mon negotiating point—then call the *last* person who offered the package and the job, and ask if there is any room to negotiate the package you just received. Do not wait the full period you requested to confirm the offer. If you asked for a week in which to get back with your answer, then you should make this call in the first day or two.

Once you have opened the door for this discussion, you should be ready to work in a businesslike manner: no playing games and no waffling. You should be firm, forthright, and confident. If you are not sure you can marshal this atti-tude, then consider not getting into this situation. There is nothing worse than entering into negotiating and then cowering down and folding. In negotiating, as the quote at the heading of this Key states: The one who speaks first comes on the short end of the stick. This is why it is best not to bring the salary ques-tion first; let the manager raise it. This is further fortified in the examples below. Yet another nugget of wisdom is to hang on to those items you have decided you can surrender, until the end; giving them too early may make you look anxious and like a patsy!

A typical dialog with an HR person—the last person who contacted you about presenting the offer—can go like this:

> John: "Hi Nina, this is John. I am calling about the offer you just gave me yesterday. I carefully looked at it, and I am won-dering if there is any room to negotiate this offer."
>
> Nina: "Let us see, John, what did you have in mind?"
>
> John: "I was wondering about the base. The range for this position is $95 K-$135 K, right?"

Nina: "Right!"

John: "My salary of $102 K is almost at the low end here, Nina. As I mentioned to you and Jim Smith (the hiring manager), I consider myself a top performer. My references will confirm that, too! In view of this, I am wondering if there is any latitude to move this figure to the right and take it beyond the mid point. This is how I was compensated at my last position. I would like to explore this to see if this can be accommodated, please!"

Nina: "So what number are we looking at here, John?"

John: "Well, Nina, I did not want to throw out a number, but something that reflects my superior performance and my previous seniority would be a good consideration!"

Nina: "John, I'll have to get back to you on this. I need to consult with Jim Smith and my HR manager before I can give you an answer here."

John: "That makes sense. When would you know, Nina? I have committed to confirming my answer back to you by Friday, and that gives us four more days. I am very interested in this position and am looking forward to working with General Electronics and Jim Smith. Actually, I am quite excited about it!"

With this conversation, you have left an option open to the employer to get back to you. If they decide not to make the change then you know you have explored it. If they did give you the increase then take it and do not haggle, even if that number now is still to the left of the one you were *thinking*. If this conversation took place in the way the script is laid out, then more than likely you will get what you went looking for, and perhaps even more!

Nina can come back and say that she is sorry that she could not do anything to change what has already been offered. Your best recourse, then, is to accept what is offered and agree to come on board. This assumes you have no other offers or options. While accepting, you can put a caveat. Remind them that you are a top performer and that General Electronics should watch you perform for six months, and then make an adjustment to your salary commensurate with that performance. Even if this is then changed to the full year, they are now on notice to honor that. When you offer this counter proposal, sometimes, the employer comes back with a response and a number that is pleasantly surprising! This is because not many companies conduct reviews in six months (see "Sally's tale" on the following page).

Yet another creative way to explore getting a higher salary is to carefully look at the entire offer and see if you have not tapped into some aspect of the offer because of how you are situated. Let us say that the employment package offers a relocation allowance. You do not need to claim it because you are already local to the company.

In one particular instance a client was *not* able to negotiate a higher starting salary but was able to split the relocation allowance as the hiring manager said, upon the client making an observation about this allowance, that he would be happy to give him half of the amount of the relocation allowance, as that equaled to the salary increase the client was seeking in his base pay. The manager perhaps thought to himself that the relocation funds came from another budget— probably HR funds—so he was able to swing the deal without any impact on *his* budget!

Do not haggle over benefits and other details, because to HR, these are policy matters, and they are unwilling to make exceptions.

Another area that is a sticking point to some senior employees starting in a new place of employment is their vacation—a mere two weeks every year—as it is for all new employees. This can be approached, not at the HR level, but at the individual manager level. Upon *accepting* the offer, approach your hiring manager in person, and explore if there is any latitude or discretion in the way your start date can be structured. Explain that you had been used to six weeks vacation at the previous employer, and you would appreciate some consideration. One way that can work is to start officially on a certain date and ask the manager to consider your showing up to work at a later date. The manager ignores that period that you are not at work and you treat it as vacation. This "hidden" vacation approach can work only during the first year.

Negotiating: Sally's Tale

This incident shows that anyone can negotiate if they are positioned correctly from the start, even in a seemingly impregnable situation. Having a clear understanding of what is worth

negotiating, having a script, and having practiced that script with contingent scenarios, and then having an exit strategy can be of help. Never enter a negotiation without a clear exit strategy.

Sally was an administrative assistant who lost her job in the middle of 2001 from a Fortune-10 company. She was single, in her mid 50s, and was discouraged at the prospects of finding anything in the Valley, as the layoffs mounted. She had pulled together a résumé that was a compilation of her past, and had sent over 250 responses. She abandoned hope when she did not even get one call in return. She was frustrated at the impregnable nature hiring process, as she found it impossible to contact anyone where she had sent her résumés.

In November, Sally had reconciled herself to selling her condo in the Valley and moving to a modest locale out of California—perhaps in the Midwest.

Sally, in her last act of resignation, decided to redo her résumé per the suggested template—Résumé Showcase, Key-3—and selectively target companies with a well-researched cover letter. To her surprise, she got calls for interviews, and within five weeks, had two job offers. One was from a mid-sized law firm, and another, from Stanford University, as an administrator for a senior executive. The offer, however, was about $5,000 below her needs.

Sally wanted the Stanford job badly because of the prestige and benefits. She was terrified to consider negotiating the offer, as she was sure she would lose it— she had never negotiated in her life and was raised in the belief that you get what you deserve, and not what you negotiate!

With some coaching, Sally marshaled enough courage to initiate negotiating the Stanford offer. The following script summarizes the dialog that took place:

Sally: "Hi James (Stanford's HR Rep) this is Sally. Thank you for your offer yesterday. I am calling to explore if there is any way we can negotiate this offer, as I am very interested in accepting the position. I was looking for a base more in line with the value I bring to this position."

James: "Let me go and check. I shall call you tomorrow."

James: "Hi Sally, this is James. As I checked the possibilities I found that there is no way to make any upward adjustment to the base. We have many candidates interested in this position, as you can imagine."

Sally: "I am sorry to hear that, James. I'll tell you what, though, since I am so interested in this position, and I am so confident that I can do a great job there, I am willing to join you at the salary you offered. As I have mentioned before, I consider myself a top performer, and my references will attest to that, and you will see that for yourself as well. If I accept what you are offering now, can we have an understanding that three months after I start working there, my salary is adjusted commensurate with what I deliver, and what you observe?"

James: "Let me go and check. I shall call you later today."

James: "This is James again, Sally. I checked with our senior staff and they all said that we review only once a year, regardless of any circumstances. That is our policy. However, if we offered you $10,000 more to your base now, would you still be interested in joining us?"

Sally: "That is an interesting number, James. Let me think it over and call you tomorrow."

The next day Sally accepted the offer!

Sometimes when you are turned down, you still need to stay in control and salvage what is still available without losing face. As it played out in Sally's case, she had an exit strategy that worked well for her, and she did not have to execute her ace card, as at the end she got what she was looking for and then some. Also read Mike's tale that follows, in contrast.

Negotiations are not as difficult as most believe they are. You just have to take a close look at the entire package and then decide why you want to negotiate certain elements of it. If you are convinced that this is a fair and reasonable thing to do, then you will probably succeed getting what you want and, sometimes, even more! Always wait to start negotiating *after* an offer is made.

Negotiating: Mike's Tale

Mike was a software quality engineer who was laid off and was looking for nearly a year. He finally found a contract-hiring agency that offered a position that would place him at their client's company as a QA lead. The following transpired, resulting in Mike's offer being withdrawn:

Mary: "Looks like we have made our decision and we are going to make you an offer, Mike! We're going to offer $40 per hour as a QA lead and get you started right away at Harris Electronic Arts."

Mike: "Wait a minute, Mary, that is not the number I had in my mind. I was thinking more along the lines of $60 per hour. I have checked the salaries for the region and industries in the geography and looking at what I was making from the last job just a few months back, your number is way below the market."

Mary: "In that case we'll get back to you. I'll talk to my boss and see what he thinks."

The following day Mary sent Mike a terse email stating that as a result of his demands, they had decided to go back to other candidates and search some more. Mike, now desperate, tried repeatedly calling her and sending her emails, pleading that he was willing to come on board for what they originally offered, and suggesting that they observe his performance after he came on board and then decide about the hourly rate.

Mary did not respond to Mike's pleas!

Reloading Mike

The following hypothetical dialog is presented here to show how Mike might have approached the situation differently and perhaps would have landed a different outcome:

> **Mary:** "Looks like we have made our decision and we are going to make you an offer, Mike! We're going to offer $40 per hour as a QA lead and get you started right away at Electronic Arts."

> **Mike:** "Thank you, Mary. May I reflect on this and get back to you in a day or so. This is exciting! EA can wait a day or so, right?"

> **Mary:** "Of course, they can! I am looking forward to hearing from you tomorrow, then, Mike."

> **Mike:** "Thanks, again, Mary for your offer yesterday. I am excited. I just wanted to check with you if there is any room in the number you gave me. Can you please tell me now or do you want to check and get back to me on this?"

> **Mary:** "Did you have a number in mind, Mike?"

> **Mike:** "No, no, Mary. I was just reflecting on my exit salary at General and what I did there for a number of years. That was a higher number by a significant amount and I just did not want to casually dismiss that without at least checking to see if the market now is shifted that much."

> **Mary:** "It actually has, Mike! With all the jobs going to India now, we can get a good QA person for even less. We thought we are offering you top dollar."

> **Mike:** "I understand. I'll tell you what, Mary, I would like to start on this assignment. I would like to show you what I could do for you and EA within the next few months. If I am able to deliver greater value than you expect can we revisit this then?"

> **Mary:** "Maybe, we can. Does it mean that we can count on you to start there next Monday?"

> **Mike:** "Yes, Mary, you can!" And, thank you, again!

With this dialog, Mike sends his acceptance by email to Mary, and mentions their conversation about the last part and sees how things go for the next three months.

Approaching an earnest offer in this spirit would have Mike employed again after being out of work for so long and would have given him an opportunity to "plug in" with the market; a definite plus.

Accepting the Offer

Accepting the offer should be done after considering all aspects of negotiating the final points without stickling over minutia.

This is also the time to shake loose and leverage offers from others, who have gone through their process and are just waiting. In a tough economy, the hiring process is long and often several weeks or months can go by between subsequent interviews. An offer from *any* employer can change that. How? For example, if you have had two rounds of interviews with another company and you feel as though it is dragging its feet, the best tactic is to call and mention that you have a *bona fide* offer from one of the companies you were pursuing. You must also state that by a certain date you have committed to accepting that offer. You do not—and must not—disclose the name of the company or the salary for *any* reason. Requesting to move the process along before that date to get an offer from them because of your continued interest there is appropriate. If this can be done before starting negotiations with the first company, it is even better. This is why getting a longer period to accept any offer is advantageous because of the possibility of multiple offers.

A well-managed job search can result in multiple offers in a short time if the final steps of the process are handled with finesse. Having multiple offers can create problems for some. They find it difficult to manage this important part of making the final choice, without alienating some employer. The challenge here is to *not* do that to the one who is the most desirable. That is why handling the process during this step with great professionalism is critical.

A temptation you may feel when a company is getting close to making an offer is to *assume* that the offer will be forthcoming and leveraging that assumption to get others to make offers. This is lying, and is not recommended! Do not ever lie about an offer, if you do not have one *in* your hand. The person at the other end has an ability to sense this from the tone of your voice, no matter how clever you think you are at disguising it! If an offer is pending or is imminent, stating it forthrightly is appropriate—"I am expecting an offer in the next day or so and just wanted to give you a heads up. Can you do anything to accelerate your process to get me an offer, as I am very interested in working at your company?" This works most of the time if the circumstances are favorable.

Having to decide between multiple offers, even in a tough job market is not that unusual if the overall campaign is handled as laid out in the discussion throughout this book. One word of caution: after concluding negotiations with the original employer, going back and reopening the offer is generally not a good idea. The only exception to this is that after concluding the negotiations with one employer ("B" or "C" company), another offer (an "A" company), looks better. In that case calling the original employer and stating why the offer is being declined in a *diplomatic* manner is the right thing to do. If a counter offer is made, then all factors have to be considered once again, before moving ahead and the disparities between the companies ("A," "B," or "C") reconciled.

Once an offer is acceptable, calling the person who made the offer and orally accepting it is appropriate, including the start date. The signed offer should be in the mail in a day or so confirming this call and then calling to make sure that it *was* received.

Accepting the offer does not mean that you have to honor it! If something happens to change that—another offers comes along *after* confirming the first one—confirming the one you want to accept and then *calling* the contact at the company that made the original offer is appropriate.

The next section shows how to do this with an actual example.

Declining the Offer

Having to decline an offer can happen for a variety of reasons:

- You got a better offer elsewhere
- You changed your mind because you learned something adverse about the company
- You changed your mind because your circumstances changed since your acceptance
- You want to continue to look for a better opportunity
- You simply changed your mind about working and want to retire

Whatever the reason, occasionally you end up in a situation where you have to decline an offer, even after your accepting it or indicating that you would be accepting it. As long as you are honest to yourself, and present that honesty in a message that is not offensive to the company, where you are declining the offer, it is fair game. The reason for taking some trouble to do this is that you want to protect yourself from any future need you may have of this employer, or those who worked with you during this process. You want to stay in good stead with this company that considered you worthy of their trust in addition to protecting your own prospects with those who may leave the company and move on to other opportunities.

The following sample letter (an actual case, with names disguised) shows how this can be done gracefully. But before sending a written response, calling first is recommended!

Victor Smiths
4456 Acorn Way
Alameda, CA 97665
510-554-0944: Victor2212@yahoo.com

November 21, 2003
James Garragos
Director,
Product Development
General Electronics
2121 Osaka Way,
San Jose, CA 95131

Dear Jim,

Thank you for your ongoing dialog during this difficult time in making my final decision.

As I explained to you over the phone, my personal situation prevents me from joining General Electronics, primarily because of the commute. From where I now reside, it is a five-hour drive for me each day. My wife works, too, and we have three small children. This is an extreme hardship and will be a major factor in negatively impacting my work-life balance.

Originally, when I negotiated your offer, I was not that concerned about the distance, although it was on my mind. Since we concluded our negotiations, I was surprised to get a very attractive offer from Lockheed, which is only 25 minutes from my home. The job is challenging and I am excited about the possibilities. I had not considered this as a viable alternative as I entered your employment negotiations.

I hope that you understand my situation and agree that my choice is based on what is best for us mutually in the long term.

I hope that we get a chance to work together in a future opportunity. I feel that you are an excellent manager and I can learn much from you!

Once, again, thank you for your confidence in offering me the position.

Cordially,

Victor Smiths

♠The Ethics of a Job Offer

Once an offer is accepted many wonder what their obligation is to honor it. This issue has become more important as the job market has become increasingly more competitive, and, at the same time, rivalry for the star performers has become intense to keep competitive advantage.

When a company presents you an offer it has gone through much trouble narrowing down the list of candidates through a rigorous process. Often, after making an offer it gets negotiated in good faith, which increases the obligation on the part of the new hire to accept that offer and then honor it.

Between the time an offer is presented, negotiated, and accepted and the start date for the new job, any number of factors can supervene the intent of the accepted offer. If an offer comes as you continue to pursue other employers and another offer comes after you have accepted the offer you thought was best until then, it creates a quandary for many because there are no clear answers that can guide you in such situations. The following guidelines may help in how to handle such situation (s):

1. When an employer is about to make an offer it is a good idea to request that you need some time to review and accept the offer. If you disclose that you are still interviewing with others, then it is your obligation to let them know that you would consider their offer and then decide whether to continue the process with other employers. You may decide to not disclose every aspect of your development if you chose not. But, do not dissemble or misrepresent. As before, never lie. But, this does not entail *full* disclosure, either!

2. If an employer then goes ahead and makes an offer, decide if you must negotiate that offer. This part is in the previous discussion in this chapter.

3. Once you agree to the terms, you must accept the offer promptly and send the acceptance in writing.

4. If you now get an offer that trumps the one you just accepted, do *not* go back to the first employer and reopen the negotiations. That deal is now closed and re-opening it may put you at a disadvantage because of the perception it creates. One way to explore this is to communicate why you are considering another offer and see if they come back for yet another round of negotiations. They must initiate this, not you!

5. If you decide that the latest job offer is the one you now want. Make sure that you negotiate the terms the way you like and then accept the new offer.

6. Notify the first employer as soon as possible, by calling on the phone and then sending a letter or email. Although some wait until they start their job to notify the other employer, this is not advisable.

7. If a recruiter is involved in the case of the employer on whom you just reneged, their retainer may be at stake. The recruiter may persuade you to reconsider to protect their interest. Do not succumb to these persuasions if you have already made up your mind about what is best for you. Remember, though, that the recruiter and the employer (particularly the hiring manager) will not view you favorably in the future. Although this can trouble a few, it should never be an overriding consideration.

8. Always remember that you must protect your own interest in the matters of what is best for you. Do not delegate that to others who have their own interests. protect Also, how you handle the backing out is also important to soften the blow of your decision. Just imagine if the situation were reversed: On the eve of your joining the new employer, you get a call that they found someone more qualified after they extended you the offer and after you accepted it. Remember the WGACA principle of Chapter-2: Tools and Rules of Transition.

♠Starting Your New Job

Starting a new job is exciting. It is a new chapter in a career journey filled with anticipation and hope. Starting a new job is also an opportunity to create and manage expectations for what is to come. If you have not done this in past jobs, it is time now to start.

The first day on the new job is important in setting and managing expectations. The following checklist will help for the better management of that day with some sense of control. If you do not do this on the first day or soon thereafter, it is difficult to go back and recover:

1. If you have not been successful negotiating the salary you wanted, and, in fact, accepted a lower salary in your new job, the time to bring it up is in your first meeting with the manger. State that you are glad to be part of their team and are looking forward to making the overall team look good to the customers, competitors, and others within the company.

   Mention to the manager that you were unable to get the salary you hoped, but decided to come on board and demonstrate what you said during the process: superior performance. Ask the manager that if you were to demonstrate a superior performance, if he has any discretion in giving you an adjustment to the salary commensurate with that performance at the end of the year. It is unlikely that anyone would respond negatively to this idea.

2. Once this is out of the way, you can have a discussion about your assignment, organization, and other details. Following that meeting, send an email to your manager thanking them for the welcome and that you were glad to be on their team. At the end, mention the agreement you just made about the performance and the salary adjustment at the end of the year. This way if the manager moves on, having this document covers you when the time comes, regardless of who is writing the performance review.

3. Have a discussion about how the assignments will be made and how your performance will be measured. How often you will meet and how the manager would like to receive reports from you or by what means. If there is an intermediate level between you and the manager, ask how that arrangement will work from a reporting standpoint and how he will have access to how you perform. Reiterate that you are trying to circumvent the command structure, but get clarity about your expectations.

4. If you have anything else on your mind before starting your new job, this is the time to air it so that there are no surprises. It is much easier to get clarity on things that can impede good performance than waiting for an adverse situation to develop.

5. If you have any special needs that are circumstantial, this is the time to bring it up. For example, if your expectant wife is concerned about her delivery complications in two months, mentioning this early will create awareness. You may want to explain what the needs may be when the time comes—"I may have to suspend my travel within a month or so until the situation is cleared up"—so that there are no surprises.

6. If you have any special support needs that are situational or acute, mention them at this time so that there are no surprises and that the manager can accommodate them. The manager may also feel more comfortable communicating that to the rest of the team so that you feel welcomed!

There is no magic or mystery here. It is about being forthright, honest, and making sure that yours and your manager's expectations are made clear at the same time. For many, the first few days set the tone for the tenure in that organization; you want to do nothing to compromise it.

♠Keeping Yourself Employed and Employable

If you have just been re-employed after your first job loss, treat this as a wake-up call. This may be one of many such situations, if you are in the early part of your career. If you were able to transition from a job to another one smoothly, consider yourself fortunate. Your best defense against being out of work is to keep yourself valuable and useful at all times. The following guidelines will help manage this well:

1. Keep looking for opportunities of growth in the company. Compare them to outside jobs as they are posted and evaluate what skill sets can make you get there. Specifically ask for those assignments during your meetings with your manager. Seek these out and make sure that you position yourself well for being assigned those projects. If you keep your eyes and ears open and keep good networks within the organization this should be a natural process for you!

2. If you see anything that can jeopardize your future—an impending merger, acquisition, or a reorganization—make sure that you have some way to get an early warning and that you have someone who can help you find a position that is safer. Once the process starts, everyone is going to jump ship and you may be at a disadvantage. No matter how well you think you have done or are doing, do not defer the inevitable. Look out for yourself!

3. Take on high-visibility and tough assignments. Once you take these on, you'd be surprised how help comes your way and how much easier they are because of the support you get from others. Everyone loves a hero! So, become one!

4. Do not complain and do not explain is the simple mantra to stay out of trouble. When hard times hit those who complain or spend more time explaining why they failed are the first to go!

5. Keep yourself well networked and well liked. No one wants to forget the ones who pitch in or are well connected.

6. Do not forget to credit openly those who helped you by sending thank you notes that are distributed. Everyone likes to be visibly acknowledged for a good job they did.

7. Much of your success at the new job—any job for that matter—will depend less on your knowledge and how smart you are, but more on your attitude to get along with others and your cooperation to get things done, even though you may not always be in agreement with the cause.

Remember the adrenaline factor discussed in Chapter-2: Tools and Rules of Transition: : Managing your Chemicals. You do not want those around you to have their adrenaline flowing when you just show up in the room, instead you want their endorphin flowing!

8. Always keep your résumé current, looking to build it up as you grow in your job, so that you are a desirable commodity in rapidly changing markets. Ask for résumé-building assignments. This is why constantly scanning for job opportunities and what skills are in demand will allow to you to seek those assignments that are résumé builders and not just résumé fillers!

9. Develop relationships with those whom you want to be your references at the new place of employment. Create special bonds with those by getting to know their family and personal life to the extent it is proper.

10. Go out of the way to become valuable in company events and showcase your skills by speechmaking, acting as an MC or helping out some cause that puts the company or your organization in a good light. Make sure that you get visibility for that volunteer work!

Summary Chapter-10: Negotiating the Offer

Getting the prospective employer to make an offer is a matter of confidence and will that you display and the professionalism with which you navigate through the hiring process.

Do not raise salary issues before it is presented during the selection process. The only time it should come is when the offer is being made. For details see how to navigate through this dialog in Win-Win Negotiations.

Do not give out a salary number unless it is absolutely necessary any time during your hiring process. Avoid giving numbers. Never lie about your salary (up or down). Always give a range unless someone asks for a number specifically.

Temper your anxiety to get an offer by being relaxed at all stages of the interview process and during the follow-ups. The more you are relaxed about it the more likely that you'll get what you are looking for. The offer may even pleasantly surprise you!

Carefully look at the whole offer in the way it is presented. Look at the table: Compensation Package.

Using the momentum that you have built in getting interviews at multiple employers it is easy to get multiple offers. How to handle this well is worth learning by reading the details in that section.

Negotiating the Offer: If you are skittish about negotiating an offer, don't be! Remember the saying: You do not get what you deserve, you get what you negotiate. But, do not wait till the last minute to present your case for a higher salary. You should position your value and expectations throughout the process that culminated your being brought to the offer table.

Always wait to negotiate until an offer is made in writing or just before it so that you are sure that the offer is being made in earnest and that the potential employer has some commitment to your joining the company. Revisit Win-Win Negotiations, Multiple offers, Accepting the Offer, Declining the Offer, and The Ethics of a Job Offer to review how an offer is negotiated, leveraged, accepted, or declined. Before you enter negotiations, have a walk-away threshold. This figure or criterion gives you your own exit point; if you do not get what you are looking for, you should be prepared to walk away from the offer *with no regrets!*

You have some latitude in how you position the offer you accepted until the time you start your job. Read Starting Your New Job to see why. To keep your employment on solid footing and to keep yourself employable, read Keeping Yourself Employed and Employable.

Epilogue

"Knowledge comes, but wisdom lingers."
—Alfred Lord Tennyson, poet (1809–1892)

This book was prompted by a sudden and growing need stemming from the current social and economic scene that involves our society's most important demographic—the mid-career professionals, specifically, the baby boomers. Baby boomers are those born between 1946 and 1964. This segment is important because the potential of what they represent in untapped value and also because the erosion of their ability to earn as they age into an older workforce can create an economic whiplash at the national and global levels. A mid-career professional is anyone who has worked for between 15 years and until their "typical" retirement age—65 in the U.S.—can be considered to fit this demographic. Incidentally, this experience bracket puts them also in the well identified category of our society's demographic. They typically belong to the baby boomer generation and are nearly 75 million strong!

Although this scenario at the macro level has the ability to potentially have serious effects on a nation's overall affairs, its affect at the individual level is devastating. The book has deliberately chosen to keep its focus at the individual level so that what needs to be done to change the situation for an individual is actionable. This book focuses its scope and aims at what an individual in the baby-boomer age group can do themselves and must do to regain their control in career-related matters. There are no allusions to any government or social initiatives.

With ever-accelerating technology dissemination and constant focus on automation to eliminate rules-based labor, knowledge jobs are rapidly disappearing. The impact of this trend on the manufacturing sector of the labor force alone has been singularly devastating. This trend has resulted in a loss of nearly 45 percent of the manufacturing jobs during the past decade. The same trend has now gripped the high-tech sector. Especially hard hit in the high-tech sector are those in IT and software development, where off shoring, increased automation, and a general slowdown in technology upgrades have decimated the ranks of these professionals, too.

The fallout of these trends on the mid-career professionals has been alarming. Baby boomers are the most affected professionals in this demographic and as the trend has continued during the past decade, they have looked more for someone on the outside to help them—as the governmental agencies for regulatory relief—than taking charge of their own destiny. The governmental intervention is going to be disappointing at best, if it ever happens.

So, what does a mid-career professional or a baby boomer need to do today to protect their career and prepare for their ongoing work-life? The following list may be helpful:

1. **Manage your career:** In the past putting your faith in your employer to look after your welfare in work-related matters was expected. Starting in the mid 1970s this began to change, and, after the meltdown of 2001, this obligation shifted entirely on the job holder. Recent media coverage about major companies as GM, several national airlines, and others is a reminder to us all about how these employers have changed their views on their current obligations to employees, including jobs, benefits, and pensions. This steady drumbeat of bad news has brought into sharper focus how much the expectations between the provider and the employee have changed over just a short period of time.

   What this implies is clear. Someone in their career now, no matter where, must look at making themselves constantly valuable in what they do. It is not merely enough to have a job that appears stable. They must evaluate how that job creates value in the changing ecosystem and how they must fashion what they do to keep their value-generation process on the cutting edge. In Chapter-4: The Baby-boomer Advantage, we presented the concept of hyper-human work. One must be vigilant, constantly looking out for those components of their work that cannot be off shored, outsourced, or eliminated. If they do not readily appear identifiable, then part of the obligation you have to yourself—and your employer—is to continually identify new components of your job that cannot be sourced.

2. As already pointed out in the Preface, if you expect your employer to terminate you, either through a layoff, retirement, or retrenchment, do not assume that it is a foregone conclusion and that it is *fait accompli*. Make a case to your manager—and your chain of command—why you need to continue for *their* benefit. See if you can reconfigure your employment compact before it runs out, so that you are not faced with a period of unemployment.

3. **Develop your brand:** In the old job and career paradigms you did the job that was assigned to you. Sometimes, the job did not even create economic value, even though the intentions for that assignment were imminently lofty. With the increasing focus on relentless value creation in each step of a value chain, everyone is under increasing scrutiny to develop their own way of adding value that results in the end customer seeing it as an enhanced experience. In this revised perspective, everyone is expected to develop their own imprint on the final customer experience. This is the branding concept and everyone is expected to develop it, own it, communicate it, and leverage it in all their endeavors.

4. **Know and Own your genius:** The central tenet of this book (and all my other books in this genre) is that we all have our genius about us that differentiates us from others. Using this genius as a portfolio of our Unique Skills and building a value proposition based on this genius is our brand that has a staying power. Skills based on the genius are adaptable skills and they become transferable across different jobs and careers.

   Your Unique Skills, presented in the résumé as a centerpiece of your value message, have to power to bridge between yesterday and tomorrow ("A résumé is about tomorrow.") and also between what you represent and what the potential employer is looking for! Using this force of your transportable genius makes changing industries or careers an easily attainable transformation, especially "late" in your life.

5. **Develop your network:** As you navigate through your career, develop contacts that go beyond your daily interactions. Join professional groups and social clubs that promote personal development. The Toastmasters is once such organization that brings together those who want to improve their communication skills through public speaking, and more broadly, manifesting their leadership. Also join an online network as LinkedIn. (www.linkedin.com). Keeping in touch with important contacts with the networks that you develop is also just as important.

6. **Venture out with ideas:** If you see some opportunities are being ignored, where a company can do better by adopting one of your ideas, start with you employer first and see how that can work for you in your own growth. Once you develop confidence, expanding this concept to outside companies that interest you can be a good way to keep yourself marketable. See examples of how this is done in Chapter-6: Building Your Platform. Additional examples are in Chapter-7: Write to the Point with Letters! Most of the prospecting letters in this chapter have new ideas on how to do things differently and innovatively.

7. **Be Vigilant:** As you see yourself getting stagnant in what you do, do not wait for your boss to come and give you a challenging assignment (see #5). Do not go in denial over your situation. Identify something that could benefit the organization, your company, or even your community and then take some risk and prepare a compelling proposal. If the proposal is approved, more than likely, you will be running the show. Make sure that such opportunities are résumé builders.

8. **Expand horizons:** Many professionals stick to their area of work and often miss out on assignments that can be theirs if they had a broader experience base or connections inside their own organization. Becoming more visible stems from expanding your reach and taking it beyond merely delivering on what is assigned to you. As you seek more responsibilities you make yourself less vulnerable to being laid off in leaner times.

9. **Continue learning:** With the ever expanding knowledge in a variety of areas and new career opportunities being identified continually, it is a good idea to expand your academic credentials by joining on-line or continuing education services. Learning, however, does not come from formal coursework alone. It comes from curiosity, imagination, and risk taking. In many instances employers pay for such formal coursework. It is much easier to complete a degree or certification when you are living in a structured routine (such as having a regular job) than it is when you are not. Do not procrastinate on your plans to advance your academic frontiers.

10. **Volunteer time:** In this age of high stress, opportunities to donate your time to social causes are plentiful. Social services organizations (battered wives, abused children, suicide hotline, among others) are some of the organizations that reflect the state of our human existence in this stressed out world. Volunteering at such organizations will open up your perspective, give you new contacts with others who also do similar work, and provide you with an experience otherwise difficult to get.

11. **Develop confidence:** As you grow professionally, developing yourself as an individual is equally important. One way to develop self-confidence is your constantly challenging yourself. Often, diffidence comes from your own limiting beliefs, not from something inherent. Remember what Eleanor Roosevelt said, "*No one makes you feel inferior without your consent.*" One antidote for self-doubt is to risk doing something new every day. If you do something—just one thing—each day that scares you, you will soon realize that nothing does!

The best strategy for the mid-career professionals—including the baby boomers—is to look at the shifted employment market with a new perspective and use some or all of the advice offered here to stay in control of your own future.

Good luck!

Appendix-I: Retirement Cash Flow Needs

"The universe always provides for our need, but never for our greed."

—Mahatma Gandhi (1869–1948)

This appendix is presented to show how your financial situation at the time of a major transition towards retirement can set the tone for the remainder of your life. The example[2] shown as an Excel spreadsheet is for illustrative purposes only. Using this template you can modify this example and create something that fits your own situation by simply changing some of the parameters. Because of the instant response of the Excel application, it is easy to see interactively how your cash flow changes as you manipulate some of the key parameters and their timing in the flow of events. Of course, what is presented in the following pages is simply a snap shot and, hence, is static.

In the illustrative example shown, two cases of a person "retiring" at 60 are showcased. This is purposely chosen to reflect the current situation with many baby boomers. Many in their 50s have lost their jobs and are despaired because it is difficult to get traction in this job market. Many feel that it is too early to retire because their finances need shoring up. Although many of their concerns are well founded, they are misguided on two fronts: although there are fewer jobs, especially for older workers, there are many opportunities—the main purpose for this book. Secondly, many underestimate the financial power of their own situation. The example shown is presented to assuage their concerns and empower them to look at what they have, differently.

It is relatively easy to load this example in Excel and change key parameters as age, the size of investable income, and the Social Security payout to build your specific financial picture for yourself.

The following pages show two specific cases of a person "retiring" at 60, earning $110,000 in annual salary and other income. This is chosen primarily to reflect the 59-1/2 year threshold for the cashing in of the 401-K accounts

---

2   Thanks to my friends S.G. Kane, who came up with this simple approach to cash flow and S. S. Naik who made critical comments about its validity

without penalty. Although the available amount of $500,000 is shown, it may not merely be derived from the proceeds of the 401-K account. In August 2005, an average 401-K account held $66, 234. The amount—$500,000— used in the example could be from a combination of retirement accounts, your own savings, and other means available *after* taxes. For someone making $110,000 annually, the size of this fund is realistic at this age.

In the first case of this person, they are assumed to have gone into "retirement" at 60 and then engaging in an income-producing activity (consulting, business, part-time job) that generates substantially smaller income ($24,000 annually, post tax, in the third year, item # 8)

In the second case, the same person, after "retiring" from a job that earned $110,000 annually, reinvents and gets another job at $85,000 annually, in the second year, a job that continues till the age of 75.

The difference this strategy makes to the bottom line for this person is dramatic in available cash and financial freedom during the later years in their life. Bottom line: Immediately upon leaving your job you must reinvent and get another job that keeps you engaged productively and at a level of financial compensation comparable to the previous job.

Between the two cases, the final difference in the financial status of the two cases is worth noting.

Although the level of income assumed in this example is high for average U.S. wage earners ($37,500), the various parameters are scalable. For example, someone earning $75,000 annually at that age (60) would have commensurately smaller annual expenditure (not $60,000, as shown in the example, but perhaps $45,000).

The following assumptions are the basis for what is presented in the example. The numbers themselves are instructive to read to see how they create their own dynamic—and dread—over time, as one gets more and more dependent and infirmed.

1. The hypothetical person in the cited examples (two cases) is slated for "retirement" at 60. They may even have lost their job through a layoff and are not willing to go back into the work force because of a variety of reasons.

2. The main residence is owned free and clear and there is no ongoing mortgage payment at 60. The taxes and insurance are part of the ongoing monthly expenses, which are included in the Annual Expenditure

3. Reverse mortgage refers to the option available to many seniors now when they turn 62 (youngest spouse) and where an avenue to generating a steady monthly income from the equity built into their primary

residence is available. In the examples shown the person chooses to get a monthly check for the rest of their life. The home can continue to appreciate and the benefit of that increase is held by the owner.

4. An inflation rate of 3 percent is assumed to be flat over the 30 year span of the model

5. A second property, already owned, is expected to be liquidated at 75, and on which capital gains tax (10 percent) applies, which is then available for reinvestment. Selling and other costs bring the total expenses to 15 percent of the sell price. The reason this property is shown to appreciate at 7.5 percent annually (compared to the 5 percent for the residence) is because of its investment potential.

6. Social Security Payments (after taxes) start as shown in the two cases and stay constant for the remainder of life.

7. A source of income from consulting, business or a part-time job is expected to ramp up upon entering the "retirement." This is for a person who does not reinvent to find a "comparable job."

8. A person who reinvents and gets another job immediately following retirement (within a year) has an earning capacity at 80 percent of the previous salary.

9. Investment income can be derived from your 401-K or other retirement account. The amount shown ($500,000) is expected to be available after all taxes and the liquidation of your credit card and other consumer debts. In the U.S. an average 401-K account has about $66,000 (2005 data). The investment income (post tax) is shown at 3 percent.

10. An equity portfolio (includes some bonds) is expected to grow at 5 percent annually. This portfolio is liquidated as shown in the two cases. In the case of the person who reinvents (case-II), the cash is invested in savings bonds at 76 that provide a 2.5 percent return and then that portfolio, too, is cashed out at 94. This is triggered by an otherwise negative cash flow that year. In the case of the person with only a part-time job (case-I), the portfolio is held longer—till age 81 and then the after-tax proceeds ploughed back into the investment fund. This ensures a longer positive cash flow. The person in this case takes a greater risk with the stock portfolio, depending on the conditions, by holding it longer (by five years). The income (post tax) is assumed at 2.5 percent.

11. In the example cited (case-I) the person who does not reinvent to get another job runs out of money at 85!

12. In the second example the person who reinvents and gets a comparable job runs out of money at 95!

13. The appreciated home can be sold after their death by the survivors (in either example).

14. Beyond this ten-year gap, financial disparity for the two cases grows with time and the two cases end up with substantially different negative investment funds.

15. The annual expenditures are assumed as flat in constant dollars. This is not true, especially for the demography in question. Government data show that actual expenses go down as a person ages. The U.S. Department of Labor (www.DOL.Gov) publishes Consumer Expenditure data from year to year and they have consistently shown that in this age bracket, there is a steady decline in expenditures, overall. This may be more because those in this age group do not have disposable income to keep up with expenses. Increases in healthcare and other costs for the elderly can take a toll on their budget.

16. The federal tax rates for the two cases shown are different because of the size of the annual income. State taxes are expected to be low or none.

17. As one advances towards besetting infirmity, more and more assets should be converted to cash. This is because maintaining other assets as real estate, valuables, and art are subject to neglect, loss, theft, and plunder by unscrupulous acquaintances or even family members. Liquidating an asset in dire circumstances can often lead to a transactional disadvantage.

18. Frequently reviewing your last will and testament and updating it as circumstances change is critical.

19. Both spouses must be intimately familiar with their finances as they enter their twilight years.

20. Those who cannot afford to retire in the U.S., may want to consider settling in other countries purely because of the cost of living and medical care. India, parts of Europe, and other English-speaking countries are some possible destinations. The healthcare is considerably more affordable in those countries as well and the dollar, as an international currency, is still king.

CASE-I: Hypothetical Retirement Cash Flow Statement (1/5)

Case-I: A person retires and engages in some minor income-generating activity (All pecentage firgures are annual)

Year into "Retirement:" (@ 60 years)	1	2	3	4	5
1. Annual Expendeture- Basic (5% Inflation)	$60,000	$61,800	$63,654	$65,564	$67,531
2. Annual Expendeture- Special (5% Inflation)	$3,000	$3,090	$3,183	$3,278	$3,377
3. Annual Cash Flow Out: (1+3)	$63,000	$64,890	$66,837	$68,842	$70,907
4. Investment Funds Available at Beginning	$500,000	$454,985	$426,719	$401,251	$378,673
5. Net Investment Funds Available (4-3)	$437,000	$390,095	$359,882	$332,409	$307,766
6. Investment Income @ 3% on (5) after taxes	$13,110	$19,505	$17,994	$16,620	$15,388
7. Taxed (@20%) Fixed Annuity Income (SSI Payout)	$0	$0	$0	$0	$0
8. Post-tax Consulting/Part-time job/Business (5% growth)	$0	$12,000	$18,000	$24,000	$25,200
9. Equity Portfolio including bonds (5% growth)	$75,000	$78,750	$82,688	$86,822	$91,163
10. Post-tax income from equities 2.5% of (9)	$1,875	$1,969	$2,067	$2,171	$2,279
11. Occupied Home (5% value growth) Free & Clear	$150,000	$157,500	$165,375	$173,644	$182,326
12. Reverse Mortgage Income (monthly for life)	$0	$0	$0	$0	$0
13. Second Property (7.5% annual increase)	$65,000	$69,875	$75,116	$80,749	$86,805
14. Net income: second property (5% growth)	$3,000	$3,150	$3,308	$3,473	$3,647
15. Sell second property after 15% taxes etc.	$0	$0	$0	$0	$0
16. Sell equity portfolio for cash (after tax amount)					
17. Net Annual Cash Flow (6+7+8+10+12+14+15)	$17,985	$36,624	$41,369	$46,264	$46,514
18. Carry Over Investable Funds for Next Year	$454,985	$426,719	$401,251	$378,673	$354,279

CASE-I: Hypothetical Retirement Cash Flow Statement (2/5)

	6	7	8	9	10	11	12	13	14	15
	$69,556	$71,643	$73,792	$76,006	$78,286	$80,635	$83,054	$85,546	$88,112	$90,755
	$3,478	$3,582	$3,690	$3,800	$3,914	$4,032	$4,153	$4,277	$4,406	$4,538
	$73,034	$75,225	$77,482	$79,807	$82,201	$84,667	$87,207	$89,823	$92,518	$95,293
	$354,279	**$347,189**	**$339,672**	**$331,125**	**$321,512**	**$310,796**	**$298,941**	**$285,912**	**$271,674**	**$256,194**
	$281,245	$271,964	$262,190	$251,319	$239,311	$226,129	$211,734	$196,089	$179,156	$160,901
	$14,062	$13,598	$13,110	$12,566	$11,966	$11,306	$10,587	$9,804	$8,958	$8,045
	$19,200	$19,200	$19,200	$19,200	$19,200	$19,200	$19,200	$19,200	$19,200	$19,200
	$26,460	$27,783	$29,172	$30,631	$32,162	$33,770	$35,459	$37,232	$39,093	$41,048
	$95,721	$100,507	$105,533	$110,809	$116,350	$122,167	$128,275	$134,689	$141,424	$148,495
	$2,393	$2,513	$2,638	$2,770	$2,909	$3,054	$3,207	$3,367	$3,536	$3,712
	$191,442	$201,014	$211,065	$221,618	$232,699	$244,334	$256,551	$269,378	$282,847	$296,990
	$0	$594	$594	$594	$594	$594	$594	$594	$594	$594
	$93,316	$100,315	$107,838	$115,926	$124,621	$133,967	$144,015	$154,816	$166,427	$178,909
	$3,829	$4,020	$4,221	$4,432	$4,654	$4,887	$5,131	$5,388	$5,657	$5,940
	$0	$0	$0	$0	$0	$0	$0	$0	$0	$152,000
	$65,944	**$67,708**	**$68,935**	**$70,193**	**$71,485**	**$72,812**	**$74,178**	**$75,585**	**$77,038**	**$230,539**
	$347,189	**$339,672**	**$331,125**	**$321,512**	**$310,796**	**$298,941**	**$285,912**	**$271,674**	**$256,194**	**$391,441**

CASE-I: Hypothetical Retirement Cash Flow Statement (3/5)

	16	17	18	19	20	21	22	23	24	25
	$93,478	$96,282	$99,171	$102,146	$105,210	$108,367	$111,618	$114,966	$118,415	$121,968
	$4,674	$4,814	$4,959	$5,107	$5,261	$5,418	$5,581	$5,748	$5,921	$15,000
	$98,152	$101,097	$104,129	$107,253	$110,471	$113,785	$117,199	$120,715	$124,336	$136,968
	$391,441	**$331,645**	**$265,963**	**$194,017**	**$115,408**	**$29,716**	**-$63,504**	**$19,682**	**-$86,290**	**-$201,364**
	$293,289	$230,548	$161,833	$86,763	$4,937	-$84,069	-$180,702	-$101,033	-$210,626	-$338,331
	$14,664	$11,527	$8,092	$4,338	$247	-$4,203	-$9,035	-$5,052	-$10,531	-$16,917
	$19,200	$19,200	$19,200	$19,200	$19,200	$19,200	$19,200	$19,200	$19,200	$19,200
	$0	$0	$0	$0	$0	$0	$0	$0	$0	$0
	$155,920	$163,716	$171,901	$180,496	$189,521	$198,997	$185,000	$0	$0	$0
	$3,898	$4,093	$4,298	$4,512	$4,738	$4,975	$4,625	$0	$0	$0
	$311,839	$327,431	$343,803	$360,993	$379,043	$397,995	$417,894	$438,789	$460,729	$483,765
	$594	$594	$594	$594	$594	$594	$594	$594	$594	$594
	$0	$0	$0	$0	$0	$0	$0	$0	$0	$0
	$0	$0	$0	$0	$0	$0	$0	$0	$0	$0
	$0	$0	$0	$0	$0	$0	$0	$0	$0	$0
							$185,000			
	$38,356	$35,414	$32,183	$28,645	$24,779	$20,565	$200,384	$14,742	$9,263	$2,877
	$331,645	**$265,963**	**$194,017**	**$115,408**	**$29,716**	**-$63,504**	**$19,682**	**-$86,290**	**-$201,364**	**-$335,454**

CASE-I: Hypothetical Retirement Cash Flow Statement (4/5)

	26	27	28	29	30	31	32	33	34
	$125,627	$129,395	$133,277	$137,276	$141,394	$145,636	$150,005	$154,505	$159,140
	$15,450	$15,914	$16,391	$16,883	$17,389	$17,911	$18,448	$19,002	$19,572
	$141,077	$145,309	$149,668	$154,158	$158,783	$163,547	$168,453	$173,507	$178,712
	-$335,454	**-$480,563**	**-$637,372**	**-$806,598**	**-$989,000**	**-$1,185,378**	**-$1,396,577**	**-$1,623,487**	**-$1,867,050**
	-$476,531	-$625,872	-$787,040	-$960,756	-$1,147,783	-$1,348,925	-$1,565,030	-$1,796,994	-$2,045,761
	-$23,827	-$31,294	-$39,352	-$48,038	-$57,389	-$67,446	-$78,251	-$89,850	-$102,288
	$19,200	$19,200	$19,200	$19,200	$19,200	$19,200	$19,200	$19,200	$19,200
	$0	$0	$0	$0	$0	$0	$0	$0	$0
	$0	$0	$0	$0	$0	$0	$0	$0	$0
	$0	$0	$0	$0	$0	$0	$0	$0	$0
	$507,953	$533,351	$560,018	$588,019	$617,420	$648,291	$680,706	$714,741	$750,478
	$594	$594	$594	$594	$594	$594	$594	$594	$594
	$0	$0	$0	$0	$0	$0	$0	$0	$0
	$0	$0	$0	$0	$0	$0	$0	$0	$0
	$0	$0	$0	$0	$0	$0	$0	$0	$0
	-$4,033	**-$11,500**	**-$19,558**	**-$28,244**	**-$37,595**	**-$47,652**	**-$58,457**	**-$70,056**	**-$82,494**
	-$480,563	**-$637,372**	**-$806,598**	**-$989,000**	**-$1,185,378**	**-$1,396,577**	**-$1,623,487**	**-$1,867,050**	**-$2,128,255**

CASE-I: Hypothetical Retirement Cash Flow Statement (5/5)

	35	36	37	38	39	40
	$163,914	$168,832	$173,897	$179,114	$184,487	$190,022
	$20,159	$20,764	$21,386	$22,028	$22,689	$23,370
	$184,073	$189,595	$195,283	$201,142	$207,176	$213,391
	-$2,128,255	-$2,408,151	-$2,707,840	-$3,028,485	-$3,371,314	-$3,737,620
	-$2,312,329	-$2,597,746	-$2,903,123	-$3,229,626	-$3,578,490	-$3,951,011
	-$115,616	-$129,887	-$145,156	-$161,481	-$178,924	-$197,551
	$19,200	$19,200	$19,200	$19,200	$19,200	$19,200
	$0	$0	$0	$0	$0	$0
	$0	$0	$0	$0	$0	$0
	$0	$0	$0	$0	$0	$0
	$788,002	$827,402	$868,772	$912,211	$957,822	$1,005,713
	$594	$594	$594	$594	$594	$594
	$0	$0	$0	$0	$0	$0
	$0	$0	$0	$0	$0	$0
	$0	$0	$0	$0	$0	$0
	-$95,822	-$110,093	-$125,362	-$141,687	-$159,130	-$177,757
	-$2,408,151	-$2,707,840	-$3,028,485	-$3,371,314	-$3,737,620	-$4,128,768

CASE-II: Hypothetical Retirement Cash Flow Statement (1/6)

Case-II: A person "retires" at 60; reinvents to get a job (80% of old salary). (All pecentage figures are annual)

Year into "Retirement:" (@ 60 years)	1	2	3	4	5
1. Annual Expendeture- Basic	$60,000	$61,800	$63,654	$65,564	$67,531
2. Annual Expendeture- Special	$3,000	$3,090	$3,183	$3,278	$3,377
3. Annual Cash Flow Out: (1+2)	$63,000	$64,890	$66,837	$68,842	$70,907
4. Investment Available at Beginning- ICF	$500,000	$455,008	$476,343	$500,036	$526,311
5. Net Investment Funds Available (4-3)	$437,000	$390,118	$409,506	$431,194	$455,404
6. Investment Income @ 3% of (5) After taxes	$13,110	$19,506	$20,475	$21,560	$22,770
7. Fixed Annuity Taxed at 30% (SSI Payout)	$0	$0	$0	$0	$0
8. Reinvention job (30% post taxed) (5% p.a. increase)	$0	$61,600	$64,680	$67,914	$71,310
9. Equity Portfolio including bonds (5% growth)	$75,000	$78,750	$82,688	$86,822	$91,163
10. Post-tax income from equities 2.5% of (9)	$1,875	$1,969	$2,067	$2,171	$2,279
11. Occupied Home (5% annual increase)	$150,000	$157,500	$165,375	$173,644	$182,326
12. Reverse Mortgage Income (monthly for life)	$0	$0	$0	$0	$0
13. Second Property (7.5% annual increase)	$65,000	$69,875	$75,116	$80,749	$86,805
14. Net income from second properry	$3,000	$3,150	$3,308	$3,473	$3,647
15. Sell second property after 15% taxes etc.	$0	$0	$0	$0	$0
16. Sell all bonds for cash (conversion tax free)					
17. Net Cash Flow (6+7+8+10+12+14+15+16)	$18,008	$86,225	$90,530	$95,117	$100,006
18. Carry Over Investable Funds Next Year	$455,008	$476,343	$500,036	$526,311	$555,410

CASE-II: Hypothetical Retirement Cash Flow Statement (2/6)

	6	7	8	9	10	11	12	13	14
	$69,556	$71,643	$73,792	$76,006	$78,286	$80,635	$83,054	$85,546	$88,112
	$3,478	$3,582	$3,690	$3,800	$3,914	$4,032	$4,153	$4,277	$4,406
	$73,034	$75,225	$77,482	$79,807	$82,201	$84,667	$87,207	$89,823	$92,518
	$555,410	**$587,591**	**$623,136**	**$662,346**	**$705,547**	**$753,087**	**$805,344**	**$862,722**	**$925,656**
	$482,375	$512,366	$545,654	$582,540	$623,346	$668,421	$718,138	$772,899	$833,138
	$24,119	$25,618	$27,283	$29,127	$31,167	$33,421	$35,907	$38,645	$41,657
	$0	$0	$0	$0	$0	$0	$0	$0	$0
	$74,875	$78,619	$82,550	$86,677	$91,011	$95,562	$100,340	$105,357	$110,625
	$95,721	$100,507	$105,533	$110,809	$116,350	$122,167	$128,275	$134,689	$141,424
	$2,393	$2,513	$2,638	$2,770	$2,909	$3,054	$3,207	$3,367	$3,536
	$191,442	$201,014	$211,065	$221,618	$232,699	$244,334	$256,551	$269,378	$282,847
	$0	$0	$0	$0	$0	$0	$0	$0	$0
	$93,316	$100,315	$107,838	$115,926	$124,621	$133,967	$144,015	$154,816	$166,427
	$3,829	$4,020	$4,221	$4,432	$4,654	$4,887	$5,131	$5,388	$5,657
	$0	$0	$0	$0	$0	$0	$0	$0	$0
	$105,216	**$110,770**	**$116,692**	**$123,007**	**$129,741**	**$136,924**	**$144,585**	**$152,757**	**$161,474**
	$587,591	**$623,136**	**$662,346**	**$705,547**	**$753,087**	**$805,344**	**$862,722**	**$925,656**	**$994,613**

CASE-II: Hypothetical Retirement Cash Flow Statement (3/6)

	15	16	17	18	19	20	21	22	23
	$90,755	$93,478	$96,282	$99,171	$102,146	$105,210	$108,367	$111,618	$114,966
	$4,538	$4,674	$4,814	$4,959	$5,107	$5,261	$5,418	$5,581	$5,748
	$95,293	$98,152	$101,097	$104,129	$107,253	$110,471	$113,785	$117,199	$120,715
	$994,613	**$1,243,479**	**$1,233,418**	**$1,219,763**	**$1,202,240**	**$1,180,561**	**$1,154,420**	**$1,123,491**	**$1,087,433**
	$899,319	$1,145,327	$1,132,322	$1,115,633	$1,094,987	$1,070,090	$1,040,635	$1,006,293	$966,718
	$44,966	$57,266	$56,616	$55,782	$54,749	$53,505	$52,032	$50,315	$48,336
	$0	$26,500	$26,500	$26,500	$26,500	$26,500	$26,500	$26,500	$26,500
	$116,156	$0	$0	$0	$0	$0	$0	$0	$0
	$148,495	$140,000	$140,000	$140,000	$140,000	$140,000	$140,000	$140,000	$140,000
	$3,712	$3,500	$3,500	$3,500	$3,500	$3,500	$3,500	$3,500	$3,500
	$296,990	$311,839	$327,431	$343,803	$360,993	$379,043	$397,995	$417,894	$438,789
	$825	$825	$825	$825	$825	$825	$825	$825	$825
	$178,909	$0	$0	$0	$0	$0	$0	$0	$0
	$0	$0	$0	$0	$0	$0	$0	$0	$0
	$152,000	$0	$0	$0	$0	$0	$0	$0	$0
	$344,159	**$88,091**	**$87,441**	**$86,607**	**$85,574**	**$84,330**	**$82,857**	**$81,140**	**$79,161**
	$1,243,479	**$1,233,418**	**$1,219,763**	**$1,202,240**	**$1,180,561**	**$1,154,420**	**$1,123,491**	**$1,087,433**	**$1,045,879**

CASE-II: Hypothetical Retirement Cash Flow Statement (4/6)

	24	25	26	27	28	29	30
	$118,415	$121,968	$125,627	$129,395	$133,277	$137,276	$141,394
	$5,921	$15,000	$15,450	$15,914	$16,391	$16,883	$17,389
	$124,336	$136,968	$141,077	$145,309	$149,668	$154,158	$158,783
	$1,045,879	**$998,445**	**$935,376**	**$864,840**	**$786,332**	**$699,322**	**$603,247**
	$921,543	$861,478	$794,300	$719,531	$636,664	$545,164	$444,464
	$46,077	$43,074	$39,715	$35,977	$31,833	$27,258	$22,223
	$26,500	$26,500	$26,500	$26,500	$26,500	$26,500	$26,500
	$0	$0	$0	$0	$0	$0	$0
	$140,000	$140,000	$140,000	$140,000	$140,000	$140,000	$140,000
	$3,500	$3,500	$3,500	$3,500	$3,500	$3,500	$3,500
	$460,729	$483,765	$507,953	$533,351	$560,018	$588,019	$617,420
	$825	$825	$825	$825	$825	$825	$825
	$0	$0	$0	$0	$0	$0	$0
	$0	$0	$0	$0	$0	$0	$0
	$0	$0	$0	$0	$0	$0	$0
	$76,902	$73,899	$70,540	$66,802	$62,658	$58,083	$53,048
	$998,445	$935,376	$864,840	$786,332	$699,322	$603,247	$497,512

CASE-II: Hypothetical Retirement Cash Flow Statement (5/6)

	31	32	33	34	35	36
	$145,636	$150,005	$154,505	$159,140	$163,914	$168,832
	$17,911	$18,448	$19,002	$19,572	$20,159	$20,764
	$163,547	$168,453	$173,507	$178,712	$184,073	$189,595
	$497,512	**$381,489**	**$254,513**	**$115,882**	**$104,854**	**-$86,317**
	$333,966	$213,036	$81,006	-$62,830	-$79,220	-$275,912
	$16,698	$10,652	$4,050	-$3,141	-$3,961	-$13,796
	$26,500	$26,500	$26,500	$26,500	$26,500	$26,500
	$0	$0	$0	$0	$0	$0
	$140,000	$140,000	$140,000	$140,000	$0	$0
	$3,500	$3,500	$3,500	$3,500	$0	$0
	$648,291	$680,706	$714,741	$750,478	$788,002	$827,402
	$825	$825	$825	$825	$825	$825
	$0	$0	$0	$0	$0	$0
	$0	$0	$0	$0	$0	$0
	$0	$0	$0	$0	$0	$0
				$140,000	$0	$0
	$47,523	**$41,477**	**$34,875**	**$167,684**	**-$7,097**	**-$26,766**
	$381,489	**$254,513**	**$115,882**	**$104,854**	**-$86,317**	**-$302,678**

CASE-II: Hypothetical Retirement Cash Flow Statement (6/6)

	37	38	39	40
	$173,897	$179,114	$184,487	$190,022
	$21,386	$22,028	$22,689	$23,370
	$195,283	$201,142	$207,176	$213,391
	-$302,678	**-$546,932**	**-$822,056**	**-$1,131,330**
	-$497,961	-$748,074	-$1,029,232	-$1,344,721
	-$24,898	-$37,404	-$51,462	-$67,236
	$26,500	$26,500	$26,500	$26,500
	$0	$0	$0	$0
	$0	$0	$0	$0
	$0	$0	$0	$0
	$868,772	$912,211	$957,822	$1,005,713
	$825	$825	$825	$825
	$0	$0	$0	$0
	$0	$0	$0	$0
	$0	$0	$0	$0
	$0	$0	$0	$0
	-$48,971	-$73,982	-$102,098	-$133,647
	-$546,932	**-$822,056**	**-$1,131,330**	**-$1,478,368**

Bibliography

"Life affords no higher pleasure than that of surmounting difficulties, passing from one stage of success to another, forming new wishes and seeing them gratified."

—Samuel Johnson, lexicographer (1709–1784)

Chapter-1: The Retirement Dilemma

Adrienne, Carol. *The Purpose of Your Life: Finding Your Place In The World Using Synchronicity, Intuition, and Uncommon Sense.* Harper Collins, 1999.

Briggs, Isabel Myers, with Peter B. Myers. *Gifts Differing: Understanding Personality Type.* Consulting Psychologists Press, Inc., Reprint Edition, 1995.

Bronson, Po. *What Should I do with My Life? The True Story of People Who Answered the Ultimate Question.* Random House, 2003.

Buckingham, Marcus, Curt Coffman. *First, Break All the Rules: What the Worlds Greatest Managers Do Differently.* Simon & Schuster Adult Publishing Group, 1999.

Carnegie, Dale, Dorothy Carnegie (Editor), Arthur R. Pell, (Editor). *How to Win Friends and Influence People.* Simon & Schuster Adult Publishing Group, Revised Edition, 1982.

Covey, Steven R. *The 7 Habits of Highly Effective people: Powerful Lessons in Personal Change.* Simon & Schuster Adult Publishing Group.1990.

Embree, Marlowe. *Type Reporter* No. 79, 12/00. Chapel Road, Fairfax Station, VA 22039; 703-764-5370.

Freidman, Thomas L. *It's a Flat World: A Brief History of the Twenty-first Century.* Farrar, Strauss and Geroux, 2005.

Goldman, Daniel. *Emotional Intelligence: Why it can matter more than IQ.* Bantam Books, Inc., 1997.

Ibarra, Herminia. *Working Identity: Unconventional strategies for reinventing your career*. Harvard Business Press. 2003

Johnson, Spencer. *Who Moved My Cheese? An Amazing Way to Deal With Change in Your Work and Your Life*. Simon & Schuster Adult Publishing Group, 1999.

Kiviat, Barbara. *The End of Management? Time*, July 12, 2004, special section, Future Shock,

Laney, Marti Olsen Laney. *The Introvert Advantage: How to Thrive in an Extraverted World*. Workman Publishing, 2002.

Nemko, Marty. *Cool Career for Dummies*. For Dummies, 2nd edition, 2001

Osborne, Carol. *The Art of Resilience: 100 Paths to Wisdom and Strength in an Uncertain World*. Crown Publishing Group, 1997.

Ray, Michael, Rochelle Myers. *Creativity in Business*. Double Day & Company, Incorporated, a division of Bantam Doubleday, 1981.

Saraf, Dilip G. *The 7 Keys to a Dream Job: A Career Nirvana Playbook!* iUniverse Publishers, 2004

Saraf, Dilip G. *Pathways to Career Nirvana: An Ultimate Success Sourcebook!*, iUniverse Publishers, 2004

Saraf, Dilip G. *Reinvention through Messaging: The Write Message for the Right Job!* iUniverse Publishers, 2004

Susan J. Jeffers. *Feel the Fear And Do It Anyway* Fawcett Book Group, 1996.

Tieger, Paul D., Barbara Barron-Tieger, Deborah Baker, (editor). *Do what You Are: Discover the Perfect Career for You Through the Secrets of Personality Type*. Little Brown & Company, 2001.

Chapter-2: Tools and Rules of Transition

Adrienne, Carol. *The Purpose of Your Life: Finding Your Place In The World Using Synchronicity, Intuition, and Uncommon Sense*. Harper Collins, 1999.

Bolles, Richard. *What Color is Your Parachute? A Practical Manual for Job-Hunters and Career Changers*. Ten Speed Press, 2004.

Buckingham, Marcus, Curt Coffman: *First, Break All The Rules: What the Worlds Greatest Managers Do Differently.* Simon & Schuster Adult Publishing Group,1999.

Covey, Steven R. *The 7 Habits of Highly Effective people: Powerful Lessons in Personal Change* Simon & Schuster Adult Publishing Group, 1990.

D'Alessandro, David F. Michelle *Ownes: Career Warfare: 10 Rules for Building Successful Personal Brand and Fighting to Keep it.* McGraw Hill Companies, 2004.

Damp, Dennis V, Salvatore Conciald (Illustrator). *The Book of U.S. Government Jobs, 8th Edition, Where They Are, What's Available, and How to Get One.* Brookhaven Press, LLC, 2002.

Goldman, Daniel. Emotional Intelligence: *Why it can matter more than IQ.* Bantam Books, Inc. 1997.

Hamilton, Leslie, Robert Tragert. *100 Best non Profits to Work For.* Thompson Learning, 2000.

Jeffers, Susan J. *Feel the Fear And Do It Anyway* Fawcett Book Group, 1996.

Krannich, Ron L., Caryl Ray Krannich, et. al. *Job Hunting Guide transitioning from College to Career.* Impact Publishing, VA, 2003.

Segal, Nina, Erich Kocher. *International Jobs and where They Are and How to Get Them.* Perseus Publishing, 2003.

Saraf, Dilip G. *The 7 Keys to a Dream Job: A Career Nirvana Playbook!* iUniverse Publishers, 2004

Saraf, Dilip G. *Pathways to Career Nirvana: An Ultimate Success Sourcebook!,* iUniverse Publishers, 2004

Saraf, Dilip G. *Reinvention through Messaging: The Write Message for the Right Job!!* iUniverse Publishers, 2004.

Chapter-3: Managing Transitions

Adrienne, Carol. *The Purpose of Your Life: Finding Your Place In The World Using Synchronicity, Intuition, and Uncommon Sense.* Harper Collins, 1999.

Bolles, Richard. *What Color is Your Parachute? A Practical Manual for Job-Hunters and Career Changers.* Ten Speed Press, 2004.

Crispin, Gary, Mark Mehler. *CareerXRoads 2003: The Directory to Job, Resume, and Career Management sites on the Web.* MMC Group, 2002.

Damp, Dennis V, Salvatore Conciald (Illustrator): *The Book of U.S. Government Jobs, 8th Edition, Where They Are, What's Available, and How to Get One.* Brookhaven Press, LLC, 2002.

D'Alessandro, David F., Michelle Owens: Career Warfare: *10 Rules for Building Successful Personal Brand and Fighting to Keep it.* McGraw Hill Companies, 2004.

Lucht, John: *Rites of Passage at $100,000 to $1 Million+: Your Insider's Lifetime Guide to Executive Job Changing and Faster Career Progress in the 21st Century.* Henry Holt & Company, Incorporated, 2000.

Krannich, Ron L., Caryl Ray Krannich, et al. *Job Hunting Guide transitioning from College to Career.* Impact Publishing, VA, 2003

Leslie, Hamilton, Robert Tragert. *100 Best non-Profits to Work For.* Thompson Learning, 2000.

Montag, William E.; *CareerJournal.com Resume Guide for $100,000 Plus Executive Jobs* John Wiley & Sons, Incorporated, 2002.

Riley, Margaret Riley Dikel, Francis E. Roehm. *Guide to Internet Job Searching.* McGraw Hill, Company, 2002.

Saraf, Dilip G. *The 7 Keys to a Dream Job: A Career Nirvana Playbook!* iUniverse Publishers, 2004

Segal, Nina, Erich Kocher. *International Jobs and where They Are and How to Get Them.* Perseus Publishing, August 2003.

Chapter-4: How Your Genius *Helps* You

Adrienne, Carol: *The Purpose of Your Life: Finding Your Place In The World Using Synchronicity, Intuition, and Uncommon Sense.* Harper Collins, 1999.

Bolles, Richard. *What Color is Your Parachute? A Practical Manual for Job-Hunters and Career Changers.* Ten Speed Press, 2004.

Conniff, Richard: *Reading Faces*. Smithsonian, Volume 32, Number 10, January 2004, pp 44-50.

D'Alessandro, David F., Michelle Ownes. *Career Warfare: 10 Rules for Building Successful Personal Brand and Fighting to Keep it*. McGraw Hill Companies, 2004.

Porot, Daniel. *The Pie Method for Career Success: A unique Way to Find Your Ideal Job*. JIST Works, Inc., Indianapolis, IN, 1996.

Ryan, Robin. *60 Seconds & You're Hired!* Penguin Books, 2000.

Saraf, Dilip G. *The 7 Keys to a Dream Job: A Career Nirvana Playbook!* iUniverse Publishers, 2004

Saraf, Dilip G. *Reinvention through Messaging: The Write Message for the Right Job!* iUniverse Publishers, 2004

Veruki, Peter, Peter Venki. The 250 Job Interview Questions You'll Most Likely be Asked and the Answers That Will Get You Hired. Adams Media Corporation, 1999.

Chapter-5: The Baby-boomer Advantage

Adrienne, Carol. *The Purpose of Your Life: Finding Your Place In The World Using Synchronicity, Intuition, and Uncommon Sense*. Harper Collins, 1999.

Black, Joe D., L. Tyler Nelson. *The Leadership of Change: A Workshop for Leaders and Managers*, 1991.

Briggs, Isabel Myers, with Peter B. Myers. *Gifts Differing: Understanding Personality Type*. Consulting Psychologists Press, Inc., Reprint Edition, 1995.

Bronson, Po. *What Should I do with My Life? The True Story of People Who Answered the Ultimate Question*. Random House, 2003.

Buckingham, Marcus, Curt Coffman. *First, Break All the Rules: What the Worlds Greatest Managers Do Differently*. Simon & Schuster Adult Publishing Group, 1999.

Carnegie, Dale, Dorothy Carnegie (Editor), Arthur R. Pell, (Editor). *How to Win Friends and Influence People*. Simon & Schuster Adult Publishing Group, Revised Edition, 1982.

Covey, Steven R. *The 7 Habits of Highly Effective people: Powerful Lessons in Personal Change.* Simon & Schuster Adult Publishing Group.1990.

Embree, Marlowe. *Type Reporter* No. 79, 12/00. Chapel Road, Fairfax Station, VA 22039; 703-764-5370.

Goldman, Daniel. *Emotional Intelligence: Why it can matter more than IQ.* Bantam Books, Inc., 1997.

Johnson, Spencer. *Who Moved My Cheese? An Amazing Way to Deal With Change in Your Work and Your Life.* Simon & Schuster Adult Publishing Group, 1999.

Laney, Marti Olsen Laney. *The Introvert Advantage: How to Thrive in an Extraverted World.* Workman Publishing, 2002.

Osborne, Carol. *The Art of Resilience: 100 Paths to Wisdom and Strength in an Uncertain World.* Crown Publishing Group, 1997.

Ray, Michael, Rochelle Myers. *Creativity in Business.* Double Day & Company, Incorporated, a division of Bantam Doubleday, 1981.

Tieger, Paul D., Barbara Barron-Tieger, Deborah Baker, (editor). *Do what You Are: Discover the Perfect Career for You Through the Secrets of Personality Type.* Little Brown & Company, 2001.

Chapter-6: Building Your Platform

Saraf, Dilip G. *The 7 Keys to a Dream Job: A Career Nirvana Playbook!* iUniverse Publishers, 2004

Saraf, Dilip G. *Pathways to Career Nirvana: An Ultimate Success Sourcebook!,* iUniverse Publishers, 2004

Saraf, Dilip G. *Reinvention through Messaging: The Write Message for the Right Job!!* iUniverse Publishers, 2004.

Whitcomb, Susan Britton, Pat Kendall. *EResumes: Everything You Need to Know About Using Electronic Resumes to Tap into Today's Hot Job Market.* McGraw Hill Companies, 2001.

Trautman, Kathryn Kraemer, Barbara Guerra (Ed.). *Ten Steps to a Federal Job! Navigating the Federal job System, writing Federal Resumes, KSAs and Cover Letters with a Mission.* The Resume Place, 2002.

Chapter-7: Write to the Point with Letters

Dumaine, Deborah. *Instant Answer Guide to Business Writing: An A-Z Source for Today's Business Writers.* iUniverse 2003

Saraf, Dilip G. *The 7 Keys to a Dream Job: A Career Nirvana Playbook!* iUniverse Publishers, 2004

Saraf, Dilip G. *Pathways to Career Nirvana: An Ultimate Success Sourcebook!,* iUniverse Publishers, 2004

Saraf, Dilip G. *Reinvention through Messaging: The Write Message for the Right Job!!* iUniverse Publishers, 2004.

Chapter-8: Marketing the Product—You!

Saraf, Dilip G. *The 7 Keys to a Dream Job: A Career Nirvana Playbook!* iUniverse Publishers, 2004.

Saraf, Dilip G. *Pathways to Career Nirvana: An Ultimate Success Sourcebook!,* iUniverse Publishers, 2004

Saraf, Dilip G. *Reinvention through Messaging: The Write Message for the Right Job!!* iUniverse Publishers, 2004.

Chapter-9: Acing the Interview

Adams, Bob: *Everything Job Interview Book.* Adams Media Corporation, 2001.

Medley, Anthony K. *Sweaty Palms: The Neglected Art of Being Interviewed.* Ten Speed Press, 1991

Ryan, Robin. *60 Seconds and You are Hired!* Penguin Books, 2001

Saraf, Dilip G. *The 7 Keys to a Dream Job: A Career Nirvana Playbook!* iUniverse Publishers, 2004

Saraf, Dilip G. *Pathways to Career Nirvana: An Ultimate Success Sourcebook!,* iUniverse Publishers, 2004

Saraf, Dilip G. *Reinvention through Messaging: The Write Message for the Right Job!!* iUniverse Publishers, 2004.

Chapter-10: Negotiating the Offer

Bolles, Richard: *What Color is Your Parachute? A Practical Manual for Job-Hunters and Career Changers.* Ten Speed Press, 2004.

Chapman, Jack: *Negotiating Your Salary: How To Make $100,000 a Minute.* Ten Speed Press, 2001.

D'Alessandro, David F., Michelle Ownes. *Career Warfare: 10 Rules for Building Successful Personal Brand and Fighting to Keep it.* McGraw Hill Companies, 2004.

Jeffers, Susan J. *Feel the Fear And Do IT Anyway.* Fawcett Book Group, 1996.

Krennich, Ronald, Caryl Krannich. *Dynamite Salary Negotiations: Know What You're Worth and Get IT.* Impact Publications, VA, 2000.

Laney, Marti Olsen Laney: *The Introvert Advantage: How to Thrive in an Extraverted World.* Workman Publishing; 2002.

Porot, Daniel, Saniel Porot with Frances Bolles Haynes. *101 Salary Secrets: Negotiate Like a Pro.* Ten Speed Press, 2001.

Ray, Michael and Rochelle Myers: *Creativity in Business*: Doubleday, A Division of Bantam Doubleday Dell Publishing Group, New York, 1989.

Saraf, Dilip G. *The 7 Keys to a Dream Job: A Career Nirvana Playbook!* iUniverse Publishers, 2004

Saraf, Dilip G. *Pathways to Career Nirvana: An Ultimate Success Sourcebook!,* iUniverse Publishers, 2004

Saraf, Dilip G. *Reinvention through Messaging: The Write Message for the Right Job!!* iUniverse Publishers, 2004.

Index

"Not everything faced can be changed, but nothing can be changed until it is faced."

—James Baldwin, author (1924–87)

"Not to know is bad. Not to want to know is worse. Not to hope is unthinkable. Not to care is unforgivable."

—Nigerian Proverb

978-0-595-36258-5
0-595-36258-3

LaVergne, TN USA
28 October 2009
162226LV00001B/96/A

9 780595 362585